D1609907

FASCISM AND CONSTITUTIONAL CONFLICT

Fascism and Constitutional Conflict

The British Extreme-Right and Ulster
in the Twentieth Century

JAMES LOUGHLIN

LIVERPOOL UNIVERSITY PRESS

First published 2019 by
Liverpool University Press
4 Cambridge Street
Liverpool
L69 7ZU

ISBN 978-1-78694-177-0 cased

Typeset by Carnegie Book Production, Lancaster
Printed and bound in Poland by BooksFactory.co.uk

For Lochlainn

Contents

Figures

Abbreviations

AGM	Annual General Meeting
AIA	Anglo-Irish Agreement
BBL	British Brothers' League
BF	British Fascists
BNP	British National Party
BPP	British People's Party
BU, CRL	University of Birmingham, Cadbury Research Library
BUF	British Union of Fascists
C18	Combat 18
CPI	Communist Party of Ireland
DUP	Democratic Unionist Party
FOM	Friends of Mosley
IFL	Imperial Fascist League
INA	Irish National Archives
INLA	Irish National Liberation Army
ITP	International Third Position
LEL	League of Empire Loyalists
LHMA	Liddell Hart Military Archives
NAK	National Archives, Kew
NF	National Front
NILP	Northern Ireland Labour Party
OUP	Official Unionist Party [also UUP]
PD	People's Democracy

PR	proportional representation
PRONI	Public Records Office of Northern Ireland
PUP	Progressive Unionist Party
RUC	Royal Ulster Constabulary
SDLP	Social Democratic and Labour Party
UCP	Ulster Constitutional Party
UDA	Ulster Defence Association
UDI	unilateral declaration of independence
UF	Ulster Fascists
UKIP	United Kingdom Independence Party
ULF	Ulster Loyalist Front
UM	Union Movement
UNA	University of Northampton Archive
USC	Ulster Special Constabulary
UUUC	United Ulster Unionist Council
UVF	Ulster Volunteer Force
UWC	Ulster Workers' Council
VPP	Volunteer People's Party
WNP	White Nationalist Party
YNF	Young National Front

Preface

As an academic subject the Northern Ireland problem has been exhaustively researched, and continues to be so. Nevertheless, there exist some areas that remain relatively unexplored. This work addresses one of these: namely, the relationship between the British extreme-Right and Ulster/Northern Ireland in the twentieth century. Studies of British fascism have not entirely ignored the subject, especially with reference to the recent troubles, and anyone entering the field of British fascist studies will find themselves indebted to the specialists who have made it their own: specialists such as Richard Griffiths, Roger Griffin, Roger Eatwell, Stuart Rawnsley, Colin Holmes, Thomas Linehan, Nigel Copsey, Richard Thurlow, Matthew Goodwin, Graham Macklin and Paul Jackson, among others; not least Tom Villis whose work on British Catholics and facism in the inter-war period has illuminated an important under-researched area. However, their perspective, for understandable reasons, has been primarily focused on Britain. Irish independence in 1921 removed the large Irish presence from the House of Commons and thus the Irish question from the heart of British politics, while regional autonomy in Northern Ireland under its own administration was allowed to proceed with little oversight from Westminster for 50 years, a period in which a host of grievances developed that ultimately led to the Northern Ireland conflict from the late 1960s. But Northern Ireland had been a constitutionally problematic entity from the beginning, and it is in this context that the case for examining the region in the context of fascism should be seen.

Central to British fascist ambitions was belief in the emergence of a great national crisis that would discredit the established political parties and thus create the space for a fascist takeover, but the envisaged crisis never occurred. The only part of the United Kingdom that could be said to have approximated those conditions was Ulster/Northern Ireland. In the years from 1912 to the outbreak of the Great War in 1914 the Ulster crisis came close to pulling the United Kingdom as a whole into a state of civil war, while from 1921 the region was under attack from both constitutional nationalism and republican paramilitarism until the IRA ceasefire of 1994 and the Belfast/Good Friday Agreement of 1998. These crisis conditions cultivated a loyalist population characterised by ultra-patriotism, a sense of national threat and a commitment to British institutions and national symbols such as the monarchy and the Union flag comparable to that of the extreme-Right. Accordingly, the region should have provided a congenial arena for extreme-Right growth to a degree greater than in Britain, where such conditions did not apply. But it failed to do so. Central to understanding that failure is deeply entrenched local parties and political traditions, and the barrier they constitute to all mainland British parties attempting to organise in the region, not just those of the extreme Right. How the latter attempted to negotiate that barrier is a central concern of this study. It is explored through private papers, Government and police papers, together with party newspapers, the mainstream press and personal information communicated to the author.

The subject of fascism and Ireland more generally has been the focus of a number of important works since Maurice Manning's study of the Blueshirts in the early 1970s.[1] Mike Cronin expanded greatly on the subject in his *Blueshirts and Irish Politics*,[2] while the Blueshirt leader General O'Duffy's political career has been comprehensively investigated by Fearghal McGarry.[3] More recently, R. M. Douglas has produced an exhaustive study of Ailtirí na hAiséirghe (Architects of the Resurrection) of the 1940s,[4] following

---

[1] Maurice Manning, *The Blueshirts* (Dublin: Gill & Macmillan, 1970).
[2] Mike Cronin, *The Blueshirts and Irish Politics* (Dublin: Four Courts Press, 1997).
[3] Fearghal McGarry, *General Eoin O'Duffy: A Self Made Hero* (Oxford: Oxford University Press, 2005).
[4] R. M. Douglas, *Architects of the Resurrection: Ailtirí na hAiséirghe and the Fascist 'New Order' in Ireland* (Manchester: Manchester University Press, 2009).

earlier work on British fascism and the Irish question.[5] This study attempts to make a similar contribution to knowledge with regard to British fascism and Ulster/Northern Ireland.

I have incurred many debts in writing this book, especially in the provision of research materials and expertise. The late James Kelly, veteran reporter for the *Irish News* and *Irish Press*, shared his recollections of attending Ulster Fascist meetings in Belfast in 1934; Daniel Jones, Archivist at the University of Northampton, provided expert guidance through the archive of *Searchlight* magazine; Amanda Bernstein, Rare Books librarian at Sheffield University generously contributed an image of Oswald Mosley (Figure 5); and Johanne Devlin Trew of Ulster University was of great assistance by researching military records for the book. Paul Bew gave informed consideration to the inter-war chapters; Paul Rowlandson and Tom Fraser of Ulster University provided copies of important fascist publications. My former colleague at Ulster University, Gerard O'Brien, conducted research on my behalf at the Irish National Archives; Jeffery Wallder and Keith Thompson of the commemorative organisation, Friends of Oswald Mosley, provided copies of political literature directed at the Irish community in Britain; Eamonn O'Ciardha of the School of Irish Language and Literature at Ulster University translated a significant article bearing on British fascism, while additional material was provided by Shaun Canny and Matthew Collins when doctoral students at the university; Billy Kelly, formerly of Ulster University, together with Bill Breslin of Wholesale Newspaper Services, Derry, facilitated access to copies of the *Irish Daily Telegraph*; Terry Curran of Technical Services at the Magee campus of Ulster University upgraded the quality of illustrations and photographs. Thanks are also due to Liverpool University Press's readers for advice offered on the improvement of the text and the staffs of the following libraries and research centres: Cadbury Research Library, University of Birmingham including permission to quote from the Mosley and Jeffrey Hamm papers; British Library, especially its newspaper division; Caird Library, National Maritime Museum, Greenwich; Liddell Hart

[5] R. M. Douglas, 'The swastika and the shamrock: British fascism and the Irish question, 1918–1940', *Albion*, vol. 29, no. 1 (1997).

Military Archives, King's College London: Magee and Coleraine campuses of Ulster University; Linenhall Library, Belfast; Berkeley Library, Trinity College Dublin, and especially the staff of its book repository at Santry; National Library of Ireland; Central Library, Derry; Belfast Public Library, newspaper division, especially Louise Wasson of the library's Ulster and Irish Studies department who located important press images; the Public Records office of Northern Ireland, in particular the Deputy Keeper of the Records for permission to quote from the Cahir Healy papers (D2991); National Archives, Kew.

More personally, additional support was provided by Simon Doherty, who contributed essential computer expertise on several occasions, while Greg and Carmen Penlington generously provided accommodation on research trips to London.

Figure 1   Map of Northern Ireland
The region consists of six of the nine counties of the province of Ulster,
the others in the Irish Republic being Donegal, Cavan and Monaghan.
    These counties were also variously affected by Northern Ireland's
political troubles. Accordingly, the terms 'Ulster' and 'Northern Ireland'
are both used in referring to the region.

Introduction

Ulster and the Context of British Fascism

On his re-election as leader of the Northern Ireland Labour Party (NILP) in 1966, Revd Albert McElroy described 'Ulster Toryism' as 'a state of mind which, psychologically, bears a close resemblance to the obscurantism and the essential unreason of Fascism.'[1] During the civil rights struggle of the late 1960s the perception of the Stormont Government as 'fascist' was widespread among nationalists – a perception expressed in Nazi salutes and the derogatory anti-Royal Ulster Constabulary chant 'SS-RUC'.[2] The historical reference these perceptions embodied, however, was less than comprehensive. In particular, they obscured the attraction that fascism and movements inspired by fascism had for many people in Britain and Ireland in the inter-war years, though not enough to achieve political success.

The reasons for fascism's failure in the British context have been firmly established. An academic consensus exists on four main themes, if not the degree of significance accruing to each: fascist misunderstanding of the crisis facing British society; fascism's incompatibility with British culture; the weakness of the British Union of Fascists (BUF); State management of fascism and the opposition of the Left.[3] The specificity of the reasons for fascism's failure, however, contrasts with the difficulty of coming to terms with the phenomenon itself.

---

[1] 'Northern Toryism "resembles fascism"', *Irish Times*, 10 January 1966.

[2] See, for example, *Londonderry Sentinel*, 20 November 1968.

[3] Richard Thurlow, 'The failure of the fascists', in Andrew Thorpe (ed.), *The Failure of Political Extremism in Inter-War Britain* (Exeter: University of Exeter, 1989), p. 67.

The term is conceptually ambiguous: 'there still exists no definition [of fascism] ... acceptable to all, or recognised as universally valid',[4] though in the British context a highly influential definition has been provided by Roger Griffin, who claims that an essential characteristic of an authentic fascist movement is the presence of a 'palingenetic' myth of national rebirth.[5] At the same time, a distinction must be made between the academic preoccupation with defining what was and was not authentically fascist in a discrete phase of history now past and the attitude of contemporary political actors, lacking the benefit of hindsight and believing themselves to be working with a fascist grain of history, or zeitgeist. Academic and contemporary attitudes to Salazar's Portugal illustrate the difference. The consensus among the former that Portugal was authoritarian rather than fascist[6] contrasts with contemporary British fascist – and anti-fascist – commentaries that regarded Salazar's dictatorship as indicative of developments suggesting future international fascist hegemony.[7] Different States might be travelling at different speeds, but in contrast to the academic verdict on fascist eligibility was a more fluid contemporary outlook which recognised no rigid barriers to the deliverance of a fascist future. And for many British commentators and political actors the

---

[4] Zeev Sternhell, 'Fascist ideology', in Walter Lacqueur (ed.), *Fascism: A Reader's Guide* (Harmondsworth: Pelican, 1976), pp. 325–26; Roger Eatwell, *Fascism: A History* (London: Chatto & Windus, 1995), pp. xx–xxi.

[5] This characteristic of fascism as a form of 'revolutionary nationalism' is well established in the secondary literature, but Griffin's is the most exhaustive treatment: Roger Griffin, *Modernism and Fascism: The Sense of a New Beginning under Mussolini and Hitler* (Basingstoke: Palgrave Macmillan, 2007), *passim*; Roger Griffin, *The Nature of Fascism* (London: Pinter, 1991), pp. 44–45.

[6] Juan Linz, 'Some notes towards a comparative study of fascism in sociological perspective', in Lacqueur, *Fascism: A Reader's Guide*, p. 21; Stanley Payne, *Fascism: Comparison and Definition* (Madison: University of Wisconsin Press, 1980), p. 139; Martin Kitchen, *Fascism* (Basingstoke: Macmillan, 1982), p. 88; Michael Sanfey, 'On Salazar and Salazarism', *Studies*, vol. 95, no. 368 (2003), 405–11.

[7] See, for example, Vicomte Leon de Poncins, 'Oliveira Salazar', *British Union Quarterly*, vol. 1, no. 1 (January/April 1937), 51–65; John Gibbons, 'Salazar of Portugal: portrait of a dictator', *Action*, 19 June 1937; F. A. Ridley, *The Papacy and Fascism: The Crisis of the Twentieth Century* (London: Martin Secker and Warburg, 1937), pp. 239–40.

United Kingdom was not excluded from that future. There were a number of reasons for thinking so, but especially the implications for the stability of the British State of the Ulster crisis of 1912–14.

British Fascism: Pre-War Precedents

The Ulster dimension to the debate on inter-war fascism has been almost completely ignored in the academic literature. In one of the relatively few references to Ulster in the British fascist context, Robert Benewick, while noting that some BUF spokesmen made a genealogical link between their movement and the pre-war Ulster Volunteer Force (UVF), denied that the UVF had any substantive relevance to inter-war British fascism: it lacked revolutionary character and had a 'one-dimensional' objective – the defeat of Irish Home Rule: 'The fact that the Ulster Volunteers were organised on a military basis did not make them Fascist.'[8] In fact, there is no historiographical consensus on whether even their paramilitary preparations in 1913–14 were in earnest, as opposed to being merely another weapon in an essentially constitutional campaign against Home Rule.[9] The paramilitary posturing of Ulster Unionists in the mid-1880s, for instance, was found, on police investigation, to have little substance.[10] However, the crisis of 1912–14 was much more serious: the Parliament Act of 1911 reduced the House of Lords' power over Commons' legislation to a two-year veto, making the passage of Home Rule inevitable after that period, but also allowing time for a loyalist paramilitary force to be mobilised in Ulster. But whether serious in rebellious intent or not, the impact of inter-war fascism was such that the pre-war period could easily seem freighted with proto-fascist developments.

Post-Great War perspectives tended to invest the Edwardian era with a rosy glow, an era of imperial greatness and prosperity

---

[8] Robert Benewick, *The Fascist Movement in Britain* (London: Allen Lane, 1972), pp. 23–25.

[9] For the latter view, see Alvin Jackson, *Sir Edward Carson* (Dublin: Historical Association of Ireland, 1993).

[10] James Loughlin, *Gladstone, Home Rule and the Ulster Question, 1882–93* (Dublin; Gill & Macmillan, 1986), chap. 6.

that constituted a condition of affairs which it was desirable to approximate. Writing during the Second World War, E. H. Carr noted the prevalence of this outlook among the victorious powers in the inter-war period: 'The aim was now to retrieve a false move, to undo what had been done, to erase from the fair page everything written on it since 1914.'[11] In Britain, certainly, this attitude extended beyond the political and economic elite. Richard Bellamy, northern organiser of the BUF, recorded of his Blackshirt comrades that often their 'minds lay rooted in the halcyon past which had ended abruptly in 1914'.[12] But a significant element of that past was a pervasive antisemitism. Even King Edward VII was subject to catcalls of 'King of the Jews' on a visit to Aldershot in June 1902. A commentator noted: 'if his patronage is meted out so much to the Hebrews his action will be bitterly resented.'[13] Certainly, antisemitism was a powerful factor in the growth of the British Brothers' League (BBL) in the years 1901–05, a movement inspired by Irish developments.

The Irish question was a perennial feature of the parliamentary timetable in the late nineteenth century and the success of nationalist political agitations had impressive results – that of the Land League in 1879–82 initiated a transformation in tenant farmer rights that concluded with land ownership on a massive scale from 1903, and with it the end of the Anglo-Irish landed elite's power, while the Irish Home Rule agitation had converted the towering figure of William Ewart Gladstone to the cause of Irish autonomy.[14] That British politicians, such as David Lloyd George, would ape Irish agitational practices for political effect is not surprising;[15] nor that

[11] E. H. Carr, *Conditions of Peace* (London: Macmillan, 1943), p. xvii.
[12] Bellamy, cited in Stephen Dorril, *Blackshirt: Sir Oswald Mosley and British Fascism* (London: Penguin 2007), p. 247.
[13] Diary entry, 21 June 1902, in John Vincent (ed.), *The Crawford Papers: The Journals of David Lyndsey, Twenty-Seventh Earl of Crawford and Tenth Earl of Balcarres, 1871–1940 during the Years 1892 to 1940* (Manchester: Manchester University Press, 1984), p. 67.
[14] There is a wealth of literature on these subjects. For examples, see Paul Bew, *Land and the National Question in Ireland, 1858–1882* (Dublin: Gill & Macmillan, 1979); J. L. Hammond, *Gladstone and the Irish Nation* (London: Longman, 1938).
[15] John Grigg, *The Young Lloyd George* (London: Methuen, 1973).

Captain William Stanley Shaw, the founder of the BBL, an organisation established to combat the influx of European Jews to Britain's
urban centres, especially London, would also seek to do so. The
term 'League' was common in the titles of political movements in
the pre-Great War period, but the Irish Land League, later National
League, had political achievements to its credit few others could
match. It was hardly surprising, therefore, that Shaw in promoting
the BBL should threaten to bring Land League practices to the
pursuit of his cause.[16]

The academic literature on the BBL has little to say about
Shaw.[17] A 'Colonial of Irish descent' born in Middlesex in 1878, his
grandfather and father were 'Connaught men' from county Sligo
and his mother from Redruth in Cornwall.[18] The year of his birth
preceded the outbreak of the Irish land war of 1879–82 which began
in Connacht and of which his Anglo-Irish father and grandfather
would have had direct experience. Shaw regarded his Connaught–
Cornish parentage as endowing him with an authentic British
identity; though like many antisemites of the inter-war years, he was
careful not to specify 'Jews' when raising alarm about the supposed
alien invasion, referring only to impoverished 'foreigners'. This
allowed him to stimulate xenophobia while avoiding an accusation
of obvious rabble-rousing, something that would have compromised
his position as an officer of the London Metropolitan Police Mission.
His choice of the xenophobic *Daily Mail* as the organ through which
to exploit the issue was effective for the purpose.[19]

The BBL, with Shaw as president, acquired a popular following
of 45,000, though his leadership and organisational limitations
were soon exposed and by 1902 he had resigned to be replaced by
Major W. Evans-Gordan, the Tory MP for Stepney, East London.
The organisation existed to pressure the Government to restrict

[16] '"British Brothers": Irish Land League methods for east London', *Daily Mail*, 14 September 1901.
[17] Colin Holmes, *Anti-Semitism in British Society, 1876–1939* (London: Edward Arnold, 1979), p. 89; Bernard Gainer, *The Alien Invasion: The Origins of the Aliens Act of 1905* (London: Heinemann, 1973), p. 238.
[18] *Daily Mail*, 14 September 1901; 'England's oldest inn', *Daily Mail Atlantic Edition*, 31 January 1924; Shaw to the editor, *Daily Mail*, 3 May 1954.
[19] Shaw to the editor, *Daily Mail*, 18 October 1901.

alien immigration, and when this duly transpired with the Aliens Act of 1905 it quickly dissolved leaving little direct trace.[20] Its relative brevity of existence, limited recruitment area and lack of an over-mastering leader partly accounts for its failure to register with inter-war political opinion as an indicator of the fascist era to come. The antisemitism on which it traded, however, remained a virulent strain in right-wing political discourse from the Edwardian years to the inter-war period, as David Cesarani's account of the career of the Tory Cabinet minister Sir William Joynson-Hicks amply demonstrates.[21] And other features of the pre-war period allowed proto-fascist indicators to be identified.

Following a visit to Nazi Germany, the cultural commentator John Gloag saw in Rudyard Kipling's imagining of a militaristic United Kingdom, 'The Army of a Dream' (1904),[22] 'something like Fascism or Nazism'.[23] In his assessment of the reign of George V (1935), D. C. Somervell identified in the Suffrage movement led by the authoritarian Pankhursts an organisation on what 'one may call Fascist lines.'[24] In the Ulster context proto-fascistic developments could also be identified. For W. S. Armour, son and biographer of the Ulster Presbyterian Home Ruler Revd J. B. Armour, pre-war Toryism in Ulster was 'Fascism before the term was ever known ... Those acquainted with the atmosphere of Irish Unionism find themselves completely at home either among fascists or Nazis.'[25] Hostile assessments such as these were countered by those for whom

---

[20] See Shaw–Board of Trade correspondence in *The Times*, 23 January 1902; Gisela C. Lebzelter, 'Anti-Semitism: a focal point for the British radical right', in Paul Kennedy and Anthony Nicholls (eds), *Nationalist and Racialist Movements in Britain and Germany before 1914* (Basingstoke: Macmillan, 1987), p. 95.

[21] David Cesarani, 'The anti-Jewish career of Sir William Joynson-Hicks, cabinet minister', *Journal of Contemporary History*, vol. 24, no. 3 (July 1989), 461–82.

[22] Rudyard Kipling, 'The Army of a Dream', in *Traffics and Discoveries* (London: Macmillan, 1904), pp. 243–301.

[23] John Gloag, *Word Warfare: Some Aspects German Propaganda and English Liberty* (London: Nicholson and Watson, 1939), p. 120.

[24] D. C. Somervell, *The Reign of King George V: An English Chronicle* (London: Faber & Faber, 1935), p. 61.

[25] W. S. Armour, *Mankind at the Watershed* (London: Duckworth, 1936), p. 64.

fascism represented a future, enlightened new age of 'national re-birth', to use Griffin's term, and which had a closer focus on contemporary political movements and leaders.

In writing her biography of Charles Stewart Parnell, the Irish nationalist leader of the 1880s,[26] Joan Haslip was advised by the Nazi sympathiser Arthur Bryant,[27] and when the book appeared it was reviewed by William Joyce (the future Lord Haw-Haw) in the Mosleyite print, *Action*. Joyce condemned Home Rule, but identified in Parnell a heroic proto-fascistic leader who was simply before his time, evident in how his oppositional practices at Westminster had exposed the 'cowardice' and decadence of parliamentary democracy,[28] a theme very much at the heart of Blackshirt propaganda. And in this context, Sir Oswald Mosley's own impression of Parnell might be noted, the latter's parliamentary exploits communicated by a grandfather who was a Tory MP in the 1880s.[29] But relevant to contemporary conditions as Parnellism appeared to be, the apparently fascistic connotations of pre-war Ulster Unionism have much greater import for our concerns, primarily because of the British establishment support Sir Edward Carson, the Ulster Unionist leader, attracted and what it appeared to indicate in the event of another serious crisis facing the State.

Pre-War Ulster and Post-War Relevance

The degree to which Ireland, and especially Ulster, informed British politics in the inter-war period was a product of a variety of factors. The creation of the two Irish constitutional entities in 1921 may have taken the Irish question out of *mainstream* British politics; nevertheless, the sense of threat that Ireland posed was real, especially for the radical Right. During the negotiations for the Anglo-Irish Treaty of 1921, Lloyd George drew a direct parallel between the violence of the paramilitary Ulster Special

---

[26] Joan Haslip, *Parnell* (London: Cobden-Sanderson, 1936).

[27] Joan Haslip to Arthur Bryant, n.d. [early 1930s] (King's College London, Liddell Hart Military Archives, Arthur Bryant papers, C4).

[28] William Joyce, 'Here lies a brave enemy', *Action*, 3 September 1936.

[29] Oswald Mosley, *My Life* (London: Nelson, 1968), pp. 19–20.

Constabulary (USC) and that of Italian fascists.[30] But Rightist assessments of British conditions in the immediate post-war period easily identified Sinn Fein/communist-inspired social upheaval as the real threat, though for the mainstream Right that threat would gradually dissipate during the inter-war period as the Anglo-Irish conflict of the early 1920s receded into the past. For the British Left, however, Ireland, especially Ulster, had far greater significance and for much longer.

It was bound to register in popular memory in a way that informed post-war politics, not least because of the continued parliamentary presence of politicians who had been active in the pre-war era, such as Carson and Joseph Devlin, the leader of the Ulster nationalists who forged a close friendship with Oswald Mosley when he campaigned against Black and Tan atrocities in Ireland. Devlin liked to identify the Ulster 'rebellion' with treasonous links to Germany before the war,[31] and to establish a causal connection to the 1916 Rising and imperial unrest thereafter: 'He [Carson] started the first rebellion. Out of that rebellion sprang the Irish rebellion. The spirit that was created in Ireland wafted itself to Egypt and to India.'[32] And to the continued presence of Irish politicians like Carson and Devlin can be added many Labour and Tory politicians of the inter-war period, such as the party leaders Ramsay MacDonald and George Lansbury, together with the Tory politicians Andrew Bonar Law, Lord Birkenhead, William Joynson-Hicks and many of their followers.

Certainly, pre-war Ulster Unionist connections and sympathies were evident among leading members of Stanley Baldwin's Government in the mid-1920s – Sir Douglas Hogg (Lord Hailsham), the Attorney General; Viscount Cave, Lord Chancellor; Ronald McNeill (Lord Cushendun), Financial Secretary to the Treasury; Sir W. Mitchell Thompson, MP for a Scots seat and a former MP

[30] Michael Laffan, *The Partition of Ireland, 1911–1925* (Dublin: Dublin Historical Association, 1983), p. 95.
[31] See Devlin, Hansard, HC, vol. 267 (17 June 1932), cols 736–737. George Lansbury had earlier made the same point: Hansard, HC, vol. 197 (25 June 1926), col. 748.
[32] Devlin, Hansard, HC, vol. 260 (24 November 1931), cols 334–335.

for county Down, appointed Postmaster-General in 1924.[33] Again, Winston Churchill, who had been a Liberal Home Ruler in the pre-war period, had now moved back to the Tory Party and was Chancellor of the Exchequer. Inheriting a property in county Antrim in the 1920s,[34] he would become a trenchant defender of the Unionist regime. Strong support for Ulster Unionism existed even among Cabinet members with no Ulster connections. This was especially the case with the already noted Sir William Joynson-Hicks – 'Jix' – the Home Secretary. A virulent antisemite, convinced of the existence of a worldwide Jewish conspiracy against the British Empire, the antisemitism that informed his intense national chauvinism was allied to hostility to other 'aliens', such as Germans and communists. He had both the friendship of Sir James Craig (from 1927 Lord Craigavon), Prime Minister of Northern Ireland, and the firm support of Baldwin.[35]

Baldwin himself could claim an Ulster background, his maternal great-grandfather having been born in Ballinamallard, county Fermanagh, in 1761.[36] Behind the avuncular country squire image Baldwin liked to project lay a strong strain of the Tory Diehard, the influence of which was well represented in the Cabinet and the Tory Party in general. As David Cesarani put it, while Baldwin's hands remained unsullied, 'he gave free rein to the wild men in his party who had been preaching xenophobia … allies [who] trawled for votes in the popular prejudice against foreigners, "aliens", "agitators".'[37] It was a mindset sympathetic to strong executive action in aid of preserving 'order' and found expression in the warm welcome Tory leaders gave to Mussolini's accession to power in 1922.

[33] See *Impartial Reporter*, 20 November 1924.
[34] *Cookstown News*, 3 March 1926; Lady Craigavon Diary, 28 February 1926 (PRONI: D1415/B/38).
[35] Cesarani, 'Anti-Jewish career of Sir William Joynson-Hicks', *passim*; Craigavon Diary (PRONI: D1415/B/38).
[36] *Impartial Reporter*, 21 August 1924.
[37] David Cesarani, 'Joynson-Hicks and the radical right in Britain after the First World War', in Tony Kushner and Kenneth Lunn (eds), *Traditions of Intolerance: Historical Perspectives on Fascism and Race Discourse in Britain* (Manchester: Manchester University Press, 1989), p. 133.

This was especially the case for the Prime Minister, Andrew Bonar Law, whom Mussolini telegrammed to express his concern simply 'to safeguard the supreme interests of the country, which are in accordance with the interests of peace and civilization';[38] a view, undoubtedly, that Bonar Law, who had close Ulster family connections, took of his own support for Carson in the pre-war years, support justified given the seriousness of the crisis as perceived by the Right – a disjuncture between the 'national will' and a nationally unrepresentative Parliament.[39] And he was impressed by Mussolini personally on their meeting at the London conference on post-war reparations in December 1922.[40]

In fact, a close similarity of view on political mastery between Carson and Mussolini can be identified. The former's opinion that 'the nation (like a woman) loves a strong man' for whom 'the country is calling out',[41] was echoed in the Duce's statement, 'The crowd loves strong men. The crowd is like a woman'.[42] More specifically, and as his correspondence with Lady Londonderry indicates, Carson had a proto-fascistic yearning for the emergence of the representative individual, the national autocrat who, by a triumph of will, would authentically embody the national spirit and crush the revolutionary designs of 'Jacobin' Liberals and their Irish nationalist and socialist allies.[43] Both Carson and Mussolini would inspire Britain's first fascist movement, Rotha Lintorn-Orman's British Fascists (BF).[44] While Mussolini provided the international

---

[38] Mussolini to Bonar Law, cited in Robert Graves and Alan Hodge, *The Long Weekend: A Social History of Great Britain, 1918–1939* (London: Readers Union, 1941), p. 249.

[39] Lord Willoughby de Broke, 'The constitution and the individual', in *Rights of Citizenship: A Survey of Safeguards for the People* (London: Warne, 1912), p. 46; James Loughlin, *Ulster Unionism and British National Identity since 1885* (London: Pinter, 1995), pp. 53–54.

[40] Robert Blake, *The Unknown Prime Minister: The Life and Times of Andrew Bonar Law, 1858–1923* (London: Eyre & Spottiswoode, 1955), pp. 485–86.

[41] Carson to Lady Londonderry, n.d. [early 1910], 29 August 1911 (Londonderry papers, PRONI: D2846/1/1/40, 68).

[42] Quoted in Christopher Hibbert, *Mussolini: A Biography* (London: Reprint Society, 1962), p. 54.

[43] Loughlin, *Ulster Unionism and British National Identity since 1885*, pp. 63–64.

[44] See James Loughlin, 'Rotha Lintorn-Orman, Ulster and the British Fascists

inspiration for Lintorn-Orman, Carson's success in preventing the imposition of Home Rule on north-east Ulster offered a template and example of what could be achieved in the British context.

The Duce appeared to be Italy's national saviour. He had come to power without a specifically fascist programme, something which only developed gradually in the later 1920s. Especially significant for his right-wing British admirers was his defence of the monarchy and religion.[45] As with Carson's defiance of a nationally 'unrepresentative' Liberal Government in 1912–14, so in October 1922 had Mussolini mobilised the Italian national will to remove an similarly unrepresentative Liberal Government and class of politicians who had ill-served crown and country; he had done it while avoiding *mass violence* and in doing so received the endorsement of the King, Victor Emmanuel III,[46] not unlike the apparent endorsement King George V had bestowed upon the Unionist regime during the inauguration of the Northern Ireland Parliament in June 1921. That George V visited Italy in 1923, conferred the Insignia of the Order of the Bath on Mussolini and credited his wise leadership with delivering Italy from its recent crisis,[47] would no doubt have reinforced the resonance. And just as with the approval conferred on Carson's paramilitarism by the 'respectable' classes in Britain up to 1914,[48] so too did the same class approve of Mussolini's accession to power in 1922,[49] while the Foreign Office, Conservative – and other –politicians, together with the press, had a largely uncritical attitude to Italian fascism until Mussolini's invasion of Ethiopia in 1935 and his antisemitic measures of 1938.[50] Lord Haig said of the Duce:

movement', *Immigrants & Minorities: Historical Studies in Ethnicity, Migration and Diaspora*, vol. 32, no. 1 (March 2014), 62–89.

[45] Colin Cross, *The Fascists in Britain* (London: Barrie and Rockliff, 1963), p. 58; Denis Smith, *Mussolini* (London: Paladin, 1993), pp. 138–42.

[46] Hibbert, *Mussolini*, pp. 54–55.

[47] Christopher Duggan, *Fascist Voices: An Intimate History of Mussolini's Italy* (London: Bodley Head, 2014), p. 75.

[48] D. M. Jackson, *Popular Opposition to Irish Home Rule in Edwardian Britain* (Liverpool: Liverpool University Press, 2009), *passim*.

[49] B. S. Farr, *The Development and Impact of Right-Wing Politics in Britain, 1903–1932* (New York: Garland, 1987), p. 54.

[50] Alistair Hamilton, *The Appeal of Fascism* (London: Anthony Blond, 1971),

'What a man! He really is exceptional.'[51] And for our purposes it is important to note that support for Mussolini was no less evident among Ulster Unionists and the nationalist community.

On his accession to power the *Belfast Telegraph* declared, 'Socialism has lost its stranglehold. The methods beloved by Lenin for the overthrow of society are frustrated',[52] while the passion of individual opinion leaders could be quite unbounded. Thus the Anglican Primate of All Ireland, Charles Frederick D'Arcy, who as Lord Bishop of Down, Connor and Dromore had signed the Ulster Covenant of 1912 in the company of Sir Edward Carson,[53] enthused over 'the wonderful success of the Fascist movement' following a family visit to Italy in 1926.[54] Carson also, if less obviously, was impressed by Mussolini.[55]

For its part, the leading nationalist paper, the *Irish News*, concerned at first about Mussolini,[56] soon accommodated itself to his rule – he restored display of the crucifix and Catholic religious teaching in schools in his first year in office.[57] It registered shock when the mentally unstable Lady Violet Gibson, a daughter of the Irish peer Lord Ashbourne, almost succeeded in assassinating the Duce in 1926,[58] while the Lateran Treaty of 1929 which created the Vatican State ensured that Italian fascism generally got sympathetic coverage thereafter.[59]

pp. 157–79; John Brewer, *Mosley's Men: The British Union of Fascists in the West Midlands* (Aldershot: Gower, 1984), pp. 4–5.

[51] Lord Haig, quoted in *Fascist Bulletin*, 27 March 1926.

[52] *Belfast Telegraph*, 30 October 1922; also *Belfast News-Letter*, 30–31 October; 1, 3 November 1922.

[53] Ronald McNeill, *Ulster's Stand for Union* (London: John Murray, 1922), p. 121.

[54] C. F. D'Arcy, *The Adventures of a Bishop* (London: Hodder & Stoughton, 1934), p. 268.

[55] Dorril, *Blackshirt: Sir Oswald Mosley and British Fascism*, p. 256.

[56] 'Militarists on top!', *Irish News*, 30 October 1922.

[57] Virginia Crawford, 'The rise of fascism and what it stands for', *Studies*, vol. 12 (1923), 550.

[58] *Irish News*, 8 April 1926. The attempt is exhaustively discussed in F. S. Saunders, *The Woman Who Shot Mussolini* (London: Faber & Faber, 2010).

[59] 'Signed and sealed', *Irish News*, 12 February 1929.

For the British Left, however, Italian fascism, Toryism, Ulster and the connections between them, carried a very different resonance. Certainly, the relationship between Tory support for Ulster paramilitarism in the pre-Great War period and sympathy for Italian fascism was a significant element in leftist calculations about the possibilities of a successful fascist movement in Britain, especially in the context of Government action and legislation which appeared to curtail freedom of assembly and expression. For the Left, these inevitably brought the pre-war Ulster scenario into view.

A Labour motion of censure on the Baldwin Government in 1925 for prosecuting communists urging the overthrow of capitalism in general included speeches by Ramsay MacDonald and George Lansbury highlighting the support given by the Home Secretary, William Joynson-Hicks, to the army 'mutineers' in 1914[60] – a reference to what for the Left was the most serious aspect of the pre-war Ulster crisis, the apparent willingness of the army's officer class to disobey possible Government orders to suppress the Ulster resistance.[61] They were followed in similar vein by the Labour leader J. R. Clynes[62] and the future Labour Chancellor of the Exchequer Hugh Dalton, for whom the use of Tory Party premises for the drilling and training of BF members was of a piece with the party's support for Ulster rebellion in 1914: 'When [will] a Conservative conference … pass a resolution excluding Fascists from membership of the Conservative Party? We are waiting for that.'[63]

[60] Ramsay MacDonald, George Lansbury, Hansard, HC, vol. 188 (1 December 1925), cols 2079–2080, 2137–2138.
[61] No mutiny as such took place. Rather, in March 1914, Brigadier General Hubert Gough and sixty cavalry officers at the Curragh camp at Kildare resigned their commissions rather than obey orders they believed would entail them being deployed to coerce Ulster Unionists into accepting Home Rule. When the War Office, without Government permission, refused the resignations, telling the officers the Government did not intend to use the army for this purpose, the Government's authority over this branch of the armed services was seriously compromised. K. Jeffery, 'Curragh incident', in S. J. Connolly (ed.), *The Oxford Companion to Irish History* (2nd edn, Oxford: Oxford University Press, 2002), pp. 138–39.
[62] Clynes, Hansard, HC, vol. 188 (1 December 1925), col. 2168.
[63] Dalton, Hansard, HC, vol. 188 (1 December 1925), col. 2155. See also debates on the Trades Disputes and Trade Unions Bill of 1927 – which

With the onset of the Great Depression just as the second Labour Government took office in 1929 and the split in the Labour Party that followed Ramsay MacDonald's creation of the National Government with Baldwin's Tory Party in 1931 – continued under Baldwin's leadership following the general election of 1935 – Britain, as a stream of repressive Government measures unfolded,[64] seemed to be developing conditions in which the emergence of fascism was only too likely. John Strachey, a former close colleague of Sir Oswald Mosley and who had followed him out of the Labour Party and into his short-lived New Party in 1931, claimed, the 'rise of some form of Fascism is … latent in the whole political and economic situation of Great Britain'.[65] Not all leading Labour figures took this view. For G. D. H. Cole, a fascist revolution in Britain was highly unlikely given that Britain had not experienced defeat in war, or a devastating economic collapse such as had occurred in Germany.[66] But for Strachey this was much too complacent a view.[67] Britain was not 'basically different from the rest of the world. She is only a little behind-hand. The same processes are at work with us that we can see in their fruition in Europe.'[68] A fascist zeitgeist, or spirit of the age, was very much present and was likely to find hegemonic expression in Britain 'just so soon as they [British capitalists] are sufficiently alarmed'.[69]

---

restricted the right to strike and constrained Union membership and funds. C. L. Mowat, *Britain between the Wars, 1918–1940* (London: Methuen, 1966), p. 336; also Richard Wallhead, Hansard, HC, vol. 205 (5 May 1927), col. 1869.
[64] Thus, punitive sentences on supporters of sailors at Invergordon protesting at severe pay cuts by refusing to obey orders in 1932. Mowat, *Britain between the Wars*, pp. 403–06; George Buchanan, Hansard, HC, vol. 263 (23 March 1932), col. 1146; unwarranted arrests in December 1932 of communists involved in the National Unemployed Workers Movement (George Buchanan, George Lansbury, Hansard, HC, vol. 273 (22 December 1932), cols 1288–1289); Government use of coercion in July 1933 to suppress the Indian Congress movement (Lansbury, Hansard, HC, vol. 280 (17 July 1933), cols 1565–1566).
[65] John Strachey, *The Menace of Fascism* (London: Gollancz, 1933), p. 218.
[66] G. D. H. Cole in *New Statesman*, 7 April 1933, cited in Strachey, *Menace of Fascism*, pp. 166–67.
[67] Strachey, *Menace of Fascism*, pp. 167–69.
[68] Ibid., p. 176.
[69] Ibid., p. 178.

What made the fascist threat especially worrying was the difficulty of specifying exactly how it might manifest itself: 'It would be fully consonant with the traditions of our governing class if British Fascism appeared in an almost unrecognisable form.'[70] As Malcolm Muggeridge put it in his assessment of the 1930s, fascism could mean 'one thing at one moment and another at another'.[71] Significantly, Strachey's *The Menace of Fascism* appeared *after* the emergence of Mosley's BUF in 1932, and it clearly was not regarded as the organisation that would *necessarily* define the fascist threat. Harold Laski, Professor of Political Science at the London School of Economics and a leading Labour Party intellectual, shared Strachey's analysis, noting the speed with which the Nazi regime had effected 'so startling a transvaluation of all German values'.[72] The former – and later – Labour MP for Jarrow, Ellen Wilkinson, also detected 'well-marked tendencies in Britain which may lead to a different type of fascism from Mosley's, and may undermine his leadership'.[73] What made alternative forms of fascism to Mosley's BUF more likely was, W. A. Rudlin argued, that the Tory Diehards 'are already [seen] in the public mind as statesmen of experience, whereas Sir Oswald Mosley is known to be experienced in almost everything except the business of statesmanship'.[74]

For Wilkinson, the National Government itself was the agency through which it could develop:

> It has all the features which distinguish Fascism from pure and simple reaction. ... Its leader [Ramsay MacDonald] is a former Socialist, like every other Fascist leader, and there is much Socialist phraseology left in his speeches to the masses.

---

[70] Ibid., pp. 178–79.

[71] Malcolm Muggeridge, *The Thirties in Great Britain* (1971; London: Fontana, 1940), p. 39. See also Robert Skidelsky, *Oswald Mosley* (London: Macmillan, 1981), p. 300.

[72] Harold Laski, Foreword to Robert A. Brady, *The Spirit and Structure of German Fascism* (London: Gollancz, 1937), p. 13.

[73] See Ellen Cicely Wilkinson and Edward Conze, *Why Fascism?* (London: Selwyn & Blount, 1934), p. 58.

[74] W. A. Rudlin, *The Growth of Fascism in Great Britain* (London: Allen & Unwin, 1935), p. 116.

> ... By relying more and more on Orders in Council, whether
> to get through quota schemes or put through economy
> proposals such as the Means Test, it is following the Fascist
> tradition of dispensing with parliament as much as possible.[75]

Nor could the supposed resilience of 'English national character' be
relied upon as a bulwark against the fascist temptation. Wilkinson
reminded her readers that the 'Black-and-Tans were British of the
British, and rejoiced of their super-patriotism'.[76] Visiting Belfast in
November 1933 to support Harry Midgley, then a leading member
of the NILP and its candidate for the Dock division of the city at the
Stormont election of that year, she identified in the northern regime
an example of 'Tory Fascism',[77] a regional indicator of the type of
Government the Tories might have in mind for Britain – effectively
a one-party State arrayed with a range of repressive measures such
as the Special Powers Act, an instrument for interning without
trial anyone it did not like, and one which Lord Rothermere
would recommend to Sir Oswald Mosley as a model the Blackshirt
movement should aim for (see Chapter 2).

It was in this context of repressive measures and unease about
the future of British politics that the Labour MP, Major James
Milner, opined of the Incitement to Disaffection Bill in November
1934:[78] 'I dread to think, as many others must, of what might
happen under this Bill ... if a Fascist Government came into
power in this country.'[79] But the fundamental significance of
the authoritarian tendencies of Tory and National Government
supporters in the context of the pre-war Ulster precedent was its
implications should a Labour Government come to power on a

[75] Wilkinson, *Why Fascism?*, pp. 65–66.

[76] Ibid., pp. 232–33.

[77] *Irish News*, 28 November 1933; and for the election more generally,
Graham Walker, *The Politics of Frustration: Harry Midgley and the Failure of
Labour in Northern Ireland* (Manchester: Manchester University Press, 1985),
pp. 67–70.

[78] Buchanan, Hansard, HC, vol. 293 (30 October 1934), col. 100; Major
Gwilym Lloyd George, Hansard, HC, vol. 288 (16 April 1934), cols 775–776;
Earl of Kinnoull, Hansard, HL, vol. 94 (6 November 1934), cols. 149–150.

[79] Major James Milner, Hansard, HC, vol. 293 (2 November 1934), col. 570.

radical reforming programme. In 1934, the Labour Party leader George Lansbury declared:

> Hardly a meeting do I address without people putting questions to me on these lines: 'Do you really believe that the possessing classes will allow you to do by Act of Parliament the things that you want to do?' and when I say 'Yes,' they immediately shout: 'What about Ulster?' *No one can get away from that fact.* (my italics)[80]

That General Gough, a leader of the army 'Curragh mutiny' of 1914, had, among other leading military figures, become associated with the Blackshirt-linked January Club in early 1934 – the period in which Lord Rothermere's support was greatly boosting BUF membership levels – made MI5 concerned that dangerous links were being made with the army.[81] Nor did 'the Ulster mutiny of 1914' lose its precedental importance in this respect as the decade wore on.[82] Britain's unwritten constitution could easily facilitate a fascist triumph: it 'is no less "unwritten" and flexible [now] than it was in 1914'.[83] In fact, in facilitating pre-war Ulster paramilitarism it had the consequence of problematising issues of public assembly and intent in the inter-war years. As we shall see, Sir Oswald Mosley in a famous case successfully defended his political utterances and behaviour by arguing that what he had said and done paled beside the outright promotion of treason and armed rebellion against the State engaged in by Sir Edward Carson, a leader of the Bar.

What gave such considerations practical import was that the massive majority MacDonald's National Government enjoyed in 1931 had, by 1935, suffered a number of by-election defeats to the Labour Party, successes mirrored in local Government with the party gaining a majority for the first time on the London County

---

[80] Lansbury, Hansard, HC, vol. 293 (2 November 1934), col. 537; Isaac Foot, Hansard, HC, vol. 293 (2 November 1934), col. 542; Mr Knight, Hansard, HC, vol. 293 (2 November 1934), col. 557; James Maxton, Hansard, HC, vol. 293 (2 November 1934), cols. 563–564.

[81] Dorril, *Blackshirt: Sir Oswald Mosley and British Fascism*, p. 275.

[82] Laski, Foreword to Brady, *The Spirit and Structure of German Fascism*, p. 13.

[83] Rudlin, *Growth of Fascism*, pp. 115–16.

Council. And these successes were gained by a party whose policies had taken a radical socialist turn.[84] That the National Government was returned to office at the general election of 1935 under Baldwin's leadership only exacerbated opposition fears at a time (1936–37) when British pro-Nazi sentiment reached a peak,[85] and when, with the outbreak of the Spanish Civil War in 1936, the Tory Party overwhelmingly supported General Franco's insurrection against the Republican Government.[86]

Referencing Carson and the 'Curragh mutiny' of 1914, Lieutenant Commander R. T. H. Fletcher warned: 'The truth is that events in Spain have revealed a latent drift towards Fascism in the Conservative party, and it will be a disaster for this country if that drift is not checked, and the ideals of democracy are not recaptured.'[87] Certainly, some Conservatives were now less likely to be embarrassed about their support for Ulster paramilitarism in 1914, about which they had hitherto maintained an embarrassed silence: 'If Edward Carson had a good case General Franco had a very much better case.'[88] Harold Laski had that association in mind when writing the Foreword to Robert Brady's *The Spirit and Structure of German Fascism*: the British army was 'the least democratic of any important State' apart from the pre-revolutionary army of Spain.[89] Laski did not exclude the possibility of fascism triumphing in Britain even after the outbreak of war with the European dictators.[90]

[84] Ibid., pp. 132–33.
[85] Richard Griffiths, *Fellow Travellers of the Right: British Enthusiasts for Nazi Germany* (Oxford: Oxford University Press, 1983), p. 4.
[86] Ibid., pp. 261–64.
[87] Lieutenant Commander Fletcher, Hansard, HC, vol. 326 (19 July 1937), cols. 1887–1888.
[88] Lord Rankeillour, Hansard, HL, vol. 112 (9 March 1939), col. 110.
[89] Laski, Foreword to Brady, *The Spirit and Structure of German Fascism*, p. 13.
[90] Harold Laski, *Where Do We Go from Here? An Essay in Interpretation* (Harmondsworth: Penguin, 1940), pp. 95, 115.

Conclusion

In one of its dictionary definitions, a 'vector' is described as 'a carrier of disease or infection'.[91] For our purposes this can be usefully applied as a political metaphor for the Left in the inter-war period, with Tory support and legislation for repressive measures acting as a vector of memory calling forth the threatened Ulster rebellion of 1912–14 as a factor signalling a fascistic outcome in contemporary Britain. The ambiguity of meaning that attached to the term 'fascism' facilitated anxieties in this respect. But, arguably, the effect of the pre-war Ulster precedent was to provide a distorting prism that stereotyped debate in overly stark, contrasting hues, blinding leftist commentators to the realities of the British political environment, certainly failing to appreciate the variety of opinion about fascism on the political Right as European fascism became increasingly nasty in the later 1930s. Laski's concern about the triumph of fascism in Britain *after* the outbreak of the Second World War suggests the extent to which it functioned in this respect.

For British fascist organisations in the inter-war period, however, the Ulster 'rebellion' of the pre-war period had a more varied reference and meaning, ranging, for instance, from inspiration for Rotha Lintorn-Orman's BF; 'evidence', for William Joyce, that the fascist era of national rebirth had long been developing and was now close to realisation; a factor, for Oswald Mosley, in determining legally permissible behaviour in the public arena, while others could read into it a warning against conceding self-government to India. In the post-Second World War period, and up to the present, though in rather different ways, 'Ulster' would continue to be a significant reference point for the British extreme-Right.

---

[91] J. M. Hawkins (ed.), *The Oxford Reference Dictionary* (Oxford: Oxford University Press, 1988), p. 908. For a discussion of vectors of memory in the post-Second World War period, see Nancy Wood, *Vectors of Memory: Legacies of Trauma in Postwar Europe* (Oxford: Berg, 1998).

I

Ulster and Fascism
in the Inter-War Period

1

Rotha Lintorn-Orman, Ulster and the British Fascists Movement

The emergence of British fascism in the early 1920s was a response to perceived related external and internal threats to the United Kingdom and its Empire. For the extreme-Right the idea of national peril was exacerbated by a number of alarmist publications that appeared in the post-war period, especially the notorious *Protocols of the Learned Elders of Zion*, a work that remained influential despite the exposure of its forged nature as early as 1921.[1] A leader of the National Front (NF) in the 1970s admitted that it 'was probably a forgery but that it nonetheless retained its value as a work of prophecy of what the Jews are actually planning and doing in reality.'[2] In the paranoid atmosphere of the post-Great War years the view quickly developed that communism was but one aspect of a worldwide Jewish conspiracy responsible for provoking subversion throughout the British Empire, especially in Ireland and India.[3] From 1921, Ireland, in alliance with international communism, was seen to threaten further constitutional upheaval.

Colonel A. H. Lane's *The Alien Menace* identified Ireland's independence struggle as a Jewish–communist conspiracy,[4] as did the

---

[1] 'Anti-Semitism', in Walter Theimer, *The Penguin Political Dictionary* (Harmondsworth: Penguin, 1939), pp. 23–24.
[2] See Joseph Pearce, *Race with the Devil: My Journey from Racial Hatred to Rational Love* (Charlotte, NC: Saint Benedict Press, 2013), p. 84.
[3] Gisela Lebzelter, *Political Anti-Semitism in England, 1918–1939* (London: Macmillan, 1978), *passim*.
[4] Colonel A. H. Lane, *The Alien Menace: A Statement of the Case* (2nd edn, London: Boswell, 1928), *passim*.

more influential Nesta H. Webster. In *World Revolution* she brought together antisemitism and contemporary post-war anti-Germanism in her argument on the 'Illuminati', a 'terrible and formidable sect' that had originated in mid-eighteenth-century Bavaria and was responsible for all forms of 'subversion' and plans for 'World Revolution'.[5] Familiar with a pre-war Ireland inhabited by 'gay, happy-go-lucky ... peasants',[6] the only explanation for its subsequent rebellious state was manipulation by forces located in Germany engaged in 'a great conspiracy against the British Empire':[7] 'It was ... Germany who [*sic*] fanned the flames of civil war now raging in Ireland. ... The same organisation is at work in India.'[8] Webster repeated and reinforced the arguments of *World Revolution* in *Secret Societies and Subversive Movements* (1924) and *The Surrender of an Empire* (1931), each embodying the central theme of varied and multiple revolutionary manifestations manipulated by a single driving force: 'each seems to form part of a common plan, which, like the separate pieces of a jigsaw puzzle, convey no meaning, but when fitted together make up a perfectly clear design.'[9] Not for nothing would Webster become known as the queen of conspiracy theorists, her publications remaining consistently influential with fascists and neo-fascists, as Joe Pearce's account of his NF education in the late 1970s indicates.[10]

It was to meet the challenge to Christianity and Empire that Lane and Webster outlined that the British Fascists (BF), the first such British movement, was established. Both would become BF supporters and contributors to the organisation's press outlets.[11]

---

[5] Nesta Webster, *World Revolution: The Plot against Civilisation* (London: Constable, 1921), pp. 8–10.

[6] Nesta Webster, *Spacious Days: An Autobiography* (London: Hutchinson, 1949), p. 96.

[7] Ibid.; Webster, *World Revolution*, pp. 75–78, 180–81, 242–45.

[8] Webster, *World Revolution*, p. 308.

[9] Webster, *Secret Societies and Subversive Movements* (London: Boswell, 1924), p. 348.

[10] Pearce, *Race with the Devil*, pp. 85–89.

[11] See 'The name "fascists" justified', *Fascist Bulletin*, 16 January 1926; 'Communism or fascism', *Fascist Bulletin*, 1 May 1926. For Lane, see Colonel A. H. Lane, 'Report on Professor Harold J. Laski', *British Lion*, March 1929; 'The alien menace', *British Lion*, no. 27 [May] 1928.

On officially joining the organisation in January 1927, Webster was immediately elected on to the BF Grand Council,[12] Lintorn-Orman crediting her work with bringing before the public 'the evils of Socialism and Bolshevism more than anything else'.[13] Given the seriousness of the threat to the British State and Empire, the BF was anxious to identify domestic evidence of its existence, finding it especially in occultism,[14] an evil expressed via a number of bodies, but especially the 'Kibbo Kift Kindred', an organisation whose activities involved 'pagan rites', totem poles and 'the cult of nudity'. But most seriously it had close connections with communism, in the service of which it, 'like German agents' before 1914, was busily engaged in mapping Britain's communications system for the purpose of subversion. In this context Lintorn-Orman feared party politicians would 'hesitate to take decisive steps until revolution has actually broken out ... Civil war will require something more than Special Constabulary'. Until a State crisis erupted the BF would continue to warn the people of its developing nature, as national life was corrupted racially by the immigration of 'foreign and hybrid elements represented by paper Britishers' and 'alien [Jewish] financiers who had an increasing stranglehold on the country's economic lifeblood'.[15] As for revolution's Irish dimension, Brigadier-General R. B. D. Blakeney, who would serve as BF President for a time, described it succinctly: 'The Red Army is no chimera. The Irish Republican Army is in being.'[16] This was an outlook firmly embedded in the mentality of Britain's emergent secret services,[17] no less than the BF, another of whose leading members

[12] *British Lion*, 27 January 1927.
[13] 'Mrs Nesta H. Webster on fascism', *British Lion*, 27 January 1927.
[14] See Webster, *Secret Societies and Subversive Movements*, chap. 4; 'A Theosophical symbol', *Fascist Bulletin*, 29 May 1926; 'The subversive occult movements', *British Lion*, [January 1928].
[15] *Fascist Bulletin*, 5 June 1926. For extensive discussion of the political anxieties the BF was subject to, see Colin Holmes, *Searching for Lord Haw-Haw: The Political Lives of William Joyce* (London and New York: Routledge, 2016), chap. 3.
[16] R. B. D. Blakeney, 'British Fascism', *Nineteenth Century*, 97 (1925), 132–41.
[17] Directorate of Intelligence, *A Survey of Revolutionary Feeling in the Year 1919* (National Archives, Kew (NAK), CAB24/96/CP462), 4–5; Report no. 48:

was Brigadier-General Sir Ormonde Winter, former Deputy Chief of Police and Director of Intelligence in Ireland (1920–22),[18] and who for two years after his Irish sojourn was supplied both with a revolver for his own defence and police protection.[19] His sense of national peril and the need to combat it led him to join the BF.[20]

Founded by Rotha Lintorn-Orman in 1923, the British Fascists (formerly British Fascisti) was the Rightist movement with the closest Ulster links. This chapter focuses on that dimension of BF activities, pointing up the Ulster influence on the BF sense of the crisis the United Kingdom faced in the later 1920s and early 1930s and how it should be dealt with; the close ideological, class and personal links between the BF and Ulster loyalists; and also how an examination of BF activities in Northern Ireland can provide insights on Ulster Unionism.

The BF, Organisational Crisis and Ulster

Lintorn-Orman, whose mother had established the Girl Guides in the pre-war period, came from a military background and had served courageously with an ambulance corps in Serbia in 1916, twice earning the Serbian Cross of Mercy (Croix de Charité). The 'bitter experiences of front-line death and destruction were a factor in … [her] fear that a similar cataclysm might occur within the British Empire – even within Britain itself.'[21] In 1922, an example of how to prevent such an outcome presented itself with Mussolini's accession to power and the rapidity with which he imposed order on an increasingly chaotic Italian political system.

'Report on revolutionary organisations in the United Kingdom', 30 March 1920 (NAK, CAB24/103/CP1009).

[18] Robert Benewick, *The Fascist Movement in Britain* (London: Allen Lane, 1972), p. 32.

[19] Sir Ormonde Winter, *Winter's Tale: An Autobiography* (London: Richards Press, 1955), p. 347. Winter makes light of these security measures and fails to mention the BF and his role in it.

[20] Brigadier-General Sir Ormonde Winter, 'A statement on fascist policy', *Fascist Bulletin*, 29 August 1925.

[21] B. S. Farr, *The Development and Impact of Right-Wing Politics in Britain, 1903–1932* (New York: Garland, 1987), p. 54.

Figure 2   Emblem of the British Fascists
Author

Like the Italian dictator, her movement had 'Fascist' in the title, but with no fascist programme as such. In the academic literature this has led to the denial that the BF ever had any authentic fascist ambition.[22] G. C. Webber encapsulates the academic consensus in his statement: 'It borrowed the name, but not much else from Italy.'[23] Certainly, the BF fails the test of a 'Fascist minimum' as defined by Roger Griffin – a movement informed by a modernist 'palingenetic' myth directed to 'realizing a totalising vision of national or ethnic rebirth'.[24]

[22] Colin Cross, *The Fascists in Britain* (London: Barrie and Rockliff, 1963), pp. 58–63; Roger Eatwell, *Fascism: A History* (London: Chatto & Windus, 1995), pp. 175–77; J. V. Gottlieb, *Feminine Fascism: Women in Britain's Fascist Movement* (London: I.B. Tauris, 2003), pp. 32–34.

[23] G. C. Webber, 'Tolerance and discretion: conservatism and British fascism, 1918–1926', in Tony Kushner and Kenneth Lunn (eds), *Traditions of Intolerance: Historical Perspectives on Fascism and Race Discourse in Britain* (Manchester: Manchester University Press, 1989), p. 163.

[24] Roger Griffin, *Modernism and Fascism: The Sense of a New Beginning under Mussolini and Hitler* (Basingstoke: Palgrave Macmillan, 2007), pp. 181–82; also Roger Griffin, *The Nature of Fascism* (London: Pinter, 1991), pp. 44–45.

A reactive outlook, concerned mainly to stem the perceived collapse of the traditional power structure and values, rather than a modernist, socially transformative, national vision, initially informed the BF as a movement. Its outlook was reflected in the movement's original badge that included a crown, which had to be removed apparently at the same time as a loyalty oath to the King included in the BF membership pledge was declared illegal. Nevertheless, Lintorn-Orman shared with Italian fascism the belief that the existing parliamentary system of Government was incapable of solving the crisis facing the State, and emphasised a masculine 'return to *VIRILITY* … a determination to get the right Kingdom *regardless of immediate consequences*' (my italics).[25]

The BF was the ideal agency for this project because 'it has no past [parliamentary] traditions to fetter its actions.'[26] Her thinking in this respect was significantly different from that of the leading Ulster member of the organisation's leadership, Lord Ernest Hamilton. Just a fortnight later he would utilise the letter columns of the *Morning Post* to offer the services of the BF to Conservative Party election candidates,[27] thereby doing much to facilitate the view that the BF was blindly subservient to Tory interests. But if dictatorial intent was not explicitly aimed for it was at least implicit in Lintorn-Orman's arguments. In fact, the BF would come to accept that dictatorship might be necessary in the national interest and ultimately actively to promote it, though Lintorn-Orman's attempts to demonstrate the 'virility' she promulgated often resulted in a 'mannishness' that invited ridicule.[28] Accordingly, while she would remain the most prominent personality in the BF, the official leadership of her organisation was male, and for our purposes what is significant is the Ulster dimension.

Lord Garvagh, owner of 15,000 acres in county Londonderry, initially held the position of President,[29] while Lord Ernest Hamilton's definition of fascism was based on a perceived disjuncture

---

[25] *Fascist Bulletin*, 26 September 1925.
[26] Ibid.
[27] Lord Ernest Hamilton to the editor, *Morning Post*, 13 October 1925.
[28] Gottlieb, *Feminine Fascism*, pp. 16–22.
[29] 'Irish Fascisti Peer', *Irish Independent*, 20 November 1923.

between the parliamentary system and authentic British national feeling that had been gestating from the 1880s, when Gladstone's Home Rule plans first appeared to threaten Ulster's membership of the United Kingdom.[30] Thus: 'The first duty of Fascism … is to combat this insane love-our-enemies craze which is hurrying the country post-haste towards suicide.'[31] Outside the landed elite, the Unionist propagandist H. M. Pim offered his services to the BF,[32] while William Joyce (later Lord Haw-Haw), was an early member.[33] Joyce's view that the pre-war UVF was an authentic progenitor of British fascism – he regarded Sir Edward Carson as a 'political god'[34] – and would have developed as such had not the Great War intervened,[35] is hardly convincing. Nevertheless, it indicates clearly enough the significance the UVF had for the BF and much of the British extreme Right (the *Morning Post* described the Ulster loyalists as 'the first of all the Fascists, although an Orange sash, and not a shirt, was the badge of their allegiance')[36] in the crisis Britain appeared to be facing, while, as we shall see, Lintorn-Orman would seek Carson's personal endorsement for her organisation.

Interpretations of the UVF and Ulster Orangeism such as that provided by the BF and the *Morning Post*, however, were too narrowly framed: BF literature could describe the Irish Marxist Labour leader James Connolly as 'Jim Connolly', a 'traitor … justly executed in Dublin during the Irish Rebellion in 1916',[37] without recognising

---

[30] Lord Ernest Hamilton, *Forty Years On* (London: Hodder & Stoughton, 1922), p. 223.

[31] *Fascist Bulletin*, 25 July 1925.

[32] See 'The old flag', *Fascist Bulletin*, 27 June 1925. For a short biographical account of Pim, see Patrick Maume, 'Herbert Moore Pim, 1883–1950', in James Quinn and Patrick Maume (eds), *Ulster Political Lives, 1886–1921* (Dublin: Royal Irish Academy, 2016), pp. 247–49.

[33] J. A. Cole, *Lord Haw Haw: The Full Story of William Joyce* (London: Faber & Faber, 1964), pp. 56, 197.

[34] Holmes, *Searching for Lord Haw-Haw*, p. 64.

[35] 'Quis Separabit' [obituary of Lord Carson], *Fascist Quarterly* (January 1936), 27–29.

[36] *Morning Post*, quoted in editorial, *Irish News*, 24 July 1933.

[37] British Fascists, *The 'Red Menace' to British Children* (2nd edn, London: British Fascists, [1926]), p. 4.

the crucial role that Carson's pre-war mobilising and arming of the UVF had played in providing the template for the 1916 rebels and the consequent break-up of the United Kingdom in 1922. Fixated on the Soviet threat to western civilisation, of which militant Irish republicanism was a perceived aspect, it was inconceivable for the BF that the Ulster-based inspiration for combating that threat might actually have inspired the republican dimension of it. And while Carson provided Lintorn-Orman with an example of politically triumphant will to emulate, irrespective of 'immediate consequences', hers did not reflect a homogeneity of outlook among the movement's leadership in the run-up to what seemed the most serious contemporary threat to the State, the General Strike of 1926: the BF's offer of assistance to the Government was accepted only on condition that it change its name and register as a non-political organisation.[38]

Lintorn-Orman's refusal occasioned a split in the organisation, with Brigadier-General R. B. D. Blakeney, who had succeeded Lord Garvagh as President, and much of the male leadership, including Lord Ernest Hamilton,[39] resigning.[40] For Lintorn-Orman, only her movement could be expected to deal effectively with a serious threat to the State and that a leadership role in that context would transform its political fortunes. Thus its present weakened state, while disappointing, was not necessarily a reason for despair; indeed,

---

[38] However, Government rejection of BF assistance was, in practice, less definite than it appeared. It was quite happy to use BF personnel on an individual and ideological basis, and on the premise that they act under Government direction: John Hope, 'Fascism and the state in Britain: the case of the British Fascist, 1923–31', *Australian Journal of Politics and History*, vol. 39, no. 3 (1993), 367–80.

[39] H. R. Boyd to Lord Stamfordham, 23 June 1926, Report on the British Fascists (NAK, HO144/19069).

[40] *Fascist Bulletin*, 17 October 1925. Hamilton's resignation ended his overt involvement in politics, but he was later a member of the elite Anglo-German Fellowship in the later 1930s, while his daughter, Mary, held membership of Captain A. H. Maule Ramsay's pro-Nazi Right Club. See Nigel West, *MI5: British Security Service Operations, 1909–1945* (London: Triad Granada, 1983), p. 168; Robin Saikia (ed.), *The Red Book: The Membership List of The Right Club, 1939* (London: Foxley Books, 2010), p. 105; British Fascists, *'Red Menace'*, pp. 8–11.

the departure of the moderates could be seen as the removal of its weakest elements. A need to restore its membership levels was an important factor in the decision to extend BF activities to Northern Ireland following the strike.[41] And certainly from a BF perspective the region was seriously in need of constitutional defence.

It was singular in a number of respects: as a factor in Anglo-Irish relations; geographically, by sharing a border with another, perceptibly hostile, State; and by having its own autonomous Government, dominated by one ethnic – Protestant and Unionist – group and where the Catholic and nationalist minority was not only excluded from power but agitated actively for unity with the Irish Free State. Whereas the Catholic population of Britain in the inter-war period stood at 2,964,000 dispersed among a total population of around 45,000,000,[42] accounting roughly for only one in 15 of the population and posing no threat to State interests, in Northern Ireland disaffected Catholics constituted one-third of a total population of around 1,500,000, rendering the region constitutionally unstable, while constitutional uncertainty and anti-partitionist propaganda exacerbated Unionist fears facilitating repressive security policies directed against the Catholic population.

Northern Ireland in the Post-War Period

Given that the failure of fascism which historical hindsight allows was not perceivable to contemporary observers, the nature of the crisis the United Kingdom was experiencing in the inter-war period was very much determined by the angle and geographic position from which it was viewed. A Belfast perspective would identify a British State constitutionally fragile, a London perspective one fundamentally secure. And while the Northern Ireland Government attracted the support of the BF leadership when the Boundary Commission was established to settle the region's border with the

---

[41] Subscription income apparently dropped from £6,848 in 1925 to £604 in 1928 and less than £400 per year thereafter: Richard Thurlow, *Fascism in Britain: A History, 1918–1985* (Oxford: Blackwell, 1987), pp. 52–53.
[42] Tom Villis, *British Catholics and Fascism: Religious Identity and Political Extremism between the Wars* (Basingstoke: Palgrave Macmillan, 2013), p. 1.

Irish Free State in late 1924,[43] it had otherwise merited only a brief, unspecified, inclusion in BF policy on 'the development of agriculture and afforestation in Britain and Ireland',[44] when, in fact, it was the only part of the United Kingdom that had evidenced the kind of socio-political upheaval the BF expected in Britain. A regional parliament excluded from the remit of Dublin rule may have been achieved by January 1922, but amid civil and paramilitary conflict, exacerbated when some northern units of the IRA went on the offensive from the start of May 1922, attacking Unionist property and security installations, with attendant killings of the Unionist MP W. J. Twaddell and members of the Ulster Special Constabulary (USC) – a security organisation a great expansion of which the Unionist premier Sir James Craig had succeeded in persuading the Imperial Defence Committee, chaired by a sympathetic Winston Churchill, to fund. Eventually, local forces at the regime's command would total 48,000, with one estimate putting one adult male Protestant in four 'in some section of the security forces'.[45] Furthermore, serious problems developed in the post-war years within the Unionist family itself as large numbers of demobilised soldiers found themselves without employment.

A solution to their difficulties was found in giving the labour issue a sectarian twist, with the claim that during the war northern industries had been subject to 'peaceful penetration' by 'tens of thousands' of Catholics from the south and west. The upshot was loyalist mass expulsions of 'Bolsheviks' and Catholics from northern industries in the early 1920s, endorsed by a Unionist leadership concerned to maintain its hold over a loyalist working

[43] See 'British Fascisti and Sir James Craig', *Cork Examiner*, 6 September 1924. For a comprehensive account of the Anglo-Irish settlement, in particular in its Ulster aspects, see Nicholas Mansergh, *The Unresolved Question: The Anglo-Irish Settlement and its Undoing, 1912–1972* (New Haven, Conn. and London: Yale University Press, 1991), parts III–V.

[44] *British Lion*, [late June] 1926.

[45] Graham Walker, *A History of the Ulster Unionist Party: Protest, Pragmatism and Pessimism* (Manchester: Manchester University Press, 2004), pp. 129–30, 144; Michael Farrell, *Arming the Protestants: The Formation of the Ulster Special Constabulary and the Royal Ulster Constabulary, 1920–1927* (Dingle: Brandon Books, 1983), pp. 127–29.

class increasingly inclined to violent autonomous action,[46] and in the process prepared to approve the abandonment of impartiality in the exercise of their duties by the northern security forces. Indeed, the conditions in which the statelet was born – republican attack, nationalist boycott and fluctuations in British State interests – would determine a consistent leadership tendency of accommodating sectarian loyalist grass-roots demands as the price of political management.[47]

That tendency found striking expression in 1922 when, in contravention of the Government of Ireland Act of 1920, the northern regime abolished proportional representation (PR) in local government elections. Introduced to enhance the protection of minorities, PR had resulted in significant loss of Unionist power at the local elections of 1920, especially in Derry city where nationalists won control of the corporation for the first time since the 1680s. Westminster's initial refusal of the royal assent dissolved when faced with the regime's threat of resignation and the prospect of London having to administer the region. The episode was of profound significance for the future. It established both the unhindered control of regional Government by Unionist administrations and also the Westminster convention of non-intervention in Northern Ireland's affairs.[48] At the same time, the latter was accompanied by increasing Tory support for Northern Ireland's constitutional position that would have an important influence on the outcome of the Boundary Commission in 1925.

The Commission had been established in clause 12 of the Anglo-Irish Treaty of 1921, and intended to convince the republican signatories that in the event of Ulster Unionists refusing inclusion in the Irish Free State it would determine the boundary between Northern Ireland and the south, something republicans expected

---

[46] Paul Bew, Peter Gibbon and Henry Patterson, *Northern Ireland, 1921–1996: Political Forces and Social Classes* (London: Serif, 1995), pp. 25–27; Walker, *History of the Ulster Unionist Party*, pp. 55–56.

[47] Walker, *History of the Ulster Unionist Party*, pp. 58–60.

[48] Paul Canning, *British Policy towards Ireland, 1921–1941* (Oxford: Oxford University Press, 1985), pp. 64–65; Patrick Buckland, *A History of Northern Ireland* (Dublin: Gill & Macmillan, 1989), pp. 52–54.

– given the large nationalist areas of the west and south of the region – to result in substantial swathes of Northern Ireland being transferred to the Free State. However, when Unionist rejection quickly followed the publication of the Treaty, the expected rapid establishment of the Boundary Commission failed to emerge. Southern divisions and a subsequent civil war over the terms of the Treaty were partly to blame, but so too were illnesses affecting political leaders, north and south, changes of Government in Britain and, especially, the blank refusal of Sir James Craig to appoint a commissioner to represent his regime's interests; a difficulty only resolved when Westminster made arrangements to appoint an Ulster commissioner. Accordingly, it was late 1924 before the commission seriously began to address the boundary issue.[49] Thus from the establishment of the northern entity through to late 1925, when the commission's proceedings collapsed following a damaging, but accurate leak of its likely findings in the *Morning Post* – far from the Irish Free State gaining large tracts of northern territory it would actually lose part of east Donegal[50] – constitutional uncertainty hung over the region. By then, however, and despite ongoing irritations in the Belfast–Westminster relationship,[51] Ulster Unionist leaders had successfully cultivated British Conservative support and secured the region's position within the British State. As Stanley Baldwin had put it, if the commission determined on transfers of counties from north to south (counties Tyrone and Fermanagh had nationalist majorities), 'then of course Ulster couldn't accept it and we should back her'.[52] For its part, and in return for economic concessions by Westminster, the Free State accepted the existing border.[53] Thus the Ulster regime had established its virtually unfettered control of the domestic administration of the region and consolidated its

[49] Michael Laffan, *The Partition of Ireland, 1911–1925* (Dublin: Dublin Historical Association, 1983), pp. 98–100.
[50] Ibid., pp. 103–04.
[51] For instance, changes to the royal title which failed to identify Northern Ireland's membership of the United Kingdom (*Belfast Telegraph*, 23 November 1926; *Belfast News-Letter*, 24 November 1926).
[52] Baldwin to Edward Wood (later Lord Halifax), 6 September 1924, quoted in Canning, *British Policy towards Ireland, 1921–1941*, p. 86.
[53] Laffan, *Partition of Ireland*, pp. 104–05.

relationship with the Tory leadership and party, which apart from the brief Labour Government of Ramsay McDonald in 1924 would be in power from 1924 to the end of the decade.

As compared with other areas of the United Kingdom, Northern Ireland would remain a politically volatile frontier region and a likely location for constitutional upheaval. Nevertheless, while such factors gave the region the appearance of needing a BF presence, that the Unionist regime had effectively consolidated the region's constitutional position by 1926 meant that the state of acute crisis Lintorn-Orman saw as conducive to political success had passed; and with it the utility of an organisation like the BF. Accordingly, despite a close harmonisation of BF ideological outlook with the loyalist Orange and Black organisations,[54] and the opportunity the BF presence apparently offered the northern authorities to extend and consolidate their mainland British links, the organisation's growth in Northern Ireland would be disappointing.

The Ulster Command

The Ulster dimension to BF activities is acknowledged in the academic literature,[55] but only briefly, and while its important feminine aspect is referenced, it is greatly underdeveloped, in particular the crucial personal relationship the BF founder, Lintorn-Orman, formed with the Waring family of Lisnacree in south county Down, especially Dorothy Grace Harnett, and which would be crucial to the centrality that Ulster would have in BF affairs in the late 1920s. But it was the formation of the BF's Belfast centre that initially registered the organisation's presence in Northern Ireland.

Formed in late summer,[56] and having apparently established a significant membership, the Ulster Command had its first public

---

[54] See report of arguments made at the annual Royal Black celebrations in August 1926 in *British Lion*, 11 September 1926.
[55] Richard Griffiths, *Fellow Travellers of the Right: British Enthusiasts for Nazi Germany* (Oxford: Oxford University Press, 1983), pp. 92–93; Gottlieb, *Feminine Fascism*, pp. 34, 149, 168.
[56] *British Lion*, 25 September 1926.

meeting in Belfast on 22 November 1926, chaired by Captain
E. G. Morgan, the platform party (Figure 3) evidencing the organisation's pitch to both women and men. Speakers lauded the fascist
example set by Mussolini and his definition of fascism as 'National'
rather than 'International' in nature. There would, however, be
no association with Italian fascists *in* Belfast or elsewhere in the
north. Members of the resident Italian community, whose activities
were confined chiefly to maintaining links with the homeland,
were overwhelmingly Catholic with close ties to the local Catholic
clergy,[57] though the BF 'Irish Command' in the Irish Free State did
communicate to the Italian community its great relief at Mussolini
surviving Lady Violet Gibson's assassination attempt in 1926.[58] It
was to assert clearly the Ulster Command's very different identity
that Captain Morgan informed the press that the BF had no
connection whatsoever with Italian fascism and disapproved of its
ideas and methods. As the BF understood it, fascism 'is simply the
binding together of all loyal people who uphold the traditions of our
country, who are of British birth and extraction', whose religion was
'the teachings and principles of Christ'. If any attempt was made by
force or otherwise to 'overthrow the constitution of our land we
shall be on the side of the Government of the day'.[59]

At the Ulster Command inaugural meeting, Captain
W. Turner-Coles, the movement's Chief of Staff at the London
GHQ, more vehemently defined its political position and objectives:
'Britain for the British', expressed in the mantra, 'firstly, for
God; secondly, for King; and thirdly, for Country',[60] pursued
through 'methods best suited to conditions here'.[61] The meeting,
however, descended into chaos and violence – occasioning hospital
treatment for Captain Morgan, reported variously as a broken arm

[57] See, for instance, 'Belfast fascists: new flag blessed', *Irish Times*, 11 June
1925; *Derry Standard*, 3 July 1935; *Irish News*, 14 August 1935; Robert Fisk,
In Time of War: Ireland, Ulster and the Price of Neutrality, 1939–45 (London:
Paladin, 1987), p. 50.
[58] 'Irish fascists' message', *Irish Examiner*, 3 November 1926.
[59] E. G. Morgan to the editor, *Weekly Telegraph*, 25 September 1926.
[60] See also BF enrolment form (British Fascists documents, PRONI:
D3783/A/2).
[61] *British Lion*, 4 December 1926.

Figure 3   Platform Party at the Inaugural Meeting of the British Fascists
Ulster Command, Belfast, 22 November 1926
Reproduced from *Irish Daily Telegraph*, 23 November 1926,
courtesy of A. & G. Baird and the *Belfast Telegraph*

or dislocated shoulder[62] – when Turner-Coles declared that those
who disagreed with the BF creed should 'get out' of the country.[63]
In Belfast political violence usually had a sectarian origin, but the
savage inter-ethnic violence that characterised the early years of
the regime had now ceased, and there is nothing in reports of the
meeting to suggest a nationalist presence, though the local political
culture was reflected in the definition of 'a Socialist' as a 'Rebel'.
What was unusual about the violence, was that it was occasioned by
different senses of Britishness.[64]

    That violence occurred, however, was not entirely surprising.
Turner-Coles had an aggressive approach to political agitation that
provoked violence at BF meetings in Britain,[65] while the Ulster
Command's statement of policy and aims, produced a month earlier,
was characterised by the apocalyptic belief that the State was faced
with such a treacherous and dishonourable enemy that either 'we
or our opponents must go under': 'broad-minded tolerance as often

[62] *Western Daily Press*, 23 November 1926; *Irish Times*, 23 November 1926.
[63] *Belfast Telegraph*, 23 November 1926; *British Lion*, 4 December 1926.
[64] *British Lion*, 4 December 1926.
[65] See 'Turner-Coles's activities in London: scenes at fascist demonstration',
Irish Times, 30 March 1927.

as not is but the excuse and camouflage of Moral Cowardice'. And together with constitutional upheaval societal values were also under threat, evidenced in a parliamentary bill at Westminster to amend the blasphemy laws: 'after its enactment no Criminal Proceedings will be initiated against any Person for Schism, Heresy, Blasphemy, Blasphemous Libel or Atheism.' The threat, moreover, would be directed specifically at the most vulnerable sector of British society, children: 'Karl Liebnecht the notorious [German] Communist, states "Who has the Youth has the future".'[66]

The Ulster Command's arguments evidenced mainland British concerns with a regional inflection, and as such were non-controversial in a local context. What worried the authorities, however, was the aggression with which they were expressed, and how the BF's evident lack of faith in the regime's ability to deal with constitutional subversion would lead it to act autonomously. This seemed only too likely in the context of a negative assessment of Captain Morgan and the local BF leadership made by the RUC two months earlier.

Morgan was described as 'a waster' with 'an excess of so-called loyalty', who both before and during his membership of the USC in the early 1920s 'was a source of trouble to Roman Catholics … He was actually seen writing filthy inscriptions on the walls of their houses.' Moreover, his resignation from the USC in October 1924 was compelled following a court of enquiry which found him guilty of lying to a superior officer and an 'act judged prejudicial to the good order and discipline of the Force'. Accordingly, while the principles of the BF 'are excellent … it is a pity that the local organisation should have got into somewhat undesirable hands.'[67]

In sum, Captain Morgan was a personification of the violent, sectarian and lawless elements of loyalism that had proved so troublesome to the Unionist leadership in the early 1920s. That he would lead an independent 'loyal' organisation outside the control of the Unionist leadership could only be regarded as a development to be discouraged, especially as the Northern Ireland parliamentary

---

[66] Ulster Command, British Fascists, *Who and What are the British Fascists?* (Belfast: Ulster Command, 1926) (Home Affairs papers, PRONI: HA/32/1/509).
[67] 'EWS', Note to police report on BF inaugural meeting, 22 November 1926 (Home Affairs papers, PRONI: HA/32/1/509).

election of 1925 had returned a number of Labour and Independent MPs elected at Unionist Party expense, suggesting some splintering of the broad alliance of Unionist interests.[68] Accordingly, RUC advice to Government ministers was to steer clear of the BF.[69] Of course, as a British patriotic movement, the northern authorities were unlikely actually to move against it, thus its recruitment activities proceeded.

Organising took place within the structure already existing for the British State in general: a hierarchy headed by a headquarters committee from a larger grand council spread geographically downwards to county and area commanders, the latter having 'very wide discretionary powers, much depending on their initiative when the call comes'.[70] For our purposes, this is of particular significance, for although the BF structure in Northern Ireland was organised as an 'Ulster Command', with its centre in Belfast, the region would be noteworthy mainly for the activities of the county Down division, led officially by the County Commander, Mrs Florence Waring, but substantively by her daughter, Dorothy Grace Harnett.[71] On the whole, it would prove to be more energetic than the BF organisation in the Irish Free State.

The BF 'Southern Command' based in Dublin was established before that of Northern Ireland. It defined its role as seeking to promote loyalty to the Empire through the example of 'strict discipline' in an Ireland 'very conducive to … disorder'. Numbering around 100,[72] its activities attracted State attention, though interest dissipated as the group was found to be constitutionally non-threatening.[73]

---

[68] On the election, see Michael Farrell, *Northern Ireland: The Orange State* (London: Pluto Press, 1976), pp. 103–05.

[69] E. Gilfillan to R. P. Pim, 9 September 1926 (Home Affairs papers, PRONI: HA/32/1/509).

[70] Blakeney, 'British Fascism', p. 139; Benewick, *The Fascist Movement in Britain*, pp. 30–31.

[71] Gottlieb's *Feminine Fascism*, however, confuses the identities and roles of Harnett and her mother. Harnett is listed as two separate people: 'Dorothy Waring' and 'D. G. Harnett' on page 31 and 'Mrs Dorothy Grace Warring [*sic*] (a.k.a. Harnett)' on page 345.

[72] *British Lion*, 29 September 1926.

[73] See 'Organisation of fascists in An Saorstat' (Irish National Archives (INA), Department of Justice file, JUS/H197/61).

Indeed, it was surprisingly mute on a subject both the BF in Britain and Lord Carson were increasingly exercised about – the fate of loyalists living in an apparently unstable and unfriendly constitutional environment. Southern Command activities were fully reported in the BF press, but the Irish Free State, outside the United Kingdom, offered little hope for progress. Northern Ireland, by contrast, was a region where State integrity needed defence.

The ebullience with which Turner-Coles expounded the BF creed at the Belfast inaugural meeting was informed by a promising early response to the movement's recruitment efforts.[74] Within a year a membership of 1,000 in the city was reported,[75] while the BF Women's Units in Belfast were reportedly 'looking after the welfare' of a similar number of children in the poorest districts.[76] But 1927 marked the highpoint for the Belfast centre. By June 1927, the police were satisfied that the BF's tendency to political trouble-making – which apparently included the use of Lambeg drumming to break up labour meetings[77] – had been contained;[78] despite an official membership of around 1,000 active engagement with the centre was clearly diminishing.

While the anniversary meeting of the BF's first Belfast meeting, and others outside Belfast, were honoured by the attendance of Rotha Lintorn-Orman,[79] unlike an estimated 250 that attended the inaugural meeting in 1926, in 1927 Lintorn-Orman spoke to an audience of only 80, and unlike the grand ambition then – to confront the communist menace head on – the objective the local BF membership claimed now, a membership 'largely composed of working men' was 'to help those in authority to maintain law and order'.[80] Despite an official programme of recruitment throughout the region – 'the Six Counties (outside Belfast) are just as important

---

[74] *British Lion*, 4 December 1926.
[75] *Irish Times*, 5 August 1927.
[76] *British Lion*, June 1927.
[77] See Job Stott to editor, *Irish News*, 30 June 1934.
[78] Note by 'EWS' (15 June 1927) to police report on BF meeting of 10 June 1927 (Home Affairs papers, PRONI: HA/32/1/509).
[79] 'Newcastle meeting', *Belfast News-Letter*, 2 November 1927.
[80] E. Gilfillan to Secretary, Ministry of Home Affairs, 3 November 1927 (Home Affairs papers, PRONI: HA/32/1/509).

as the city'[81] – it was effectively confined to the overwhelmingly Protestant east of the region, especially greater Belfast, and this was of some significance. For whereas in Britain the BF was concerned to emphasise its cross-confessional character, especially for the purpose of reassuring its Roman Catholic membership when occasional anti-Catholic sentiments were expressed within the organisation,[82] this would not be the case in Northern Ireland, though with no discernible benefit in terms of popular support. Even extending the movement to the Newtownards area of north Down (see Figure 1) proved problematic,[83] while Rotha Lintorn-Orman's hopes for meetings in Armagh or Londonderry in late 1927 were not fulfilled.[84] She would return to the Belfast centre the following year, supported by the Ulster Unionist MP for Queen's University, Sir John Campbell, who presided. But the attendance was even smaller than in 1927.[85]

The last, police-reported, meeting of the BF in Belfast, on 25 May 1929, reflected the centre's steadily declining fortunes. There had now been a 'complete change in personnel' with 'those who took a prominent part in the inception of the Branch' having 'either resigned or pleaded that other duties prevented them from attending'. Certainly, its new governing body, consisting of two clerks, a tramway driver and an assistant in a pawnbroker's shop,[86] registered a distinct lowering of social class from the military officers who had initiated the Ulster Command. Leadership apathy reflected a more

[81] D. G. Harnett, District Officer (co. Down), Ulster Women's Units, to Miss Robinson, 8 December 1927 (British Fascists documents, PRONI: D3783/A/2).

[82] See *Fascist Bulletin*, 13 February 1926; 'Editorial note', *Fascist Bulletin*, 27 March 1926; condemnation of state persecution of Catholics in Mexico: 'British Fascists: strong condemnation of persecution', *Irish Independent*, 2 June 1928.

[83] D. G. Harnett to Miss Robinson, 8 December 1927 (British Fascists documents, PRONI: D3783/A/2).

[84] N. G. Ray, British Fascists GHQ, London, to Mrs Waring, 12 October 1927 (British Fascists documents, PRONI: D3783/A/2).

[85] Note by 'EWS' (25 June 1928) to police report on BF meeting (Home Affairs office, PRONI: HA/32/1/509).

[86] E. Gilfillan to Secretary, Ministry of Home Affairs, 25 May 1929 (Home Affairs office, PRONI: HA/32/1/509).

general membership decline, 'believed to be due to lack of public support and enthusiasm'. Accordingly, apart from a Fascist Children's Club, 'the activities of the organisation are practically nil in Belfast.' Its hopes for the future hung on a return to power of the Labour Party in Britain and a consequent 'big fillip to the organisation'.[87] Labour did indeed return to power in 1929, but the expected rush of popular support for the Ulster Command did not take place.

Apart from the Government boycott of the BF and possible public concern about individual BF leaders, the BF in Belfast suffered from a number of weaknesses. First, in addition to the fact that by 1926 the constitutional crisis facing the regime had clearly dissipated, the BF's stated rationale for organising in Northern Ireland – because its regional Government had become constitutionally apathetic, ignoring communist 'danger signals'[88] – was hardly persuasive. Second, its 'mainland' British focus on communist subversion was of little immediate local relevance[89] – the 'communist' General Strike had made virtually no impression in Northern Ireland.[90] And compared with the enthusiastic support of the Conservative Party and the British right-wing press for Northern Ireland's constitutional position – Conservative support was reinforced by the fact that the 13 Ulster Unionist MPs at Westminster were an important addition to Tory strength given the narrow margin of victory and defeat at general elections in the 1920s[91] – there was little in terms of practical political support the BF could offer. Third, the gradually increasing antisemitic tone of BF propaganda,[92] embodied in

[87] Ibid.
[88] *British Lion*, 17 February; December 1927.
[89] 'The fighting spirit', *British Lion*, 23 October 1926; *British Lion*, 4 December 1926; 'British fascism in Ulster', *British Lion*, 17 February 1927; 'Belfast', *British Lion*, June 1927.
[90] See Stanley Baldwin–Craig correspondence, 11 May 1926 (Cabinet papers, PRONI: CAB23/53).
[91] James Loughlin, *Ulster Unionism and British National Identity since 1885* (London: Pinter, 1995), pp. 93–94.
[92] The view that antisemitism was merely a late-developing theme in BF propaganda has been effectively refuted in Kenneth Lunn, 'The ideology and impact of the British Fascists in the 1920s', in Kushner and Lunn, *Traditions of Intolerance*, pp. 150–51.

concern about the 'alien menace', had little response in Belfast. Nor did the Belfast centre prioritise it. The north's Jewish community numbered fewer than 2,000 (in 1937, 1,472, with 1,284 living in Belfast) and apparently found it a hospitable environment.[93] Fourth, despite the mainland British organisation's reporting of Catholic clerical condemnation of communism,[94] and the fact that the Ulster organisation shared an equally virulent detestation of 'Communism', the regional organisation could not hope to extend its support base across the sectarian boundary. This was precluded not only by the latter's anti-partitionism and Morgan's sectarian past but by the Ulster organisation's close association with the Orange Order.

The only part of the BF operation in Belfast to survive its effective demise was the Fascist Children's Clubs, which offered regular, practical activity. The decline of the Belfast centre, however, was not entirely mirrored outside the city. Arguably, Belfast's decline was a condition of the relative importance the county Down BF units would assume in the late 1920s.

Dorothy Harnett and the South Down Ulster Women's Units

The county Down BF units, established shortly after the Ulster Command became active, with their base at Lisnacree, outside Kilkeel, and led officially by the Area Commander Mrs Florence Waring, provided the agency through which Rotha Lintorn-Orman's Northern Ireland visits were arranged. At one level the county Down units fitted easily within the structure of the movement's Women's Units across the British State, with their emphasis on countering communist/socialist influence through children's education and welfare.[95] At another level, due mainly to the recent history of the area, they were quite distinctive.

---

[93] David Warm, 'The Jews of Northern Ireland', in Paul Hainsworth (ed.), *Divided Society: Ethnic Minorities and Racism in Northern Ireland* (London: Pluto, 1998), pp. 225–26; Gerald Moore, 'Anti-Semitism in Ireland', PhD thesis, Ulster Polytechnic, 1984; Dermot Keogh, *Jews in Twentieth-Century Ireland: Refugees, Anti-Semitism and the Holocaust* (Cork: Cork University Press, 1998), p. 58.

[94] '"Devil's work" of Communism', *Fascist Bulletin*, 27 June 1925.

[95] See, for example, 'N.W.5 Women's branch', *Fascist Bulletin*, 26 September

The security that the close of the Boundary Commission episode afforded the Unionist Government in Belfast was felt less strongly among border Unionists. The sense of grievance felt by nationalists in these areas at the disappointment of their hopes for large land transfers to the Irish Free State remained as an ambition to be fulfilled,[96] feeding local Unionist anxieties. County Down was overwhelmingly loyalist in its northern and mid-area and strongly nationalist in the south. For Unionists in the latter, especially in the Kilkeel area, the threat to their membership of the United Kingdom was clear from 1922: nationalist-controlled local authorities repudiated the authority of the northern parliament and declared their allegiance to the Irish Free State.[97] Ulster Unionist perceptions of southern events in this period – mirrored to a limited extent by those in the south who perceived Northern Ireland coming under the control of 'the Ku Klux Klan'[98] – tended to be lurid, often diverging widely from reality.[99] Thus when the leader of the irregular forces that had instigated the Irish Civil War, Eamon de Valera, led his new party, Fianna Fail, into the southern parliament in 1927 on an anti-imperial and anti-partitionist platform, drawing on popular support that made electoral success in the near future likely, border Unionist anxieties intensified. In this context, the Government influence that served to quarantine the Belfast centre of the BF was less effective in south Down: the sense of Unionist vulnerability, together with the closer personal familiarity common to rural communities, acted to mitigate it.

1925; 'Children's club (London, W.14)', *British Lion*, 25 September 1926; 'Fascist children's clubs', *British Lion*, June 1927; *The Young Fascist: A Monthly Magazine of the Fascist Youth Movement*, June 1934 (British Fascists documents, PRONI: D3783/A/2).
[96] Enda Staunton, *The Nationalists of Northern Ireland, 1918–1973* (Dublin: Columba, 2001), pp. 109–10.
[97] Laffan, *Partition of Ireland*, chap. 6; Eamon Phoenix, *Northern Nationalism, Partition and the Catholic Minority in Northern Ireland, 1890–1940* (Belfast: Ulster Historical Foundation, 1994), pp. 167–68.
[98] Director of Intelligence to Minister of Defence and Chief of the General Staff, 4 January 1924: 'Report: Ku Klux Klan in the six counties' (INA, Irish Military Archive, MS 334).
[99] Dennis Kennedy, *The Widening Gulf: Northern Attitudes to the Independent Irish State 1919–1949* (Belfast: Blackstaff Press, 1988).

Thus while none of Belfast's sixteen Unionist MPs engaged with the city's BF centre – Sir John Campbell's presence at the Belfast meeting in 1928 was an exception – the BF in south Down apparently had a closer involvement with the district's Unionist MP, Robert McBride.[100] Also, while the Belfast centre could not boast of any elite or aristocratic involvement in its activities, in the south Down–south Armagh area the Earl and Countess of Kilmorey of Mourne Park, Newry, gave their support, with Countess Kilmorey taking a significant role in the activities of the BF Children's Clubs.[101] Earl Kilmorey would be appointed Commander of the Ulster Division of the Royal Naval Volunteer Reserve in 1930,[102] reflecting the greater social engagement with, and respectability of, the BF in the area. Even the level of military rank was generally higher than the Captains who controlled the Belfast centre.

BF meetings in the south Down–south Armagh area could assemble platform parties at the Major, Colonel and Brigadier-General level, in addition to others drawn from the senior professional class, though individual BF officers from the Belfast area keen to remain active were also present.[103] The annual excursions of the Belfast Fascist Children's Clubs to the south Down area[104] pointed up, no less, the prominence of its formations. But, most importantly, in a context where the fraught experiences of the early 1920s seemed about to be repeated, south Down produced, in Dorothy Grace Harnett (Figure 4: Harnett is holding the wreath) the most dynamic and influential member of the Ulster Command, though she was not an unmixed blessing.

Harnett, a member of the local gentry, had, along with her parents, been temporarily imprisoned by the IRA during the independence struggle while their home, Lisnacree House, was searched for weapons. Subsequently she proved to be a highly

---

[100] See, for example, McBride's speech at Royal Black demonstration, August 1926, reported in *British Lion*, 11 September 1926; BF meeting notice for Town Hall, Dromore, co. Down, 28 November 1927 (British Fascists documents, PRONI: D3783/A/2).

[101] See *British Lion*, June 1929.

[102] *Irish Times*, 6 January 1936.

[103] See, for example, *Down Recorder*, 13, 18 August 1927; 30 June 1928.

[104] See *Newry Telegraph*, 2 July 1932; 1 July 1933.

Figure 4   British Fascists' Wreath-Laying Party, Cenotaph, London,
Armistice Day 1931
British Fascism, November 1931 © British Library Board: General Reference
Collection 1930–1934 PENP.NT124

controversial member of the USC, accused of insulting local
Catholics and, more seriously, strip-searching republican women
suspects. At first defended by the northern regime, her activities
eventually became so controversial that both local Unionist and
nationalist complaints led, in March 1923, to her services being
dispensed with.[105] Accordingly, while the BF centre of gravity in
Northern Ireland moved from Belfast to south Down in the later
1920s, the prominence of Harnett in its activities would ensure
there was little prospect of the northern authorities changing their
boycott policy towards the organisation. Police reports recorded her
'somewhat unenviable notoriety while acting as a female searcher

---

[105] Gordon Gillespie, 'The secret life of D. G. Waring', *Causeway* (spring
1998), 43–45; also 'Old families of the Mourne county: no. 6. The Warings
of Lisnacree', *Mourne Observer*, 6 July 1956.

in the Kilkeel district',[106] suggesting all too clearly similarities of character with Captain Morgan. Nevertheless, from her enlistment in the movement in 1926 Harnett's progress was swift.

By July 1927, she had been appointed District Officer, Ulster Women's Units and was taking a leading role in their affairs[107] as Lisnacree House became the primary base for BF activities in Northern Ireland.[108] In May 1928, both Harnett and her mother, the County Commander, were awarded 'The Order of the Fasces', third class, for meritorious service.[109] Central to Harnett's progress was a close relationship with the movement's founder, Rotha Lintorn Orman.

This had sources in social background, military service and personality, as well as ideology. From virtually identical officer-class military backgrounds and close in age,[110] Harnett, like Lintorn-Orman, had served with ambulance units (the Red Cross)[111] during the Great War, if to less meritorious effect. In fact, Harnett, strong-willed, having an abrasive personality with similar 'virile' characteristics, was virtually a mirror image of Lintorn-Orman, personally embodying the Ulster dimension to BF ideology in the same way as the latter did the mainland British. She was, thus, the very model of the active, engaged, recruit for an organisation Lintorn-Orman envisaged as entailing as practical a role for women in combating 'the Red Menace' as she did for men. At the same time, Harnett's growing influence coincided with, and was facilitated by, a deterioration in Lintorn-Orman's health, derived mainly from her wartime experience, but undoubtedly exacerbated by the recent split in the movement. Her

[106] 'EWS' note (25 June 1928) to police report on BF meeting of 19 June 1928 (Home Affairs papers, PRONI: HA/32/1/509).

[107] *British Lion*, [July]; 20 October 1927; also Harnett to 'Miss Robinson', Acting O/C, Belfast Women's Units, 8 December 1927 (British Fascists documents, PRONI: D3783/A/2).

[108] I. N. G. Ray, Assistant Chief of Staff, Women's Units, GHQ, London, to Mrs Waring, 2 December 1927 (British Fascists documents, PRONI: D3783/A/2).

[109] *British Lion*, May 1928.

[110] Lintorn-Orman was 32 in 1927, Harnett, 35.

[111] Gillespie, 'Secret life of D. G. Waring', 43.

visits to Northern Ireland facilitated a close friendship. Harnett remarked: 'L[intorn]-O[rman] is still a brick to me and seems glad to have me to talk things over with.'[112] Her confidence in Harnett led to the latter taking over the editorship of the BF paper, *British Lion*.

As her health declined Lintorn-Orman was prone to make unsubstantiated claims of communist arms dumps and Russian plans for revolutionary uprisings, claims that inevitably irritated the police who had to investigate them,[113] and which tended to discredit the BF. If its credibility was to be a function of national crisis, evidence of the latter's emergence was desperately needed. In this context Northern Ireland was important. It was almost the only major issue on which BF propaganda had significant credibility and Harnett was well placed to exploit it.

The BF and Communal Violence

Campaigning by Lintorn-Orman and the London headquarters staff in Northern Ireland (in addition to the Belfast visits, at least one visit to the Dublin section took place[114] together with meetings in Dromore, Newcastle, Newry and Kilkeel) was a central element of a strategy to revive the BF's declining fortunes. Remedies would also include the introduction of humorous/human interest content in *British Lion* to give the movement wider public appeal;[115] the promotion of Kenneth Reavell, a BF volunteer who had lost his life in an railway accident during the General Strike, as the movement's first martyr;[116] and, not least, a sustained campaign in the pages of *British Lion* together with public – often alarmist – addresses in Britain by Harnett.

[112] Harnett to 'Darling Ma', 3 February 1928 (British Fascists documents, PRONI: D3783/A/2).
[113] Thurlow, *Fascism in Britain*, p. 55.
[114] I. N. G. Ray, Assistant Chief of Staff, Women's Units, GHQ, London, to Mrs Waring, 12 October 1927 (British Fascists documents, PRONI: D3783/A/2); *British Lion*, December 1927.
[115] 'The future of the British Fascists', *British Lion*, August 1927; [March 1929].
[116] *British Lion*, October/November 1927.

In fact, Harnett shaped the BF narrative of impending revolution in Ireland, one heavily informed by her own traumatic family and community experiences of the early 1920s. A return of 'the wholesale nocturnal murders of 1921–23' was prophesised, and would be a *precursor* to wider state and imperial disruption: 'when the trouble starts in Ireland it will also begin in London, Glasgow, Liverpool, Bristol and Cardiff and other towns too numerous to mention here.' The only way to eradicate the evil that de Valera, 'the Spanish Jew', represented, was an invasion of the south, where thousands of loyal Irish longed for the return of British rule. As things stood, southern Ireland 'was really becoming a German colony'; 'half the shops in Dublin' were becoming German owned and they 'were inter-marrying with the native population'. Moreover, nationalist/ republican scheming, north and south, abetted by Soviet–German subversion, was facilitated by weak Government in both Irish constitutional arenas.[117]

Concern about a national catastrophe facing Ireland, north and south, was not the sole preserve of border Unionists and the BF, it was common to northern Unionist opinion in general in the late 1920s.[118] However, the relative salience of the republican menace as perceived by the Belfast Government, as distinct from Unionists in the border area, allowed for a more considered approach on how to meet it, one that would consolidate Unionist unity. Bearing in mind how PR at the Northern Ireland election of 1925 had facilitated splintering of the Unionist bloc, Craigavon now took steps to abolish it in favour of the first-past-the post system. The effect at the election of 1929, an election inevitably centred on the constitutional question, was the elimination of Independents.[119] Given the regime's unfettered control of the region, powers of organisation and influence through the loyal orders and the

---

[117] See 'Fooling the simple Saxon', *Irish Independent*, 25 January 1928; also, District Officer, Ulster Women's Units, 'The Peril in Ulster', *British Lion*, December 1927; 'The Irish gunmen', *British Lion*, [April 1928]; 'Moscow plot in Ireland', *British Lion*, [June 1928]; 'Irish republicans in London', *British Lion*, [November 1928]; Irish Loyalist [Harnett], 'The Achilles heel', *British Lion*, March 1929.
[118] Kennedy, *Widening Gulf*, pp. 141–42.
[119] Ibid., pp. 142–43.

patronage at its disposal to enhance popular Unionist compliance, the BF's influence continued to be limited. Effectively, it was restricted to the south Down–south Armagh area where local constitutional anxieties, given the right stimulus and circumstances, could find violent expression.

The BF belief in an impending national catastrophe in this period – the 'present crisis in national affairs' – is reflected in an alliance with the extreme imperialist group Unity Band.[120] It was heightened by the Imperial Conference of 1931, which finalised a process of dominion independence from London initiated by the conference of 1926.[121] The BF, sharing with Lord Carson a long-standing concern for Irish loyalist interests, immediately perceived how these might be further endangered by the opportunity now existing for the Irish Free State to break all connections with the United Kingdom.[122]

As the general election of March 1932 in the Irish Free State approached, Harnett's warnings of constitutional upheaval looked prescient: the Cosgrave Government, claiming that an armed conspiracy against the State already existed, banned twelve organisations, including the IRA and the Friends of Soviet Russia,[123] and warned of constitutional anarchy if de Valera came to power.[124] On attaining office, de Valera declared his intention to abolish the Oath of Allegiance to the King and the right of Irish citizens to appeal to the Privy Council in London from the Supreme Court in Dublin, while releasing imprisoned republicans[125] and lifting the ban on the IRA. His close relationship with

---

[120] 'British fascists and the Unity Band', *British Fascism*, July 1930; Griffiths, *Fellow Travellers*, p. 90.

[121] George Woodcock, *Who Killed the British Empire?* (London: Reader's Union, 1974), pp. 243–45.

[122] 'The last link', *British Fascism*, November 1931; also *British Fascism*, 6, 20 February 1926; *British Fascism*, March 1932; H. M. Hyde, *Carson* (London: Heinemann, 1953), pp. 485–86.

[123] Donal O'Sullivan, *The Irish Free State and its Senate* (London: Faber & Faber, 1940), pp. 264–65.

[124] Lord Longford and T. P. O'Neill. *Eamon de Valera* (London: Arrow, 1974), pp. 273–74.

[125] O'Sullivan, *Irish Free State*, p. 295.

the latter[126] gave colour to the belief that he would give violent effect to his anti-partitionism, raising the expectations of border nationalists that the great land transfers they had been cheated of in 1925 would now be forthcoming,[127] though, in reality, and as the latest study of de Valera emphasises, he was always opposed to any attempt militarily to coerce Ulster Unionists to abandon partition.[128] But, with Ireland *apparently* on the verge of revolution, and signalling the great national crisis she had long warned of, Lintorn-Orman sought to address a central weakness in a movement now steadily haemorrhaging membership to Mosley's British Union of Fascists (BUF)[129] – the lack of a charismatic male leader. Thus, having joined Harnett in a public appeal for support of 'loyal Ulster' and a British reoccupation of southern Ireland,[130] Lintorn-Orman sought endorsement of the BF from the great icon of pre-war Ulster paramilitarism, Lord Carson.

Requesting an interview 'at the earliest possible convenience' for a deputation that would include herself and Harnett, Lintorn-Orman claimed to have 'a number of men and women' ready to defend Ulster, together with 'aircraft' and the necessary 'organisation'.[131] Reference to an earlier agreement by Carson for an interview that was not followed through, however, and her regret that he and Lady Carson were unable to attend a BF 'reception' the previous day,[132] were not good auspices. Carson shared Lintorn-Orman's anxieties, but now in his late seventies and in poor health, he declined to associate himself publicly with the BF. Thereafter, the BF's gradual decline continued as unsuccessful attempts were made to combine

---

[126] T. D. Williams, 'De Valera in power', in Francis MacManus (ed.), *The Years of the Great Test, 1926–39* (Cork: Mercier, 1967), pp. 36–37.

[127] Staunton, *The Nationalists of Northern Ireland*, pp. 109–10.

[128] See Ronan Fanning, *Eamon de Valera: A Will to Power* (London: Faber & Faber, 2016), pp. 208–18.

[129] See 'Who began fascism in Britain', *British Fascism*, 1 March 1933; Gottlieb, *Feminine Fascism*, pp. 24–25, 30, 40.

[130] Harnett, 'Shall we lose Ulster?'; Lintorn-Orman, 'The Empire's need of loyal Ulster', *British Fascism*, February 1933.

[131] Rotha Lintorn-Orman to Lord Carson, 11 February 1933 (Carson papers, PRONI: D/1507/A/48/7).

[132] Ibid.

with other fascist organisations, and as Lintorn-Orman's own health and behaviour became increasingly problematic.[133] Nevertheless, Lintorn-Orman, like Sir Oswald Mosley in turn, retained a belief in the centrality of her movement to national salvation. And Ireland continued to provide colour to the expectation of State crisis: at the Stormont election of November 1933, de Valera, already embarked on constitutional and economic conflict with Britain, was elected as an abstentionist MP for south Down.[134]

De Valera's choice of constituency was significant. Down was a heartland county of Northern Ireland, but its ethno-national make-up no less suggested constitutional vulnerability. Moreover, north Down had been represented since 1921 by the northern Prime Minister, Lord Craigavon, so de Valera's south Down candidacy gave the county's elections symbolic import as a territorial and constitutional struggle. In reality, de Valera's candidature was a mere gesture of support for a nationalist minority whose material grievances – and partition – he could do little to resolve,[135] but for Harnett and the BF it was an indicator of the long-feared onslaught on Ulster and the Empire, abetted by the 'treasonous' activities of border nationalists. Newry Urban Council added to its rejection of the northern regime and pledge of loyalty to the Irish Free State in 1922 by ending the policy of flying the Union flag on council buildings in 1932. Given the perception that 'Newry is the Gap of the North'[136] – a geographical point of entry from the south – the flag incident took on wider significance.[137] The scenario of constitutional threat, however, was not all it seemed.

De Valera's nomination had begun as newspaper speculation which he then decided to follow through on. South Down nationalists were enthusiastic about Irish unity, but they had not been consulted on de Valera's candidature and were initially inclined to

---

[133] Thurlow, *Fascism in Britain*, p. 56.

[134] John Bowman, *De Valera and the Ulster Question, 1917–73* (Oxford: Oxford University Press, 1983), p. 132.

[135] Ibid., pp. 132–33.

[136] J. W. Nixon et al., Northern Ireland Parliamentary Debates, HC, 29 November 1932, cols. 185–204.

[137] See *Newry Telegraph,* 1, 22 September, 20 October, 5, 17 November, 8, 10 December 1932.

stick with the sitting MP: only emotive warnings of 'a terrible slur on Mr de Valera' persuaded them otherwise.[138] This was a reality the BF, as many Unionists, would have been incapable of appreciating, though there were differences in their approach to the perceived constitutional threat. For Unionists, the problem of disloyalty the flag controversy reflected was one chiefly affecting Northern Ireland, but for the BF it was indicative of a connected and growing pattern of disloyalty across the whole British State.[139] Also, Unionist protests were limited to the verbal and written: Edward, Prince of Wales had affirmed emphatically the constitutional security of Northern Ireland when he inaugurated the Stormont parliament buildings in November 1932.[140] In the south Down–south Armagh area, however, Unionist anxieties, exacerbated by the State-wide sense of crisis that characterised the BF mentality, would produce a violent response to de Valera's northern initiative.

In October–November 1933, Dorothy Harnett and Wing Commander A. W. F. Whitmore – an English guest speaker and leading member of the BF in Britain – campaigned in the border counties. In Armagh city Whitmore emphasised the primacy of Ulster as an arena of BF operation: the 'trouble was starting as it had before ... there had been two murders already'.[141] The Armagh meeting, however, elicited no great popular response and succeeded in recruiting only 'a few members'.[142] For this the city's distance from the border (see Figure 1), a relatively favourable local religio-ethnic balance and the lack of an established BF branch, may all have played a part.

The situation in south Armagh-south Down was very different. With de Valera's candidature for the constituency, it represented the front line of the coming struggle. When Whitmore held a meeting in Newry Town Hall in early November his speech was subject

---

[138] James Kelly, *Bonfires on the Hillside* (Belfast: Fountain Publishing, 1995), pp. 86–88.

[139] 'Gentlemen-the King', *British Fascism*, October 1932.

[140] See, for instance, *Illustrated London News*, 26 November 1932.

[141] See report of BF meeting in Armagh: 'Fascist move in six Counties', *Irish Press*, 20 October 1933.

[142] Ibid.

to constant interruption and the town's reputation as a bastion of republican–communist subversion was confirmed when his request at the end of the meeting for his listeners to stand and sing 'God Save the King' was met with a virtually complete walk-out.[143] Thus the political temperature of the area was volatile when, with the purpose of mobilising the local loyalist population, a series of BF meetings was organised for the Kilkeel district under the auspices of Harnett's mother, Mrs Florence Waring, who in October 1931 had been raised to the Second Order of the Fasces.[144] The Unionists of this loyalist outpost in an overwhelmingly nationalist area proved a receptive audience for the aggressive and apocalyptic rhetoric of the BF.

The Kilkeel meetings were arranged to begin at the same time as de Valera's first election meeting in the south Down constituency,[145] and, with Whitmore and Harnett to the fore, ran over three days. Whitmore had not informed the police of his intention to hold public meetings[146] and their absence ensured that inflammatory rhetoric rapidly produced sectarian conflict in which local Catholics were the primary victims and which lasted for almost a week.[147] According to one source, Whitmore had urged the driving of Catholics into the 'republic' they were so fond of,[148] and violence only subsided when police reinforcements arrived, at the same time as further planned BF meetings were cancelled.[149] Violence associated with BF activities in Britain was not uncommon, but it was usually a transient occurrence which left little or no local trace when the meetings which occasioned it were over. In Northern Ireland, however, riots such as those provoked by BF speakers in Kilkeel exacerbated deeply entrenched and geographically specific

[143] 'Fascism in the north', *Irish Examiner*, 6 November 1933.
[144] See *British Fascism*, October 1931.
[145] *Irish News*, 29 November 1933.
[146] Report headed 'Disturbance in Kilkeel', 8 December 1933 (Home Affairs papers, PRONI: HA/32/1/509).
[147] 'Prolonged reign of factionist terror in Kilkeel', *Irish News*, 6 December 1933.
[148] Statement of local Parish Priest, cited in 'Disturbances in Kilkeel', 8 December 1933 (Home Affairs papers, PRONI: HA/32/1/509).
[149] *Irish News*, 7 December 1933; *Belfast News-Letter*, 7 December 1933.

religio-ethnic antagonisms which ensured that violence would be prolonged. At the same time, controversy surrounding the Kilkeel disturbances carried echoes of the crisis facing the BF in Britain. Concerned that a 'Fascist' was being blamed as the instigator of the Kilkeel violence, 'The Organiser' of the recently formed Ulster Fascists (UF) – a movement with a very different approach to partition (see Chapters 2 and 3) – condemned BF activities in the area: 'Real Fascism stands for peace, progress and prosperity, not for meetings of the Kilkeel type, which embitter the people, cause party feeling, and end in extra police being called out'.[150] The UF was a regional offshoot of Mosley's BUF,[151] then successfully engaged in undermining the BF in Britain. Its commentary on the Kilkeel disturbances was its own small contribution to that process.

The BF was in crisis at this time, with opposition to Lintorn-Orman's style of leadership and her attempts to 'Ulsterise' the British national crisis led by E. Mandeville Roe and Neil Francis-Hawkins. They were attracted particularly by Mosley's leadership credentials and his more obviously fascist, in particular corporatist, ideas of Government.[152] While no less concerned about imperial disruption than the BF, it was indicative of the very different approach to Northern Ireland of the BUF that the significance of de Valera's victory in south Down was seen chiefly in terms of making 'the Stormont junta ... look rather ridiculous'.[153] The BF and BUF may have shared the same 'fascist' rubric but they were different movements, and for our purposes Ulster/Ireland registered one of most significant aspects of that difference.

Whether it was a direct result of his activities in Northern Ireland is unclear, but on his return to London shortly afterwards Whitmore immediately became a focus of attention for the security services. Its report on BF activities of January 1934 illustrates the

---

[150] *Irish News*, 7 December 1933.

[151] See James Loughlin, 'Northern Ireland and British fascism in the inter-war years', *Irish Historical Studies*, vol. 19 (November 1995), 543–52.

[152] Steven Woodbridge, 'Fraudulent fascism: the attitude of the early British fascists towards Mosley and the New Party', *Contemporary British History*, vol. 23, no. 4 (2009), 493–507.

[153] *Fascist Week*, 8–14 December 1933.

importance of the Ulster scenario to the movement. Whitmore was identified as 'a leading member of the organisation' actively engaged in plans to reorganise the BF in Northern Ireland. Making his pitch to 'several influential members of the Bath Club',[154] Whitmore claimed to have been a member of the 'old Ulster Volunteer Force and had participated in gun-running in 1914'. His plan was to 'organise the British Fascists in Northern Ireland on the same basis as the old Ulster Volunteer Force', for which purpose he returned to Northern Ireland on 2 January 1934.[155] Whitmore's plan, however, had no chance of coming to fruition. Financial difficulties resulting from the BF's declining fortunes had been greatly exacerbated when Rotha Lintorn-Orman's mother cut off financial support in 1933, believing the movement had been taken over by disreputable elements manipulating her daughter through the use of alcohol and drugs.[156] Dorothy Harnett also lost sole control of the editorship of the successor to *British Lion*, *British Fascism*, at this time.[157]

The BF and Ulster: Crisis and Demise

The movement's financial difficulties came to a head when the BF's bank pressed for payment of a large overdraft. Colonel H. C. Bruce Wilson, a past member of the BF management council,[158] stepped forward to guarantee it, thereby acquiring a controlling influence in the movement. Wilson took over the editorship of *British Fascism*, which from early 1934 reflected an enhanced emphasis on his own particular concerns, especially antisemitism, pro-Nazism and the forging of an alliance with Mosley's BUF, something Lintorn-Orman had firmly rejected. The change in direction was marked by the creation of a new emblem for the movement. Inspired by the Swastika, he introduced an abstract Spiral, suggestive, he

[154] Opened in 1894; closely associated with the Conservative Party.
[155] See A. Canning, Special Branch, 'Report on the British Union of Fascists and others', 22 January 1934 (NAK, Home Office papers, HO45/25386/33).
[156] NAK, Home Office papers, HO45/25386/37–40; Thurlow, *Fascism in Britain*, p. 56.
[157] Griffiths, *Fellow Travellers*, p. 93.
[158] Frederic Mullally, *Fascism inside England* (London: Claud Morris, 1946), p. 20.

argued, of energy, drive and general forward fascist development.[159]
Its introduction stimulated discussion which included the Red Hand
symbolism of the ancient O'Neill clan, 'the Chiefs and Kings of
Ulster': 'the Red Hand of Ulster ... was the symbol then as now,
of the Right Hand of God'.[160] For Dorothy Harnett, however, such
sympathetic referencing of Ulster's premier native clan was unlikely
to have been welcome, nor the symbolic transformation of the BF
the Spiral registered.

Harnett's public profile in Northern Ireland greatly increased
in 1934 when she made an inflammatory speech at a loyalist rally
to protest about a controversial letting in May of the Ulster Hall in
Belfast, a citadel of Ulster Unionism, to the Catholic Truth Society.[161]
She recklessly urged young men in the audience – a packed Ulster
Hall with 3,000–4,000 outside – to follow the example of Mussolini
and Hitler and choose 'a man with a single heart and in whom you
have absolute confidence' for the purpose of paramilitary action.
The speech earned a charge of incitement to disorder resulting in
her being bound over to keep the peace for a year.[162] But for our
purposes the result of the court proceedings is of less significance
than Harnett's evidence.

She disclosed that she had resigned from the BF on the grounds
that its policy was detrimental to the northern Government.[163] She
did not explain in what way, and according to one academic source
she was, in fact, BF Propaganda Officer in May 1934.[164] However,
an MI5 report[165] and her encouragement of independent fascist
formations in Northern Ireland indicate clearly enough that she
had left the movement. The explanation involves an interrelation of
personal and policy factors.

Harnett's loss of influence at the movement's London headquarters
was undoubtedly a function of the effective displacement of

---

[159] 'The symbolism of the spiral', *British Fascism*, April 1934.
[160] 'The antiquity of symbolism', *British Fascism*, May 1934.
[161] 'Protest against Catholic missionary exhibition', *Irish News*, 25 May 1934.
[162] Police report, *Irish News*, 13 June 1934.
[163] *Belfast Telegraph*, 13 June 1934.
[164] Gottlieb, *Feminine Fascism*, p. 345.
[165] Report of 14 June 1934, MI5, 'Activities of the Fascist Organisations in the UK (excluding the British Union of Fascists)' (NAK, KV3/58).

Lintorn-Orman, who had ceased to take an active part in BF activities,[166] together with her opposition to Colonel Wilson's plan to effect a merger between the BF and Mosley's BUF. Given its distinctly anti-partitionist bent, that Harnett would regard the BF under Colonel Wilson's direction as inimical to the Unionist Government's interests is understandable, and her resignation logical.

The mid-1930s were landmark years for the BF: 1935 witnessed the death of Lintorn-Orman and the winding up of her movement; 1936 the demise of the southern constitutional threat. By then it was clear that de Valera's constitutional innovations would have no implications for Northern Ireland, while fears of an IRA-led invasion of the north were put to rest when he imposed a crackdown on the organisation.[167] For Harnett, 1936 marked her reinvention as Dorothy Gainsborough Waring, author of popular fiction with an Ulster/British background, her early work sharing space on her publisher's list with novels by Vladimir Nabokov.[168] Insofar as her fiction offers an insight into her political outlook, however imperfectly, it suggests a gradual disengagement from the *extremes* of her fascist commitments of the previous decade.

It was evident in a more nuanced attitude to 'aliens' and Jews; ambivalence towards the European dictators, albeit still regarding Mussolini and Hitler as great men; and criticism of 'fanatically' extreme patriotic organisations – her last pre-war novel, *The Day's Madness*, took Arnold Leese's miniscule and rabidly antisemitic Imperial Fascist League (see Chapter 2) as the model for the 'Imperial Brothers Organisation', run by a 'tin-pot dictator'.[169] Nevertheless, she was still open to the idea of international conspiracies working against the interests of the British nation,[170] while holding in reverence the memory of her late mentor and friend, Rotha

---

[166] On Lintorn-Orman at this time, see Gottlieb, *Feminine Fascism*, p. 318.
[167] Williams, 'De Valera in power', p. 36.
[168] Nabokov's *Camera Obscura* and *Despair* included in the John Long catalogue, in endpapers of Waring's *Nothing Irredeemable* (London: John Long, 1936).
[169] D. G. Waring, *The Day's Madness* (London: John Long, 1939), p. 6.
[170] Waring, *The Oldest Road* (London: John Long, 1938), pp. 30–31; also, *The Day's Madness*, pp. 5–7.

Lintorn-Orman.[171] This outlook characterised her later involvement in the Ulster branch of the Anglo-German friendship organisation, The Link, founded by Admiral Sir Barry Domvile.[172]

Conclusion

It is a truism that the shadow of the Great War hung over the inter-war period. It could do so in many ways. For our purposes it is the war's consequences for the British extreme Right that is of importance, and, specifically, the first fascist manifestation, the BF. The Great War produced a perceived legacy of constitutional crisis in the United Kingdom, which the BF, inspired by Mussolini's accession to power in Italy, sought to meet. That the British post-war crisis as understood by the BF never actually emerged goes far to explain why the movement failed; however, for Northern Ireland a more regionally specific explanation is needed.

Here a crisis of the State certainly took place; the Unionist Party was subject to severe internal pressures, while the regime's nationalist/republican enemies posed a serious constitutional and paramilitary threat to the region's membership of the United Kingdom. If, as has been argued, the pre-war constitutional crisis threatened the 'Ulsterization' of British politics,[173] this was precisely the objective the BF aimed to achieve in the late 1920s and early 1930s as it sought to confront the apparent threat posed by de Valera. However, as against the factors that seemed to facilitate a successful BF mobilisation in Northern Ireland there were others that militated against it.

Thus, and in addition to the imperfect fit between the BF conception of national crisis and the political realities of the region, by the time the movement began to organise in Northern Ireland

---

[171] Dedication: 'To R.B.L-O. in memory', in Waring, *Oldest Road*, p. v.

[172] See James Loughlin, 'Hailing Hitler with the Red Hand: The Link in Northern Ireland, 1937–40', *Patterns of Prejudice*, vol. 50, no. 3 (July 2016), 276–301.

[173] John Stevenson, 'Conservatism and the failure of fascism in inter-war Britain', in Martin Blinkhorn (ed.), *Fascists and Conservatives: The Radical Right and the Establishment in Twentieth Century Europe* (London: Routledge, 1990), p. 265.

the worst of the region's contemporary crisis was over; and just as the BF clearly failed to appreciate that the collapse of the General Strike of 1926 marked the end of serious threats to the socio-constitutional order in Britain, so too did it fail to appreciate the significance for Northern Ireland of the collapse of the Boundary Commission proceedings in 1925. Thereafter, an entrenched Unionist regime was well placed to defend its constitutional position without needing to engage with the BF. Moreover, given leadership concern about management of the Unionist movement, it was a misfortune for the BF that despite an essential commonality of British values with Ulster Unionism its Belfast leadership was such that official engagement and support would not be forthcoming. Thus both confidence and concern at Unionist leadership level combined to damage BF prospects in Northern Ireland. But if State influence served to constrain BF development in Belfast the activities of the county Down units no less allows an insight into its limits.

While grassroots Unionism could, on occasion, act autonomously and violently for varying reasons at locations across Northern Ireland in this period (Belfast would experience an orgy of loyalist violence in mid-1935)[174] the BF's exacerbation of Unionism's constitutional anxieties in south Down pointed up an often problematic relationship between heartland and periphery in general that would complicate the governance of Northern Ireland throughout the life of the regime.

---

[174] Farrell, *Northern Ireland*, pp. 136–40.

2

The British Union of Fascists and Northern Ireland (I)

The Ulster Question in Blackshirt Perspective

A comparison of Rotha Lintorn-Orman's British Fascists (BF) with Sir Oswald Mosley's British Union of Fascists (BUF) offers both similarities and contrasts. Both movements were concerned with the same fundamental issues – the preservation of the British Empire and thwarting the advance of international communism – in the furtherance of which they sought to provide an alternative to a weak parliamentary system incapable of recognising and defeating the forces of subversion facing the State. Also, both movements were founded by individuals with a record of courageous war service, and for whom the conflict had a profound influence on their political outlooks. Both were inspired by Mussolini and created movements which privileged 'will' and local/regional initiative in furthering their causes. Both developed an increasingly antisemitic and racist outlook. The differences between them, however, were more significant.

Most obviously, at leadership level, Mosley had the personal qualities to provide the masculine leadership that Lintorn-Orman clearly could not (Figure 5). He also had financial resources much superior to those of Lintorn-Orman, and while the BF only gradually came to accept the need for dictatorship, Mosley's BUF more readily advocated it and had a much clearer idea of the corporatist political system that would replace parliamentary democracy; though it might be noted that when the BF was formed it was on the basis of an Italian template whose fascist characteristics developed only gradually, whereas Mosley's BUF, founded a decade later, had the fully formed Italian and German templates as a basis for construction. Furthermore,

Figure 5   Oswald Mosley inspecting the women's formation of his
organisation's Limehouse branch, 4 July 1937
Courtesy of Sheffield University

Mosley's more developed conception of an alternative fascist political
order was informed by a 'palingenetic' vision completely lacking in
the BF – that of a new era emerging out of the wreckage of the Great
War and the discrediting of the old parties and institutions whose
betrayal of the war generation had rendered them morally unfit and
politically redundant. In this conception fascism was the historically
inevitable vehicle to deliver on the promise of the new era.[1] But
of particular significance for our purposes, while the outlooks of
both Lintorn-Orman and Mosley were influenced by recent Irish

---

[1] This characteristic of fascism is well established in the secondary literature,
but for the most exhaustive treatment of the intellectual and ideological roots
of fascism as a form of 'revolutionary modernism', see Griffin, *Modernism and
Fascism, passim*. Mosley's movement underwent a number of minor name
modifications: British Union of Fascists (1932); British Union of Fascists and
National Socialists (1936); British Union (1937).

developments, they were influenced by different developments. Whereas the BF was prompted by Sir Edward Carson's pre-war paramilitary mobilisation of Ulster Unionists against the third Home Rule Bill, Mosley, though he made reference to Carson for personal purposes, took his cue from the Irish War of Independence during which, and on the subject of which, he established his reputation as a brilliant parliamentary debater, especially as a vocal and highly effective opponent of atrocities perpetrated by British forces. This chapter attempts to locate the place of Blackshirt anti-partitionism within the overall context of the movement's politics.

Ireland, Catholicism and Blackshirt Politics

Mosley's stance on Ireland earned him the support of leading constitutional nationalists such as T. P. O'Connor and the Ulster nationalist leader Joseph Devlin, facilitated the considerable Catholic and/or Irish membership of the BUF and also significant Irish sympathy throughout his life.[2] Moreover, his engagement with the Irish question had no small influence on the movement's consistently conciliatory approach to the Catholic Church and to a pro-nationalist approach to the Northern Ireland problem: his first intervention on the Ulster dimension of the Irish question occurred in March 1921 when he effected the release from Londonderry prison of one James O'Donnell, held for nine weeks without charge or trial.[3] Until recently, the website of the commemorative organisation, the Friends of Mosley (FOM),[4] carried the iconic image of Bishop Edward Daly waving a white handkerchief as he led to safety a group of people carrying a man seriously wounded by British paratroopers in Derry on 'Bloody Sunday', 31 January 1972, a visual reference in direct lineal descent from Mosley's critique of Black and Tan actions in Ireland during the War of Independence.

As for the Catholic dimension to the Blackshirt movement's relationship with its Irish supporters, important in this context was

[2] See Oswald Mosley, *My Life* (London: Nelson, 1968), chap. 8, p. 213; Robert Skidelsky, *Oswald Mosley* (London: Macmillan, 1981), chap. 5.
[3] Skidelsky, *Mosley*, p. 102.
[4] See www.oswaldmosley.com.

the precedent for church–State relations established by Mussolini's concordat with the Papacy of 1929. By the mid-1930s, a symbiosis of Catholicism and fascism was apparent to many, especially a close similarity of view on the idea of a corporate State. Mussolini and Hitler had both been Catholics, while the 1929 Lateran Treaty with Italy had been followed in 1933 by a Concordat with Salazar's Portugal and in 1934 by another with Nazi Germany. In Ireland the symbiosis between right-wing regimes and the church was reinforced by the latter's obsession with communism,[5] while the church's organisation for societal improvement, Catholic Social Action, was seen as a model for adoption elsewhere, not least to fascist States: 'The State has nothing to fear, but everything to gain, from a properly understood Catholic Action movement'.[6] As a movement for social reconstruction serving the *national* (as opposed to any party political) interest, it was welcomed by the BUF, thus greatly easing the path of Catholic recruitment. The north of England organiser of the BUF, Richard Bellamy, remarked that while clergymen of the Church of England were the most likely representatives of religious denominations actually to join the Blackshirt movement, priests of the Catholic Church 'more often expressed in private their approval of our ideals and most aspects of policy, notably our support for the corporate state and opposition to atheistic Marxism than did the clergy of the Protestant denominations'.[7]

By May 1935 the *Blackshirt* could report that 12 per cent of leading BUF officials were Catholics,[8] and as such represented a substantially larger proportion of the movement than Catholics were of the general population, something that Stuart Rawnsley has pointed out 'was also true of the BUF membership in general'.[9] In

---

[5] Gerald Moore, 'Anti-Semitism in Ireland', PhD thesis, Ulster Polytechnic, 1984, pp. 147–48.

[6] See A. M. Crofts OP, *Catholic Social Action: Principles, Purpose and Action* (London: Catholic Book Club, 1936), pp. 186–87.

[7] Richard Bellamy, *We Marched with Mosley: The Authorised History of the British Union of Fascists* (London: Black House Publishing, 2013), pp. 62–63.

[8] *Blackshirt*, 17 May 1935.

[9] Stuart Rawnsley, 'The membership of the British Union of Fascists', in Kenneth Lunn and Richard Thurlow (eds), *British Fascism* (London: Croom Helm, 1980), pp. 161–63.

this context it might be noted that, while during the period when
he was concerned to attract Italian funding Mosley temporarily
suppressed Blackshirt antisemitism and attacked Nazi race doctrine,[10]
later in the 1930s, when he was closely supportive of Hitler's regime,
the only serious criticism of Nazism that the Blackshirt press allowed
itself was in reference to its repressive policies towards the Catholic
Church.[11] Indeed, it argued that if Blackshirt fascism resembled
'any other country's fascism it would probably be that of [Salazar's]
Portugal', the merits of which were given significant coverage.[12]
During the Spanish Civil War, it complained that under 'Red' rule
in Madrid only Protestants were allowed a place of worship, not
Catholics.[13] For its part, the Executive Committee of the Catholic
Truth Society refused a request to issue a pamphlet on fascism
in 1938 on the grounds that it would be seen as an attack on the
BUF and thus incompatible with its policy of avoiding criticism of
political parties.[14] But while the pro-Catholic strand of Blackshirt
politics integrated symbiotically with the anti-partitionism with
which Mosley was associated and its accompanying criticism of
the Ulster regime, the referencing of Northern Ireland *in general*
within the BUF was wider and more diverse, reflecting the different
interests and viewpoints the movement encompassed.

Sports coverage, for instance, reported the Ulster Grand Prix
purely on its merits,[15] while the movement's agricultural expert,
Jorian Jenks, a founder member of the Soil Association in 1946,
always took a United Kingdom approach to his subject, including
'our fellow-Britons and near-neighbours in Ulster', and generally

[10] Stephen Dorril, *Blackshirt: Sir Oswald Mosley and British Fascism* (London: Penguin 2007), p. 235.
[11] See, for example, Clement Bruning, 'Shot and Shell', *Blackshirt*, 6 February 1937.
[12] H. W. J. Edwards, 'The dissidents', *British Union Quarterly*, vol. 2, no. 3 (July–September 1938), 47.
[13] 'Further facts about red rule in Malaga and Madrid', *Action*, 24 April 1937.
[14] Kester Aspden, *Fortress Church: The English Roman Catholic Bishops, 1903–63* (Leominster: Gracewing, 2002), p. 21; Tom Villis, *British Catholics and Fascism: Religious Identity and Political Extremism Between the Wars* (Basingstoke: Palgrave Macmillan, 2013), p. 38.
[15] 'Sport', *Action*, 27 August 1936.

praised the Stormont regime's agricultural policy,[16] though other Blackshirt comment, noting the region's apparent dependence on Russian flax, attacked the regime for failing to support its own flax industry.[17] For the movement's philosopher, Alexander Raven Thomson, the most significant lesson of the Ulster problem was the portent it held for ill-considered ideas about the introduction of democracy to India, where the enmity between the minority Muslim, and the much larger Hindu, communities was greater than inter-ethnic hostility in Ireland and where democracy would simply be the agency for conflict greater than Ireland experienced.[18] In a variation on this theme, the Blackshirt leader in Scotland, James Little, citing Lord Carson, argued for retaining British control of India by reference to the weakness of safeguards for southern Irish loyalists in the Anglo-Irish Treaty of 1921.[19] Similarly, A. K. Chesterton, author of the hagiographical *Oswald Mosley: Portrait of a Leader* (1936), railed against the way the 'anti-British traitor in Ireland' – as in Egypt and India – could be sure of getting 'his wounds ... licked in Britain'.[20]

W. P. Leaper, a leading journalist, rather dubiously argued that *all* Irishmen respected Carson for his concern for the welfare of Irish loyalists, a concern, he pointed out with quotation, Mosley shared. Both men had criticised Westminster's betrayal of southern loyalists in the settlement of 1921: 'I [Mosley] have always insisted that this small minority should be given the option of evacuation with compensation' following on 'the withdrawal of the English troops'.[21] Leaper's commentary was related to a strain of opinion in

---

[16] Jorian Jenks, 'Pigs is pigs', *Action*, 25 September 1937; 'Ulster lesson', *Action*, 12 March 1938; 'Linum', 'Flax culture in the British Isles', *Fascist Quarterly*, vol. 2, no. 4 (October 1936), 545–46; 'Another 1,300 farms gone', *Action*, 19 August 1939.

[17] 'Big Russian ships in Belfast', *Blackshirt*, 23 August 1935.

[18] A. R. Thomson, 'India and Ireland: why democracy disrupts both', *Action*, 3 July 1937.

[19] 'Misrepresentation of fascism', *Blackshirt*, 4 January 1935.

[20] A. K. Chesterton, 'The problem of decadence', *Fascist Quarterly*, vol. 2, no. 1 (January 1936), 65.

[21] *Fascist Week*, 22–28 December 1933. See also 'The ups and downs of politics', *Blackshirt*, 6 July 1934.

the Blackshirt movement that sought to differentiate Carson from the regime in Northern Ireland that he played such a central role in establishing. It found expression in criticism of the northern authorities for constructing a statue at Stormont to a leader who, it was argued, could only have been pained by the act given his pre-war declaration: 'We will not have Home Rule'.[22] But undoubtedly the most important individual reference to Carson was made by Mosley himself during a libel case he brought against *The Star* newspaper, which had accused him of planning a violent takeover of the State.

The paper strongly defended the action, but Mosley's evidence in the witness box was telling, responding, as follows, to Sir Norman Birkett's suggestion of illegality in Mosley's admission that there were conceivable circumstances of national anarchy in which he would have to use guns: 'No. Lord Carson said hundreds of things far worse than that at a time when he was a leader of the Bar (Laughter)'. Mosley won the case and was awarded £5,000 in damages.[23] If Carson's threatened rebellion against the Liberal Government in 1914 without restraint was constitutionally permissible, then it was impossible to argue convincingly that Mosley's far more circumspect and hypothetical comments on the circumstances in which he would use weapons was outside the law. As Colin Cross has argued, the importance of the court proceedings was that they established 'once and for all that the BUF was a constitutional movement'.[24] Nor was Mosley's reference to Carson's threatened rebellion in the pre-war years an offhand comment. The Blackshirt movement was very much alive to the significance of Carson's pre-war activities in problematising contemporary issues of political assembly and intent. Under the heading, 'Wisdom of the Ancients', *Fascist Week* had already carried a quotation from Carson in July 1912: 'Don't be afraid of illegalities.'[25] But while the precedent of Carson's pre-war

---

[22] 'Northern irony', *Blackshirt*, 30 September 1933.
[23] 'The leader awarded £5,000 damages', *Blackshirt*, 9 November 1934; Mosley, *My Life*, pp. 352–53.
[24] See Colin Cross, *The Fascists in Britain* (London: Barrie and Rockliff, 1963), pp. 143–44.
[25] *Fascist Week*, 12 January 1934.

activities helped to create the political space for the Blackshirt movement to operate, it was nationalist opposition to the partition of Ireland Carson was central to establishing that Mosley regarded as best serving his political ambitions.

While Mosley's effecting the release from Londonderry prison of James O'Donnell suggested deep sympathy with the politically oppressed, as Robert Skidelsky has remarked, Mosley had no interest in people as such: 'He viewed people entirely externally ... They were "instruments" for his purpose, [like] tools a mechanic uses to fix a car.'[26] Colin Cross had earlier come to a similar conclusion: 'Although he was on occasion very kind-hearted [to his followers], he showed little sign of personal feeling towards them.'[27] The same can be said about Mosley's attitude to the issues the BUF pursued more generally, including Irish unity. His attacks on Black and Tan atrocities, for instance, were driven primarily by a *moral* impulse, by how their activities affronted the ethics of warfare in a way that besmirched Britain's reputation. Likewise, his support for a dominion solution to the Irish question was based on a simple recognition that it was necessary and was best conceded in generosity rather than compelled by necessity.[28] With the advent of European fascism, however, and Mosley's own attempt to replicate the success of Mussolini and Hitler in Britain, the flaws in the British approach to the Irish question in the immediate post-war period took on a wider significance, as evidence of the corruption and decadence of a parliamentary system that had failed the British people and which fascism was destined to supersede in the national interest. That in the Irish context Mosley's pro-unity stance went together with attacks on Westminster Governments for having abandoned southern Irish loyalists was simply a way of reinforcing his case. And if the latter was a less evident factor in Blackshirt propaganda than pro-nationalism this was because the southern loyalists, unlike Irish Catholic nationalists, had no substantive corresponding constituency in Britain to be

[26] Robert Skidelsky, 'Great Britain', in S. J. Woolf (ed.), *European Fascism* (New York: Random House, 1968), p. 235.

[27] Cross, *The Fascists in Britain*, p. 135.

[28] A. K. Chesterton, *Oswald Mosley: Portrait of a Leader* (London: Action Press, 1936), pp. 31–32.

mobilised in the Blackshirt interest. In other words, the pursuit of any issue was a function of its relative utility for Mosley and his organisation, and that was a product of the intersection between political dynamics, the movement's interests and the personal disposition of individual BUF figures. By the same token, Mosley's lack of subjective identity with Irish nationalism created space for views on Ulster to be expressed not identical to his. And for our purposes, the irony is that despite the pro-Irish unity reputation of the Blackshirt movement, in the organisation's developmental period, 1932–37, the most influential Blackshirt commentators were associated with, and sympathetic to, Ulster Unionism if not the Stormont regime.

W. E. D. 'Bill' Allen and Ulster

Of leading commentators on Ulster/Ireland the most important was undoubtedly W. E. D. Allen, former Ulster Unionist Party (UUP) MP for West Belfast. Elected at the general election of 1929, he was never likely to be happy within the UUP's Westminster contingent, for whom political conformity was the chief priority: 'I believe men are in politics, not sheep.'[29] Having ancestors among the radical Presbyterians involved in the 1798 Rebellion and later constitutional nationalism with whose activities he clearly had some sympathy,[30] Allen soon fell foul of his Westminster colleagues for his independent views before defecting two years later to Mosley's New Party, and, to the fury of his former colleagues, resolutely refusing to resign the seat he had won with Unionist votes.[31] Allen argued that resignation was unnecessary as his defection to the New Party did not entail any abandonment of his Ulster Unionist principles, and published 'the Mosley Plan' for Britain's economic recovery in the local press to explain his actions.[32] He was later to claim that he would have

[29] Allen cited in *Larne Times*, 14 March 1931.
[30] See W. E. D. Allen, *David Allens: The History of a Family Firm, 1857–1957* (London: John Murray, 1957), chaps 3 and 4; 'Mr W.E.D. Allen: An Appreciation', *Irish Times*, 1 October 1973.
[31] See 'Ulster Unionist Party: Mr W.E.D. Allen and the secretaryship', *Irish Times*, 7 November 1930; 'Mr W.E.D. Allen, M.P.: called on to resign', *Irish Times*, 14 March 1931.
[32] 'The Mosley plan: Mr Allen's views', *Irish Times*, 13 March 1931.

preferred to continue representing West Belfast as a fascist MP, an option foreclosed by the UUP's determination to be rid of him.[33] The short-lived New Party was the pathway to Allen's association with the BUF.[34]

Described long after by Mosley as 'a tremendously boastful man ... who simply lived in a dream world',[35] in the early to mid-1930s, Allen was regarded differently. Mosley attached great importance to his adhesion, not because of his Ulster Unionist background but because 'it emphasised the non-Labour and "national" character of the New Party'.[36] But Allen's recruitment was of much greater significance. He would be an important financial contributor to the BUF and reputedly the facilitator of funding Mussolini provided to the BUF, while also playing a leading role in shaping a historical and national context for the organisation; in particular, in attempting to create an 'authentic' British identity for a movement suffering from the 'un-English' perception of its fascist persona. At the same time, his relationship with the BUF was quite complex: he never actually held BUF membership, and was also, if erroneously, thought to be an MI5 informer.[37]

As to Northern Ireland, despite his professed fidelity to partition, his desertion of Ulster Unionism and his association with Mosley would inevitably be viewed as treasonous. Rowel Friers, the celebrated political cartoonist of the Northern Ireland troubles of the later twentieth century, worked in Allen's family business – poster production and display – in the 1930s, and remarked that possibly 'the most unpopular poster we printed – though undoubtedly the most historic – was one for recruitment to Sir

---

[33] Security Service note on Allen, 1938 NAK, Security Service, Personal Files: W. E. D. Allen, KV/2/879).

[34] This phase in Allen's political career is covered comprehensively in Paul Corthorn, 'W. E. D. Allen, Unionist politics and the New Party', *Contemporary British History* (2009), vol. 23, no. 4, 509–25.

[35] Mosley, quoted in Nicolas Mosley, *Beyond the Pale: Sir Oswald Mosley, 1933–1980* (London: Secker & Warburg, 1983), pp. 174–75.

[36] John Strachey, *The Menace of Fascism* (London: Gollancz, 1933), p. 158.

[37] Comment on Allen, 26 March 1934 (NAK, Security Service, Personal Files: W. E. D. Allen, KV/2/879); Dorril, *Blackshirt: Sir Oswald Mosley and British Fascism*, 153.

Oswald Mosley's British Union of Fascists'.[38] Indeed, according to a Special Branch report of 1937, Allen also used a Belfast bank account to channel money to support Mosley's movement from Nazi Germany.[39]

Allen's approach to the Ulster question in the context of Mosley's movement was to locate it within a conception of British history whose culmination would be the triumph of fascism, following the route to power pursued by Mussolini and Hitler. With European fascism as a framing context,[40] Allen posited Mosley's Blackshirt movement as a force shaping British nationalism to confront 'the demoralising effects of the mechanistic conditions of life which the uncontrolled development of modern capitalism has produced'. And while de Valera in Ireland and Gandhi in India had also reacted against it, they did so merely by burying their heads 'in the Irish bogs and the Indian temple, invoking the old gods of the Gael and the Hindu to save them from the horrors of the modern world,' an argument that in its Irish aspects was a variation of a long-standing Unionist view which contrasted a modernising Ulster against a backward southern Ireland. But Allen's discussion went well beyond the Ulster Unionist perspective in his critique of the Whig champions of 'the present parliamentary system': they had confused the struggle for the 'freedom of the Englishman' with the 'laissez faire struggle for the freedom of the market and had no wish to confront the selfish, anti-national capitalist order'. Thus 'the United Kingdom of Great Britain and Northern Ireland' had experienced Highland depopulation, deserted English farmlands and the throwing away of Ireland 'as not worth the holding'.[41] Only fascism, in the shape of Sir Oswald Mosley's Blackshirt movement, could transform this situation,[42] and pre-war Ulster provided the

[38] Rowel Friers, *Drawn From Life: An Autobiography* (Belfast: Blackstaff Press, 1994), p. 83.
[39] Colin Holmes, *Searching for Lord Haw-Haw: The Political Lives of William Joyce* (London and New York: Routledge, 2016), pp. 100–01.
[40] Allen, 'The Fascist idea in Britain', *Quarterly Review*, vol. 261, no. 518 (October 1933), 224–25.
[41] Ibid., 228.
[42] Ibid., 232, 236–37.

proof that the British people 'will not fail ... to respond to the proper stimulus':

> The Ulster movement was, in fact, the first fascist movement in Europe, and its spontaneous development, not only in Northern Ireland [*sic*], but everywhere throughout Great Britain, is the best answer to those sophists who proclaim that the principles of modern Fascism can find no response in the British character.[43]

Thus Allen was concerned, not just to locate Northern Ireland and its Unionist population as authentic elements of the British State and nation, but to accord 'Ulster' the privilege of being the foundation site of contemporary British fascism. But while Allen neatly integrated Unionism and fascism that would not mean support for the Stormont regime. He would develop his Ulster fascist argument at greater – book – length in his promotional work on Mosley and the BUF published in 1934 under the pseudonym 'James Drennan',[44] a work in which Scottish and Welsh nationalists, together with the Bretons and Basques, were described as movements similar to de Valera's in their rushing to 'hide from the glaring horror of the future'.[45]

The period of the book's preparation witnessed the massive influx of new members that followed the press baron Lord Rothermere's alliance with Mosley from the late summer of 1933 to July 1934: branch numbers rose from around 300 to nearly 500 with an increasing membership of approximately 40,000 to 50,000.[46] The tone of the work, accordingly, is imbued with what Richard Thurlow has described as 'an almost chiliastic belief in the BUF attaining power within a few months',[47] thereby lending its Ulster dimension enhanced

[43] Ibid., 238.

[44] James Drennan, *B.U.F.: Oswald Mosley and British Fascism* (London: John Murray, 1934).

[45] Ibid., pp. 192–93.

[46] Martin Pugh, *'Hurrah for the Blackshirts!': Fascists and Fascism in Britain between the Wars* (London: Jonathan Cape, 2005), 152; G. C. Webber, 'Patterns of membership and support for the British Union of Fascists', *Journal of Contemporary History*, vol. 19, no. 4 (1984), p. 577.

[47] Richard Thurlow, *Fascism in Britain: A History, 1918–1985* (Oxford: Blackwell, 1987), p. 150.

significance. In this context, Allen was tempted to exclude Mosley's anti-Black and Tan activities from the work as 'being not relevant to the main theme', though conceding 'that they show you in a rather favourable light, and the section about the [southern] loyalists is bound to impress Tories who may be sympathetic to Fascism, but who may have had rather a misunderstanding *of your old attitude to Ireland*' (my italics). The latter comment suggests that Allen assumed Mosley's pro-unity approach to Ireland in the early 1920s had changed. He asked for 'your views on this point'.[48] We do not have explicit evidence of Mosley's reply – many of Allen's private papers were destroyed in the Blitz[49] – but its nature can be garnered clearly enough, for Mosley's Irish activities remained, though Allen's preference can be identified in *how* they were recorded, which was in the briefest possible compass, amounting to barely a page.[50] Doing so privileged Carson's pre-war activities in making the Blackshirt case to the British public, presenting them as reflective of British opinion on politics and consti-tutional issues in general. And the pre-war Ulster mobilisation offered a number of positions to advance the Blackshirt cause.

Thus the Tories' 'treasonous' complicity in Carson's 'rebellion' allowed him to assert the greater ethical and constitutional integrity of the BUF – the Blackshirt movement was entirely law-abiding in its political ambitions – though given that on achieving power Mosley intended to dismantle parliamentary democracy, pre-war Ulster loyalism was referenced to demonstrate that

> the British people have no blind faith in the infallibility of the democratic methodology, and they are never prepared to see the vital interests of the nation – whether those interests happen to be in Ulster, as in the past, or in England and throughout the Empire, as at present – sacrificed to the pretensions of vicious and corrupt theories.[51]

[48] W. E. D. Allen (Mullagh Cottage, Killough, co. Down) to Mosley, 15 August 1933 (Sir Oswald Mosley papers, University of Birmingham, Cadbury Research Library (BU, CRL): OMN/B/7/2/2).
[49] See Allen to Mosley, 25 November 1971 (Jeffrey Hamm papers, BU, CRL: MS124/1/1/71).
[50] Drennan, *B.U.F.*, pp. 45–46.
[51] Ibid., pp. 291–93.

Significantly, the Ulster arguments were positioned at the end of the book, effectively as the culmination of Allen's case for Blackshirt fascism. Yet whatever persuasive value these arguments may have had, they no less reflected Allen's perceptual limitations, especially with reference to the Catholic and Irish constituencies.

For example, Allen's claim that in both Italy and Germany fascism 'has shown itself well capable of confronting the reactionary influence of the Roman Catholic Church'[52] was widely at variance with Blackshirt opinion in general and Mosley's in particular. Also flawed, though in a different way, was Allen's claim that while in Germany antisemitism was rife, 'such phases must be passing, for the new Fascist nations will justify their pride of nation within themselves and not in extrovert antagonisms'.[53] This last, naive, opinion in part reflected the lack of antisemitism in the early BUF,[54] but also Allen's Northern Ireland background, a region quite unlike Britain or southern Ireland, in that antisemitism had little significant social influence. Yet again, while Allen argued that the 'integration' of the United Kingdom of Great Britain and Northern Ireland would be the first task of fascism, his referencing of the Ulster Fascists' (covered in Chapter 3) membership of the New Empire Union, together with 'the New Guard of Australia, the New Guard of New Zealand, [and] the New Guard of South Africa',[55] suggests he thought that Northern Ireland's constitutional status as an autonomous region within the British State also entailed autonomous imperial status.

While Allen's propaganda efforts were directed chiefly at the British public, it was not the only constituency the BUF had to address. It had also to be mindful of its own membership. The first half of 1934 was one of great growth for the BUF, but it was also a period when de Valera's policy of dismantling the Irish Free State's imperial links and refusal to pay annuities due under land acts passed in the pre-independence period were taking effect.[56] In the

---

[52] Ibid., pp. 191–93.
[53] Ibid. p. 221.
[54] Cross, *The Fascists in Britain*, pp. 119–20.
[55] Drennan, *B.U.F.*, pp. 258–59.
[56] Deidre MacMahon, 'Economic war', in S. J. Connolly (ed.), *The Oxford*

context of fraught Anglo-Irish relations concern existed about the unity of BUF members from Irish Catholic/nationalist and Ulster Protestant/Unionist backgrounds.

Anglo-Irish Difficulties and Blackshirt Unity

Academic attention to the Irish dimension of BUF membership has had a natural focus on Catholicism/nationalism. Little attention has been paid to its Ulster Protestant/Unionist membership. And yet it certainly existed. The former Blackshirt John Charnley recorded his own experience of 'the two Ashworth brothers from Belfast, the older of the two vehemently anti-Sinn Fein, and yet the closest of Blackshirt companions with Mick Carter. They had fought on opposite sides in Ireland but Mosley bonded them together in common endeavour ... in many a B.U.F. branch, Southern Irish Catholics and Northern Protestant [*sic*] worked together amicably'.[57] In the same vein, William Joyce – son of an Irish Catholic father and Ulster Presbyterian mother – claimed that one of fascism's most redeeming features was its nationally unifying effects, including Protestant and Catholic.[58] Allen, the former Ulster Unionist MP, expressed what was undoubtedly in the minds of the Blackshirt leadership at this time when he warned, 'It is up to ... Irishmen of all persuasion in the ... the B.U.F. ... to keep their heads, and see that they are not hustled into breaking each other's heads ... by such hypocritical adherents of the dying cause of Social Democracy as Messrs de Valera and [J. H.] Thomas [British Dominions Secretary]'.[59]

The difficulty was that addressing the Irish Catholic constituency was much easier than addressing the Ulster Protestants, not least because the latter had no obvious ethnic identifiers. Unlike the singularity of national identity, religion and anti-partitionist ambition that marked out the Irish nationalist constituency, BUF

Companion to Irish History (2nd edn, Oxford: Oxford University Press, 2002), pp. 176–77.
[57] John Charnley, *Blackshirts and Roses: An Autobiography* (1990; 2nd edn, London: Black House Publishing, 2012), p. 47.
[58] William Joyce, 'The philosophy of conflict', *Fascist Week*, 5 January 1934.
[59] 'Lucifer', 'Current cant and fascist fact', *Fascist Week*, 12 January 1934.

members from the Ulster Unionist community appear to have been much smaller and had no such singular markers, tending to blend into the general British membership. A case in point is that of William Samuel Bogle.

Bogle, a former member of the full-time 'A' Special Constabulary, had been a chauffeur for Lord Charlemont, a former Minister of Education in Northern Ireland, after which he became unemployed and was then identified 'with the Fascist Organisation' before moving to London. Detained in May 1940 under Defence Regulation 18b as a member of the BUF, his wife responded by appealing to Charlemont, claiming that her husband had only been briefly a BUF member in the late 1930s, through dire economic necessity. Bogle's case was taken up by both Charlemont and Lord Craigavon, the Northern Ireland Prime Minister, before being dropped quite abruptly, undoubtedly when it was discovered that Bogle had not, as his wife claimed, long distanced himself from the BUF, but was in fact a District Inspector of its London administrative centre.[60] The BUF, however, seems to have had no knowledge of his Northern Ireland background, nor did the commemorative organisation, the FOM, when it detailed his biography and contribution to the BUF in 2006.[61] In the absence of a definable constituency to address within the BUF, movement propaganda such as that provided by Allen filled the space. In addition to authoring *B.U.F.* he was also a significant contributor to *Fascist Week*.

Allen had been invited by Rex Tremlett, a senior BUF official and one of the movement's leading journalists,[62] to assist in the production of, and write for, the publication.[63] Established to capitalise on the support for the Blackshirt movement provided by Lord Rothermere, it aimed at a somewhat more intellectual

[60] See correspondence of Mrs Bogle to Lord Charlemont; Lord Charlemont to Lord Craigavon, June 1940 ('Suspected Persons (General Correspondence)', Home Affairs papers, PRONI: HA/32/1/770); John Anderson, 'A face in the crowd', *Comrade: Newsletter of the Friends of Oswald Mosley*, no. 60 (April 2006).

[61] Anderson, 'A face in the crowd'.

[62] Cross, *The Fascists in Britain*, p. 87.

[63] Rex Tremlett to Allen, 8 August 1933 (Sir Oswald Mosley papers, BU, CRL: OMN/B/7/2/19).

audience than *Blackshirt*, and for the duration of its existence had a circulation of around 30,000 copies per week as against 25,000 for its sister print.[64] That Allen was not actually a member of the BUF meant that he was not involved in the internal faction-fighting that consumed the BUF leadership at this time,[65] and was thus free to devote his efforts to press commentaries. This he did chiefly in the weekly feature, 'Current Cant and Fascist Fact' written under the pseudonym 'Lucifer',[66] and which had a focus on Irish affairs, north and south, his contributions informed by the belief that Mosley's accession to power would occur in the near future:

> Fascism in Britain is entering into the classic phase of persecution through which it passed in Italy and Germany before it emerged to power. The Old Gangs have discovered … that 'Fascism in this country is no longer a thing to be treated jocularly [quotation from Stanley Baldwin]', and in their fear they will try every means to defeat the inevitable. Fascists are facing the hour of trial, and Fascists do not flinch. During the next few months every man and woman in the Movement will be on their mettle, and there are few who will be found wanting.[67]

This was the context in which Allen's expressed concern for unity among Ulster Protestants and Irish Catholics in the BUF has to be seen; and the expectation of fascist triumph included Ireland no less than Britain: 'In Ireland Fascism is progressing no less rapidly. In the North the Ulster Fascists have been organising and in the South, the Blueshirts look like sweeping all before them during the coming year'.[68] And, just as in *B.U.F.*, where he cited Carson's pre-war

---

[64] Thurlow, *Fascism in Britain*, pp. 64–66; Dorril, *Blackshirt: Sir Oswald Mosley and British Fascism*, pp. 244–45, 262, 277; Pugh, '*Hurrah for the Blackshirts!*', pp. 129–31.

[65] On these disputes, see Daniel Tillies, *British Fascist Anti-Semitism and Jewish Reponses, 1932–40* (London: Bloomsbury, 2014), pp. 80–83.

[66] Commentary on Allen, 18 April 1934 (NAK, Security Service, Personal Files: W. E. D. Allen, KV/2/879); Bryan Clough, *State Secrets: The Kent–Wolkoff Affair* (Hove: Hideaway, 2005), p. 171.

[67] *Fascist Week*, 2 March 1934.

[68] Ibid.

activities to place Northern Ireland at the heart of British fascism, so Ireland's historical grievances for which Britain was held responsible could be exploited as the background to a future Anglo-Irish fascist future,[69] as well as to defend European fascism. When *The Times* condemned the Nazi regime for atrocities associated with the Reichstag fire and subsequent trial in 1933, 'Lucifer' pointed up its hypocrisy by referencing its support for the Black and Tan atrocities in Ireland a decade earlier, and which Mosley had played a leading role in ending.[70]

Nevertheless, the southern Irish arena of fascist activity was, like Britain, also fraught with threat: when de Valera moved in February 1934 to introduce a Wearing of Uniform (Restriction) Bill to combat the Blueshirt movement Allen noted, presciently, that he was just 'a little ahead' of Baldwin, 'the patron of the armed I.R.A. as the Tories once were of the armed Ulster Volunteers'.[71] A Public Order Bill on the wearing of uniforms was duly enacted by the Baldwin Government on 18 December 1936.[72]

Fascist Week, the emergence of the Ulster Fascists, and the nature of Allen's commentaries were all products of the 'palingenetic' phase of national rebirth that the BUF believed it was living through. That phase, however, would cease in mid-1934 when Rothermere ended his links with Mosley's movement, and Allen would make a significant contribution to that outcome.

Allen, Lord Rothermere and the 'Fascist drive in Ulster'

Rothermere, whose mother came from county Down, was a committed supporter of the Unionist regime, though no anti-Catholic bigot.[73] He had reacted rather hysterically to de Valera's accession to

---

[69] See 'Lucifer', 'Current cant and Fascist fact', *Fascist Week*, 22 December 1933; 29 December 1934.

[70] *Fascist Week*, 5 January 1934.

[71] Ibid.

[72] Cross, *The Fascists in Britain*, p. 106.

[73] See journal entry, 29 November 1938, in N. J. Crowson (ed.), *Fleet Street, Press Barons and Politics: The Journals of Collin Brooks* (Cambridge: Cambridge University Press for the Royal Historical Society, 1998), pp. 230–31.

power in 1932, fearing an immediate threat to partition.[74] Accordingly, in this period, Rothermere's popular print, the *Daily Mail* – blatantly pro-fascist in its European and Irish Free State coverage[75] and apparently more widely read in Northern Ireland than any regional Unionist paper[76] – was a site wherein support for both the BUF and the Unionist regime was demonstrated. Eulogies to Lord Craigavon, 'Ulster's Great Leader', who occupied a similar position in Northern Ireland to that of Hitler in Germany, accompanied enthusiastic encouragement of the BUF,[77] goodwill that, at the time, was heartily returned.[78] Rothermere's support was certainly of great significance: membership fell from 50,000 to around 5,000 after his compact with Mosley ended, but even while it endured the activities of the UF and support for its critique of the Unionist regime in the BUF press would produce strains in the Mosley–Rothermere relationship.

Preparing the ground for public demonstrations in Northern Ireland by the UF, a major article in *Fascist Week* – 'Fascist drive in Ulster: Tories degrading the National flag' – carried a wholesale condemnation of the Stormont regime:

> Without close contact with the facts it is difficult for you to appreciate all the jobbery and corruption – the intimidation and the suppression – the camouflage and treachery behind all this panoply of 'Unionism' and 'loyalty' in Ulster.
>
> Surely no part of the Empire has suffered so much from the malevolent activities of the political lawyer and the political parson. Mob psychology and sectarian fanaticism,

---

[74] See Lyndan Macassey to Lord Craigavon, 30 January 1933 (Cabinet papers, PRONI: CAB 9F/123/7).

[75] '6,000 benefit by Italian amnesty: triumph of fascism', *Daily Mail*, 5 November 1932; 'Hitler's key position in Germany', *Daily Mail*, 8 November 1932; 'Hitler's momentous talk to the *Daily Mail*', *Daily Mail*, 17 February 1934.

[76] See J. A. Acheson to J. M. Andrews, 14 October 1937 (Cabinet papers, PRONI: CAB 9F/123/3A).

[77] Geoffrey Harmsworth, 'Ulster's great leader', *Daily Mail*, 20 April 1934; 'Hurrah for the Blackshirts', *Daily Mail*, 15 January 1934; 'The Blackshirts will stop war', *Daily Mail*, 25 January 1934.

[78] See, for instance, 'Lord Rothermere: patriot', *Fascist Week*, 19 January 1934.

resulting in a general mass hypnosis and self delusion, are the stock in trade of these two curses in Ulster.[79]

Moreover, criticism of Unionist abuse of the Union flag as a sectarian party emblem and the shameful abandonment 'of three of the finest counties in the province [Donegal, Monaghan and Cavan] ... by as devilish a piece of political treachery and cowardice [partition] as ever disgraced a political party' went together with praise for 'that famous veteran, the late Mr Joe Devlin'. Through Unionist misrule, the north was now a fertile recruiting ground for republican–communist subversion, something which could only be effectively combated by fascism, the advance of which the youth of the region was now recognising.[80] The article would have significant consequences.

In the week it appeared a *Derry Journal* editorial picked up on its arguments, focusing especially on the 'shameful' betrayal by Carson and the Ulster Unionist establishment of their fellow-Unionists in Donegal, Cavan and Monaghan in 1921, and suggesting that the betrayed loyalists of the excluded counties were now being recruited into the Blueshirt movement.[81] The editorial expressed surprise that the BUF should have 'got the measure of the Orange warlords here to a nicety': there would have been less surprise had it been known that 'the measure' of the Orange warlords had been taken by the former Ulster Unionist MP for West Belfast, Bill Allen. For its part, the regime could well have been aware through Rothermere that the renegade Unionist, Allen, was the article's author. Having considerable leverage with the press baron, it moved immediately to exercise it.

Following the article's appearance Lord Rothermere was invited to visit Northern Ireland as a guest of the Stormont authorities, with Craigavon taking care to cultivate his goodwill.[82] Rothermere duly praised the 'disinterested' patriotism of Ulster Unionists in cleaving to the United Kingdom, even at financial cost to themselves – a reference to de Valera's cancellation of land annuities paid to Britain

---

[79] 'Fascist drive in Ulster', *Fascist Week*, 23 March 1934.
[80] Ibid.
[81] Editorial, *Derry Journal*, 26 March 1934.
[82] See Craigavon to Rothermere, 24 March 1934; Craigavon to Thomas Cromie, 6 April 1934 (copies) (Cabinet papers, PRONI: CAB 9F/123/7).

on his accession to power in 1932, but which were still paid by farmers in Northern Ireland.[83] And having been made aware of Craigavon's concerns about 'Fascist drive in Ulster' he quickly responded.

Writing to Mosley on 12 April, Rothermere warned him of the 'grave mistake' of his papers criticising the Northern Ireland Government: 'I am intensely interested in that country, as perhaps you know. My forebears come from there.' Referencing 'Fascist drive in Ulster' Rothermere specified Allen, who also contributed to Rothermere's own prints,[84] as the main culprit: 'I do not want my enthusiasm for your cause to be diminished by such an unnecessary and unfair attack. Will you tell Allen this?'[85] Rothermere effectively presented Mosley with an ultimatum that, given the great expansion in membership the BUF was accruing from the Rothermere connection, he may well have felt he had no option but to accept. The upshot was not just a toning down in Allen's commentaries on the Unionist regime – which he may very well have refused to accept – but the complete removal of the 'Lucifer' series from *Fascist Week*. Moreover, according to Rothermere, he also succeeded in persuading Mosley that 'Ulster must have from now on unyielding support'[86] and moved to offset the negative propaganda of the Blackshirt press through enhanced favourable coverage of Northern Ireland in the papers he controlled, especially the national paper, *Daily Mail*: four separate promotional articles appeared between 11 and 24 April alone.[87]

A significant effect of the 'Fascist drive in Ulster' controversy was in providing Rothermere with a model for the kind of administration he felt Mosley should be aiming to establish. The

[83] *Irish News*, 12 April 1934.

[84] Commentary on W. E. D. Allen, 26 March 1934 (NAK, Security Service, Personal Files: W. E. D. Allen, KV/2/879).

[85] Rotheremere to Mosley, 12 April 1934 (copy) (Cabinet papers, PRONI: CAB 9B/216/1).

[86] Rothermere to Sir Charles Blackmore, Cabinet Office, 23 April 1934 (Cabinet papers, PRONI: CAB 9B/216/1).

[87] See Viscount Rothermere, 'How Ulster has weathered the [economic] storm', *Daily Mail*, 11 April 1934; 'Farming as the life blood of Ulster', *Daily Mail*, 20 April 1934; 'How Ulster trains her young farmers'; 'Ulster may have greatest airport', *Daily Mail*, 24 April 1934.

secondary literature on the Mosley–Rothermere alliance records their break-up as being due to Rothermere's realisation that Mosley's ideas of fascist dictatorship was much more than he could stomach.[88] But it fails to specify exactly what form of administration he preferred. His correspondence with Mosley on Northern Ireland provides the clearest indication – a one-party right-wing regime of the Ulster type permanently in office. He informed the fascist leader: 'The Government of N[orthern] Ireland is so far better than Westminster or Dublin that it is almost an impertinence to compare it with the other two', while the region could provide 'the most valuable recruiting ground [for the BUF] of anywhere in the United Kingdom'.[89]

The lead provided by Rothermere was duly taken up by Lord Craigavon, who claimed that members of the Orange Order, the Black Brotherhood or the B Specials could substitute as fascists,[90] an opinion reminiscent of an already recorded *Morning Post* view that 'the organised Loyalists of Ulster … were the first of all the Fascists, although an Orange sash and not a shirt was the badge of their allegiance'.[91] It also appears that the regime approached the UF with a view to gaining the organisation's support, something Job Stott, its chief publicist, claimed was contemptuously rejected.[92]

Although he appears never to have been in contact with the movement, in the British context Rothermere's conception of fascism was closer to that of Rotha Lintorn-Orman in the early 1920s than Mosley's. Her organisation had been founded before the defining characteristics of fascism had emerged and had identified closely with Ulster loyalism. But by the mid-1930s, with both the

[88] See, for example, Mosley, *Beyond the Pale,* pp. 64–66. The author cites correspondence between Mosley and Rothermere on their differences, especially Rothermere's view that he thought Mosley would act to reinvigorate 'Conservative forces'; Benewick, *The Fascist Movement in Britain,* p. 155.

[89] Rothermere to Mosley, 12 April 1934 (Cabinet papers, PRONI: CAB 9B/216/1).

[90] Job Stott indignantly rejected the idea: Stott to editor, 'The fascists and Lord Craigavon', *Irish News,* 3 May 1934.

[91] *Morning Post,* quoted in *Irish News,* 24 July 1933.

[92] Stott to the editor, *Irish News,* 8 May 1934.

Nazi and Italian models to hand, the BUF was concerned to establish
its radical political identity and ambitions: when its revolutionary,
dictatorial aims became clear – the constitutional reconstruction
Mosley had in mind was as far away from the Stormont model as
it was possible to get – Rothermere's alliance with Mosley ended,[93]
though he would remain an admirer of Hitler and Mussolini.[94] But
even before then the seeds of alienation had already been sown in
the 'Fascist drive in Ulster' controversy and how Mosley and the
BUF responded to Rothermere's advice.

Despite the latter's impression that Mosley was now committed
both to wholehearted support of the Stormont regime and hostility
to de Valera's Government, the reality was more prosaic. 'Lucifer'
and all his works may have been removed from the pages of *Fascist
Week*, but the result was not active support for the Unionist regime:
rather, a brief pledge to 'defend Northern Ireland from any southern
aggression, a policy for which the Leader has stood throughout his
career'. And while Mosley did now voice his opposition to aspects
of Government policies in the Irish Free State, this also tended to be
expressed in brief, unemotional, matter-of-fact terms:

> Fascist policy today is not the reconquest of Ireland … Our
> policy is the exclusion of Irish goods from the British market
> until Southern Ireland behaves herself as a member of the
> Empire. As Ireland is entirely dependent on the British
> market that method would be … effective … and would
> entail no loss of British lives.[95]

Mindful of the significant pro-Irish, Irish and Catholic elements
among the BUF membership and supporters – in March 1934
the pro-nationalist writer J. B. Morton had refused to join the
Mosley-sponsored January Club partly because of his compact
with Rothermere[96] – Mosley tended to restrict his very occasional

[93] See 'Lord Rothermere and Sir Oswald Mosley', *Daily Mail*, 19 July 1934.
[94] See Crowson, *The Journals of Collin Brooks 1932–40*, *passim*.
[95] 'Lord Beaverbrook and fascism', *Fascist Week*, 4 May 1934; 'A policy for
Ireland: making Free State behave', *Sunday Dispatch*, 6 May 1934; '"Play the
game": Attitude of British fascists to Free State', *Irish Examiner*, 6 July 1934.
[96] J. B. Morton to Capt. H. W. Luttman-Johnson, 3 March 1934 (Imperial

references to Irish Free State policy to this brief statement.[97] In this context, it is noteworthy that the foundation document of the BUF, Mosley's *The Greater Britain* (1932, republished in a revised edition in 1934), makes no reference to the problems that the Irish Free State was posing for imperial unity, even though by then de Valera's programme of dismantling the Free State's imperial links was well under way. While the BUF's Catholic and Irish constituency is important in this respect, it should also be seen against the background of the state of the Blackshirt movement following Rothermere's abandonment of his connection with Mosley.

An internal report entitled 'APATHY' disclosed, among other things, English public alienation derived from Mosley's increasing sympathy with the Hitler regime when taking Italy 'as a model' would be more acceptable.[98] Accordingly, Mosley was really in no position seriously to offend his Irish and Catholic membership through virulent attacks on de Valera. Nor may there have been any personal inclination to do so. De Valera may have been determined to combat the Blueshirt movement in the Irish Free State, but in June 1933 he had made a tumultuously received visit to Italy during which he declared 'his great admiration for Fascism'.[99]

As for Allen, his departure from *Fascist Week*, which itself ceased publication as an independent print in May 1934 when it was 'merged' with *Blackshirt*, was followed by residency in Northern Ireland 'where for the last three years they [Mr and Mrs Allen] have been living entirely [since 1934]'.[100] His contribution to Blackshirt

War Museum, Captain H. W. Luttman-Johnson papers, microfilm, 94-5). Morton was English, and author of widely popular humorous prose. He developed strong pro-Irish sympathies following his marriage to an Irish doctor, Mary O'Leary, in 1927, to whom he was devoted.

[97] See, for instance, Mosley at Ipswich, 5 July 1934 in *Irish News*, 6 July 1934; also *Londonderry Sentinel*, 7 July 1934.

[98] C. S. Geroult, Memorandum on the state of the BUF entitled 'APATHY', late 1934 (Sir Oswald Mosley papers, BU, CRL: OMN/B/7/2/8).

[99] '"Up Dev." in Italian', *Irish Times*, 6 June 1933.

[100] See *Irish News*, 18 January 1937. The information was disclosed as part of an explanation to discount rumours that Mrs Allen was having an affair with the Duke of Kent; also 'Northern Ireland today: Mr W. E. D. Allen's views', *Irish Times*, 6 February 1938.

propaganda now consisted of an occasional piece on European fascism under the pseudonym 'James Drennan'.[101] This reflected a gradual distancing in his relationship with Mosley which was on a downward track by the later 1930s. When a BUF candidate performed relatively well in the East End at the London municipal elections of 1937, Allen telegrammed his congratulations,[102] but a year later their relationship reached a nadir. Allen complained about Mosley's failure to repay loans he had made on his behalf, leaving him 'in a difficult financial position': 'I have really nothing but pity for a man who has to refer to a lawyer before being able to write an (unsigned) letter to his one surviving friend.'[103]

Their deteriorating relationship coincided with, and in part reflected, a change in the balance of opinion within the Mosley movement on Ireland, one in which pro-nationalism was now firmly in the ascendant. That was inevitable with both the ending of the Mosley-Rothermere compact, the loss of leverage on the Blackshirt movement by Unionists it entailed, and the removal of the movement's other influential commentator with an Ulster loyalist connection, William Joyce. Joyce's influence on the propaganda output of the BUF was registered in 1935, the year following Allen's departure from *Fascist Week*.

William Joyce, the BUF and Ulster

Joyce was a brilliant, if vitriolic, platform speaker who would become deputy leader to Mosley and an influential contributor to Blackshirt literature – especially in its more highbrow journal, *Fascist Quarterly* – on fascist and Marxist political philosophies, international relations and constitutional issues.[104] His commentaries on Ireland, however,

[101] See, for instance, James Drennan, 'The Nazi movement in perspective', *Fascist Quarterly*, vol. 1, no. 1 (January 1935).
[102] Allen to Mosley, 5 March 1937 (Sir Oswald Mosley papers, BU, CRL: OMN/B/7/2/19).
[103] Allen to Mosley, 22 August 1938 (Sir Oswald Mosley papers, BU, CRL: OMN/B/2/2/15).
[104] See, for instance, William Joyce, 'Collective security', *Fascist Quarterly*, vol. 1, no. 4 (1935), 422–30; Joyce, 'Analysis of Marxism', *Fascist Quarterly*, vol. 2, no. 4 (October 1936), 530–42; Joyce, 'Notes on the difference between

were largely shaped by familial influence and personal experience. Of mixed religious parentage, his upbringing was shaped by a Jesuit education and his mother's anti-Catholicism, the latter evident in his preference for describing Christmas as 'Christ-tide' so as to avoid the papist connotations of the traditional name.[105] Joyce could employ European Catholicism as a weapon to attack communist influence in the Spanish Civil War,[106] but his personal anti-Catholicism was of a visceral, indeed 'rabid' nature,[107] quite different from Allen's unemotional perception of the Catholic Church as internationally a reactionary influence, and undoubtedly reinforced by the bitter personal experience of being forced out of Ireland with the Black and Tans in 1921, for whom he had been an informer in the Galway area.[108] At the same time, and as we have seen, while Joyce had no time for Irish nationalism in any form, he could identify Parnell as a leader whose political practice presaged the fascist era in how it exposed the 'decadence' of the parliamentary system, and Sir Edward Carson as a direct progenitor of Sir Oswald Mosley[109] but, unlike Allen, who made the same connection, Joyce was a supporter of both Northern Ireland's constitutional position and the Unionist regime. Moreover, he was virulently antisemitic, something that coloured his commentaries on political developments.

Joyce's sense of personal bitterness at the outcome of the War of Independence is evident in his references to the murder of Admiral Somerville in county Cork in March 1936, attacking British betrayal of Irish loyalists, especially the Royal Irish Constabulary, the plight of whose ex-members he had seen in London and compared with

observing and preserving the British Constitution', *Fascist Quarterly*, vol. 2, no. 1 (January 1936), 131–40.

[105] J. A. Cole, *Lord Haw Haw: The Full Story of William Joyce* (London: Faber & Faber, 1964), pp. 56, 197.

[106] William Joyce, 'The world, the flesh – and financial democracy', *Action*, 19 December 1936.

[107] This was the opinion of Sir Vernon Kell, head of MI5 (David McKitterick, 'Opened files name backers of Mosley', *Irish Times*, 10 November 1983).

[108] Cole, *Lord Haw-Haw*, pp. 23–24; Holmes, *Searching for Lord Haw-Haw*, chaps 1–2.

[109] William Joyce, 'Quis separabit?', *Fascist Quarterly*, vol. 2, no. 1 (January 1936), 27–29.

the supposedly better treatment Britain offered to German Jewish refugees.[110] His pro-Unionism and antisemitism were neatly married in the article, 'A martial Jew', which quoted Carson to the effect that the Jewish people had lacked any military tradition 'since the crossing of the Red Sea'.[111] His particular focus in 1936, however, was the National Council for Civil Liberties (NCCL), which had produced a damning indictment of the Stormont authorities and the repressive instruments at its disposal following the regime-facilitated violence against the Catholic community in Belfast the previous year. Joyce claimed: 'It is highly probable that the Northern Irish Government has been compelled to adopt repressive measures to preserve the peace, in view of the constant inroads made upon Ulster by paid emissaries of Irish republican organisations.' With more accuracy, he ridiculed critics who described these measures as 'Fascist' simply to draw attention 'to anything they dislike'.[112] Yet, despite Joyce's undoubted political talents and oratorical ability, by 1937 he would be out of the Blackshirt movement. This was due to a combination of financial cuts and intra-movement factional antagonism, while the bitterness with which Joyce reacted to his dismissal earned Mosley's vehement hostility.[113]

Finance was an important factor in Joyce's dismissal – Mussolini had ceased the secret funding of Mosley's movement he had hitherto been providing[114] – but the fact was that the abrasiveness Joyce displayed in print and on the platform was believed to be alienating possible public support, while his dominance in the role of Director of Propaganda and the range of Blackshirt publications that bore his name rather than Mosley's gave the impression 'that he is now to all intents and purposes the Movement'. Many 'older and saner officers are asking quite frankly whether this officer is an asset or a liability'.[115] Arrogant, ambitious, irredeemably given to intrigue that

---

[110] William Joyce, 'Searchlight over Britain', *Action*, 2 April 1936.
[111] 'A martial Jew', *Action*, 21 May 1936.
[112] Joyce, 'The world, the flesh – and financial democracy'.
[113] Dorril, *Blackshirt: Sir Oswald Mosley and British Fascism*, p. 413.
[114] Ibid., p. 340.
[115] See Hugh Vaughan-Henry to The Leader, 25 July 1934; Geroult, 'APATHY' (Sir Oswald Mosley papers, BU, CRL: OMN/B/7/2/13; OMN/B/7/2/8).

created influential enemies within the movement and with a public profile that appeared to infringe on Mosley's status as leader,[116] his departure when a suitable opportunity arose is hardly surprising. But, for our purposes, Joyce's sacking removed a committed defender of the Unionist regime at the heart of the Blackshirt movement. And that presence was further reduced when, disillusioned by Mosley's leadership, A. K. Chesterton, who was as vexed about British betrayal of Irish loyalists as Joyce, resigned in March 1938.[117] Thereafter, though the Unionist regime would still have many supporters on the British Right in general – among them the small Imperial Fascist League (see Chapter 3) and Arthur Bryant, who had family connections with Northern Ireland and who would only narrowly escape internment in 1940[118] – commentary on Ireland, north and south, in Britain's most significant fascist movement carried an unmistakeable pro-nationalist imprint unopposed by any effective Ulster counter-narrative. Certainly, Mosley personally never located the origins of his movement in Carson's threatened rebellion of the pre-war years.

The BUF and Partition: An Increasing Nationalist Embrace

The Catholic and Irish nationalist presence in the BUF, of course, had never been absent, the issues that concerned it a staple of Blackshirt press comment,[119] and which an article celebrating Archbishop Hinsley's promotion to Cardinal in January 1938, 'An honour to England', exemplified.[120] That focus intensified following

---

[116] Holmes, *Searching for Lord Haw-Haw*, chap. 6.

[117] Cross, *The Fascists in Britain*, p. 186.

[118] See 'Betty' to Bryant, 8 March 1921 (King's College London, Liddell Hart Military Archives, Bryant papers, C9); 'Loyal Ulster', in Arthur Bryant, *Humanity in Politics* (London, [1938]), pp. 65–68; Bryant to Lord Craigavon, 24 February 1939 (Cabinet papers, PRONI: CAB 9F/123/3); Andrew Roberts, 'A Nazi sympathiser and supreme toady', *Spectator*, 23 July 1994, 13–14.

[119] See 'Fascism and the Roman Catholics', *Blackshirt*, 1 July 1933; 'Bishop attacks fascism', *Blackshirt*, 15 July 1933; 'Catholic doubts about the corporate state', *Blackshirt*, 24 April 1935; 'Can Catholics support fascism?', *Blackshirt*, 19 December 1936.

[120] 'An honour to England', *Action*, 13 January 1938.

the great reduction in membership that followed the breakdown of the Rothermere–Mosley compact and especially the associated loss of revenue. Keen to cultivate Nazi support from 1934 largely for this purpose,[121] Mosley sought unsuccessfully – if the post-war testimony of an Abwehr typist is to be believed – to sell his movement to the Abwehr as an organisation working on its behalf, for the purpose of which he intimated that 'he could arrange for members of the I.R.A. to be used in a similar capacity'.[122]

Blackshirt propaganda also developed an Anglo-Irish cultural aspect. Thus, while the Anglo-Irish economic war was ongoing,[123] Francis McEvoy argued for cultural unity based on a fusion of the rich spiritual and rural culture of Ireland and the BUF's ambition to break the stranglehold of bourgeois financiers on British life: 'An England freed from the canker of commercialised pandering to the lowest instincts and the whole corrupt and poisonous materialism of financial democracy will ... find in Erin ... an eager partner in the building of the Greater Britain which your leader Sir Oswald Mosley has set before you as your ultimate task.'[124]

The theme of Anglo-Irish cultural fusion had another focus in the promotion of the Blackshirt movement in Scotland, a region in which it was extremely weak in the late 1930s.[125] The Irish and the Scots had made a shared contribution to British civilisation – 'When the illiterate

[121] See Holmes, *Searching for Lord Haw-Haw*, pp. 105–07.

[122] Testimony of Gerda Wiesner, Abwehr typist in the mid-1930s, during interrogation by British Field Security in Germany on 5 September 1946 (NAK, MI5 report, 9 April 1948, KV2/893).

[123] The conflict was a dispute between Westminster and Dublin having economic, constitutional, financial and defence issues. Initiated by de Valera's abolition of the oath of allegiance to the King and refusal to pay annuities due under various pre-independence land acts, the British Government retaliated by imposing special duties on Irish imports, especially cattle and dairy produce, and which, in turn, provoked the Irish Government to impose emergency duties on British coal, machinery, and iron and coal goods. The conflict proceeded until settled by the Anglo-Irish Agreements of 1938 (Deirdre McMahon, 'Economic War', in Connolly, *Oxford Companion to Irish History*, pp. 176–77).

[124] Francis McEvoy, 'Anglo-Irish reconciliation through cultural renaissance', *British Union Quarterly*, vol. 1, no. 2 (April/June 1937), 78–83.

[125] Cross, *The Fascists in Britain*, p. 180.

Anglo-Saxons came to Britain their first alphabet was an adaptation of that of the Irish Celt' – something that was demonstrating a revival in 'the rising of Ireland from the [constitutional] tomb in recent years'. And, like the Irish, 'all history records that a leader is what they [the Scots] desire in all national movements' rather than 'mere representative government by which the votes of a larger country could swamp those of a smaller allied nation', something Mosley's organisation would prevent.[126] Nevertheless, despite the intense cultivation of the Catholic/nationalist interest and corresponding sympathetic coverage of the BUF in general,[127] the late 1930s also saw rising Catholic concern about the 'frightening' antisemitism of the BUF together with its apparent support for compulsory sterilisation of the 'unfit', a subject on which no satisfactory answers were given.[128] And, though one Blackshirt candidate did relatively well in the East End of London at the municipal elections of 1937 (none was actually elected), it is significant that the BUF failed to carry the Irish vote, a decisive setback.[129]

In this context, Blackshirt criticism of the Ulster Unionist regime became more important as a factor in neutralising possible Catholic alienation. The *Catholic Herald*, which was to the fore in raising concern about antisemitism and sterilisation, was also to the fore in attacking the Ulster 'Orange' regime.[130] Thus, when J. H. Robb, Minister of Education in Northern Ireland, expressed his sympathy for European Jewry in the persecution it was experiencing,[131] *Action* listed the number of Catholics and nationalists held by the Stormont regime without trial and in the absence of any charges being brought against them,[132] while an integration of anti-Unionism and the Blackshirt theme of corrupt parliamentary democracy was found

---

[126] Scotia, 'Seen through Gaelic eyes', *Action*, 11 June 1938.

[127] *Catholic Herald*, 10 June 1938; Bellamy, *We Marched with Mosley*, p. 63.

[128] Cross, *The Fascists in Britain*, pp. 187–88.

[129] Dorril, *Blackshirt: Sir Oswald Mosley and British Fascism*, p. 412.

[130] See, for example, *Catholic Herald*, 10 July 1936, 30 July, 13 August 1937, 27 January, 10 February 1939, 12 September 1941.

[131] See James Loughlin, 'Hailing Hitler with the Red Hand: The Link in Northern Ireland, 1937–40', *Patterns of Prejudice*, vol. 50, no. 3 (July 2016), 290–93.

[132] See '"Would some god the giftie gie us …"', *Action*, 6 August 1938.

in Thomas Somerset, Unionist MP for North Belfast, who, *Action* demonstrated, was among a group of MPs benefiting financially from directorships while drawing a parliamentary salary.[133] Nevertheless, the BUF was occasionally compelled by 'Ulster' interests to clarify its position on religious denominations in general.

The perceived need to respond to the virulently anti-Catholic *Ulster Patriot*, which had claimed the Papacy had 'nobbled' Mosley and British fascism, required the point to be made that Mosley's movement welcomed all Christians.[134] Even though there had been no Blackshirt-affiliated presence in Northern Ireland since the demise of the UF in 1935, the BUF paid close attention to how it was reported in the region. All criticism was responded to. Just as with the *Ulster Patriot*, when the *Belfast News-Letter* claimed links between the British and German fascist movements in early 1938, Olive Hawks, a leading female officer, rejected the accusation – something we now know to be completely untrue. She also stated, more accurately, that the BUF 'is unconnected with any other organisation in either Great Britain or Northern Ireland'.[135] Vigorous rebuttal of Unionist criticism was an essential part of the anti-partitionist case, though not all proposals to effect Irish unity were welcomed uncritically.

Thus, when Bill Allen addressed the partition issue in February 1938, suggesting unity within the Commonwealth as a solution to the region's economic problems,[136] and again, following the Anglo-Irish economic war, when he argued that the defence of the British Isles be consolidated by establishing Irish unification on a dominion basis,[137] he incurred Mosleyite ridicule by proposing that Northern Ireland be given dominion status as the first step, largely with reference to the likely fate of Catholics under a regime freed

[133] '£600 a year plus ...', *Action*, 11 February 1939.
[134] Michael Goulding, 'Behind the news', *Action*, 11 February 1939; 'Ulster and the British Union': Revd Ellis G. Roberts to the editor, *Action*, 5 February 1938.
[135] Olive Hawks (For the British Union of Fascists and National Socialists) to the editor, *Belfast News-Letter*, 19 March 1938.
[136] 'Northern Ireland today', *Irish Times*, 6 February 1938.
[137] W. E. D. Allen, 'An Irishman urges a united Ireland', *Evening Standard*, 27 January 1939.

of the constraints entailed by subordination to Westminster.[138] The
failure of Allen's unity proposal, however, was due not only to its
individual weaknesses (apart from the fate of Catholics there was
little evidence of a demand from Ulster Unionists for dominion
status at this time) but to the Mosley movement's more radical stance
on partition, evident in its attitude to the IRA's English bombing
campaign in 1939, the 'S Plan', designed to solve the Ulster issue by
violent means.

The S Plan ran from mid-January to August 1939 causing at
least six deaths and a multiplicity of injuries and continued despite
a strenuous security response.[139] But no condemnatory comment or
article appeared in the Mosleyite press: only, as *Action* claimed, that
there could be no firm basis for Anglo-Irish relations until the partition
issue was settled.[140] A reference to the campaign was made in a reader's
letter of February in *Action*, but merely as an accompaniment to the
main purpose of the communication: an attack on Allen's dominion
status for Northern Ireland proposal – and even then it was not critical
but excusatory. It was not the authentic IRA perpetrating the outrages
but dupes being manipulated by those who wished 'the break-up of
the British Empire'.[141] This was vague enough to imply either Jews or
communists, or both, something that others would more explicitly
claim, such as the virulently antisemitic Catholic Tory MP Captain
Archibald Maule Ramsay.[142] Only in July 1939, when the Home
Secretary Sir Samuel Hoare claimed there was 'internal assistance' for
the IRA – which the Mosleyites believed was an attempt to target
fascists – did it explicitly address the issue, pointing out that it was
from the British left and the Irish-American community, not fascists,
that support for the IRA traditionally came.[143]

Mosley's organisation could not publicly endorse the IRA
bombing campaign, but it had connections with Irish republicanism

---

[138] John O'Brien, 'More Ulster nonsense', *Action*, 4 February 1939; T. J. Doran,
letter to the editor, *Action*, 11 February 1939.
[139] West, *MI5: British Security Service Operations, 1909–1945*, pp. 398–99.
[140] Book review of J. B. Morton, *The New Ireland* in *Action*, 11 March 1939.
[141] T. J. Doran to the editor, *Action*, 11 February 1939.
[142] Captain A. H. Maule Ramsay, *The Nameless War* (London: Britons
Publishing Society, 1954), pp. 78–80.
[143] 'Home Secretary and the IRA', *Action*, 29 July 1939.

through, for instance, the National Headquarters official, Michael Joseph Goulding, who boasted of personal contacts with IRA leaders.[144] Also, its approach to the IRA campaign had, as it developed, a wider context. The German Abwehr, impressed by its impact, made contact with the IRA in February, contacts that would eventually lead to Berlin's English language service broadcasting anti-partitionist propaganda focused on the Unionist regime's treatment of the region's Catholic community.[145] As he was preparing to broadcast to Britain from Berlin, William Joyce was instructed to avoid criticism of the IRA.[146] At the same time, MI5 reports on his organisation in the spring of 1940 detailed Mosley's own apparent connections with southern Ireland and the IRA, including an individual who claimed to be his 'right-hand man', while Mosley was also reported to have two flats in the same London building with an 'abnormal number of Southern Irish employees'.[147] Whether soundly based or not, such reports could only have contributed to the decision to intern Mosley and his followers under Regulation 18b – a regulation introduced under the Emergency Powers Act of 24 August to deal with the IRA – as would the fact that pro-Nazis drawn into close contact with Mosley and his movement in 1939 on the shared basis of preventing war between Britain and Germany took a similar line on partition, especially Admiral Sir Barry Domvile, founder of The Link.[148]

---

[144] Metropolitan Police (Special Branch) Report, Scotland House, on BUF, 5 March 1940 (NAK, Metropolitan Police Files, online access). For assessments of the IRA in the twentieth century, see Brian Hanley, *The IRA, 1926–1936* (Dublin: Four Courts Press, 2002); J. Bowyer Bell, *The Secret Army: The IRA* (3rd edn, Dublin: Poolbeg Press, 1998); T. P. Coogan, *The I.R.A.* (revised edn, London: HarperCollins, 2000); Richard English, *Armed Struggle: The History of the IRA* (London: Pan, 2012).

[145] 'Nazis urge ending of Irish partition', *Irish News*, 3 August 1939.

[146] Richard Griffiths, *Patriotism Perverted: Captain Ramsay, The Right Club and British Anti-Semitism, 1939–40* (London: Constable, 1998), p. 263.

[147] MI5 Report, 'Oswald Mosley', January–April 1940 (NAK, MI5 Intelligence Reports, KV2/884).

[148] Loughlin, 'Hailing Hitler with the Red Hand', *passim*; Griffiths, *Patriotism Perverted*, chap. 15. But see Clough (*State Secrets, passim*) for the argument that Tyler Kent and Anna Wolkoff were interned to avoid Anglo-American political embarrassment.

It is noteworthy, however, that the parliamentary reaction to the introduction of the Emergency Powers Act was indicative of the extent to which the politics of pre-war Ulster continued to colour contemporary developments. The Labour MP D. N. Pritt argued that, among other things, the bill could 'have been put forward with at least as great force in respect of Lord Carson and his Irish colleagues in 1913'.[149] Only with the onset of war with Nazi Germany would that perspective be decisively undermined. Northern Ireland's loyalty to the British war effort as against the neutrality of 'Eire' (so designated under de Valera's new Irish constitution of 1937, and how he recommended Ireland be referred to)[150] registered a new frame of reference in Anglo-Irish relations. It was thus in very different conditions – free of the taint of fascism – that in 1942 the Unionist regime publicist, Hugh Shearman, could speculate on the apparent demise of British parliamentary democracy: 'A two-party system seems largely a thing of the past in Great Britain, and never existed in Ireland'.[151]

[149] For Pritt's contribution and the debate in general, see Hansard, HC, vol. 350 (24 July 1939), cols 1047–1127.
[150] Nicholas Mansergh, *The Unresolved Question: The Anglo-Irish Settlement and its Undoing, 1912–1972* (New Haven, Conn. and London: Yale University Press, 1991), p. 299.
[151] Hugh Shearman, *Not An Inch: A Study of Northern Ireland and Lord Craigavon* (London: Faber & Faber, 1942), p. 171.

3

The British Union of Fascists
and Northern Ireland (II)
The Ulster Fascists

The extension of Blackshirt fascism to Northern Ireland under the title, Ulster Fascists (UF) occurred just as the BF in the region was going into decline, which could be seen as a happy coincidence: a competitor for popular support was leaving the political stage. That the BF had not prospered in the region, however, was a portent the UF failed to recognise, certainly did not acknowledge. That it did not do so reflects the very different conception of fascism – informed by a Griffinesque palingenetic myth of inevitable national rebirth – the UF, like its parent body in Britain, subscribed to during the period of rapid growth the Rothermere–Mosley compact produced, and the political confidence it facilitated. This chapter assesses its relative progress during the compact and the problems it encountered as it struggled to survive thereafter.

The UF: The Regional Context

To assist the formation of the UF, in August 1933, Dr Robert Forgan, Deputy Leader to Sir Oswald Mosley, wrote to a former member of the Ulster Command of the BF in Belfast requesting his assistance in establishing the UF Belfast centre. This initiative – basing Blackshirt branches on the organisation and personnel of BF converts – clearly reflected British practice where the BUF attracted many former BF members. Forgan, however, received an angry rebuff,[1]

---

[1] See E. Williams to Secretary, Ministry of Home Affairs, 21 September 1933 (Home Affairs papers, PRONI: HA/32/1/509).

undoubtedly informed by knowledge of the BUF's attitude to northern Unionists and their regime. The Belfast Centre was subsequently established at 35 High Street. This, however, was a very minor irritant compared with the difficulties that Northern Ireland presented as an arena for political recruitment.

In this context, the appeal to a 'betrayed' war generation that was central to BUF propaganda in Britain could not register effectively, because the motives for war service in 1914–18 – informed by the need to validate the cases for and against Home Rule – were significantly different from those that obtained in the rest of the United Kingdom. For Unionists, war service had done much to safeguard their place within the British State, effected, respectively, by the Government of Ireland Act of 1920, the terms of the Anglo-Irish Treaty of 1921 and the conclusions of the Boundary Commission in 1926.[2] Thus, for Ulster Unionists, the question of what the war had been fought for could be given a more satisfactory answer than was the case in Britain. As for Ulster Catholics, who had also volunteered for war service in numbers equivalent to Protestants, they became victims in the post-war years of a reconfigured nationalist/republican narrative which regarded their sacrifices of little account: at worst, an example of national betrayal; at best, colossal wrong-headedness. The resultant sense of demoralisation among Catholic ex-servicemen made asserting the public acknowledgement of that experience difficult, especially as at the same time Ulster Unionists were engaged effectively in a propaganda exercise to reduce public perception of Ulster's wartime contribution to that of the Ulster Volunteer Force (UVF) in its military configuration the 36th Ulster Division.[3] Thus, if for different reasons, the Catholic war generation would be no more easy to address for UF purposes than the Protestant.

Just as in Britain, the wartime promise of a golden post-war future for ex-servicemen was no more delivered on in Northern

---

[2] For a discussion, see James Loughlin, 'Mobilising the sacred dead: Ulster Unionism, the Great War and the politics of remembrance', in Adrian Gregory and Senia Paseta (eds), *Ireland and the Great War: 'A War to Unite Us All?'* (Manchester: Manchester University Press, 2002), pp. 133–54.

[3] Ibid., pp. 139–40.

Ireland, but regional Ulster and wider Irish narratives of meaning had so shaped Unionist and nationalist perspectives that the 'golden future' betrayal hardly registered in popular opinion. Certainly, the 'war generation' in Northern Ireland did not exist as a potential pro-fascist body in the way it was imagined in Britain by the BUF.

At the same time, the continuing controversy over partition which dominated politics in Northern Ireland made the establishing by the UF of a *via media* between nationalism/republicanism and Unionism extremely difficult, but something the palingenetic mindset that shaped the BUF outlook at this time prevented the UF from appreciating.

The UF marked its presence with a declaration which addressed partition in a way intended to negotiate both nationalist and Unionist positions: the border was deplored as 'a political handicap to the peace, progress and prosperity of the people and the country as a whole' and the very existence of Northern Ireland itself 'a costly blunder'; nevertheless, the UF did not intend that it 'would be trifled with in any way likely to assist the setting up of an all-Ireland republic'. Irish unity would only be acceptable in the form of a 'dominion of Ireland within the British empire of Fascist nations', hopes for the realisation of which were identified in the Blueshirt movement in the Irish Free State.[4]

Having framed the overall objective of the organisation, it was important to establish the UF's cross-community credentials, something the BF-inspired sectarian violence at Kilkeel, county Down of the previous year was useful as a comparative reference point in doing.[5] At the same time, the significance of sectarianism in Northern Ireland society was denied with the claim that it 'is not sectarianism that divides our island – it is Ulster's defiance and hostility to any suggestion of unity with those who abhor everything British'.[6] The organisation's position on partition closely reflected

---

[4] *Keesing's Contemporary Archives* (20–21 September 1933), 957; '"Ulster Fascists": new political party in six-counties', *Irish Press*, 21 September 1933.
[5] See promotional notice, *The Ulster Blackshirts* [1933] (Home Affairs papers, PRONI: HA/32/1/509).
[6] 'A modern Ulster loyalist' to editor, *Blackshirt*, 22 July 1933.

that of Bill Allen, whose controversial 'Fascist drive in Ulster' article was intended primarily as a boost for the UF. Like Allen, the UF combined support for the region's constitutional position with denunciation of the Stormont regime. Nevertheless, over time, UF commitment to partition would vary in line with the organisation's fortunes, determined by the very Ulster-specific difficulties that lay in the path of political progress, especially the intensity with which the religio-ethnic myths of nationalism and Unionism informed everyday life in the region.

The UF: Leading Personnel and Policies

The public face and to a large extent the driving force of the UF was Job Stott (Figure 6). A native of Yorkshire, born in 1883 but long resident in Belfast, he enlisted in the British Army in 1901 during the Boer War, but spent his army service entirely in the United Kingdom, leaving in January 1913. It was a less than wholly successful career. Having advanced to the rank of Lance Corporal in late August 1903, he lost this rank in February 1905, and although he fulfilled the statutory twelve years of a 'Short Service' contract – which specified seven years with the Colours and five in the Reserve – only just over five years of that service counted towards a pension.[7] In the Ulster context it may be of some significance that he changed his religion from Wesleyan to Roman Catholic in December 1903.[8] Stott returned to the armed forces on the outbreak of the Great War in which he served with some distinction, seeing action on the Somme from July to August 1916, together with the Battles of Ypres and Loos, among others, and being awarded the Meritorious Service Medal.

---

[7] Job Stott, Military Service Record (1901–13). I am grateful to Johanne Devlin Trew, Ulster University, for supplying me with a copy of this document.

[8] The entry in Stott's military service record is stroked through but the conversion appears real enough. Stott's death notice in April 1943 appeared only in the leading print of the Catholic and nationalist community, *Irish News* (6 April). A misprint in the notice cites him as 'Joe', but the Army Roll of Honour provides a corrective (https://search.findmypast.co.uk/search-world-records-in-military-armed-forces-and-conflict).

Figure 6   Job Stott, *c.*1922
Courtesy of the *Belfast Telegraph*

Following his war service in 1919 he was appointed Secretary of the Ulster District Selective Committee of the Appointments and Training Branch of the Ministry of Labour, concerned with securing employment for ex-servicemen. In this capacity he established a network of sub-committees across the north to facilitate the Committee's work. In this capacity, and having a keen interest in social and labour conditions, Stott was credited with placing 700 officers and 3,200 men, completing his service in October 1922.[9] His continuing militaristic inclinations are evidenced in membership of both the Ulster Special Constabulary (USC) for a time in 1921 and one of the oldest fascist movements in the Empire, the Australian New Guard.[10]

Stott's engagement in politics was first registered in opposition to the Presbyterian-sponsored campaign for extension of the prohibition of alcoholic drinks (Local Veto) to Northern Ireland in the late 1920s. He produced a substantial pamphlet, significant for the insight it provides into his political outlook at this time. Stott argued against prohibition on the basis of the primacy and autonomy of the individual as against the coercive intrusion into everyday life of the State,[11] reinforcing his argument with the claim that 'Prohibition is alien and unpatriotic to the British Empire' and antagonistic to 'all the ethics of the British Constitution'.[12] It was a position that his later commitment to fascism and the centrality of the State that it entailed would see almost entirely reversed.

Stott's biography provides a very clear indication of why he would have been attracted to Mosley's paramilitary Blackshirt movement, especially its theme of a 'war generation' betrayed by 'old gang' political parties – 'EX-Servicemen of all creeds on the scrap-heap is a nice reward from the IMPERIAL PROVINCE, which they saved in its hour of danger'[13] – a betrayal the BUF would remedy; and a war generation in Northern Ireland whose welfare he

[9] 'Mr J. Stott's record', *Weekly Telegraph*, 21 October 1922.
[10] [10] *Londonderry Sentinel*, 21 April 1934; *Irish News*, 6 July 1934.
[11] See Job Stott, *The Case against Prohibition and the Local Veto* (Belfast: Ulster Anti-Prohibition Council, 1927), pp. 1–5.
[12] Ibid., p. 5.
[13] Ulster Fascists, *Fascism in Ulster* (Belfast: Ulster Fascists, [1933]), pp. 5–6.

had been directly concerned with. However, while Stott would be the most prominent face of the UF, the organisation was actually established by Captain T. W. Armstrong.

Of Scots-Irish background, Armstrong had been a member of the old pre-war UVF, and after joining the Blackshirt movement was sent over by the London headquarters to organise the Northern Ireland Blackshirt formation in August 1933. He named it 'Ulster Fascists' and was known initially as 'Staff Officer, BUF, attached Ulster Fascists' before assuming the title 'Chief of Staff'.[14] But while sponsored by the London BUF headquarters, as Dr Forgan informed Armstrong: 'I get the impression some Ulster Fascists are inclined to regard the B.U.F. National Headquarters as their own H.Q. As a matter of fact, as you know, the Ulster Fascists are an entirely separate body from the B.U.F., although, of course, our every wish [is] for your success'.[15] But, if the umbilical cord with London was broken, the family resemblance was obvious in the UF's policies and programme, which wholeheartedly rejected the decadent post-war 'Old Gang' politicians whose era was about to be superseded by a national rebirth embodied in the emergence of fascism and the creation of a corporate State, the only means by which Ulster could meet twentieth-century conditions successfully.[16]

The UF's political arrival was registered in an 'exclusive' interview with the *Irish News*. Recruitment was apparently proceeding vigorously, 'with quite a number of influential men in this area' already associated with the movement, though given that the organisation was still in its gestation stage activity would focus initially on propaganda work instead of public demonstrations or contesting elections. The movement would adopt a shirt, almost certainly based on that of the BUF, though its specific design had yet to be defined,[17] and would enhance its identity through

[14] On Armstrong's background and role in establishing the UF, see the following: Armstrong, W. Clayton Travis to the editor, *Irish News*, 27 March 1935; Job Stott to the editor, *Irish News*, 28 March 1935.

[15] Dr Forgan to Armstrong, 19 March 1934, quoted in Stott to the editor, *Irish News*, 30 March 1935.

[16] Ulster Fascists, *Fascism in Ulster*, *passim*.

[17] 'Birth of new Blackshirt movement in Six Counties', *Irish News*, 20 September 1933.

symbolic representation. Whereas the BF had merely subsumed the Ulster Command within the symbolic compass of the movement in general, something also true of Scottish Blackshirts in regard to the BUF, the UF produced their own identifier (the axe and bundle of sticks against the background of a hand intended to represent the Red Hand of Ulster) and associated interpretation:

> The bundle of sticks symbolises 'Strength of Unity'. Divided – They can be broken. United – They are invincible.

> The Axe symbolises the Supreme Authority of the Organised State, cuts away the weeds of Party Control, and clears a road to Unity, Peace, and Progress.

> ### 'Ulster First' and 'Up Fascism.'

> The Red Hand of Ulster symbolises the Stop signal to Communism, Unrest, Unemployment, Party Government, Party Strife, Party Bitterness, and Ruinous State Expenditure and Graft.

> ### TODAY

> **The Red Hand of Ulster is the Grasping Hand of Communism and the Grabbing Fist of Party Government.**[18]

Fascism in Ulster presented nothing less than the reconstruction of 'Ulster' as a 'corporate state', a State 'organised like a human body' in which all individual interests, whether of 'employers, trade unions, banking or professional interests' would be subordinate but 'woven into the permanently functioning machinery of CORPORATE GOVERNMENT'.[19] In sum:

> Fascism is the system of the next stage of Civilisation. It is the creed of the twentieth century. It comes to subordinate the interests of PARTY and CLASS to the interests of the STATE as a whole. The mission of Fascism is to create in ULSTER the Twentieth Century State. We fight not only

---

[18] Ulster Fascists, *Fascism in Ulster*, p. 1.
[19] Ibid., p. 3.

for the material salvation of our PROVINCE, WE fight also for the re-birth of the BRITISH SPIRIT.[20]

While the path of rebirth would be pursued through remedying the evils and failures of the contemporary Unionist administration, those of communism and republicanism were also targeted, and if it was necessary to eliminate these only through a fascist dictatorship, then 'we will have a Dictator'.[21]

The UF acknowledged the importance of loyalty to 'King and Empire' and defending the region's constitutional position, but the major focus of its activities was a sustained critique of the northern regime and its practices,[22] criticisms that resonated strongly with the Catholic community. The space given to Catholic and nationalist grievances – completely ignored by the BF – reflected very much the disposition of the BUF on the Irish question, evidenced by an advertisement in *Fascism in Ulster* for *The Truth about Stormont* by 'QX', a historico-political indictment of the Stormont site and parliamentary building produced as a counter to the celebrations surrounding the inauguration of the Stormont parliament buildings in November 1932; and authored not, like the other publications, by leading BUF members, but by a reporter from the *Irish News*.[23] The *Irish News* would reproduce almost the entire contents of *Fascism in Ulster*,[24] thus ensuring that through its approximately 30,000 daily sales[25] the nationalist community throughout the north was familiarised with its message and programme. Moreover, while the UF rejected *enforced* Irish unification, the Blueshirt movement held out the prospect of agreed unity: 'A Dominion of Ireland within the British Empire of FASCIST NATIONS would receive our full support.'[26]

[20] Ibid.

[21] Ibid., pp. 8–10.

[22] Ibid.

[23] Ibid., p. 17; James Loughlin, 'Consolidating "Ulster": regime propaganda and architecture in the inter-war period', *National Identities*, vol. 1, no. 2 (1999), 171–72.

[24] 'Birth of new Blackshirt movement in six counties', *Irish News*, 20 September 1933.

[25] Lord Camrose, *British Newspapers and their Controllers* (London: Cassell, 1947), p. 142.

[26] Ulster Fascists, *Fascism in Ulster*, pp. 12–13.

This disposition inevitably made difficult the charting of an independent course between Northern Ireland's indigenous political factions, something that may have been underrated by the palingenetic belief that 'Fascism is the system of the next stage of Civilisation' and which the UF's membership, together with the BUF, of the fascist New Empire Union,[27] may have seemed to provide evidence for; as would, within the UK, the contemporaneous emergence of a fascist organisation in Scotland. Both Belfast and Edinburgh would have Blackshirt-linked organisations by November 1933, while *Fascism in Ulster* paralleled that of *Fascism and Scotland*. Both appeared about a year after the BUF made its official entry to the public arena in October 1932, an occasion marked by the publication of Mosley's own definitive work of fascist philosophy and policy, *The Greater Britain*,[28] the source for the UF's policies. However, the relationships of the Ulster and Scottish organisations with the BUF leadership exhibited significant differences.

Although welcoming the adoption of much BUF policy in the Scottish fascist programme, the London leadership also expressed concern about its desire for self-Government and reacted sharply against its anti-Catholicism, something that focused largely on Catholic immigration from the Irish Free State:[29] '*We disagree ... entirely with their attitude towards Roman Catholics*' (my italics).[30] In the most significant contribution to date on fascism in Scotland, Stephen Cullen argues that this position, reflecting the BUF's attempt to chart an equidistant course between religious denominations, was mistaken: 'in trying to do so, the BUF handicapped itself in the struggle for support'.[31] But while this may well have been true, Cullen underrates the degree to which the BUF's attitude to Catholicism was ideologically based, while also underestimating its

[27] Ibid., p. 5.
[28] A. K. Chesterton, *Oswald Mosley: Portrait of a Leader* (London: Action Press, 1937), p. 119. A misprint on the page gives the year as 1933.
[29] See Steve Bruce, *No Pope of Rome: Anti-Catholicism in Modern Scotland* (Edinburgh: Mainstream, 1985), chap. 2.
[30] 'Fascism in Scotland: A disclaimer', *Blackshirt*, 16 June 1933.
[31] Stephen Cullen, 'The fasces and the saltire: the failure of the British Union of Fascists in Scotland, 1932–1940', *Scottish Historical Review*, vol. 87, no. 2 (October 2008), 324–25.

material advantage outside Scotland. As the enduring pro-Catholic theme in BUF propaganda suggests, that constituency was too important to sacrifice for the uncertain gains to be made in Scotland by an organisation which, while receiving a degree – if inadequate[32] – of material and personal support from the London centre, was *explicitly* designated as 'entirely independent of the British Union of Fascists'.[33] As we have seen, a statement of the separate status of the UF from the BUF was also made, but it was done privately by Dr Forgan: no emphatic public declaration to this effect was produced.

The UF's optimism about its prospects, nevertheless, could only have been encouraged by the contemporaneous emergence of a Scottish Blackshirt formation, while in terms of comparative growth the UF appears initially somewhat better placed than its Scottish counterpart. For whereas Blackshirt progress in Scotland was hampered by the presence of several pre-existing small fascist organisations,[34] the UF emerged just as the only other active fascist movement in the region was in the process of dissolution, something the UF sought to hasten through a moral indictment that added BF attacks on 'peaceful and lawful' Labour meetings in Belfast to its responsibility for the Kilkeel violence.[35]

Certainly, contrasted with the BF, UF propaganda was informed by a positive vision of Northern Ireland's future, one characterised by promise rather than paranoid fear for the constitution, though one that Jews, especially, would soon have reason to doubt. While the concern to emphasise the ethical character of the UF was evident in an emphatic rejection of antisemitism – 'We are NOT Anti-Jewish – Our Brand of Fascism is BRITISH'[36] – reflecting the lack of antisemitic feeling in the region, the BUF in Britain would soon be distinctly antisemitic and the UF would, if half-heartedly, follow its example. But, initially at least, the UF apparently made significant progress. By September 1933, when *Fascism in Ulster*

---

[32] Cullen, 'Fasces and saltire', 313.
[33] *Blackshirt*, 16 June 1933.
[34] Cullen, 'Fasces and saltire', 310.
[35] Ulster Fascists, *Fascism in Ulster*, pp. 4–5.
[36] Ulster Fascist leaflet, *The Ulster Blackshirts* [1933] (Home Affairs papers, PRONI: HA/32/1/509).

was produced, up to eight branches were reported already to have been established, the most recent in south Fermanagh,[37] while the BUF prints, *Blackshirt* and *Fascist Week*, offered consistent support for the UF in its gestation period, including the reproduction of encouraging letters from fascists in Northern Ireland.[38]

Reflecting the optimism and enthusiasm that followed the emergence of the Rothermere–Mosley compact, *Blackshirt* heralded the emergence of the UF as 'a Godsend to end Party bitterness, Strife and Religious insults … Under Fascism the Flag of Empire will not continue to be turned into a PARTY or RELIGIOUS banner'.[39] Thus, with the northern regime now in existence for over a decade, and with its discriminatory, sectarian and oppressive characteristics fully in evidence, the presence of the UF could be justified as not just a political and constitutional, but a *moral* necessity.[40] Unlike the BUF critique of the National Government at Westminster, which focused chiefly on its decadence and incompetence, the sectarian nature of the northern regime allowed for a more trenchant critique: the Minister of Agriculture, Sir Basil Brooke's anti-Catholic diatribes could find unpleasant echoes at street level, such as the view that Catholics were 'parasites' who should 'not be allowed to live among Ulster people'[41] – a form of abuse bearing close similarity to Nazi antisemitism – while a body calling itself 'the Ku Klux Klan' would circulate anonymous letters to Protestant butchers in Belfast urging the sacking of their Catholic employees, though it seems without much success.[42] Furthermore, Government corruption, together with the sterility of Orange–Green politics, served to explain a woefully inadequate response to dire economic circumstances.[43]

[37] Police report of UF progress (Home Affairs papers, PRONI: HA/32/1/509).
[38] 'A.N. Irishman', Belfast to the editor, *Blackshirt*, 16 June 1933; 'A modern Ulster loyalist' to the editor, *Blackshirt*, 22 July 1933.
[39] 'Fascism comes to Ireland', *Blackshirt*, 7 October 1933.
[40] Ibid.
[41] See Orange demonstration reported in *Newry Telegraph*, 11 July 1933.
[42] 'Ku Klux Klan begins boycott campaign in Belfast', *Irish News*, 6 October 1933.
[43] Belfast Fascist, 'Ulster's wage war', *Blackshirt*, 18 March 1933.

Political Activity and its Difficulties

The Great Depression had impacted on Northern Ireland, as in the rest of the United Kingdom, in terms of mass unemployment, near-starvation subsistence levels, and employer insistence on reducing already inadequate wage levels. These had produced a working-class response characterised, unusually, by cross-community opposition and collective action by a range of industrial and political organisations from labour unions to republican and communist groups.[44] The UF appetite for action was whetted when 'The Friends of the Soviet Union' established a branch in Belfast, invited the Belfast Trades Council to affiliate and offered trips to the USSR.[45]

Its emergence in Belfast at this time was hardly accidental, coming in the wake of a particularly violent phase of socio-political agitation which had begun in November 1932 when Irish Railway companies moved to enact a 10 per cent wage cut, resulting in a strike which drew in British rail unions, Revolutionary Workers Groups and leftist IRA members. The employers' use of blackleg labour escalated the conflict which took on an extremely vicious turn as the Unionist authorities redefined the struggle as a republican/communist attempt to force Northern Ireland into an Irish republic. Initially, however, common interests and cross-community mobilisation – 'They seem now, at long last, to have realised that "Hail Marys" will not save seventy thousand unemployed, and that Orange drums will not march them through the Twentieth Century'[46] – appeared to present a promising basis for UF action, against a background in which the London BUF prints, *Blackshirt* and *Fascist Week*, not only provided a consistent critique of the Unionist regime and regional parties but also a wider British context of meaning for UF activities.

Of the two, *Fascist Week* provided the closer Ulster/Irish focus, especially in Bill Allen's series, 'Current Cant and Fascist Fact', which

[44] For discussions, see Michael Farrell, *Northern Ireland: The Orange State* (London: Pluto Press, 1976), chap. 6; Paddy Devlin, *Yes, We Have No Bananas: Outdoor Relief in Belfast* (Belfast: Blackstaff Press, 1979).

[45] See 'Who are the Belfast "Friends of the Soviet Union"', *Irish News*, 7 October 1933.

[46] 'Belfast Fascist', 'Ulster's wage war', *Blackshirt*, 18 March 1933.

would explain why the UF recommended supporters to buy that print in particular.[47] Allen described the UF decision not to contest the Stormont election of November 1933 as inspired – 'The Fascists did well to hold their hand, for despair is fast breaking down the old parties and old allegiances in Northern Ireland'[48] – though the reality was that the organisation was simply too weak to do so. Moreover, the success of General Eoin O'Duffy's Blueshirt movement in southern Ireland, added to that of the UF in Northern Ireland and the BUF in Britain, would create a context in which all of the problems affecting Anglo-Irish relations would be successfully resolved.[49]

Inspired by the excessive optimism that characterised the BUF at this time, Allen was, perhaps excusably, over-optimistic. O'Duffy banned BUF members from joining his movement and on Northern Ireland was preoccupied with the traditional nationalist objective of ending partition, grounding his hopes on the assumption that many Unionists believed partition to be based on a 'rotten foundation' and 'secretly hoped' that a movement such as his would come along to remove it.[50] O'Duffy reiterated his unity message throughout the autumn of 1933.[51] Not surprisingly, his organisation – officially the National Guard – was banned in Northern Ireland as soon as it was formed,[52] and far from complementing UF progress in Northern Ireland, as Allen thought, would function seriously to damage it. But, even within Northern Ireland, Allen's expectation as to the progress the UF was likely to make was misconceived.

---

[47] See leaflet entitled *The Ulster Blackshirts* (Home Affairs papers, PRONI: HA/32/1/509).

[48] 'Up fascism', *Fascist Week*, 8 December 1933. See also 'The fate of Ulster', *Fascist Week*, 22 December 1933.

[49] See 'Lucifer', 'Current cant and fascist fact', *Fascist Week*, 22 December 1933; 29 December–4 January 1934; 'Fascism in Britain and Ireland', *Fascist Week*, 5 January 1934.

[50] *Irish News*, 21 July 1933; Mike Cronin, *The Blueshirts and Irish Politics* (Dublin: Four Courts Press, 1997), pp. 194–95. For other assessments of the Blueshirt movement, see Maurice Manning, *The Blueshirts* (Dublin: Gill & Macmillan, 1970); Fearghal McGarry, *General Eoin O'Duffy: A Self Made Hero* (Oxford: Oxford University Press, 2005).

[51] *Irish News*, 23 October, 20, 23 November 1933.

[52] *Irish News*, 24 July 1933; Manning, *The Blueshirts*, 77–78.

In a zero-sum environment it was unlikely that the political equidistance between the region's existing parties the UF sought to establish could ever realistically be achieved: the willingness of the *Irish News* to publicise *Fascism in Ulster* was itself indicative of the difficulty the organisation would have engaging with the Protestant community. The *Irish News* would have been happy to publicise criticism of the Stormont regime at any time, but it was especially keen now, having been the victim of a vindictive prosecution by the Minister of Home Affairs, Sir Dawson Bates. The paper had severely embarrassed the regime on the occasion of the official inauguration of the Stormont parliament building by the Prince of Wales in November 1932, by disclosing that the Unionist Government had accepted a proposal to have 100,000 Orangemen provide a 'Guard of Honour' for the Prince, a story that was taken up by the *Sunday Times* and the *Manchester Guardian*. The regime responded by prosecuting, and convicting, the *Irish News* under the Special Powers Act on the basis of a reader's letter on the issue which claimed it was 'spreading false reports' prejudicial to peace and order. It was an obviously politically biased prosecution which infuriated the editor, Sydney Redwood, as an attack on the freedom of the press.[53] Accordingly, with the UF critique of the Unionist regime closely mirroring that of the nationalist community, the leading regional Unionist print, the *Belfast News-Letter*, largely ignored the UF's emergence, reflecting the stance of the Unionist press across Northern Ireland, with, it seems, the exception of the *Fermanagh Times*.[54]

As the process of putting the Belfast organisation in place developed through the autumn and winter of 1933–34, the BUF press continued to highlight Ulster and wider Irish issues, the latter stimulated by the Anglo-Irish 'economic war'. Against this background, in January 1934, the UF entered the public arena. Apparently in an attempt to confront local sectarian traditions, a

[53] See Eamon Phoenix, 'The history of a newspaper: the *Irish News*, 1855–1995', in Eamon Phoenix (ed.), *A Century of Irish Life: The Irish News and 100 Years of Ulster History, 1890s–1990s* (Belfast: Ulster Historical Foundation, 1995), pp. 28–29.
[54] '"Fascism" in Ulster', *Fermanagh Times*, 21 September 1933.

meeting to expound Blackshirt principles in Dundonald, outside Belfast, took place in the local Orange Hall.

The organisation's founder, Captain Armstrong, set out the UF vision of a distinctively British rebirth of the United Kingdom and the British Empire along fascist lines, with the region's corrupt regime being replaced by a new beginning where all interest groups would be subordinated to the national welfare in a world engaged in a struggle between communism and fascism: 'If Britain were to survive she would have to go ahead and get something done that was definite and clear-cut, and one hundred per cent British.' While the UF had adopted a black shirt – a foreign importation – this was 'because in a colour scheme it was difficult to please everyone', but as to political practice, they did not intend 'to introduce Italian or German methods. They would stick to British Fascism'.[55]

In the same period, the UF got publicity from an unlikely source. Loftus Johnson, speaking at a meeting of the Belfast branch of the Irish Communist Party (CPI) on 18 February, brought the organisation's leaflet, *The Ulster Blackshirts*, to its attention in a speech framing local political developments in a wider European context. Europe was on the 'point of a big explosion' with fascism threatening an imperialist war in France, Austria and Spain. In southern Ireland an attempt was being made to impose fascism on the working class, while in Northern Ireland 'much the same dictatorship has developed', though with the Special Powers Act at its disposal the Unionist regime did not need to follow exactly European fascist practices of smashing up 'the Trade Union machine or making illegal many more of the Working Class Parties'. Nevertheless, the emergence of the UF demonstrated that Mosleyite fascism was 'developing very rapidly so far as Belfast and the country districts around Belfast are concerned'. Moreover, the nature of the leaflet, especially the threats made to 'wipe out' communist enemies and their allies, was of as a kind that, had it been produced by the Communist Party, everyone associated with it would have been jailed. That 'not a step' was taken by the authorities against the UF demonstrated that

---

[55] See 'Fascism in Ulster', *Belfast News-Letter*, 18 January 1934.

the Fascists represent the interests of those whom you [RUC attending the meeting] are serving, namely, the Capitalist class, in this particular part of the country, and in view of the fact that they employ you to serve their interests, you would find it more than your job is worth to take any steps to prevent them from issuing any agitational literature of this description, for the wiping out of the Communist Party.[56]

Johnson's speech is illuminating in a number of ways. Ironically, his claim that the UF was spreading rapidly in the greater Belfast area would have mirrored the UF's own propaganda, but needs to be regarded with scepticism. Both movements, from directly opposite perspectives, expected momentous fascist advances affecting the United Kingdom in the very near future. But these expectations lacked a solid empirical and factual basis, and while both expectations of fascist progress appear real enough, the respective motive in each case was movement recruitment. And, in this respect, the UF was in a much weaker position than the CPI.

That Loftus Johnson was a member of the Woodworkers' Society reflected the sustained engagement of the CPI (until 1933 the Revolutionary Workers Groups) in Belfast's working class and industrial struggles, especially those over Outdoor Relief rates in 1932 and the rail workers' strike in 1933. Not by any means the dominating force in these struggles, and forever inclined to read (mis-read) prospects of inter-community working class solidarity in the cause of a 32-county socialist republic, nevertheless, the CPI's base in Belfast's working-class community is clear enough.[57] By contrast, the UF, a new arrival on the Belfast political scene, had no such base and faced a formidable task in building one. Accordingly, it could not effectively reply to Johnson's claim that lack of Government action against it proved the UF was simply a tool of

---

[56] Police Report of Meeting of the Communist Party of Ireland (Belfast Local) on Custom House steps, 18 February 1934 (Home Affairs papers, PRONI: HA/32/1/550).

[57] For a sustained critical evaluation of these struggles, see Ronnie Munck and Bill Rolston, *Belfast in the Thirties: An Oral History* (Belfast: Blackstaff Press, 1987), chap. 2.

the 'Capitalist class'. Johnson was right in claiming that the Unionist regime had not moved against the UF, but this was because, to date, it was seen to pose no significant threat to the authorities or their interests,[58] while the communist/republican threat was taken more seriously, partly because it was believed to be, and partly because it was just too useful a tool to discard when sectarianism was needed to shore up the regime's support base.

In this context it is worth noting that the report of eight UF branches having been established by 21 September 1933[59] was radically revised a month later: it 'appears that no branches have yet been formed, with the exception of one in Armagh city, which came into existence on 18th instant'. A Mr E. D. Kerr, JP, of Carrickreagh, near Enniskillen, 'has been appointed Fascist organiser for county Fermanagh, but up to the present no branches have been formed, and it is not expected that the Movement will receive much support in that county'.[60] Certainly, neither the nationalist nor Unionist papers in the area makes any reference to it in this period. But for the CPI the reality of UF region-wide weakness counted for little against the fact of its very existence. Moreover, even if the UF could have shown convincingly that it had no connection with the regime or the 'Capitalist class' in Northern Ireland, the argument that its activities 'objectively' served those interests would still have been persuasive to many.

As it happened, the authorities, having found nothing disturbing for months in UF activities, were about to pay the organisation rather more attention. Their interest was occasioned in February 1934 by reports of the circulation of UF literature, especially *Fascism in Ulster* – 'a most scurrilous production' – among members of the police.[61] This could not firmly be established, but it was a

---

[58] See handwritten note (29 March 1934) on UF leaflet, *The Ulster Blackshirts* (Home Affairs papers, PRONI: HA/32/1/509).

[59] E. Gilfillan to the Secretary, Ministry of Home Affairs, 21 September 1933 (Home Affairs papers, PRONI: HA/32/1/509).

[60] E. Gifillan, Inspector General Office, to the Secretary, Ministry of Home Affairs, 27 October 1933 (Home Affairs papers, PRONI: HA/32/1/509).

[61] C. H. Blackmore to Major G. A. Harris, Ministry of Home Affairs, 1 March 1934; Harris to Blackmore, 2 March 1934 (Cabinet papers, PRONI: CAB 9B/216).

worrying sign[62] and was followed by the controversial 'Fascist drive in Ulster' article in *Fascist Week* in late March.[63]

'Fascist drive in Ulster': The Northern Ireland Dimension

The British dimension to the controversy the article created has been covered in Chapter 2; the focus here will be on its regional aspects. It came to the attention of the Ministry of Home Affairs in early May through the agency of W. D. Scott, Permanent Secretary at the Ministry of Commerce, who suggested that it might best be responded to in the form of a rebuttal article in *Fascist Week* 'which would show this part of the world in a quite a different setting'.[64] In responding in this way Scott was acting in accordance with an established Government practice. The view of Ulster Unionism that developed through the recent troubles, and beyond, namely, of being incapable of articulating an effective media presentation of its case, belies a highly effective regime operation in the inter-war period. With substantial information resources at its command, it was highly influential in shaping how it was presented in the broadcast media (BBC), and it was generally just as effective in the less directly controllable press: unfavourable articles appearing in British newspapers were met with a direct request for the acceptance of counter-arguments ostensibly more objective in their account of Northern Ireland than the original reports.[65] The basis on which such initiatives were made, however, was that the press organ approached was open to an alternative interpretation, but in this instance it was felt that such an approach would not work: 'anything in the nature of counter propaganda would only give them opportunities and materials for further attacks'.[66] And, as we

---

[62] Harris to Blackmore, 19 March 1934 (Cabinet papers, PRONI: CAB 9B/216).

[63] *Fascist Week*, 23 March 1934.

[64] W. D. Scott to Major G. A. Harris, 8 May 1934 (Home Affairs papers, PRONI: HA/32/1/509).

[65] See James Loughlin, *Ulster Unionism and British National Identity since 1885* (London: Pinter, 1995), chap. 5.

[66] G. A. Harris to Scott, 11 May 1934 (Home Affairs papers, PRONI: HA/32/1/509).

have seen, the problem was dealt with in a more effective manner by the regime.

'Fascist drive in Ulster' was designed as a boost for the UF at a time when it was about to emerge from its initial promotional stage to active public agitation. The organisation's first public meeting took place on 19 April in Library Street, with Job Stott as speaker. The event is illustrative of the difficulties the UF would experience in advancing its cause. Stott began with remarks reflecting the sense of inevitable success the BUF generally was imbued with at this time – just a few days later Oswald Mosley would speak at the Albert Hall in the biggest fascist meeting ever held in England.[67] Those present at this inaugural meeting of the UF would, Stott assured them, 'look back on the fact that they were present at it with pride'. This, however, turned out to be a sad misreading of his audience.

For although Stott spoke for about an hour expounding BUF/UF principles, he was subjected to continuous abuse, which tended to reach a climax whenever he made any criticism of Labour or Communist Party policies, before having to close the meeting.[68] That the audience was composed chiefly of the UF's socialist and communist opponents indicated the enormity of the task the UF faced in gaining popular support. Another indicator lay in the location of the meeting: Library Street.

The traditional and most popular location for public meetings in the city was the large open space in Custom House Square. To choose the much more restricted space of Library Street, between Belfast Public Library and the offices of the *Belfast Telegraph*, just off the major thoroughfare of Royal Avenue, itself suggested – despite Stott's public confidence – some doubt about the initial level of public support to be expected. In response to the hostility attending this meeting an 'Ulster Fascist Defence Force' was apparently formed, but apart from a reference in the *Irish News*[69] it is absent from the public record.

[67] *Irish News*, 23 April 1934.
[68] *Irish News*, 20 April 1934.
[69] See W. Clayton Travis, 'Ex-A.P.O. Ulster Fascists and Unit Leader, Ulster Fascist Defence Force', to the editor, *Irish News*, 24 March 1935.

The factors limiting the progress of Blackshirt fascism in Northern Ireland, however, especially political opposition, were not entirely singular. In cities across the British midlands – e.g., Leicester, Coventry, Stoke-on-Trent – the relevance/irrelevance of the fascist message to local conditions together with the success of opponents in 'restricting the ability of local fascists to operate in outdoor locations associated with respectable politics',[70] presented similar difficulties in advancing the Blackshirt cause.

A second public meeting on 26 April in Belfast was again held in Library Street. Sensing the opposition they were likely to face the platform party was enhanced in number from six at the first meeting to 12; and with Stott now accompanied by Captain Armstrong, who spoke first. Sartorially, the form of public dress to be worn had now been finally decided upon. To accompany the black shirt, a beret was adopted. As a movement modelled on the BUF, the shirt was no surprise, but the beret was no part of the Blackshirt uniform. It had, however, been adopted for male members of the BF, and perhaps more significantly in the light of future developments was a standard item in the uniform of the Blueshirt movement.

Whereas the audience for the first UF meeting was composed chiefly of socialists and communists, now Armstrong's and Stott's perorations, which included the confident statement by Armstrong that fascism 'would soon be in power at Westminster', were met by hostile jeers representing all points on the political spectrum in Northern Ireland, apart from the Unionist Party. Thus when Stott attacked 'certain classes of Jews and alleged that Jewish financiers were helping the Communists', he was challenged to name any such financiers in Ulster; and as his anti-Jewish argument was simply borrowed from the BUF handbook of political propaganda in Britain he could not do so.[71] In fact, antisemitism would not constitute a significant element of UF arguments, and in this respect it was similar to BUF *provincial* branches where, unlike the London

---

[70] Craig Morgan, 'The British Union of Fascists in the Midlands, 1932–40', PhD thesis, University of Wolverhampton, 2008, p. 220.
[71] 'Stormy Belfast meeting: opposition to fascists', *Irish Independent*, 27 April 1934.

East End, overt antisemitism was regarded as embarrassing rather than an aid to winning support.[72]

Another note of criticism was entered when a voice in the audience asked what was the UF policy on Irish unity and freedom, to which Stott replied that 'the Free State and Northern Ireland should look after their own problems', a reply consistent with the position promoted by Bill Allen in *Fascist Week*, but which would hardly have encouraged nationalist support for an organisation whose vehement attacks on the northern regime also functioned to deter Unionists. In general, this meeting was met with as great a or a greater volume of hostility as the first.[73] That despite the enormous difficulties facing the UF the movement's leaders apparently remained confident of success can, of course, be ascribed largely to Rothermere's backing of the BUF at this time. But *how* the UF understood its experiences should also be considered.

In this respect the coverage of the organisation's activities provided by the northern newspaper that gave most space to fascism, the *Irish News*, is of importance. It was singular in the scope it gave not only to the UF but, simultaneously, to fascism in Britain and Europe: reporting of UF activities was one element in a mosaic of fascist developments that provided a wide semiotic frame of reference. That its coverage of the first UF meeting and the hostile reception it received was followed three days later by a report on Mosley's triumphant meeting in the Albert Hall[74] allowed local difficulties to be placed in a perspective of striking overall general advancement. That a similar report on the second UF meeting ran in the same column as coverage of a fascist meeting in Plymouth at which the violence was such that four people required hospital treatment[75] could both make the UF meeting appear almost 'successful' and

---

[72] Colin Cross, *The Fascists in Britain* (London: Barrie and Rockliff, 1963), p. 152.

[73] 'Ulster fascists heckled', *Irish News*, 27 April 1934.

[74] 'The fascists organising: the largest meeting ever held in England', *Irish News*, 23 April 1934.

[75] 'Four people taken to hospital: lively scenes at fascist meeting at Plymouth', *Irish News*, 27 April 1934.

hostile reaction to it as simply an aspect of the wider struggle the Blackshirt movement as a whole was undergoing as it followed the European fascist path to power: heightened conflict presaging a dramatic political breakthrough. And while as a movement the UF was never strong enough to cause the authorities to revise their opinion of it, for a Government acutely sensitive to how it was portrayed in Britain the 'Fascist drive in Ulster' controversy had illustrated how even a marginal group could occasion, or contribute to, important political developments. Certainly, from this point on, the activities of Sir Oswald Mosley and the BUF became a focus of close attention for the Unionist authorities.

External Developments and Ulster Consequences

April 1934 may have been marked by negative developments in the Ulster dimension of Blackshirt activities – the loss of *Fascist Week* and its support and the difficulties facing UF public agitation – but the millenarian expectation of epoch-transforming change sustained the latter's enthusiasm. A powerful endorsement sustaining that expectation came when an article by Benito Mussolini appeared on the front page of *Fascist Week* in early April: 'As is invariably the case, nothing could be more interesting or dramatic than this passing of an era … nothing is more fascinating or of better omen than the morning red of a new era.'[76] However, to the problems already facing UF progress was added the effects of the increasingly repressive nature of European fascism, and which critics of the UF were keen to highlight. Especially damaging was Nazi Germany's growing persecution of Catholic institutions,[77] and while this was generally not the case in Italy, here fascism's weaknesses as a system of Government was increasingly apparent.[78]

The latter was a particular focus of the proponents of Social Credit, a movement that had its evangelistic aspects with its

---

[76] Benito Mussolini, 'Twilight of the democrats', *Fascist Week*, 6 April 1934.
[77] 'The German menace', *Irish News*, 21 July 1934.
[78] See letters to editor by 'Anti-Loyalist' and 'Nimmo M. Dyce', *Irish News*, 5 May 1934.

followers adopting a green shirt as a badge of identity.[79] Founded on the ideas of Major C. H. Douglas, who envisaged permanent prosperity based on a reform of the monetary system, Greenshirts argued that Social Credit would solve the problem of poverty in Italy without the constitutional and administrative upheaval fascism entailed.[80] But the spectrum of debate was much wider and varied, denying the possibility of a hegemonic Blackshirt narrative emerging.

Thus nationalist criticism focused on both the Craigavon regime and the UF regarding 'loyalty tests for the minority', while support for the UF was countered by socialist claims that the European fascists were simply tools of finance capital. Again, a demand that Mosley be allowed to broadcast on the BBC faced a defence of the existing British democratic system as more civilised than fascism.[81] Stott's argument that criticism of European fascism emanated from 'tainted sources' was unconvincing,[82] especially as comment came not only from the politically committed but the non-aligned.[83] There was something like desperation in his attempt again to exploit the Kilkeel disturbances of the previous year. With Dorothy Harnett, late of the BF and again in the news – her conviction for breach of the peace for incitement to disorder at the Ulster Hall in May 1934 – Stott claimed the sectarian character of the Kilkeel disorder functioned not only to discredit the BF but fascism more widely. It was especially 'calculated to give a very false impression of the Ulster Fascist movement' while also facilitating 'distorted reports of religious persecution, etc., under the Hitler regime in Germany'.[84] That this argument was made in a letter to the *Derry Journal*, the leading nationalist print of the

[79] Malcolm Muggeridge, *The Thirties in Great Britain* (1940; London: Fontana, 1971), pp. 38–39.
[80] 'A.L.G.' to editor, *Irish News*, 5 May 1934.
[81] For various contributions to the debate, see, for example, 'Excelsior', 'A.L.G.', Arthur Bell, 'Anti-Loyalist', 'J.S.K.', 'A.J.C.', 'R.L.N.', C. Claxton Turner, Stott to editor, *Irish News*, 11, 15, 17, 18, 21, 24 May 1934.
[82] Stott to the editor, *Irish News*, 8, 10 May 1934.
[83] See, for instance, F. Brownlow to the editor, *Irish News*, 8 May 1934.
[84] Stott to the editor (By order of the Executive Council), *Derry Journal*, 26 May 1934.

north-west area of Northern Ireland and which had given detailed coverage to the Ulster Hall events,[85] can be seen as an attempt to establish a wider and more favourable context for the debate on fascism at a time when the *Irish News*, which hitherto had been neutral in its approach to the subject – settling largely for providing a forum for debate for its supporters and opponents – was now turning decisively against it.

Against the background of events in Germany, an especially vexing question was the relationship between fascism and Catholicism in Britain, an article on which had appeared recently in *Fascist Week*. Its tone could hardly have been more respectful, with assurance given for the autonomy of Catholic education and freedom of expression, with the line drawn only at any infringement of State sovereignty:

> What ... no reasonable man would claim is that the government of a predominantly Protestant country should bind itself to accept in permanence all Catholic values, to the exclusion of every principle which shall not have received the approval of the Vatican. Such an undertaking would create a state within a state. ... therefore, a Fascist Government ... would not and could not concede any part of its sovereignty either to any sect within the State or to any sovereign prince without the State.

The specific issues on which the State could not automatically give support to Catholic values were sterilisation and contraception, issues which, it claimed, the BUF 'had not had time to consider'.[86] The *Irish News*, however, took exception both to the Catholic Church being described as a 'sect' and also to the BUF's inability or unwillingness to declare its approach to issues on which the church had very definite views. Accordingly, readers were recommended to 'suspend judgement' on the BUF until 'these Fascists have had time to think things out'.[87] Blackshirt activity in Britain, however, would tilt the balance decidedly towards rejection.

[85] *Derry Journal*, 25 May 1934.
[86] 'Fascism in Britain and the Catholic Church', *Fascist Week*, 4 May 1934.
[87] 'An unsatisfactory pronouncement', *Irish News*, 8 May 1934.

Mosley's attempt to outdo the success of the Albert Hall meeting in March 1934 with an even bigger meeting at Olympia on 7 June was, from the perspective of BUF fortunes, a disaster: it attracted 10,000 communist and socialist counter-demonstrators determined that the Albert Hall success not be repeated. Apparently concerned to demonstrate how the BUF could deal effectively with its opponents, Blackshirt violence at Olympia was such as seriously to damage the movement's reputation and to disillusion many who would otherwise have been its natural supporters.[88] Whether the *Irish News* and its readers would fall into this category can be doubted; nevertheless, the Olympia 'hooliganism' was clearly an influence in the paper's decision to declare against fascism on 18 June 1934.

Remarking that 'by their recent activity in England' fascists have 'made Britain somewhat anxious to see the last of Fascism', the UF publication *Fascism in Ulster*, which it had extensively publicised in September 1933, was now targeted: the document's support for partition – even if on a different basis from that of Ulster Unionism – was identified as antithetical to the ambitions of the Irish people 'who wish to see unity in their country'.[89] Stott's response, rejecting any implication that the UF was either a 'White Guard' for Ulster Unionism or in the pay of the 'Craigavonites', while holding out the prospect of eventual Irish unity when fascism had triumphed throughout the British Isles,[90] evidenced the palingenetic expectation that still characterised the Blackshirt movement, but was otherwise ineffective. Nor was what seems to have been – in the wake of the *Irish News* attack – a renewed attempt to gain the support of Ulster Unionists any more successful.[91] As for the prospects of fascist success in the Dominions, which Stott had also claimed,[92] well-founded criticism contested the existence of these movements and/or their significance.[93] And difficult enough as was Stott's task in promoting

---

[88] Cross, *The Fascists in Britain*, pp. 109–16.
[89] 'No choice to make', *Irish News*, 18 June 1934.
[90] Stott to the editor, *Irish News*, 30 June, 17 July 1934.
[91] Stott to the editor, *Belfast News-Letter*, 29, 30 June 1934.
[92] Stott to the editor, *Irish News*, 30 June 1934.
[93] *Irish News*, 5, 6, 12 July 1934.

the UF cause, it was made immeasurably more difficult by contemporary events in Germany.

The 'Night of the Long Knives' on 30 June 1934, when Hitler authorised the slaughter of 90 prominent members of the leftist faction of the Nazi movement together with its chief Ernst Rohm, demonstrated the increasingly vicious character of the regime. It turned a large swathe of British opinion against fascism in general, and against the BUF as it struggled to defend the purge.[94] The *Irish News* gave expression to its sense of horror in the editorial heading: 'Thank God this is Ireland'.[95] With the breakdown of the Rothermere–Mosley compact in July and the collapse in membership and associated hopes of political triumph that followed, the BUF was in a weakened state; but the UF was much more so, its membership vulnerable to offers suggesting a better route to political success. A damaging one came, ironically, as a consequence of one of the factors that underlay the Kilkeel disturbances – Eamon de Valera's candidature for south Down at the Stormont election of 1933.

General O'Duffy's Ulster Initiative

Criticising de Valera for failing to follow up his election with any concrete strategy for ending partition, General O'Duffy appointed a 'Commissioner' for the north in August 1934 to work in conjunction with Blueshirt units to be formed in the region, with an envisaged end to partition to be associated with the restoring of the historic site of Tara to its former position as the capital of Ireland.[96] That his National Guard had been banned in the north on its formation was interpreted by O'Duffy – a native of county Monaghan – as a sign of weakness: 'Lord Craigavon saw the danger to his Administration of an all-Ireland open and constitutional organisation like ours'.[97] As for the UF, O'Duffy's initiative was undoubtedly made attractive to

[94] Cross, *The Fascists in Britain*, pp. 116–18, 162.
[95] *Irish News*, 10 July 1934.
[96] See 'Blueshirts in six counties!', *Derry Journal*, 22 August 1934; 'Blueshirt units for the north', *Irish News*, 22 August 1934; and for Unionist comment, *Londonderry Sentinel*, 23 August 1934.
[97] *Londonderry Sentinel*, 23 August 1934.

a significant section of its membership when it was rumoured that he was 'in league with Mosley'[98] (an attempt to give substance to the rumour by Mike Cronin has been vehemently rejected by Risteard Mulcahy, son of the leading Blueshirt Richard Mulcahy,[99] while decades later Mosley would state that he never met O'Duffy)[100] and therefore posed a threat to its unity.

Attention-grabbing as it was, however, the prospects for success of O'Duffy's initiative were poor. Having fused his National Guard with the former governing party, Cumann na nGaedheal, and the Centre Party, to establish Fine Gael in 1933, the new organisation was suffering its own problems – O'Duffy would be compelled to resign the leadership of Fine Gael on 21 September – while initial soundings in the north as to likely Blueshirt support had not been encouraging.[101] Nevertheless, how the UF should respond to O'Duffy agitated the organisation's leadership. The immediate response was an intensification of UF propaganda and an expansion of its political ambitions.

Late August 1934 saw the emergence of the *Ulster Blackshirt Bulletin*, heralding the UF's intention to elect representatives to Westminster, combined with an open letter to the loyal orders making the UF case for support.[102] Produced in-house, the *Ulster Blackshirt Bulletin*, which was soon brought to Government attention,[103] allowed for more extended treatment of political issues than was possible either at public meetings or letters to the press, and on its own terms,[104] though with an inevitably much smaller

---

[98] Manning, *The Blueshirts*, p. 144.
[99] Cronin, *Blueshirts and Irish Politics*, p. 195; Risteard Mulcahy, *Richard Mulcahy (1886–1971): A Family Memoir* (Dublin: Aurelian Press, 1999), pp. 236–37.
[100] See Mosley's review of Maurice Manning's *The Blueshirts*, 'The problems of fascism', *Hibernia*, 14 May 1971.
[101] 'General O'Duffy's agent in the north: revelations by a political correspondent', *Irish News*, 24 August 1934.
[102] *Irish News*, 23 August 1934.
[103] See C. S. Thomson to the Secretary, Ministry of Home Affairs, 12 September 1934 (Home Affairs papers, PRONI: HA/32/1/509).
[104] See *Ulster Blackshirt Bulletin*, 31 August 1934 (Cabinet papers, PRONI: CAB 9B/216).

circulation. It was not enough to defuse the problem posed by O'Duffy's northern initiative.

The upshot was a specially convened secret meeting of the UF Executive Council to discuss the issue on the weekend of 1–2 September, with delegates from each of the six counties present,[105] though the RUC was also officially present. It emerged that a section of the membership headed by 'a leading officer', favoured an immediate union with the Blueshirts, an option rejected by the majority of the leadership.[106] The result was a split which saw approximately 200 members opting to seek admission to the Blueshirt movement, and being promptly expelled – 'axed' – from the UF. Stott detailed the split in a frank interview with a 'special representative' of the *Irish News*; and given the absence of the organisation's records the interview provides some indications of UF membership. He disclosed that the 'axing' of the Blueshirt converts was merely the most recent of 1934: 'The first was when we had to expel a number of members because they refused to obey our order not to be associated with the extreme methods of a certain Protestant organisation.'[107] Stott did not specify which organisation he referred to but there is little reason to doubt his truthfulness. As the split was in train the UF was engaged in acrimonious debate with the extremist *Ulster Protestant*, with military service consti-tuting the standard by which to gauge the quality of constitutional loyalty: 'Mr Stott is only one Fascist with more loyal service than the whole connection of the Ulster Protestant!'[108]

As for O'Duffy's movement, Stott was frank about why 'blending' with it was unacceptable: 'As we are at present, our organisation cannot have any compromise with the Blueshirts. They are not Fascists, but merely an adjunct of a political party. Our organisation is non-political and non-sectarian, and we are equally opposed to any other party, be it Fianna Fail, Orange, or Hibernian.' Only if and when the parties of the Irish Free State

---

[105] 'Ulster Fascists and Blueshirts', *Londonderry Sentinel*, 4 September 1934.

[106] 'Ulster Fascists and Blueshirts', *Irish News*, 3 September 1934.

[107] 'Northern fascists secede', *Irish News*, 6 September 1934.

[108] 'The Ulster Protestant', *Ulster Blackshirt Bulletin*, 6 September 1934 (Cabinet papers, PRONI: CAB 9B/216).

became '100 per cent Fascist' would a new situation arise, and even then only within the context of the 'British Commonwealth of Nations'.[109] Stott's argument that the Blueshirts movement was not really a fascist movement was substantially correct,[110] but this would have been evident to the seceders also, and their enthusiasm for unity with the Blueshirts suggests Irish unity per se had an attraction that overrode questions of fascist authenticity. O'Duffy was to claim that a deputation of 26 UF members – 24 of them Protestants – met him in Cork, giving assurances of the great support he would get in the north.[111] If indeed this was the case it suggests that the majority of the 200 or so seceders were also Protestants, and thus a sizeable element of the region's Protestant nationalist community.

Stott's assertion of fascist principle which determined the expulsion of the pro-O'Duffy group came with a significant cost in terms of organisation confidence and finance. Its febrile state was evident in the strident tone of *Ulster Blackshirt Bulletin* commentary:

> Yet another … little clique has found it impossible to 'split' the ranks of REAL FASCISM. … The AXE had to be used, and we are well rid of those who wanted to rush into another organisation – doomed to failure … and although reduced in numbers, we are stronger than ever in the Fascist cause. New members will soon make up for those who would follow O'DUFFY.[112]

To make the point, this issue and the next duly reported an influx of new members,[113] while a promotional article appeared describing the role of women in the UF. But, unlike Rotha Lintorn-Orman's BF, that role was restricted to the domestic sphere: 'Motherhood is one of the highest callings, and therefore of utmost importance to

---

[109] 'Northern fascists secede', *Irish News*, 6 September 1934.
[110] On this point, see Manning, *The Blueshirts*, pp. 243–44: 'it could be said that the Blueshirts had much of the appearance but little enough of the substance of Fascism'.
[111] *Derry Journal*, 7 September 1934.
[112] 'Don't be alarmed!', *Ulster Blackshirt Bulletin*, 7 September 1934 (Cabinet papers, PRONI: CAB 9F/216).
[113] '"It's an ill wind …"' (Cabinet papers, PRONI: CAB 9F/216); 'How they lie!', *Ulster Blackshirt Bulletin*, 21 September 1934.

the State.'[114] It was unlikely to lead to a mass influx of female recruits and their membership fees. In September 1934, the *Ulster Blackshirt Bulletin* disclosed that the organisation was moving to new premises and declared: 'FUNDS ARE URGENTLY NEEDED.'[115] It was an added and unnecessary irritant at this time that, despite Stott's many attacks on the BF for the purpose of asserting the UF's own identity, the Gas Department of Belfast corporation failed to make the distinction between the two organisations and repeatedly targeted the UF for an unpaid electricity bill incurred by the BF.[116]

The turmoil within the UF occasioned by O'Duffy's northern initiative brought no assistance from the BUF in London. Mosley, however, seems to have been aware of it, taking the opportunity of a speech at Ipswich in early September to reiterate the BUF position on the Irish Free State and imperial membership.[117] As for O'Duffy, his Ulster intervention, such as it was, came to an abrupt end with his removal from the leadership of the National Guard on 21 September. It was disastrous for all concerned. It never had any real hope of success and not only contributed to his own political demise, but set in train a series of developments that would destroy the UF.

Crisis and Demise

O'Duffy's northern initiative inevitably drew increased regime attention to UF activities and its Blackshirt connections. Cabinet anxieties in this respect, against the background of Mosley's visit to Scotland in April – the first of two he would make – were exacerbated by a belief that he was soon to visit Northern Ireland, stimulating discussion on how to deter it, including whether to ban the dissemination of Blackshirt literature. In the event,

[114] 'Fascism for women and [*sic*] wives' (Cabinet papers, PRONI: CAB 9F/216).
[115] 'New premises fund', *Ulster Blackshirt Bulletin*, 21 September 1934.
[116] See Stott to 'The Manager', Gas Department Belfast City Hall, 18 September 1934; Stott to Sir Crawford McCullough, Lord Mayor of Belfast, 18 September 1934 (Cabinet papers, PRONI: CAB 9B/216).
[117] *Irish News*, 8 September 1934.

Craigavon promised to deal with the prospect of a Mosley visit personally 'at this stage', though what exactly he could do, given that Rothermere's abandonment of the BUF deprived him of any personal leverage, is difficult to envisage. Certainly, any attempt to use the Special Powers Act against Mosley to prevent his entry to Northern Ireland would have created the kind of controversy on the subject of coercion that a Government acutely sensitive to how it was perceived in Britain always sought to avoid. It is likely that this was also the reason why the proposed ban on Blackshirt literature was abandoned.[118] Nevertheless, UF activities made Mosley's likely intentions regarding Northern Ireland a focus of continuing regime attention.

In October 1934, Captain Armstrong made a visit to BUF headquarters in London for the purpose of arranging a visit by Mosley to Northern Ireland. On his return Armstrong reported that a visit would be made but that it was not expected 'until January 1935'; and, in the circumstances, until a firm date was set, projected meetings for the fascist leader in the Ulster Hall in Belfast and the Guildhall in Derry would not be proceeded with.[119] The projected visit, however, was never to happen. The closest *personal* association between Mosley and Ulster came in early November 1934, when Robert Procher, who claimed to be his valet, appeared before Rathmullan court in county Donegal charged with disorderly conduct, the judge granting bail on the reasonable assumption that 'there was no danger of the peace of Rathmullan being disturbed by a Fascisti outbreak'.[120] But while Mosley never came to Northern Ireland the BUF London headquarters, as noted in Chapter 2, continued to monitor developments and Blackshirt-related press reports in the region with corrections offered as deemed necessary.[121] Such concern for the integrity of fascism as a

[118] Cabinet conclusions, meeting of 30 August 1934 (Cabinet papers, PRONI: CAB 4/328/3-4).
[119] E. Gilfillan to Secretary, Ministry of Home Affairs, 18 October 1934 (Home Affairs papers, PRONI: HA/32/1/509).
[120] See 'Charged in Donegal: man stated to be valet to Sir Oswald Mosley', *Irish Press*, 9 November 1934.
[121] See, for example, J. A. McNab to the editor commenting on a recent review of a book on fascism authored by the leading Labour Party activist,

creed in Northern Ireland, of course, was of little assistance to the UF, which continued to suffer the debilitating consequences of the O'Duffy episode.

This was evident in UF commentaries from mid-September, with the admission that the success of fascism in Northern Ireland would have to wait upon developments in Britain: when 'Westminster becomes Fascist' Stormont would have no option but to do the same. Likewise the border problem would easily be solved once fascism was triumphant in the south.[122] But, in the meantime, the UF maintained its contribution towards that supposedly inevitable end through vigorous propaganda, and now with an enhanced overture to constitutional nationalism: 'Where are the young Redmonds, the Devlins, the Davitts etc., of today? Youngsters imbued with the right spirit of nation, morals, service, sacrifice – where are they?'[123] It was accompanied by a condemnation of 'the timid fools of 40-odd years of age, who ... "yap" about Unionism, freedom and liberty ... We have no sympathy for this type of "down and out" so-called "Unionist" ex-servicemen or "loyal" ex-Special Constables.'[124] This pitch, however, was no more likely to be successful in attracting support than previous efforts: Home Rule nationalism was constitutionally redundant and could not be resurrected. The most noteworthy aspect of the pitch, however, was its attack on a significant element of the loyalist community, the ex-servicemen whose welfare was an enduring concern of Stott in the post-war years, as well as of Blackshirt propaganda in Britain. As such it probably caused, certainly reflected, deep internal divisions within the UF, evidenced by the very public resignation of Captain Armstrong from the position of UF Chief of Staff.

Armstrong's resignation took place at the same time as the organisation changed premises, from High Street to Donegall Street, Belfast, and was associated with administrative change: control of the UF passed to a new Executive Council on 10 October, with which,

Ellen Wilkinson, *Irish News*, 19 November 1934; A. K. Chesterton to the editor, *Irish News*, 14 December 1934; 2 October 1935.

[122] *Irish News*, 20 September 1934.

[123] *Ulster Blackshirt Bulletin* items, reported in *Irish News*, 1 October 1934.

[124] *Ulster Blackshirt Bulletin* items, reported in *Irish News*, 9 October 1934.

Armstrong claimed, he had no connection. His successor, with the title of Chief Executive Officer, was Marcus J. C. Walker to whom Job Stott was responsible in the capacity of Administrative Officer of the Executive. Armstrong's breach with the UF governing body, however, was far from clear-cut. The autumn/winter of 1934–35 witnessed disputes between himself and Stott about the degree of his involvement and services to the organisation, Armstrong emphasising a minimal role, while Stott, and others, claimed that he continued to hold meetings under the UF rubric well into January 1935.[125]

What is clear, however, is that during this period Armstrong was preparing a final break with the UF. He issued a circular to UF members inviting them to assist in 'arranging the Group Organisation necessary for the British Union of Fascists (Sir Oswald Mosley, leader), Northern Ireland Branch'. It would be run under BUF discipline admitting no questioning of headquarters orders and admit to membership only proven 'loyalists'.[126] In the circumstances, this initiative is understandable, given that Armstrong originally had been a BUF member sent by the London headquarters to establish the UF. Nor is it surprising that he established his BUF branch in January 1935, the month in which he expected its prospects to be boosted by a visit from Mosley. But, as Stott pointed out, however much Armstrong might want his new Blackshirt body to be brought within the organisational structure of the BUF in Britain, Dr Forgan had already emphasised that such formations in Northern Ireland would be entirely independent.[127]

By March 1935, the UF as an organisation had disintegrated. Stott responded by setting up the Ulster Centre of Fascist Studies with himself as 'Director of Studies' at the Donegall Street address. The Ulster Centre represented a move away from direct and open street conflict with the opponents of fascism to a largely educational role promoting the virtues of fascism as a solvent for society's ills in

[125] For accounts of the intra-organisation disputes in this period, see Armstrong to the editor, *Irish News*, 29 March 1935; Stott to the editor, *Irish News*, 30 March 1935; 'Hard Facts' to the editor, *Irish News*, 30 March 1935.
[126] See W. B. M'Kay to editor, *Irish News*, 27 March 1935.
[127] Dr Forgan to Armstrong, 19 March 1934, quoted in Stott to the editor, *Irish News*, 30 March 1935.

a number of specific areas. In fact, the Centre's literature suggests a modern product consultancy, listing the range of activities offered and the institutions it hoped to cater to, e.g., 'Universities, Schools, Technical Authorities, Municipal Organisations, Welfare Centres, Churches, Film Societies, Employers' and Workers' Associations, Toc H [a Christian charitable organisation originating during the First World War as a rest house for servicemen], Ex-Service and Youth Movements, Literary and Debating Societies, and other approved centres.' Weekly study circles and correspondence courses were also offered.[128]

The Centre's 'mission statement', as it might now be called, very much bore Stott's personal imprint, especially in the high ethical character claimed for fascism, an argument that by this time was increasingly difficult to sustain. By 1935, the international profile of fascism was being shaped increasingly by a Nazi regime whose reputation for savagery the 'Night of the Long Knives' had demonstrated. It was a reality Stott refused to accept, responding, for instance, 'on behalf of the Fascist Movement throughout the world in general' to an *Irish News* review of Winthrop Stoddard's anti-Nazi, *Clashing Tides of Color*,[129] with a true believer's statement of faith in Nazism's ability, unlike decadent parliamentary democracy, to inspire a spirit of self-sacrifice and to mobilise a people's energies for the national good.[130] But with the collapse of the UF an already difficult message to sell became increasingly more so as another dispute with Armstrong began, the latter denying Stott's authority to speak for fascism, Stott querying how policies devised for 'the teeming polyglot millions of the London east end and other British areas' could apply to the unique conditions of Northern Ireland; and adding, tellingly, that fascism reflecting local conditions was completely in accord with Sir Oswald Mosley's own philosophy.[131]

---

[128] See Ulster Centre advertisement printed on Stott's communication to Sir Dawson Bates, Minister of Home Affairs, 14 May 1935 (Home Affairs papers, PRONI: HA/32/1/509).
[129] 'Dunluce', 'Racial divisions in the world today', *Irish News*, 20 March 1935.
[130] 'A fascist protest', *Irish News*, 21 March 1935.
[131] See Stott to editor, *Irish News*, 23 March 1935. Stott was supported against

Both, however, realised how politically self-defeating this kind of acrimonious debate was for their new fascist formations, and broadly compatible positions emerged on an acceptable basis for fascism in Northern Ireland: direct rule of Northern Ireland by a fascist-controlled Westminster, though also unity with the south under an Irish fascist Government, provided it was based 'on a full and equal partnership within the British Commonwealth of Nations'.[132]

The range of debate on fascism that took place in the letter columns of the *Irish News* in the latter part of March 1935 – which extended well beyond the specific issues that preoccupied Armstrong and Stott[133] – might well have continued had not the paper's editor declared the correspondence closed on 1 April, the choice of date intended perhaps to have significance. Certainly, the arguments and claims of Armstrong and Stott might well have seemed the utterances of political fantasists were it not for the belief shared by many fascists, and non-fascists, that the creed's failure in the British State was far from inevitable. The breakdown of the Rothermere–Mosley compact may have dashed the hopes of those expecting the early arrival of a Mosley Government; nevertheless, that compact still showed what was possible in the right circumstances, and from the low point of 5,000 members in 1935 BUF membership rose gradually to approximately 22,500 by September 1939.[134]

It was with this outlook that Stott raised what seemed the wholly realistic question of a dynamic fascist leader for the region: 'Sick of old gang politics ... the people eagerly await the lead, not of a

Armstrong by 'Corporate State', *Irish News*, 23 March 1935; Armstrong to the editor, *Irish News*, 22 March 1935.

[132] Stott to editor, *Irish News*, 26 March 1935; Armstrong to editor, *Irish News*, 27 March 1935.

[133] For example, the identity of Northern Ireland and what was meant by 'Ulster' – six or nine counties; a 'plague on both your houses' attack wondering how either Stott or Armstrong could believe that a fascist state could ever be established in Northern Ireland or solve its problems. See contributions to the letters section of the *Irish News*, for 24, 26, 27, 28, 29 March 1935.

[134] Thomas Linehan, *British Fascism, 1918–1939: Parties, Ideology and Culture* (Manchester: Manchester University Press, 2000), pp. 160–61.

buffoon ... but of someone with dynamic force, who is not afraid to step out in front, someone who will lift the cudgels and fight for the new life [against] any attack from whatever quarter it may be delivered.'[135] Stott had not raised this issue while the UF, with its BUF connections, was in being, but with its collapse and the splintering of fascist support it now had immediate import: a charismatic leader was a defining element of a thriving fascist movement.

Richard Thurlow has argued that the BUF was misnamed; that it was predominantly an English movement 'with its main areas of strength in London and the south-east'.[136] And for a movement based on the leadership principle it was undoubtedly the fact that its most important single asset was Mosley himself – wealthy, personally impressive and with exceptional oratorical skills. Scotland and Northern Ireland – unlike Wales which had no separate organisation and no separate BUF policy for the principality[137] – while adopting BUF philosophy and policies, were separate organisations and self-sustaining, though with some material, and rather more propagandist, support from the English BUF headquarters in London. Of the two, the UF was recognised as more separate still, having, unlike the Scottish Blackshirts, membership of the federation of fascist movements in the British Empire, the New Empire Union, and thus the issue of a charismatic indigenous leader apparently more relevant.

However, no such overarching figure of the Mosley type emerged in either Northern Ireland or Scotland; even in the Irish Free State where General O'Duffy sought to perform such a role his was a very flawed performance.[138] Having interviewed O'Duffy in this period, particularly with reference to his ambitions for Irish unity, the Belfast Protestant nationalist Denis Ireland concluded that, compared to de Valera, 'this man is a schoolboy'.[139] Given the enormity of the task facing the UF, the absence of such a figure

---

[135] Stott to editor, *Irish News*, 26 March 1935.

[136] Thurlow, *Fascism in Britain*, p. 125.

[137] Stephen Cullen, 'Another nationalism: the British Union of Fascists in Glamorgan 1932–40', *Welsh History Review*, vol. 17, no. 1 (June 1994), 114.

[138] For an exhaustive account of O'Duffy, see McGarry, *General Eoin O'Duffy*.

[139] Denis Ireland, *From the Irish Shore: Notes on My Life and Times* (London: Rich and Cowan, 1936), p. 104.

was of more consequence than it was in Scotland, which would have that deficiency compensated for, to an extent, by a visit from Mosley later in 1934, suggesting he thought the Scottish movement would, despite its autonomous existence, accept his leadership.

Certainly, it would appear that Stott was unsuited to perform the role of a charismatic leader, being just over 5 foot 8 inches in height, heavily built and with an uninspiring voice;[140] nor did he offer to perform such a role. Relatedly, given the emphasis in Blackshirt propaganda of it being a movement of youth and modernity, that Stott was 51 years old in 1934, with Armstrong, as Stott would claim, also 'in the second half of the allotted span',[141] youth was hardly evident in the leadership of the region's fascist leaders. The apparent inconsistency between a political creed emphasising youth and modernity and the region's middle-aged fascist leaders caused some comment in fascist ranks. And that it was accompanied by antagonism between Armstrong and Stott – the latter arguing that while youth was essential to the movement it needed to be guided by more mature minds, minds that had learned the lessons of the past, especially with reference to the failures and treacheries of the old parties and, of course, lessons that only his organisation, rather than Armstrong's, could be trusted to impart[142] – hardly enhanced the credibility of either. Nevertheless, what Stott lacked in leadership qualities, he compensated for in publicity promotion, taking every opportunity to exploit the print media to political advantage. But, as the 'Fascist drive in Ulster' episode demonstrated, the consequences could be negative.

Notwithstanding the closure of the debate on fascism in the *Irish News*, Stott remained a persistent contributor to its letter columns, at the same time as the nationalist bent of his politics continued, facilitated by perceived police harassment, about which

[140] Personal details in Stott's army record file supplied by Johanne Devlin Trew; information on Stott supplied to the author on 20 March 2003 by the late James Kelly. Veteran reporter for the *Irish Press* and *Irish News*, Kelly had attended UF meetings.
[141] Stott to editor, *Irish News*, 28 March 1935.
[142] For the issue, see 'In the ranks of fascism', *Irish News*, 23 March 1935; 'The call to youth', *Irish News*, 27 March 1935; 'A question of status', *Irish News*, 28 March 1935.

he complained, unsuccessfully, to Dawson Bates, the Minister of Home Affairs.[143] Lord Craigavon was condemned in late April 1935 for failing 'to assert the right of Ulster to take its lawful place in the affairs of the Irish nation', thereby depriving Ulstermen of 'their full share of control and the "plums" of office',[144] and in early May penned a critical assessment of the Social Credit programme.[145] This occurred at the same time as his involvement in an attempt to establish a Belfast branch of the Blueshirt-associated 'Thirty-Two Clubs'.[146]

Stott and the 'Thirty-Two Clubs'

This movement was devoted to Irish unity by establishing bonds of friendship through 'social, cultural, business, sporting and other … [contexts] to remove the prejudice and antagonisms that at present divide' Ireland's religio-ethnic communities. It would seek to reconstitute an independent Irish monarchy as the best way to guarantee Ireland's equal status with Britain in the British Commonwealth of Nations: club membership would be open to 'people of Irish Nationality or affiliations regardless of political or religious attachments', party politics would be rigidly avoided, the focus being on 'national and international politics in the highest sense'.[147]

It is understandable why Stott should be attracted to the Thirty-Two Clubs. The idea of serving an Irish national interest, north and south, outside the realm of party politics and within

---

[143] Stott to Dawson Bates, Minister of Home Affairs, 3 June 1935 (Home Affairs papers, PRONI: HA/32/1/509). Policemen had apparently torn down a poster advertising a fascist meeting at Finaghy, something they denied: Gilfillan to the Secretary, Ministry of Home Affairs, 15 June 1935 (Home Affairs papers, PRONI: HA/32/1/509).

[144] See 'The "plums" of office: northern fascists' grievance', *Irish Times*, 26 April 1935.

[145] Stott to the editor, *Irish News*, 2 May 1935.

[146] *Blueshirt*, 1 May 1935.

[147] C. G. Meecham, I.G., RUC, '"Thirty-Two Club" and "The Blue Shirt"', to the Secretary, Ministry of Home Affairs, 21 June 1935 (Home Affairs papers, PRONI: HA/32/1/615).

a monarchical and Commonwealth carapace was consistent with central elements of his own fascist beliefs, which he continued publicly to promote.[148] At a meeting of the Thirty-Two Clubs in Belfast on 10 April 1935, attended also by K. Newman, another former UF member and General Secretary of Stott's Centre of Ulster Fascist Studies,[149] Stott seconded the motion to establish a branch in the city. But while the *Blueshirt* reported that this was successfully done, in fact, the motion to do so failed, something which caused the Stormont regime to revise its intention to ban both the Thirty-Two Clubs movement and the *Blueshirt* newspaper.[150] In the context of the fascist project widely conceived, it was yet another failure; and for Stott personally these culminated with his response to the loyalist disorder that occurred in Belfast in the summer of 1935.

The violence was signalled on Mayday when disorderly loyalist crowds were allowed to dominate the city centre, an issue raised at Stormont by William Grant, Unionist Labour MP for Duncairn, who criticised the police for lack of control.[151] Failure to do so undoubtedly suggested that further activities of the kind could recur. When this duly transpired, it was on a much greater scale and more violent, running through July and August and with the Catholic community a focus of attack. Efforts to end the violence were made by leading Protestant churchmen, especially Revd Dr McNeice, Bishop of Down and Connor.[152] Nevertheless, it continued, with the sentiment behind it spreading to Edinburgh where threats were made against the Catholic community of the city.[153]

The loyalist disorder of Mayday was something that Stott, speaking for 'The Governing Body of the Ulster Centre of Fascist Studies', readily responded to, offering the services of its members to assist the forces of law and order in restraining violence. The offer was made in a letter to Dawson Bates, the Minister of Home Affairs

---

[148] See Stott at Larne (notice of public meeting) in *Larne Times*, 29 June 1935.
[149] *Irish News*, 28 March 1935.
[150] C. G. Meecham, I.G., RUC, '"Thirty-Two Club" and "The Blue Shirt"', to the Secretary, Ministry of Home Affairs, 21 June 1935.
[151] Stormont report, *Belfast Telegraph*, 14 May 1935.
[152] *Irish News*, 3, 8 July 1935.
[153] *Irish News*, 15, 17, 30 July 1935.

and was also sent as an open letter to the editors of the Belfast press; none, however, published it.[154] That the Unionist press did not is unsurprising, but neither did the *Irish News*. This may have been due to the fact that though Stott condemned police failings he also adopted his usual pose of condemning all Ulster political factions; and as such his letter failed to address the reality of the disturbances. Nor was his analysis of the summer violence – it was less a traditional conflict between Catholics and Protestants than due to fear in both communities about the 'encroachment' of 'the communist movement' in their communities[155] – any more convincing. But perhaps more important as a factor complicating the propagation of fascist ideas was a change in the editorship of the *Irish News*.

In mid-1935, Sydney Redwood was replaced by Robert Kirkwood, a journalist with experience on the *Catholic Herald* in London, and who combined championing Catholic causes with hostility both to communism and European fascism.[156] He was unlikely to be as tolerant of fascism in Northern Ireland as Redwood had been, especially as the assault on the Catholic community in Belfast in mid-1935 appeared to have a close similarity to the Nazi persecution of Catholics and Jews.[157] Kirkwood's concerns were reflected in the introduction of a serial column, 'Our Rome Letter', which had a particular focus on repression of the Catholic Church in Germany.[158] It was thus in a much less congenial print context than hitherto that Stott penned a ringing defence of the Nazi regime, especially a rejection of claims that German Catholics suffered oppression:

> there has been no attempt in Germany to suppress Catholics, nor to deprive them of either their religion or culture.

[154] Stott to Sir Dawson Bates, Minister of Home Affairs, 14 May 1935 (enclosing copy of open letter to press) (Home Affairs papers, PRONI: HA/32/1/509).

[155] Stott at Dublin Thirty-Two Club: 'Irish Unity in Sport', *Irish Press*, 8 August 1935.

[156] Phoenix, 'History of a newspaper', pp. 30–31.

[157] See 'Nazis and Orangemen', editorial, *Irish News*, 2 July 1935.

[158] See, for example, 'German tyranny against Catholic youth', subheading in 'Our Rome Letter', *Irish News*, 6 August 1935; also, 'German war on catholicity', *Irish News*, 29 July 1935; 'Another Nazi "drive": Catholics and Jews denounced', *Irish News*, 12 August 1935.

Dynastic egoism, political passion, patriotic blindness have no part in the Nazi regime ... The Catholic has only to free himself from the ideas, inhibitions and points of view which were forced upon him in the old-time politics – he must recognise the poison with which he has been inculcated by political opponents.[159]

As far as the *Irish News* was concerned, Stott's public presence in fascist politics now ended; nor in police files dealing with fascist activity in the region is there any further comment on Stott and the Ulster Centre of Fascist Studies. As for Armstrong's Belfast branch of the BUF, it failed to prosper and was dissolved in October 1935, an event ignored by Belfast newspapers, though it was registered by the *Irish Press*,[160] while the *Irish Independent* reported simultaneously that Stott was appointed to act as receiver in the winding up of the affairs of the UF organisation, the failure of which body he blamed on 'the anti-Fascist repressive sabotage of the official organiser [Armstrong] of the British Union of Fascists in Belfast'. Stott also declared the creation of a new organisation, 'the Ulster Blackshirts', one that 'would have no connection whatever with Sir Oswald Mosley's B.U.F.'[161] It was little more than a short-lived one-man band. Stott was to die suddenly in Nigeria while serving with the Royal Army Service Corp on 3 April 1943.[162]

The collapse of regional fascist formations, however, did not completely register the end of attempts to establish a fascist organisation in Northern Ireland. In 1937 W. E. D. Allen sought to fill the gap by persuading the dissentient Ulster Unionist MP for South Belfast at Westminster W. J. Stewart to organise 'an effective Fascist organisation in Ulster'.[163] Stewart, with a more realistic sense of

---

[159] Stott to the editor, 'Who is right?', *Irish News*, 31 October 1935.

[160] *Irish Press*, 2 October 1935.

[161] 'Ulster Black Shirts to replace the fascists', *Irish Independent*, 2 October 1935.

[162] See Job Stott, Army Roll of Honour 1939–45 database (Naval and Military Press Ltd, 2010) (https://search.findmypast.co.uk/search-world-records-in-military-armed-forces-and-conflict); Job Stott death notice, *Irish News*, 6 April 1943.

[163] See Major V. Vivian to E. Gilfillan, Office of Inspector General, RUC,

what might be possible politically, did break ranks with the UUP in 1938, but not to form a fascist organisation, rather to establish the short-lived Progressive Unionist Party which attempted to circumvent the partition issue by focusing on non-sectarian socio-economic issues.[164]

With the failure of Allen's attempt to establish another fascist organisation, the only specifically fascist presence in Northern Ireland was a mere 'point of contact' for Arnold Leese's fanatically antisemitic Imperial Fascist League (IFL). It was a tiny organisation, probably numbering at most a few hundred members during its lifetime (1929–39) and with, apparently, only eight actual branches in Britain together with a small number of 'centres for enquiry'.[165] Located in a single household in Belfast,[166] it could not even be argued that the region's 'centre for enquiry' registered a new recruit for fascism in general, for the householder was Marcus J. C. Walker, former Chief Executive Officer of the now defunct UF. In sum, the IFL had effectively no public presence in Northern Ireland and attracted no attention from the police. With reference to the Ulster problem as an issue, the organisation is noteworthy chiefly for its claim that the problem was greatly exacerbated by Jews in the City of London who controlled Ulster: 'The real enemy of Ulstermen is the enemy of the white world – the international Jew Money Power'.[167] Otherwise, the only organisational connection with fascism in Northern Ireland in the years from 1937 to 1940 was through a branch of The Link, the pro-Nazi Anglo-German friendship society founded by Admiral Sir Barry Domvile.

Anglo-Irish in identity and with a family background in Santry, outside Dublin, Domvile had somewhat conflicted political allegiances, committed to strong British defence measures but also sympathetic to Irish unity. Thus for Domvile the Ulster branch of

---

26 July 1937 (NAK, Security Service, Personal Files: W. E. D. Allen, KV/2/879).

[164] J. F. Harbinson, *The Ulster Unionist Party, 1882–1973: Its Development and Organisation* (Belfast: Blackstaff Press, 1973), pp. 219–22.

[165] Linehan, *British Fascism, 1918–1939*, p. 73.

[166] *The Fascist*, August 1938, September 1939.

[167] 'The real rulers of Ulster', *The Fascist*, November 1935.

his organisation, which had 117 members, was significant chiefly for the purpose of demonstrating the geographic spread and appeal of The Link throughout the UK, but otherwise he had no great affinity with its membership, nor did he bother to visit the branch. His pro-Nazi activities would result in his internment during the Second World War under Regulation 18b.[168]

Conclusion

Nineteen thirty-five was a landmark year for British fascism in general. It not only saw the demise of organised fascism in Northern Ireland, but was, as we have noted, the year in which Rotha Lintorn-Orman's BF movement was finally wound up; and, despite its greater strength, the year in which Blackshirt fascism in Scotland went into decline. It also witnessed the continuation of the BUF's organisational flatlining that followed the ending of the Rothermere–Mosley compact, though it would revive at the end of the decade, and, closer to home, the year in which the 'Corn-Coal' Pact negotiated between the British and Free State Governments in January took some of the energy out of the agrarian agitation on which Blueshirt activism thrived.[169] Much further afield, the Australian New Guard, the movement in which Stott had acquired his first experience of fascism, also effectively collapsed in 1935.

While the stability of existing parliamentary institutions in each of the above cases largely accounts for the weakness or failure of their fascist organisations, some singular aspects of the UF experience might be noted. The stability of the Stormont regime was based not on general, community-wide endorsement, but rather on the construction of Northern Ireland itself, designed to provide a permanent majority for one ethnic community over the other, with the prospects for cross-community political action under the UF rubric deterred by powerful community myths, a reality concealed from the UF by its palingenetic optimism about fascist success. The

[168] See James Loughlin, 'Hailing Hitler with the Red Hand: The Link in Northern Ireland, 1937–40', *Patterns of Prejudice*, vol. 50, no. 3 (July 2016), 276–301.
[169] Manning, *The Blueshirts*, p. 182.

pro-nationalist bent of UF propaganda was certainly attuned to the community apparently most likely to be susceptible to its appeal – regime hostility had driven the Catholic community into a form of internal exile centred around the Catholic Church and its institutions.[170] But this had merely reinforced a concern to see the abolition of the statelet, rather than reform of its administration so as to make its existence defensible. Ironically, the experience of the Catholic community in Northern Ireland paralleled that of those Italian Catholics in the 1930s who likewise expressed their alienation from Mussolini's fascist regime by 'retreating into the substantial network of Catholic social and cultural institutions'.[171] The alienation of faith and State, however, was much less complete in Italy than it was in Northern Ireland.

[170] For a general discussion, see David Kennedy, 'Catholics in Northern Ireland, 1926–39', in Francis MacManus (ed.), *The Years of the Great Test, 1926–39* (Cork: Mercier, 1967), pp. 138–49.
[171] See Martin Conway, *Catholic Politics in Europe, 1918–1945* (London: Routledge, 1997), p. 65.

II

Mid-Century Mosleyism
and Northern Ireland

4

Union Movement

Exploiting Partition, 1946–1966

The crushing of European fascist regimes during the Second World War and the exposure of the atrocities perpetrated by the Nazi regime made Mosley's ambition to revive his political career in the post-war years with his organisation, Union Movement (UM), established in 1948, extremely difficult. The factors that constrained Mosley's political progress in the 1930s have been noted, but fascism then was not regarded as a pariah faith in the way it would be following Second World War, one that carried a distinct stigma for those promoting it. Quite how the political environment had changed has been recorded by Trevor Grundy, a child of UM parents in the 1950s, whose mother warned him: 'You're not to tell people what we talk about in this house. It's all secret. People outside the Mosley movement would never ever understand. Just think that you and Lovene [his sister] live in two worlds, this one and the world outside 40 Blandford Square.'[1] Nor was it likely that this situation would change for Mosley personally, not least because throughout this period and after he felt compelled to defend all aspects of his past political activities and beliefs in speeches and print.[2] Accordingly, he made his own contribution to undoing his major project of this period, 'Europe-a-Nation'. Nevertheless, given his self-belief as a man of destiny whose hour would surely come, the political struggle continued.

[1] Trevor Grundy, *Memoir of a Fascist Childhood: A Boy in Mosley's Britain* (London: Heinemann, 1998), p. 26.
[2] See Oswald Mosley, *My Answer* (2nd edn, Ramsbury: Mosley Publications, 1946); *Mosley: The Facts* (London: Euphorion Distribution (England), 1957); *Mosley – Right or Wrong?* (London: Lion Books, 1961).

In this context, an issue such as anti-partitionism, which had retained its 'integrity' in political discourse on Anglo-Irish relations since the inter-war period, attracted his direct personal engagement. Unlike the 1930s when his references to the subject had been pitched at a general level, with direct attacks on the Stormont regime the preserve of his lieutenants, Mosley would now unambiguously put his personal imprimatur on his movement's anti-partitionist campaign. This chapter will focus on how partition and the immigrant Irish/Catholic community in Britain were addressed as Mosley attempted to advance his political objectives.

Cultivating the Post-War Catholic Interest

Wartime experience had enhanced that community's attraction. Portugal, a State the BUF had considered as a model for its own idea of a fascist entity before the war, had remained neutral during it, as had Europe's other two prominent Catholic countries, Spain and Eire. The latter's Taoiseach (Prime Minister) in 1945, Eamon de Valera, a leader respected by the BUF before the war, caused outrage in Britain – but not among fascists – by calling on the German Minister in Dublin, Dr Hempel, to offer his condolences on the death of Germany's Chancellor, Adolf Hitler and accepted Dr Hempel's request for political asylum.[3] Moreover, as we noted, the IRA campaign of 1939 met with no explicit condemnation from the Blackshirt movement, and during the war itself a sense of common interest was consolidated in some instances.

Adopting the traditional view that England's difficulty was Ireland's opportunity, the IRA aligned itself with the Nazi war effort, which, so far as Ireland was concerned, took shape in their 'Plan Kathleen'. This proposed a German landing in Northern Ireland in the vicinity of Derry city assisted by the IRA in county Leitrim; and although the Germans did not place much faith in the plan, they did note the possible significance

---

[3] T. D. Williams, 'Ireland and the War', in K. B. Nowlan and T. D. Williams (eds), *Ireland in the War Years and after 1939–51* (Dublin: Gill & Macmillan, 1969), p. 14.

of Irish willingness to coerce Northern Ireland.[4] For the most hardcore of Mosley's supporters, interned on the Isle of Man, an affinity with the IRA had a direct and personal dimension: they assisted an IRA/Blackshirt escape attempt from Peveril Camp and engaged in widespread disorder to deter the camp authorities from punitive punishment when the escapees were captured,[5] while a combination of Catholicism, neo-fascism and pro-IRA sentiment can be identified in the immediate post-war years. This was reflected in conversions to Catholicism, consideration of IRA methods and organisation as possible models for fascist bodies in Britain, and plans for an escape route from Britain to Eire for German prisoners of war.[6] John Wynn, convinced that 'the Catholic Religion is the foundation of a National Socialist civilisation', referenced an article in the Irish religio-historical journal *The Capuchin Annual* (1943) by 'Ultach' on 'Orange Terror' in Northern Ireland to show 'how the British Government treats those who desire to live on such a basis', and also 'why De Valera kept the British at arm's length during the war and the reason he refused them the use of the Irish Ports'.[7]

Leading extreme-Right personalities of the 1930s were also attracted to Ireland at this time. Admiral Sir Barry Domvile's post-war diaries, for instance, evidence close friendships being established with John Charles McQuaid, Catholic Archbishop of Dublin (whose sister Helen was a voluntary, unpaid personal physician to Domvile's ailing wife),[8] with Revd Denis Fahey,

---

[4] John P. Duggan, *Neutral Ireland and the Third Reich* (Dublin: Lilliput Press, 1989), p. 99.

[5] John Charnley, *Blackshirts and Roses: An Autobiography* (1990; 2nd edn, London: Black House Publishing, 2012), pp. 130–35.

[6] NAK, Security Service, Personal Files: reports on Arthur Baker, Bob Dye, 21 March 1945 (KV2/2315); John Wynn, 25 July 1945 (KV2/1362) (Wynn did not make the references to the IRA); Northern Command Monthly Intelligence Security Summary No. 78/48, 31 January 1948; Report on Wynn, 19 February 1948.

[7] Copy of letter from John Wynn to R. Rudman, P.O. Edendale, South Africa, 2 April 1945 (NAK, Security Service, Personal Files: KV2).

[8] Domvile to Healy, 6 January 1967 (Cahir Healy papers, PRONI: D2991/B/70/14).

author of the antisemitic *The Rulers of Russia* and, though no far-Right extremist, with the northern Irish nationalist MP Cahir Healy, with whom Mosley had been interned under Regulation 18b.[9] Again, William Joyce, on trial for treason in London in 1945 and unrealistically expecting an acquittal, told his wife Margaret that Ireland would be the only place for them to live.[10] Even for extreme-Right activists who had no Irish connections and took no sustained interest in partition or Irish issues generally, Eire in the post-war years could be 'dear old Ireland'.[11]

The relationship between fascism, Catholicism and anti-partitionism, however, found singular expression in Jeffrey Hamm, a Welsh Catholic convert who on the death of Alexander Raven Thomson in 1956 would become Mosley's secretary. If MI5 reports on Hamm are accurate, he expected Mosley 'eventually [to] lead a Catholic crusade in which all Jews and Communists would perish'.[12] The report may have exaggerated; nevertheless, Hamm was accurate enough in telling the *Catholic Herald* that 'many of the speakers and principal officers of the League [of Ex-Servicemen] – a feeder organisation for the inauguration of Mosley's Union Movement in 1948 – were Catholics, including himself'.[13]

Mosley's defence of his fascist activities in the 1930s was first expressed in *My Answer* (1946), which also referenced English Catholic loyalty during the Elizabethan wars with Catholic Spain[14] – a pointer to his movement's closer identification with British Catholics. While his political re-emergence in the post-war period had been met with general public hostility it attracted considerably

[9] See Domvile diaries (National Maritime Museum, Greenwich: DOM54–DOM62); Diary entries 7 January 1950 (DOM61); 15, 19 August 1951 (DOM62).
[10] Colin Holmes, *Searching for Lord Haw-Haw: The Political Lives of William Joyce* (London and New York: Routledge, 2016), p. 373.
[11] Ronald Creasy to Alexander Raven Thomson, 9 December 1954 (NAK, Security Service, Personal Files: Ronald and Rita Creasy, KV2/4023).
[12] G. R. Mitchell, 'Fascist activities in the United Kingdom, April–May 1946' (NAK, Home Office papers: HO45/25395).
[13] Gerry Sherry, 'Anti-Semitism and rowdyism in London's East End: is it a fascist danger or a communist ramp?', *Catholic Herald*, 3 October 1947.
[14] Mosley, *My Answer*, p. 11.

more interest from that constituency; and the UM press took care during this period to cultivate Catholic support.[15] In the run-up to the emergence of the UM in February 1948 Mosley had a meeting arranged with Cardinal Griffin, Cardinal Archbishop of Westminster, for the purpose of treating 'with the Vatican'.[16] But though it went off successfully – 'MOSLEY kissed his ring and appears to have behaved quite well!' – it was without practical results.[17] In fact, despite the synergy between some significant elements of Mosley's political ideas and Catholic Social Action, the strong Catholic element among Mosley's supporters and the favourable opinion held by Mosley of European Catholic authoritarian regimes, engaging substantively with the Catholic community in Britain was fraught with difficulties.

It was a community, especially at this time, conscious of having a subordinate place in a historically Protestant State, unsettled by its perceptibly close relationship with pre-war fascism and, relatedly, a position on politics which did not cohere entirely with a mainstream popular opinion informed by triumphant anti-fascism. As one Catholic commentator put it: Catholicism, regarded with 'tardy tolerance' at the best of times, saw her adherents 'become the object of suspicion and slander' as soon as the Church brought her ideas into the realm of practical politics: 'To put it simply they are called Fascists.'[18] In this context, it sought to establish equidistance between various political traditions, though trenchant in its critique of communism.[19] It was not altogether easy to do.

---

[15] 'Communist tactics: Attack on the Catholic church', *Union*, 29 May 1948; 'Catholic trade unions for a united Europe', *Union*, 13 June 1953; 'The cardinal [Griffin] condemns octopus union', *Union*, 30 October 1954; 'Catholics condemn Red visit', *Union*, 21 April 1956; 'Catholics support occupational parliament', *Union*, 28 July 1956; 'Catholics and Union Movement', *Union*, 29 June 1957.

[16] MI5, Fascist Activities, November–December 1947 (NAK, Home Office papers: HO45/25395).

[17] MI5 Intelligence Report, 9 December 1947 (NAK, Security Service Files, KV2/892).

[18] 'Fascism and democracy: is there a Catholic middle way?', *Catholic Herald*, 12 December 1947.

[19] See 'Questions of the week', *Catholic Herald*, 21 June 1946.

For instance, the *Catholic Herald* – the most widely read and representative Catholic print in London,[20] one with a close focus on the problems of the Catholic community in Northern Ireland since the inter-war period[21] and a representative site for debate concerning British Catholics – was also an organ of contact for elements of the extreme-Right. The security services noted in early 1946 that the paper's correspondence columns were being used by extreme pro-German national socialists to seek supporters for a scheme 'for the care of German, Italian and Austrian Prisoners', with the first meeting arranged for 16 March 1946 in the London home of the pacifist and socialist Lady Clare Annesley,[22] daughter of Lieutenant Colonel Hugh Annesley, 5th Earl Annesley of Castlewellan, county Down. Concern about how far the relationship between Catholicism and neo-fascism was developing prompted the *Catholic Herald* to investigate the matter during riots associated with meetings of Jeffrey Hamm's British League of Ex-Servicemen on the Dalston Road in London's East End in late 1947.

The enquiry noted both Jewish/communist and neo-fascist excesses of rhetoric and behaviour, especially antisemitic utterances by some British League members, though 'even anti-Jewish statements cannot be the full justification for saying that the League is Fascist in the sense we have always known it'. Nevertheless, 'Mr Hamm's claim that many Catholics are amongst his followers is true, and I have spoken with some of them. I found quite a few Irish', with the conclusion that the Church was in danger of being accused of sponsoring fascism.[23] A subsequent commentary on Mosley played down Catholic support and focused on his dictatorial tendencies: 'here was a new dictator, one who would be as bitter as Hitler'.[24]

---

[20] Gerald Hamilton to Mosley, 5 December 1947, intercepted letter (NAK, Security Service, Personal Files: Sir Oswald Mosley, KV2/893).

[21] See, for example, 'Catholics refused work', *Catholic Herald*, 10 July 1936; 'The country the King has visited', *Catholic Herald*, 30 July 1937; 'Ulster may have prison ships', *Catholic Herald*, 27 January 1939.

[22] Note of letter from Mary Foss to John Wynn (11 March 1946), explaining duties of the Axis prisoner organisation (NAK, Security Service, Personal Files: John Wynn, KV2/1362).

[23] Gerry Sherry, 'Anti-Semitism and rowdyism in London's east end'.

[24] 'Mosley acts and looks like a dictator', *Catholic Herald*, 13 February 1948.

Nevertheless debate for and against Mosley continued.[25] In the end, the editor had to appeal to contributors to cease writing letters on the subject of Sir Oswald Mosley;[26] but sympathetic accounts of European neo-fascism still appeared, on issues such as the Vatican's relationship with Mussolini, while locating the source of Britain and Europe's weak economic state on a willingness to satisfy the thirst for revenge of communism and 'the [Jewish?] money power of New York … on Hitler'.[27]

Despite its political sensitivities in the post-war years, there was clearly a strain of sentiment in the Irish immigrant and wider British Catholic community for the UM to mine, though there were also constraints within the UM on how far that constituency could be embraced. The perceptibly close association between the two gave rise to an erroneous rumour that Mosley was considering converting to Catholicism, apparently moving Jeffrey Hamm to hope that Mosley 'would stand forth as a leader of the true faith and that England would be purged with fire and sword'.[28] The rumour served to activate a no-popery strand among some UM members, and though it failed to emerge as politically important, evidence suggests it was significant enough to cause some concern,[29] and not just among the religiously bigoted. MI5 thought the movement's philosopher and Mosley's then secretary, Alexander Raven Thomson, 'would oppose [it] most strongly owing to his

[25] 'Mosley again?', *Catholic Herald*, 5 March 1948; N. B. Nye, 'A convert from fascism warns of its dangers', *Catholic Herald*, 7 May 1948; 'Communism and Mosley', *Catholic Herald*, 4 June 1948; also letters to editor *Catholic Herald*, 18 June 1948: 'Sir Oswald Mosley', *Catholic Herald*, 9 July 1948; 'Mosley and anti-Semitism', *Catholic Herald*, 30 July 1948.

[26] 'Was the last war necessary?', *Catholic Herald*, 3 September 1948.

[27] 'Fascism and democracy: is there a Catholic middle way?', *Catholic Herald*, 12 December 1947.

[28] Commentary on Mosley and Jeffrey Hamm, 2 November 1945 (NAK, Security Service, Personal Files: Sir Oswald Mosley, KV2/890).

[29] Report on Mosley, 18 November 1945 (NAK, Security Service, Personal Files: Sir Oswald Mosley, KV2/890); MI5 Intelligence Report, 9 December 1947 (NAK, Security Service Files, KV2/892); Comment of the leading UM member, Sid Proud, quoted in Grundy, *Memoir of a Fascist Childhood*, p. 157. Proud also considered Jeffrey Hamm a 'Pope's nark' (p. 166).

agnostic views'.[30] Mosley himself when asked by an Irish reporter at a press conference heralding the inauguration of the UM whether he had read Pope Leo XIII's encyclical on the just societal relationship between capital and labour, *Rerum Novarum* (1891) gave an ambiguous reply: 'I don't think so, but then again, I read a lot in prison.'[31]

Mosley: The Difficulties of a New Political Beginning

If any single statement registered the extent to which Mosley was 'beyond the pale'[32] of the British political mainstream in the post-war years it was surely his dismissive reference to whatever wrong 'the Jews are alleged to have suffered'[33] in *My Answer*; this at a time when the Tory Party, tainted with pro-fascism in the inter-war period, was vigorously attempting to dissociate itself from rightist groups with antisemitic or neo-fascist sentiments.[34] And yet it is questionable how far Mosley, who claimed to favour a Jewish homeland[35] and would criticise the Stalinist antisemitic purge of the early 1950s,[36] could politically afford to dissociate himself from antisemitism: its emotional impact constituted the organisation's 'only appeal to the great majority of its membership'[37] at a time when Mosley's new European focus was failing to energise some followers whose 'exaggerated Nationalism has been the core of their political faith for so long'.[38] Also, aggressive Jewish opposition to his public meetings was only too likely to

---

[30] MI5 Intelligence Report, 9 December 1947 (NAK, Security Service Files, KV2/892).

[31] 'Has Sir Oswald Mosley read "Rerum Novarum"', *Catholic Herald*, 5 December 1947.

[32] Robert Skidelsky, *Oswald Mosley* (London: Macmillan, 1981), p. 465; Graham Macklin, *Very Deeply Dyed in Black: Sir Oswald Mosley and the Resurrection of British Fascism after 1945* (London: I.B. Tauris, 2007), p. 1.

[33] Macklin, *Very Deeply Dyed in Black*, pp. 109–10.

[34] See Mark Pitchford, *The Conservative Party and the Extreme Right, 1945–75* (Manchester: Manchester University Press, 2011), *passim*.

[35] 'Britain and Israel', *Union*, 29 May 1948.

[36] See *Union*, 31 January 1953.

[37] Macklin, *Very Deeply Dyed in Black*, p. 54.

[38] MI5 Intelligence Report, January–February 1947 (NAK, Security Service Files, KV2/892); Macklin, *Very Deeply Died in Black*, pp. 54–55.

provoke visceral utterances: 'So far from declaring war against Israel, we licked the dust beneath the feet of Jewry.'[39]

Mosley's European policy was detailed in the work he regarded as his magnum opus, *The Alternative* (1947),[40] and promoted in speeches and print. It envisioned the coming together of Europe's nations in a common allegiance to ensure the continent's existence as a powerful bloc to counter those of the Soviet Union and the USA; a cooperative relationship of Europe with white-controlled Africa to deal with the former's economic problems and ostensibly existing in harmony with black Africa; a corporate system of Government in Britain to replace parliamentary democracy, and with the plan underpinned by an idealistic engagement of the spirit of the people 'for the idea of a new civilisation' and 'a new sense of service and a new morality in the State'.[41] The last was a product of Mosley's wartime reading, an intellectual diet of Greek philosophy, Goethe's *Faust*, modern psychology and Oswald Spengler, which informed his belief that only he, the embodiment of the 'Thought-Deed' man, could save Europe from chaos. For Mosley, the 'will to achievement' was the 'purpose of God', and only through constant thriving could it be effected.[42] And the time for it was now: 'Never in my life have I had such an overpowering conviction that my time is coming as I have to-day.'[43] Or again: 'The future is the Thought-Deed man; because without him the future will not be. He is the hope of the peoples and of the world.'[44] To establish the credibility of his theory Mosley looked to British history for precedents of such figures, finding one, among others, in the person of William Gladstone, 'who, in his efforts to solve the Irish problem and thus to forestall the Home Rule crisis, which might have cost the life of Britain in 1914, incurred such a savage hatred among the "respectable" classes of Great Britain'; and quite unlike his great adversary, 'the Jew Disraeli', the only man who

---

[39] 'Tear gas at Mosley meeting', *Irish Times*, 1 February 1949.

[40] Oswald Mosley, *The Alternative* (Ramsbury: Mosley Publications, 1947).

[41] 'Mosley to launch new movement', *Irish Times*, 29 November 1947.

[42] Richard Thurlow, 'The guardian of the "sacred flame": the failed political resurrection of Oswald Mosley', *Journal of Contemporary History*, vol. 33, no. 2 (1998), 247–49.

[43] NAK, MI5 Intelligence Reports, 3 October 1947, KV2/892.

[44] Mosley, *The Alternative*, p. 289.

'commanded the consistent favour of the negative mind in life and death'.[45]

Radical as was Mosley's conception of a new British civilisation, the prospects of its realisation were remote. Not only was the great national crisis that would create the conditions for it unlikely to arrive in a period of gradually increasing prosperity, but even if it did Mosley's pariah status made it highly unlikely the nation would call on his services, while the UM itself was an unlikely vehicle of national transformation. Several branches would become lethargic, with the movement suffering from maladministration, intrigues among Mosley's lieutenants (especially its organising secretary Alf Flockhart and Jeffrey Hamm),[46] the aggressive and effective opposition of the Jewish 43 group[47] and, perhaps, the appearance of Mosley himself. According to Morris Beckman, it was that of 'a middle-aged weary civilian, puffy of cheek and eye with a drooping shoulder. He would have been unremarkable in a crowd ... the charismatic orations that once inflamed his followers into ecstasies of loyalty had gone.'[48] Beckman, of course, was only too willing to describe Mosley in an unflattering light. *Picture Post* photo-essays of the same period, however, reveal a much more dynamic Mosley reminiscent of his pre-war persona, while his more corpulent frame 'in a way strengthened the aura of aggressive power'.[49]

Nevertheless, the fact remained that the respectable political arena was closed to him and his attempts to create a public space in which to promote Europe-a-Nation effectively – through book clubs; libel and slander actions against people who had called him a traitor in recent years;[50] and the manipulation of letters to the press facilitating the dissemination of his ideas – were without

[45] Ibid., pp. 38–39.
[46] Macklin, *Very Deeply Dyed in Black*, p. 50.
[47] On its activities, see Morris Beckman, *The 43 Group: Battling with Mosley's Blackshirts* (2nd edn, Stroud: History Press, 2013).
[48] Ibid., p. 135.
[49] 'Why should anyone still follow Mosley?', *Picture Post*, 1 May 1948; 'Will Mosley march again?', *Picture Post*, 2 January 1954.
[50] Security Service report on Mosley, 14 April 1945 (NAK, Security Service, Personal Files: Sir Oswald Mosley, KV2/890).

significant effect.[51] Nor was his proposal to advance his cause through publications initially well received: 'a number of people fear political persecution and victimisation'.[52] The northern Irish nationalist, Cahir Healy, later MP for Fermanagh and South Tyrone at Westminster, a close associate of Mosley in this period, advised that it might be wiser to start with works by authors of a politically neutral disposition.[53] Even the arrangement of debates with minor political organisations, such as the Young Liberals[54] and university student groups were often self-defeating when the 'race hatred' inherent in the UM was exposed.[55] Nor did the stimulus to antisemitism that followed the 1947 Jewish attacks on British military personnel in Palestine[56] prove productive of long-term UM support, despite sustained activity by Jeffrey Hamm's League of Ex-Servicemen and Women.[57] Britain gave up the Palestine Mandate in 1948, though this was after the process of forming Mosley's new movement took place.

In early February 1948, a number of groups, including the League of Ex-Servicemen and Women, the Union of British Freedom, the 18b Detainees' Aid Fund and 47 Mosleyite book clubs came together formally as the UM. But there was clearly a difficult struggle ahead; and in this context the Irish immigrant and wider Catholic community in Britain became an important factor.

---

[51] Report on Mosley and his lieutenants, 11 February 1946; copy of intercepted letter from M. E. Roberts to A. K. Chesterton, 1 March 1945 (NAK, Security Service, Personal Files: Sir Oswald Mosley, KV2/890).

[52] Security Service report on Mosley's activities, 4 April 1946 (NAK, Security Service Reports, KV2/890).

[53] Description of letter from Cahir Healy, Enniskillen, to Mosley, 18 March 1946 (NAK, Security Service, Personal Files: Sir Oswald Mosley, KV2/890).

[54] See *Union*, 6 September, 29 November, 6 December 1952.

[55] See 'A great gulf fixed', *Union*, 1 January 1953.

[56] Daniel Trilling, 'Britain's last anti-Jewish riots', *New Statesman*, 23 May 2012 (https://www.newstatesman.com/2012/05/britains-last-anti-jewish-riots). Accessed 28 April 2014. Trilling acknowledges Tony Kushner's work as a source for the article.

[57] Nicholas Hillman, '"Tell me chum, in case I got it wrong. What was it we were fighting for during the war?" The re-emergence of British fascism, 1945–58', *Contemporary British History*, vol. 15, no. 4 (2001), 3; Beckman, *The 43 Group*, pp. 71–72.

Moreover, the UM was formed just as an anti-partition campaign in Northern Ireland supported by the Irish Government and leading southern politicians was getting under way[58] – a campaign that facilitated a deepening relationship with Cahir Healy MP, the UM's most significant connection with the world of respectable politics.

The UM and Partition in a European Context

In focusing on the Ulster issue Mosley had a free hand. None of Britain's other emergent extreme-Right groups paid attention to it. When they did, in the context of the civil conflict that erupted from 1969, it was overwhelmingly in support of Ulster loyalism. There was no need for concern in this period, however, as Northern Ireland's contribution to the British war effort ensured constitutional security, reinforced by the Ireland Act of 1949, enacted following Eire's abrupt departure from the Commonwealth in 1949 to become a republic. It declared that in no event would any part of Northern Ireland cease to have membership of the United Kingdom without the consent of the Parliament of Northern Ireland,[59] though Unionist concern about constitutional security remained.[60] Only very briefly, in 1947, did the Duke of Bedford's British People's Party (BPP) consider establishing an affiliated movement in Belfast to cover Northern Ireland – the Agricultural and Industrial Party, to be organised by one John Gregg, a known fascist sympathiser. Nothing, however, came of it.[61]

Unlike the obscure Gregg, the UM had the engaged support in its promotion of Irish unity of one of the most prominent anti-partitionists in Cahir Healy. He had been interned under Regulation 18b when an MP of the regional Northern Ireland

[58] Somewhat ironically, one publication, focusing on anti-Catholic discrimination in Derry, had the title, *Ireland's Fascist City*: Frank Curran, *Ireland's Fascist City* (Londonderry: Derry Journal, 1946).
[59] Paul Arthur, *Government and Politics of Northern Ireland* (London: Longman, 1984), p. 19.
[60] See, for instance, Sir Basil Brooke to Sir Ronald Ross, 20 November 1945; R. Gransden to A. J. Kelly, 14 April 1947 (Cabinet papers, PRONI: CAB/9/J/2).
[61] MI5, 'Fascist Activities in the United Kingdom, May–June 1947', 23 June 1947 (NAK, Home Office papers: HO45/253951).

Parliament for injudicious comments on the possibilities of a German victory, something Axis propaganda outlets made much of.[62] One of few non-BUF prisoners invited to Mosley's Christmas dinner in December 1941,[63] Healy was an unusual member of the group of leading internees who would remain in close personal contact after the war and for whom their prison experience had a bonding effect. The others, which included Captain Archibald Maule Ramsay MP, Admiral Sir Barry Domvile, together with Mosley, had well-evidenced antisemitic and pro-Nazi/fascist outlooks. In Healy's case there is little evidence of these opinions, but as a founding member of Sinn Fein in 1905, having lived through the War of Independence and suffering internment without trial by the Ulster Unionist regime,[64] he readily acknowledged Mosley's contribution to the removal of the Black and Tans from Ireland, and given the close personal engagement internment facilitated was clearly influenced by Mosley's arguments for his political actions in the 1930s, as his defence of him in the late 1960s evidenced.[65] And yet, as we have noted, Mosley's motives in opposing Black and Tan terror were not primarily in aid of Irish independence, rather Britain's national honour. He had made the point in the pre-war period and restated it in *The Alternative*.[66] Healy's framing of his activities within an Irish nationalist narrative, however, made it easy for that to be obscured, and by the same token for Mosley's antisemitism to be overlooked or excused, something that extended also to Admiral Sir Barry Domvile, whose antisemitic memoir, *From Admiral to Cabin Boy*, Healy secured a review of in the *Fermanagh Herald*:[67]

[62] See Christopher Norton, 'The internment of Cahir Healy M.P., Brixton Prison, July 1941–December 1942', *20th Century British History*, vol. 18, no. 2 (2007), 186 n. 70.

[63] Ibid.

[64] For a concise assessment of Healy's political career, see Eamon Phoenix, 'Cahir Healy (1877–1970), Northern Nationalist Leader', in A. F. Parkinson and Eamon Phoenix (eds), *Conflicts in the North of Ireland, 1900–2000* (Dublin: Four Courts Press, 2010), pp. 134–52.

[65] Cahir Healy to the editor, *Irish Times*, 6 November 1968.

[66] Mosley, *The Alternative*, pp. 224–25.

[67] Diary entry, 4 October 1947 (Domvile diaries, National Maritime Museum, Greenwich: DOM60).

there is much in it with which we can agree. The Judaeo-Masonic power, which has wielded its evil influence right through the history of international relations ... is exposed and criticised, and now that the fury of wartime hate has subsided, perhaps we Irish, who can view the question objectively, may see once more through the smokescreen of the newspaper headlines and find the real culprits, not in Hitler or Mussolini or any of the men who strutted the world stage, but in the powerful figures who hurried to and fro in the wings.[68]

In this context, it might be noted that, despite Domvile's book having committed anti-partitionist content, his overt antisemitism may have led Mosley to consider him 'a grave political liability'[69] at a time when he was attempting to rebuild his political career. When the second Lord Craigavon (son of the late Prime Minister of Northern Ireland)[70] invited him to join the right-wing New Crusade, Domvile declined, considering it 'too gentlemanly' to be effective.[71]

Anti-partitionism in this period seemed a fruitful subject for the UM to exploit, coming at a problematic time in Anglo-Irish relations. The continued detention of 24 convicted republicans for their participation in the pre-war IRA bombing campaign in England seemed likely to damage relations with Eire without any compensating effect. Agitation for the prisoners' release emerged in 1947. The prisoners' only crime it was claimed, was to call world attention to 'ORANGE POGROMS against the CATHOLICS in Belfast, and the mutilation of the Irish nation by PARTITION',[72]

[68] J.O.P., 'Fellow-prisoner tells his story of Cahir Healy', *Fermanagh Herald*, 4 October 1947.
[69] Security Service, Note on Mosley, 24 January 1948 (NAK, Security Service, Report on Fascist Activities, KV2/838).
[70] 'Craigavon', *Burke's Peerage, Baronetage and Knightage* (London: Burke's Peerage Ltd, 1959), p. 56.
[71] Diary entry, 1 March 1950 (Domvile diaries, National Maritime Museum, Greenwich: DOM61).
[72] See leaflet reproductions (NAK, MI5 Intelligence Reports, October 1947, KV2/892).

while the campaign was endorsed by the Countess of Antrim, Sir Shane Leslie, Lord Killanin and the playwright Sean O'Casey.[73] Eoin O'Mahony, the State Prosecutor for Cork City and County, the leader of the campaign, also wrote to Mosley for his support.[74] The campaign took on added momentum when a coalition Government of Fianna Gael and a radical social republican party, Clann na Problachta (Children of the Republic), took office under John A. Costello in Eire in 1948, and asked officially for their release.[75] At the same time, an anti-partition campaign under way in Northern Ireland would soon direct its attention to Britain and the USA, boosted in 1948 when Eamon de Valera, following his election defeat, embarked on a tour of the USA, Australia and Great Britain, focusing relentlessly on the issue.[76] But, more importantly, with specific reference to Mosley's European project, Sean McBride, Minister of External Affairs in the southern Government, declared in July 1948 that 'the continuance of partition precludes us from taking our rightful place in the affairs of Europe'.[77]

The Irish Government's policy on partition, however, owed nothing to Mosley's Europe-a-Nation project, concerned as it was to establish international goodwill after a war in which it had played little part; and it would advise printing companies not to take business from the UM.[78] Nor for that matter, and despite a much publicised communication in 1945 from J. D. O'Connell, the 'County Solicitor for Kerry', inviting him to reside in the country as

[73] See copy of letter from Beverley Baxter, Conservative MP for Wood Green to Eoin O'Mahony, 6 October 1947 (NAK, MI5 Intelligence Reports, October 1947, KV2/892).
[74] Copy of O'Mahony to Mosley 18 October 1947 (NAK, MI5 Intelligence Reports, October 1947, KV2/892).
[75] See 'London call for release of prisoners', *Irish Times*, 19 April 1948.
[76] Cornelius O'Leary, 'Northern Ireland, 1945–72', in J. J. Lee (ed.), *Ireland, 1945–70* (Dublin: Gill & Macmillan, 1979), pp. 155–56.
[77] Nicholas Mansergh, 'Irish foreign policy, 1945–51', in Nowlan and Williams, *Ireland in the War Years and after 1939–51*, pp. 136–37.
[78] Internal External Affairs file memo sent to a Mr O'Riordan, 21 April 1953, referring to a file (External Affairs 305/89), detailing the publishing recommendation (National Archives of Ireland (NAI), Department of Foreign Affairs: Sir Oswald Mosley, 10/P/211).

a friend of Ireland,[79] did Mosley himself consider Eire a fruitful arena for the promotion of his European agenda.[80] Attempts to facilitate sales of *My Answer* were unsuccessful, the major Irish bookseller, Eason, opining that 'interest in the subject and the author ... is so slight that we would not have a sufficient demand to justify taking a supply.'[81] Nevertheless, publicly the Irish Government's stance on partition harmonised easily with Mosley's. This was first set out and published in 1948 under the title *Ireland's Right to Unite When Entering European Union.*[82]

The publication reflected the importance of the Irish immigrant and British Catholic community to the UM, registering with it in a number of ways; for instance, in the relationship Irish anti-partitionists made between the ending of partition and Ireland's involvement in European institutions; the nature of Unionist rule as an egregious example of the flawed system of parliamentary democracy to which Mosley had long been opposed; and also the correspondence between Mosley's personal experience of arbitrary imprisonment under Regulation 18b and that experienced by Catholics in Northern Ireland under the regime's equivalent of 18b: 'We had arrest and imprisonment without trial in England during the war; we have it still in Ulster today'.[83] However, now was the time to end the 'Ulster disgrace' in the context of a union of Europe composed of all western nations. Such a union would prevent the persecution of minorities, a prevention which could not exist among the narrow hatreds of smaller societies: Protestants in Northern Ireland 'have used their fear of persecution to secure from [the] British Government the means to persecute an almost equal number

---

[79] Quotation included in election flyer entitled *The Irish Stood up for Their Rights*, produced for Mosley's election campaign in North Kensington at the General Election of 1959 (copy of leaflet supplied to author, 24 January 2013, by Keith Thompson, formerly of the Union Movement).

[80] MI5, Fascist Activities, November–December 1947 (NAK, Home Office papers: HO45/253951).

[81] G. R. Mitchell, 'Fascist Activities, July–August 1946' (NAK, Home Office papers: HO45/253951).

[82] Oswald Mosley, *Ireland's Right to Unite When Entering European Union* (1948; 2nd edn, London: Sanctuary Press, 1957).

[83] Ibid.

of Catholics'. The large community of the future would guarantee freedom from persecution to such minorities: 'No further reason or excuse exist for the separate life of the Ulster State. Therefore Union Movement affirms the right of Ireland to unite and then, as a united people, to enter the wider Union of Europe.'[84] Priced at a penny a copy, nine pence per dozen and six shillings per hundred, two printings took place in 1948.[85]

In its essentials Mosley's argument on Ulster defined the UM's position on the issue for much of this period. He did not accept the British identity of the Unionist population, seeing it merely as a disaffected element of the Irish nation, but his comment on the two communities in the region being almost equal in number was erroneous – Catholics constituted only about a third of its population. Moreover, the Europe-a-Nation context in which he saw Irish reunification was hardly a context close to realisation and the great national crisis that was to facilitate Mosley's rise to power was progressively disappearing from view, though its possibility could never entirely be ruled out.[86] Moreover, while Mosley posited the context within which the Ulster problem would be resolved, his pamphlet was devoid of specific detail about exactly how this was to be done and what it would mean. As was the case with his *The Greater Britain* in the early 1930s,[87] the detail was left to the General Secretary and editor of *Union*, Alexander Raven Thomson.

Thomson was keen to stress the publication's contemporary relevance, perceiving a situation akin to that of 1914 'rapidly arising' and as with Czechoslovakia in 1938 and India in 1947, 'faced with racial and religious differences Democracy has invariably failed': 'No permanent minority will submit in the long run to the tyranny of a majority of another race or religion', hence a solution of the Ulster problem required an 'immediate revision of the democratic system on modern lines'. Thomson conceived a corporatist framework

[84] Ibid.
[85] See *Union*, 3, 10 April, 15 May, 22 May, 23 October 1948.
[86] See 'North "heading for a crash"', *Irish Times*, 22 March 1947; 'Will Mosley march again?', *Picture Post*, 2 January 1954.
[87] See Nigel Nugent, 'The ideas of the British Union of Fascists', in Nigel Nugent and Roger King (eds), *The British Right: Conservative and Right Wing Politics in Britain* (Farnborough: Saxon House, 1977), pp. 137–39.

that would protect 'special Ulster interests' through 'industrial self-government':[88]

> Orangemen feared Dublin designs on the prosperous linen and shipbuilding industries in the North, which are providing Ulster with a favourable balance of trade. No argument will dispel this fear, but the experiment of giving to these industries and others in the [Irish] Free State powers of self-government, settling their own affairs in their localities would go far to remove the misgivings of the Northern industrialists, who form the financial support of the Orange lodges.[89]

Now was the time 'for that small country, which took neither side in the recent struggle [the Second World War], to show the way by adopting corporate principles to achieve union in the common cause of Ireland and of Christendom'.[90]

Thomson's solution to the Ulster problem was of a piece with the UM's general approach to issues facing 'Celtic' nations of the British State, especially Scotland, where the corporatist solution of economic autonomy to protect essential Scottish industries from an overbearing Labour bureaucracy was also envisioned, together with freedom for the Scots, 'if they so wish', to 'vote for their own Scottish representatives to go to the Council and Assembly of Europe'.[91] But the proposed solutions for Scotland and Ireland – north and south – suffered from fundamental weaknesses. In neither Scotland nor Ireland did neo-fascist corporatism have much purchase with public or political opinion. Nor, as to southern Ireland, was there much chance of them being actively promoted: Mosley's residence in the country during the 1950s was conditional on his non-involvement in its domestic politics. Thomson himself would soon come to recognise these difficulties and admit that it was up to the Irish people to resolve the problem according to their own ideas.

[88] A. Raven Thomson, 'Ireland's right to unite', *Union*, 30 October 1948.
[89] Ibid.
[90] Ibid.
[91] 'Scottish nationalism', *Union*, 14 January 1950. Union had earlier argued that England and Scotland should unite to defend Europe (*Union*, 23 October 1948).

UM, Irish Unity and the Anti-Partition League, 1948–1951

The years from 1948 to 1951 were the most opportune for the promotion of anti-partitionism per se. The campaign for the release of IRA prisoners had indirectly raised the partition issue, which was given mass publicity through an Irish-based campaign pursued in Britain and the USA. Moreover, debates focusing on Ireland's relationship with western Europe, especially in relation to the Brussels Treaty of March 1948 and the North Atlantic Treaty of April 1949, took place at the same time.[92] Against this background, Thomson claimed that it was now 'a commonplace that the British and Irish Governments are engaged in negotiations on the possibility of re-uniting Ireland … It is also surely more than a coincidence that several Cabinet Ministers, including Mr Attlee himself, are spending their holidays on Irish soil.'[93] As Catholic Ireland now had common cause with Protestant England against atheistic communism, 'We cannot afford to enter this further struggle for European civilisation without the aid of the best fighting stock of the Commonwealth.'[94]

The Commonwealth reference echoed Mosley's plea earlier in the year – when it was clear that Ireland, like South Africa, part of the UM's European scheme, was in the process of leaving the Commonwealth – for Eire's retention in the cause of 'a wider Union which summons all who are worthy of high destiny'.[95] In this context the UM bracketed the Ulster regime with Soviet Russia as sharing 'the distinction of having been the only two Police states in Europe to have survived for some 30 years',[96] while referencing the illogicality of the Labour Government refusing 'Union to Ireland' at the same time as advocating union in Europe.[97] For its part, the Ulster regime, secure in Westminster's support, merely

---

[92] Mansergh, 'Irish foreign policy, 1945–51', pp. 136–37.
[93] 'Irish reunion', *Union*, 14 August 1948.
[94] Ibid.
[95] 'New movement in Dominions', *Union*, 20 March 1948.
[96] *Union*, 23 October 1948; also 'Behind Ulster's "Iron Curtain"', *Union*, 29 March 1952.
[97] Raven Thomson, 'Ireland's right to unite', *Union*, 30 October 1948.

noted the development of the anti-partition campaign,[98] though its paramilitary arm, the Royal Ulster Constabulary (RUC), monitored on behalf of MI5 a visit Mosley made to Ireland in 1948.[99]

Raven Thomson rehearsed his arguments on the appropriateness of corporatism to ethnically divided societies in May 1949 when de Valera made the anti-partition case at Earl's Court, London – an occasion presented in *Union* as evidencing great harmony between UM personnel and the audience, in contrast to their hostility to the sellers of the socialist *Irish Democrat*;[100] though Thomson, now aware that Ulster Unionists had a majority in four counties rather than three, adjusted his constitutional proposals accordingly, advocating 'at least a drastic revision of the existing border', though 'it would be much better to consider its complete removal'.[101]

In making the anti-partitionist case the UM was aided considerably by Cahir Healy, though it should be noted that Healy's anti-partitionism was framed within traditional Irish nationalist parameters rather than Mosley's Europe-a-Nation. He was the author of the pamphlet *The Mutilation of a Nation* (1945), which sold 20,000 copies and became the bible of every League orator, including Eamon de Valera. Healy also contributed significantly to organising the hundred-strong Friends of Ireland group in the British Parliament,[102] as well as being a rich source of information and publicity on Stormont's misdeeds.[103] Anti-partitionist campaigning, however, suffered from a number of weaknesses.

The movement was stronger on rhetoric than action and fraught with dissent. Healy was critical from 1948 of what he saw as the

---

[98] 'Campaign against Ulster', *Belfast News-Letter*, 25 October 1948.

[99] Captain G. R. Mitchell, RUC Belfast, Report on Mosley, 22 September 1948 (NAK, Security Service, Personal Files: KV2/894).

[100] 'De Valera at Earl's Court: great welcome for Irish leader', *Union*, 7 May 1949.

[101] Ibid.

[102] Eamon Phoenix, 'Cahir Healy (1877–1970): northern nationalist leader', *Clogher Record*, vol. 18, no. 1 (2003), 49–50.

[103] 'Cahir Healy comes back'; 'Censorship'; 'Ulsterman to the editor', *Union*, 8, 29 March; 19 July 1952; *Irish Times*, 18 March 1949; 27 July 1954; 21 May 1955; Healy to the editor, '"Democracy" in Northern Ireland', *Union*, 26 November 1949.

failure of both de Valera[104] and, especially, the southern Coalition Government to live up to their rhetorical radicalism on the issue: 'The Irish Government should rise to its opportunities and do something for the Northern Nationalists.'[105] Moreover, the effects of the welfare state in providing much better socio-economic benefits in Northern Ireland than existed in the Irish Republic was beginning to be a considerable disincentive to committed anti-partitionism from as early as 1950, a problem anti-partitionists had difficulty responding to convincingly.[106] Nor were Ulster Unionists likely to facilitate the campaign. An attempt to have Basil Brooke, the Northern Ireland Prime Minister (later Lord Brookeborough), debate Irish unity with de Valera at the Cambridge Union was unsuccessful, though a pro-Ulster loyalist case was made.[107] And the anti-partitionist claim was hardly energised from September 1949 when the 'Belfast Police State' dropped detention without trial along with 41 other coercive measures, even if *Union* could argue that this was due not to goodwill or political enlightenment but in response to the Republic's 'exceedingly embarrassing questions' at Strasburg, when the 'human rights' programme was being debated.[108]

At the same time, we should remember that the primary target of UM propaganda was the Irish and Catholic constituency *in Britain*, a constituency progressively less affected by the emotions surrounding the partition issue than was the case for activists in Ireland: the early 1950s would be characterised by sustained campaigning on a wide range of Irish and Catholic issues in addition to partition.[109] If partition retained its political centrality at this time, it was due to controversial constitutional changes that bore on the issue. Thus when Attlee's Labour Government enacted the Ireland Act the

---

[104] Letter to editor, 'Partition', *Irish Times*, 28 January 1948.

[105] 'Big anti-partition meeting in Dublin', *Irish Times*, 8 March 1950.

[106] See 'Pin-pointing politics', *Irish Times*, 11 March 1950.

[107] See *Irish News*, 29 October 1948; 'Campaign against Ulster … the loyalist case', *Belfast News-Letter*, 25 October 1948.

[108] '18b dropped in Belfast', *Union*, 3 September 1949.

[109] 'Manchester Gaelic League hears Union case', 'Catholics also cannot march', 'To the editor: Catholic schools', *Union*, 11 February 1950; 'Shamrock', 'Mosley on partition', *Union*, 9 September 1950; 'Shamrock', 'Truth about partition', *Union*, 16 September 1950.

UM presented it – and Labour's refusal even to debate the need for justice and civil rights in Northern Ireland – as a betrayal, unlike Mosley who had consistently pressed both issues.[110] But, even in this context, the UM faced problems.

When it offered an official alliance to the London Area Council of the Anti-Partition of Ireland League it was firmly declined.[111] Also, the radical socialist Connolly Association could argue that Mosley's Europe-a-Nation policy meant achieving Irish unity by relinquishing independence,[112] and had no difficulty in using Mosley's BUF history against the UM, especially with reference to William Joyce, the former spy for the Black and Tans, together with citing a former Blueshirt condemning the IRA prisoners. But, most seriously, a letter written on behalf of the IRA men imprisoned at Parkhurst Jail was reported, declaring that 'Fascism is a deadly enemy with which there can be no compromise ... We are prepared to fight against it anywhere.'[113]

It was almost inevitable that physical conflict between the UM and the Connolly Association would develop: it occurred in mid-July 1950 when a Connolly Association meeting in Hyde Park was attacked, its platform 'torn to pieces, its speakers ... assaulted together with members of the public who were listening'. The source of the trouble was identified as an extreme right-wing group called 'United Irishmen'.[114] A splinter group formed in 1949 from the main republican movement in Ireland, its paper, *United Irishman*, mirrored *Union* in much of its coverage; an organ of right-wing Catholicism, anti-partitionism and anti-Freemasonry,[115] in the latter respect having some affinities with the Duke of Bedford's neo-fascist BPP.[116] An

[110] 'Shamrock', 'What can the Irish voter do?', *Union*, 2 September 1950; *Union*, 27 January 1951; 'Shamrock', 'Westminster debates Ireland', *Union*, 9 June 1951.

[111] Home Office Monthly Bulletin: Fascist Activity, February 1949 (NAK, Intelligence Files: KV3/52).

[112] T. H. Jackson to the editor, *Irish Democrat*, March 1948.

[113] 'London Irish reject fascist unity stunt', *Irish Democrat*, July 1948.

[114] *Irish Democrat*, August 1950.

[115] *United Irishman*, July/August 1949; T. P. Coogan, *The I.R.A.* (London: Pall Mall Press, 1970), p. 270.

[116] *United Irishman*, October 1949; January, February 1950.

'Anti-Fascist' letter to the *Irish Democrat* implicitly, but persuasively, identified Jeffrey Hamm and another UM member as engaged in the attack.[117] But the Connolly Association was not the most effective of the UM's enemies.

That was undoubtedly the Jewish 43 Group, an organisation that went to extreme, often violent, means to deny the UM a public arena to make its case, and the activities of which Morris Beckman, a leading member, has described in detail.[118] Significantly, by 1951, it had concluded that its objectives had been so successfully achieved that it could disband, a conclusion consistent with that of the security services about their own fascist surveillance in the same year.[119] Certainly, Hamm's resort to violence at the Connolly Association meeting has all the marks of frustration at the UM's lack of political progress. At its annual meeting of February 1949 Mosley told members that they could not hope for real success at the ballot box in the ordinary course of events, but would have to wait on a major crisis.[120] Despite the recruitment of some notable personalities, such as the anthropologist G. H. Lane-Fox Pitt-Rivers and the author Henry Williamson, UM membership was somewhere between 1,000 and 1,500, with inactive members possibly numbering up to 15,000 and with little support in Scotland or the provinces.[121] In a context where the organisation

---

[117] See *Irish Democrat*, October 1950; 'London anti-fascist' to editor, *Irish Democrat*, October 1951.

[118] See Beckman, *43 Group, passim*.

[119] G. R. Mitchell to Burley, 15 March 1949; Sir Percy Sillitoe to Lt. General Sir Alexander Hood, 7 March 1951 (NAK, Intelligence Files: KV3/52).

[120] Home Office Monthly Bulletin: Fascist Activity, February 1949 (NAK, Home Office papers: HO45/253951).

[121] Report of Fascist Activities for March–April 1948; H. J. Lee to S. H. E. Burley, 2 July 1948, Report marked 'Secret'; B. G. Atkinson to Burley, Report on Fascist Activities for July–September 1948, 15 October 1948; Atkinson to Burley, Report of Fascist Activities for October–December 1948, 21 January 1949. Home Office Monthly Bulletin: Fascist Activity, 26 April, November–December 1948 (NAK, Intelligence Files: KV3/52); Hillman, '"Tell me chum"', 8; See Anne Poole, 'Oswald Mosley and the Union Movement: success or failure', in Mike Cronin (ed.), *The Failure of British Fascism: The Far Right and the Fight For Political Recognition* (Basingstoke: Palgrave Macmillan, 1996), p. 56; Home Office Monthly Bulletin: Fascist

was failing, *Union* put enhanced emphasis on Mosley's significance as a 'Thought-Deed' man, with specific reference to William Gladstone, who defied Ulster Unionist opposition in his efforts to confer Home Rule on Ireland in the late nineteenth century.[122] Such positioning may not have been intended as a preparation for it, but it was followed not long afterwards, in February 1951, by news of Mosley taking up residence in the Irish Republic.

The move was not without controversy, seen by some movement members and other Rightists as abandonment of a UM sinking ship,[123] and by the Home Office as a means of avoiding UK taxes.[124] Mosley's explanation was that England was now an 'island prison' whereas Ireland was a free country where he could better pursue his European project.[125] The move was first mooted in 1946 when Mosley was informed that a short visit would be acceptable but permanent residence was inopportune 'until international tempers had cooled'.[126] Nevertheless, though the Irish authorities tracked Mosley's political activities, especially his exploitation of partition – and would do throughout his Irish residency[127] – they accepted that there was no legal means to prevent Mosley's residency, nor indeed to do much 'about his utterances'.[128] For his part, Mosley

Activity, 26 April, November–December 1948 (NAK, Intelligence Files: KV3/52); Macklin, *Very Deeply Dyed in Black*, pp. 58–59.
[122] See *Union*, 23, 30 September, 7, 14, 21 October, 9 December 1950.
[123] Robert Saunders to Maurice Pacey, 18 March 1951 (NAK, MI5, Report on Fascist Activities in the United Kingdom, KV2/3194); Domvile to Healy, 9 July 1951 (Cahir Healy papers, PRONI: D2991/B/70/2).
[124] Home Office Monthly Bulletin: Fascist Activity: B. G. Atkinson to A. S. Oakley, 14 February 1951 (NAK, Intelligence Files: KV3/52).
[125] 'Mosley's Move to Ireland', *Union*, 31 March 1951; see also attack on hostile press interpretations of the move (*Union*, 14, 21 April 1951); J. Molloy (for Ambassador), Irish Embassy, London, to Secretary, Department of External Affairs, 21 August 1951 (NAI, Department of Defence file: G2/C/563).
[126] D. Costigan, Department of Justice, to Sean Nunan, Foreign Affairs, 27 February 1951 (NAI, Department of Justice file: 118/388).
[127] *Irish Times*, 15 May 1948; *Sunday Press*, 25 November 1951, press clippings; Dan Bryan to Sean Nunan, 19 December 1951; Denis R. MacDonald, Irish Ambassador, Paris, to Secretary, Department of External Affairs, 13 October 1960 (NAI, Department of Defence file: G2/C/563).
[128] D. Costigan, Department of Justice, to Sean Nunan, Foreign Affairs,

declared that though Ireland was now his homeland,[129] he would not become involved in its politics.[130] The controversy his presence caused at a Trinity College debate in Dublin in 1954 would undoubtedly have reinforced this decision.[131] Thus, in regard to the Irish movement with the closest ideological resonance with the UM at this time, the short-lived Aontas Naisiunta, there was no prospect of collaboration.[132] Forever on the look-out for signs of the great national crisis that would herald a new political beginning, Mosley's attention was focused firmly on Britain, where he detected a 'situation now ... developing rapidly'.[133]

For our purposes, all that can be said for the years from 1948 to 1951 was that they had seen the major themes of UM propaganda on Irish unity clarified: Labour Party betrayal of the Irish immigrant community on partition; Stormont's oppression of the Catholic community in Northern Ireland as indicative of the flaws in parliamentary democracy; Mosley's credibility on Irish unity; and the inevitability of a great national crisis that would create the conditions for the means to unite Ireland in a European context.

27 February 1951 (NAI, Department of Justice file: 118/388); Peter Berry, Department of Justice to Con Cremin, Department of External Affairs, 28 October 1960, NAI, Department of Justice file: 118/388).

[129] Mosley to Healy, 20 September 1951 (Cahir Healy papers, PRONI: D2991/B/74/11); Diana Mosley, *A Life of Contrasts* (London: Hamish Hamilton, 1977), chap. 22.

[130] 'Mosley's Statement', *Union*, 10 March 1951; *Sunday Press*, 25 November 1951, press clippings; Dan Bryan to Sean Nunan, 19 December 1951 (NAI, Department of Defence file: G2/C/563).

[131] See 'Sir Oswald Mosley Speaks in T.C.D.', *Irish Times*, 29 October 1954; 'Aftermath of Mosley's Visit to Trinity College', *Irish Times*, 30 October 1954; 'Limelight on Mosley', *Sunday Times*, 9 May 1954. Mosley, however, claimed to be well satisfied with his reception. A. Raven Thomson to Healy, 26 November 1954 (Cahir Healy papers, PRONI: D2991/A/21/104).

[132] Dan Bryan to Sean Nunan, 'Confidential', 20 February 1951 (Cahir Healy papers, PRONI: D2991/A/21/104). On Anotas Naisiunta, see Douglas, *Architects of the Resurrection*, p. 284.

[133] Mosley to Healy, 20 September 1951 (Cahir Healy papers, PRONI: D2991/B/74/11).

Electoral Politics, The European and Partition

The failures of the UM since 1948 and the problems it encountered in publicly making its case forced a consideration of various new political approaches, though not all initiatives were well informed. When Raven Thomson proposed an enhanced pro-Nazi approach to UM policies to attract back to the movement lapsed members unenthusiastic about Mosley's Europe-a-Nation project, it completely backfired as more members left, recognising that such a connection was abhorrent to the public and would ensure the UM's political marginalisation.[134] The creation of a mobile Special Propaganda Section to support the activities of undermanned branches failed due to internal intrigue; the infiltration of the Communist Party for the purpose of gaining useful information seems to have occurred only on a very limited scale and without substantive effect; decentralisation as a means of developing local initiative in provincial branches was stymied by UM headquarters' control of finance.[135] These failed initiatives ensured that partition and Cahir Healy retained their significance, evident in Mosley's close contacts with him in this period.[136]

As a Westminster MP, Healy and a fellow nationalist Michael O'Neill abandoned abstention from Westminster in 1952 with the purpose of pressing the partition issue.[137] They also petitioned the de Valera Government, unsuccessfully, to allow northern Nationalist MPs elected to Stormont seats in the southern legislature instead, though without voting rights. De Valera's refusal reflected another depressing reality for northern anti-partitionists: namely, that there was no great enthusiasm in the southern population for prioritising the issue,[138] just as there was little evidence in Britain of a groundswell of popular support for Mosleyite anti-partitionism,

---

[134] Macklin *Very Deeply Dyed in Black*, p. 53.

[135] Ibid., pp. 61–62.

[136] See, for instance, Mosley–Healy correspondence, May 1949–April 1952; in particular, letters of 28 April 1952, 18 July 1953 (Cahir Healy papers, PRONI: D2991/B/74/6–16).

[137] 'No whip for Irish MPs', *Irish Times*, 19 February 1952.

[138] See Brendan Lynn, *Holding the Ground: The Nationalist Party in Northern Ireland, 1945–72* (Aldershot: Ashgate, 1997), chap. 3.

or that the Labour Party would abandon its complicity in the 'oppression' of the Catholic community in Northern Ireland.[139]

Some slight comfort could be taken from external considerations which might compel Irish unity. Thus, Admiral Domvile informed Healy that the USA wanted to trade it off against Irish membership of the Atlantic Pact and they could very well succeed.[140] By the same token, while it is usual to regard Mosley's European project as politically unrealistic,[141] the UM was in favour of the emerging European Economic Community (EEC), even if it thought political unity should precede, not follow, economic unification, and complained that Britain seemed determined to stay out.[142] Thus it was possible to see the grain of European politics moving in a direction that might eventually make Mosley's European objective deliverable, and thus the feasibility of his solution to the Ulster problem.

As for Healy, he contributed significantly to UM political activities, supporting electoral forays (mainly local) and contributing essays and commentaries to Mosley's intellectual journal *The European*. Partition was an ongoing, dynamic issue, given the Stormont regime's reliability in producing controversial measures that Healy ensured would resonate at Westminster and whose critiques the UM could be relied upon to promote. Moreover, despite the Irish Government's hope that Mosley's Irish residency meant the abandonment of the 'remnants' of the UM, it soon became clear he was conducting UM business in Dublin.[143] As to why he was not doing so in Britain, Mosley stated, 'If you want to clear up a muck-heap you don't begin by putting yourself underneath it.'[144]

---

[139] 'Behind Ulster's "iron curtain"', *Union*, 29 March 1952.

[140] Domvile to Healy, 29 June 1951 (Cahir Healy papers, PRONI: D2991/B/70/1).

[141] For instance, Richard Thurlow, *Fascism in Britain: A History, 1918–1985* (Oxford: Blackwell, 1987), p. 245.

[142] See 'Europe unites but Britain stays out', *Union*, 10 October 1953.

[143] Bryan to Nunan, 14 March 1952 (NAI, Department of Defence file: G2/C/563); Nunan to John Chadwick, British Embassy, Dublin, 6 May 1952; Nunan to W. P. Fay, 26 September 1952; also, R. J. Callanan, Defence, to Nunan, 'Confidential', 3 October 1952; Callanan to Nunan, 28 February 1953.

[144] Mosley speaking at Cambridge Union in *Union*, 22 May 1954.

And despite the difficulties in successfully exploiting the partition issue, the issue remained a sufficiently significant one in Anglo-Irish and British–USA relations to maintain hope, evident in the claim that the Irish in Britain were now turning away from the old parties and entering the UM;[145] and sustained, respectively, by de Valera's critique of Herbert Morrison's defence of partition in a Washington speech;[146] a call by the Foreign Affairs Committee of the House of Representatives for a vote on partition by *all* the Irish people;[147] and the belief that partition was the root cause of the phenomenally high unemployment in Northern Ireland.[148] Moreover, a significant added stimulus to the partition debate emerged when a now confident Unionism made its contribution: 'Anti-Fascist Unionist' countered the claim that partition was the cause of high unemployment by referencing the difference between industrialised 'Ulster' and the agricultural Irish Republic;[149] and its presence was particularly evident in *The European*, which aimed at a more 'elevated' readership than the populist *Union*.

Edited by Lady Mosley, from its emergence in 1953 it was devoted primarily to the promotion of Mosley's European project, and intended to remedy a perceived mistake of the inter-war years: namely, excessive concentration on political action and a neglect of 'the intellectuals', allowing the communists successfully to create the impression 'that the British Union consisted entirely of morons who could neither read nor write'.[150] Though the wider British Catholic interest was catered for,[151] most contributors were not UM members and, it was argued, did not share the UM's

---

[145] 'Shamrock', 'Partition excludes Ireland from Europe', *Union*, 21 July 1951.
[146] 'Morrison defends Partition: de Valera Replies', *Union*, 29 September 1951.
[147] 'Congress for Ireland', *Union*, 17 November 1951.
[148] 'Behind Ulster's "iron curtain"', *Union*, 29 March 1952; also Ray Moat, letter to the editor, 'Conditions in Northern Ireland', *Union*, 17 May 1952.
[149] See 'Anti-Fascist Unionist' to editor, 'Northern Ireland', and editor's note, *Union*, 21 June 1952; 'Ulsterman' to the editor, *Union*, 19 July 1952.
[150] Jeffrey Hamm, *Action Replay* (London: Howard Baker, 1983), pp. 170–71; Mosley, *Life of Contrasts*, pp. 247–49.
[151] See A. J. Neame, 'Black and blue: a study in the Catholic novel', *The European* (April 1953), 26–36; Nicholas Mosley, 'A new Puritanism', *The European* (May 1953), 28–39.

political beliefs.[152] With the Ulster Unionist Party (UUP) now willing to engage in the partition debate, Mosley, inviting Healy to contribute, was 'very pleased' that an article by Jeffrey Hamm (Geoffrey Vernon)[153] attacking partition had both been 'warmly approved' in the Irish press and was vehemently assailed by the 'Ulster organisation'.[154] The purpose was to ensure that 'Ulster gets the worst of it'.[155]

Referencing the European context in which the UM envisaged Irish unity, Vernon's article ran through the gamut of Irish nationalist and Mosleyite objections to the 'Iron Curtain' dividing Ireland:[156] Irish unity 'is one step along the road which leads to the union of all Europe'.[157] The debate once started ran through to 1956. That it did so was due largely to the fact that arguments on both sides had varying degrees of strength and weakness.

For instance, W. Douglas, OBE, on behalf of the Ulster Unionist Council, could point to Vernon's error in claiming that the abolition of proportional representation for regional elections in 1929 was intended to reduce nationalist representation: this was not the case. Likewise, Douglas's claim that socio-economic benefits in Northern Ireland far transcended those in the Irish Republic was also accurate. Less convincing, however, were his reasons for the great reduction in the southern Protestant population since partition or claims for the objectivity of community treatment by the RUC. For his part, Vernon's accuracy on regime gerrymandering of electoral boundaries since 1921 went together with argument on police partisanship and the use of coercive 'special powers' in

---

[152] Hamm, *Action Replay*, pp. 71–72, 175–76.

[153] When Mosley appointed him Secretary of the UM in 1956 following Raven Thomson's death, Hamm adopted different identities for his two separate roles in politics and publishing, becoming 'Geoffrey Vernon' for his journal activities and publications, while retaining his real name for the secretaryship.

[154] Mosley to Healy, 18 July 1953 (Cahir Healy papers, PRONI: D2991/B/74/5).

[155] Mosley to Healy, 23 July 1953 (Cahir Healy papers, PRONI: D2991/B/74/3).

[156] G.V., 'The problem of Irish partition', *The European* (June 1953), 33–43.

[157] Ibid., 34–36.

Northern Ireland.[158] Healy responded to Mosley's invitation with an offer to have a member of staff in the External Affairs department in Dublin respond in a personal capacity,[159] though the offer was apparently not taken up. Otherwise, his contribution reinforced Vernon's argument on police powers by adding the Public Order Act of 1951 to the range of coercive powers the Unionist had accumulated, together with a promise de Valera had made that Unionists could retain their present powers if they transferred their allegiance to Dublin.[160] Vigorous charge and counter-charge followed.[161] In the March 1955 issue, Vernon admitted that he and Douglas could not agree, but suggested a plebiscite of nine-county Ulster to solve the partition problem, otherwise it would endure 'and its opponents will be driven to use of force'. At this point, the editor declared that the correspondence must cease.[162]

Vernon's reference to the use of force was not without point: 1956 would see a new IRA campaign begin, preceded by arms raids at British army installations in England and Northern Ireland – Felstead, Sussex (July 1953); Armagh city (June 1954); Omagh, county Tyrone (October 1954); Arborfield, Berkshire (August 1955)[163] – and boosted by an overall vote of 152,310 in Northern Ireland at the Westminster election of 1955 which saw the return of two abstentionist Sinn Fein candidates.[164] As with the absence of

[158] W. Douglas to the editor, *The European* (August 1953); G.V., letter to the editor, *The European* (September 1953), 63–64.
[159] Cahir Healy to Mosley, 23 July 1953 (BU, CRC, Sir Oswald Mosley papers: OMN/B/2/4/1).
[160] Cahir Healy to the editor, *The European* (October 1953), 61–62.
[161] Geoffrey Vernon, 'The Ulster police state', *The European* (July 1954), 22–25; Patrick Bury, letter to editor, *The European* (July 1954), 60, 226–27; Woodrow Wyatt, 'That part of Britain where one man in five is out of work', *Picture Post*, 17 December 1955, 27; Douglas to the editor; Vernon to the editor, *The European* (October 1954), 59–61; Douglas to the editor; Patrick Boyd to editor, *The European* (December 1954), 59–61; Vernon to the editor, *The European* (January 1955), 60; Douglas to the editor, *The European* (February 1955), 60–61.
[162] Douglas to the editor, *The European* (February 1955), 62.
[163] J. Bower Bell, *The Secret Army: A History of the IRA* (London: Sphere, 1972), pp. 302–25.
[164] Ibid., pp. 318–19.

overt Blackshirt criticism of the IRA's English bombing campaign in 1939, so too would this be the case with the IRA campaign of 1956–62. Indeed, UM reporting of the raids was characterised not by condemnation but attacks on 'much wild writing' in Fleet Street which missed the central point: namely, that 'this violence would not have happened if the old politicians had given Ireland justice.'[165] 'Now both parties are horrified when Irishmen use violence in reprisal … We do not condone violence – on either side! – but we say GIVE IRELAND THE RIGHT TO UNITE.'[166] For his part, however, Healy did not regard the IRA's new paramilitary campaign as of any assistance to the anti-partitionist campaign: its effect was merely to validate the actions of the Ulster B Specials in drawing full-time payment rates for part-time work.[167]

Despite Lady Mosley's closure of the partition debate in *The European*, Vernon found occasion to open it again in August 1955 with a coruscating review of Michael Sheehy's pro-partitionist *Divided We Stand*,[168] with Douglas leaping to its defence and the standard anti- and pro- partition cases being rehearsed.[169] The debate, however, also attracted a contribution which, while accepting that religious intolerance existed in Northern Ireland, argued that the large nationalist minority in the region (35 per cent) was a serious threat to State stability and went far to justify Protestant job discrimination.[170] As such, it echoed a fundamental belief of Ulster Unionism, and with it Douglas's contributions ceased. Given the

---

[165] Similarly, when Phil Clarke, successful Sinn Fein candidate, was unseated as MP for Fermanagh and South Tyrone on the grounds that he was a convicted felon, and the seat awarded to the defeated Unionist candidate following the 1955 General Election, *Union* declared it to be 'further evidence that dictatorship prevails in Northern Ireland' ('Let Ireland unite', *Union*, 20 August 1955).

[166] 'Let Ireland unite', *Union*, 20 August 1955; also, 'Dictatorship in Fermanagh', *Union*, 17 September 1955 and 'Slump in Northern Ireland', *Union*, 8 October 1955.

[167] 'Nationalist MPs deplore raids', *Irish Times*, 23 May 1957.

[168] Michael Sheehy, *Divided We Stand: A Study of Partition* (London: Faber & Faber, 1955).

[169] Vernon, review of Sheehy in *The European* (August 1955), 45–46; Douglas and Vernon to the editor, *The European* (November 1955), 63–64.

[170] W. G. Shipley to editor, *The European* (February 1956), 63.

evident failure of the IRA campaign and the strong Westminster support for the Stormont regime it occasioned, Ulster Unionist attention thereafter to Mosley's '"United Ireland" nonsense' was at best intermittent and dismissive.[171]

The partition debate in *The European* was not intended to stand alone but to run in tandem with the UM's campaign of public meetings and political controversy in Britain; a campaign in which Healy had a higher profile. On taking his seat at Westminster the UM keenly referenced the close friendship established between Healy, other Irish nationalists and Mosley's organisation when all were interned under Regulation 18b.[172] In a context where the American League for an Undivided Ireland was supposedly making great strides,[173] Healy's contribution to anti-partitionism in parliament was at one with the Labour group, Friends of Ireland,[174] though Geoffrey Bing, who had taken a leading role in publicising the Belfast pogrom of 1935 in Britain, illustrated how Healy's friendship with Mosley had soured his relations with the group when he described him as 'not worth bothering about'.[175] Though *Union* in particular sought to channel Ulster issues to the attention of the immigrant Irish and British Catholics,[176] the Friends of Ireland's anti-partitionist efforts were guaranteed much greater publicity, and certainly more than *The European* could have provided.[177]

---

[171] See, for instance *Belfast News-Letter*, 27 January 1958, press clipping (Sir Oswald Mosley papers, BU, CRL: OMD/7/1/28); '"I've won" – unheckled Mosley says', *Belfast News-Letter*, 19 September 1962.

[172] 'Cahir Healy comes back', *Union*, 8 March 1952.

[173] 'Movement to abolish Irish border making big strides in U.S.', *Irish News*, 5 June 1953.

[174] 'Speaking for the Irish Anti-Partition League at Birmingham on 5 July 1953, Healy emphasised British taxpayers bearing the cost of partition (*Irish News*, 6 July 1953); '3 northern M.P.s accuse Attlee of "studied insult"', *Irish Times*, 7 October 1954; 'Unionists giving in to extremists', *Irish Times*, 22 September 1954.

[175] Christopher Norton, *The Politics of Constitutional Nationalism in Northern Ireland, 1932–70* (Manchester: Manchester University Press, 2014), p. 106.

[176] 'Starvation in Ireland', *Union*, 18 June 1955.

[177] Apart from public indifference or hostility, the publication suffered from production and distribution difficulties.

Despite the disdain of other parliamentary anti-partitionists, Healy continued to lend support to the UM's anti-partitionist and general electoral activities. Thus he agreed to Jeffrey Hamm's request for a supporting message to the electors of Liverpool Moss Side on the occasion of a council by-election in 1952;[178] and did so again when Raven Thomson requested a letter supporting 'Germans expelled from the Eastern lands'.[179] His most significant individual contribution to UM activities, however, was his participation in a public debate on partition in December 1953 with the UUP MP for North Belfast Harland Montgomery Hyde, private secretary to the appeaser Lord Londonderry, in the late 1930s.

The event was carefully managed by the UM national organiser Alf Flockhart, confident both of strong support for Healy and of the events' success. All members of the audience – and Montgomery Hyde – would be given a copy of every issue of *The European* that contained a reference to partition, while in advertising the meeting in *Union* he had been careful not to mention Hyde's presence, in case Tory Central Office might 'bring down the curtain', though after the event his presence would certainly be announced: 'I am sure it is going to be a fine evening, for which I shall be much indebted to you.'[180] During the debate, Hyde's defence of partition was polite and tolerant, admitting that both Healy and himself were Irishmen with a love for their country, but that 'this problem of North and South had been the cause of disunity among the Irish.' The debate, *Union* averred, showed that Irishmen could discuss their differences,[181] with the implication of constitutional resolution. Hyde, however, was one of the most liberal of Ulster Unionists, quite unrepresentative of mainstream opinion in his party; and as such the debate seriously under-played the depth of visceral emotion that informed popular Unionism in Northern Ireland. Hyde

[178] Vernon to Healy, 26 March 1958 (Cahir Healy papers, PRONI: D2991/B/75/8).
[179] A. Raven Thomson to Healy, 26 November 1954 (Cahir Healy papers, PRONI: D2991/A/21/104).
[180] L. A. Flockhart to Healy, 1 October, 20 November 1953 (Cahir Healy papers, PRONI: D2991/B/71/1-2).
[181] 'Tory MP debates with Cahir Healy', *Union*, 5 December 1953.

would later claim he was drummed out of the party in 1959 for advocating abolition of the death penalty, reform of the law relating to homosexuals and the return from Britain of disputed paintings to the Lane Gallery in Dublin.[182]

Subsequent correspondence between Flockhart and Healy centred on invitations to UM events as Mosley's personal guest;[183] Healy's request for information on Protestants in Spain;[184] and especially, in the run-up to the 1955 general election, a request for Healy's endorsement in the form of a message headed 'TO THE ELECTORS FROM CAHIR HEALY M.P.', calling upon the voters of Bethnal Green and Shoreditch to vote for the UM candidate if they wanted to register a vote against communism.[185] That these activities were unattended by significant electoral or political success, and that the Irish Anti-Partition League had effectively collapsed, proved no deterrent to the continuance of the movement's efforts.

Geoffrey Vernon's article of January 1956, 'Catholics and modern politics' identified clearly the obstacle that the Labour Party presented, partly because of its economic policies and also because of its traditional anti-partitionism. Such realism, however, was accompanied by faith in the immigrant Irish community's eventual recognition of Labour's betrayal on partition in 1949; the supposed natural affinity between Catholic religious values and those of the UM, together with the apparent compatibility between the trans-national remit of the Vatican and Mosley's idea of Europe-a-Nation, as the means to change this situation.[186] Such conviction ensured the continuance of Healy's contribution to UM activities, evident in the effort Geoffrey Vernon exerted to maintain

---

[182] J. F. Harbinson, The *Ulster Unionist Party, 1882–1973: Its Development and Organisation* (Belfast: Blackstaff Press, 1973), p. 83.

[183] Flockhart to Healy, 25 March 1954 (Cahir Healy papers, PRONI: D2991/B/71/3).

[184] Flockhart to Healy, 14 July 1954 (Cahir Healy papers, PRONI: D2991/B/71/4).

[185] Flockhart to Healy, 9 February 1955 (Cahir Healy papers, PRONI: D2991/B/71/5).

[186] Geoffrey Vernon, 'Catholics and modern politics', *The European* (January 1956), 21–26.

his goodwill and which involved putting the best construction on UM efforts.[187] Thus, Healy's complaint that the Victoria Station bookstall in London had no copies of *The European* was explained as the bookstall often being out of stock,[188] when the journal's main problems were anti-fascist sentiment and lack of effective marketing.[189] Again, Healy wrote to Alf Flockhart in 1958 clearly unaware of his dismissal from the UM for 'indecency in a public convenience', a second offence for which he was imprisoned and expelled from the movement.[190] Answering Healy, Vernon omitted the Flockhart scandal, and focused instead on electoral contests, *Union* sales and an anti-de Valera demonstration.[191]

Hamm's appointment as Mosley's secretary on the death of Raven Thomson in 1956 ensured not only that the partitionist/ Catholic dimension to UM propaganda would retain its importance – by the late 1950s, 60,000 Irish immigrants a year were arriving in Britain[192] – but also how it would be dealt with. His concern to present Healy with an overly benign image of the character of the UM and its political prospects clearly reinforced Healy's own faith in Mosley as a political leader, as his response to the news that the UM leader had enthusiastically returned to active politics after an illness indicates: he hoped Mosley would be able to give the UM a big lift: people still believed in him personally.[193]

The UM found a new strand in its cultivation of Irish immigrant support in June 1956 when it picked up on a request

---

[187] Vernon to Healy, 29 February, 26 November, 21 December 1965, 18 June 1957 (Cahir Healy papers, PRONI: D2991/B/75/3, 4, 5, 7).

[188] Healy to Vernon, 26 February 1956; Vernon to Healy, 29 February 1956 (Cahir Healy papers, PRONI: D2991/B/75/2).

[189] 'Desmond' to 'Dearest Kit', 18 July 1955 (Sir Oswald Mosley papers, BU, CRL: OMN/B/4/7); Mosley, *Life of Contrasts*, pp. 247–49.

[190] On this subject, see Grundy, *Memoir of a Fascist Childhood*, pp. 112–13.

[191] Vernon to Healy, 26 March 1958 (Cahir Healy papers, PRONI: D2991/B/75/8); Vernon to Healy 23 March 1958 (Cahir Healy papers, PRONI: D2991/B/75/4).

[192] Enda Delaney, *The Irish in Post-War Britain* (Oxford: Oxford University Press, 2007), p. 119.

[193] Vernon–Healy correspondence, 26 November, 21 December 1956; 18, 21 June 1957 (Cahir Healy papers, PRONI: D2991/B/75/4, 5, 7, 8).

Birmingham City Council had made to the Irish Government asking it to dissuade Irish immigrants from coming to the city due to its appalling living conditions. Whether an expression of genuine concern or not, it suggested a nativist mindset not unusual in a decade when anti-Irish sentiments – 'no Irish need apply' – were not uncommon. Birmingham, especially, had been a particular location of anti-Irish opinion since the IRA bombing campaign in 1939, abetted by Eire's neutrality during the late war, and carrying over well into the post-war period.[194] For the UM, however, the significance of the Birmingham appeal lay in the opportunity it provided to address simultaneously two issues on which it consistently focused: 'We can get on fine with the Irish, but the Coloured invasion must stop. Give the Coloured people justice in their own lands; let Europeans live in theirs.'[195] The linking of anti-'coloured' discrimination with immigrant Irish conciliation would be a significant theme of Mosley's campaign in North Kensington at the general election of 1959,[196] though the former would be exploited to better political effect by neo-fascist groups in the economically troubled 1970s. At the same time, care had to be taken in dealing with the race issue.

By the later 1950s, the UM had a thriving correspondence with white racist groups in the USA, contacts which Mosley cultivated. However, when other British racists formed branches of the Ku Klux Klan (KKK), Mosley felt sufficiently embarrassed to proscribe membership of it:[197] any UM member joining the KKK would be expelled.[198] For our purposes, the fact that the KKK was deeply anti-Catholic meant that not to have done so could both have alienated Catholics within the UM – *Action* declared, in the context

---

[194]   Delaney, *The Irish in Post-War Britain*, p. 119.

[195]   'Keep out the Irish', *Union*, 16 June 1956; also 'Coloured question', *Union*, 16 October 1954; 'Anxiety in Birmingham', *Union*, 30 October 1954; Macklin, *Very Deeply Dyed in Black*, pp. 67–70.

[196]   Poole, 'Oswald Mosley and the Union Movement', p. 63.

[197]   Macklin, *Very Deeply Dyed in Black*, p. 70.

[198]   'The Ku Klux Klan', *Action*, 11 May 1957. *Action* was a new UM publication (though the name was a revival from the 1930s) with which *Union* would be merged in October 1957; 'The Ku Klux Klan', *The National European* (July 1965).

of an erroneous impression that the UM had communist connections: 'we ourselves are Catholics'[199] – and possibly endangered its relationship with the wider Catholic constituency the organisation was keenly concerned to cultivate. That its efforts to date in this respect had hardly been crowned with success was something the organisation chose not to acknowledge, preferring instead to read significant progress into meagre local election results together with speculation that under a European-style proportional representation system its parliamentary strength would be 'over 40 members'.[200] At the same time some attempts were made to address partition from a new perspective.

Thus, the April 1958 issue of *The European* framed Irish unity in a cultural context: the 'saintliness of Pearse, the flamboyance of Carson, the poetry and pathos of Tom Kettle [constitutional nationalist author killed in the Great War]' together formed 'a triple heritage. To take away any of these heroes is to leave Ireland the poorer, and yet divided, no matter what government rules or what area it rules over'.[201] Again, Mosley's anti-Black and Tan activities found a wider frame of reference as a critical lens through which to assess issues other than Irish partition – while implicitly keeping the Irish question in view – such as British Government handling of the Cyprus conflict and the treatment of Mau-Mau prisoners in Kenya.[202] The demise of *The European* as an independent journal in early 1959, however, was another indication of political failure, and the UM was presented with another false dawn in the race riots that swept the Notting Hill area of London in the late summer of 1958, appearing to offer a promising background for Mosley's electoral resurrection at the general election of October 1959.

---

[199] 'Catholics and Union Movement', *Action*, 29 June 1957. The last issue of *Union* appeared on 7 September 1957, being incorporated into *Action* thereafter.
[200] 'The present voting strength of Union Movement', *The European* (June 1958), 206.
[201] Eamonn Bourke in *The European* (April 1958), 98–101.
[202] 'Analysis', *The European* (November 1958), 131–32; 'No police bullying for black or white', *Action*, 23 May 1959.

North Kensington Hopes and the Political Endgame

Mosley's candidacy for the North Kensington constituency was the crucial test of his political relevance in the 1950s. Jeffrey Hamm had been living there for around six years, the UM had a branch in the area and had a long-standing record of warnings about the effects of non-white immigration. Hamm claimed that Mosley's decision to contest the seat was in response to 'much popular clamour' to do so 'as a true people's champion', but despite an intensely fought campaign by Mosley and the UM[203] the result was both disappointing and traumatic: 'Mosley was credited with 2,821 votes out of a total of 35,000, and was bottom of the poll. Not only were all our women supporters in tears, but many of the men too wept unashamedly, shocked and stunned by this anti-climax.'[204] Mosley would admit that the result was 'the biggest single shock in his life',[205] but his own electoral performance was hardly creditable, associating 'wogs' with cat food,[206] publicly condemning racist comments by his followers while indicating private tolerance,[207] and misjudging his audiences. But for our purposes, the Irish presence in the constituency is of central interest.

The UM produced two leaflets specifically directed at the Irish community, one of which married Mosley's anti-Black and Tan activities with concerns about non-white immigration. Both *The Irish Stood up for Their Rights* and *Irish Remember* made much of the former and how the Irish appreciated them together with his support for Irish unity, while the latter stressed the supposed threat to Irish jobs posed by increased 'coloured' immigration and how the 'power of question and debate' that began the job of getting the Black and Tans out of Ireland 'can get the Blacks out of North Kensington'.[208] It was

[203] Hamm, *Action Replay*, pp. 177–83.

[204] Ibid., p. 184.

[205] Grundy, *Memoir of a Fascist Childhood*, p. 192.

[206] Ibid., p. 180.

[207] Ibid., p. 176.

[208] Copies of election leaflets, *The Irish Stood up for Their Rights*, and *Irish Remember*, produced for Mosley's election campaign in North Kensington in 1959 (author's possession); see also 'Mosley's message to each elector' (Sir Oswald Mosley papers, BU, CRL: OMD/7/3/3).

a message Mosley also pressed in his speeches during the campaign,[209] together with internment without trial in Northern Ireland.[210]

Certainly, there was a substantial Irish community to address, numbering 'tens of thousands', 'immigrants to England during another period, under not completely different circumstances from the ones which forced the West Indians to come to England in the 1950s'.[211] But here also Mosley's efforts could be inept, on one occasion describing to a group of Irishwomen how he read Greek philosophy while in jail, until his peroration was interrupted by a 'huge woman': 'Sir Oswald, I don't know about your Greeks, but I've got niggers in the basement.'[212]

Trevor Grundy's canvassing indicated that, mostly, 'people were indifferent or indicated they'd never heard of Mosley'.[213] The Irish community failed to come out in sufficient numbers even to save his deposit, while the Labour Party candidate, George Rogers, who had held the seat since 1945, won by a large majority: he had a record of cultivating his Irish constituents, while during the election campaign indicated his sympathy for controlling non-white immigration.[214] It was generally assumed that the votes Mosley did gain came from former Labour voters,[215] and assuming that many of these would have been from the immigrant Irish community, he did have some degree of success with a community the UM had targeted since 1945, but not nearly enough. And while Mosley appealed against the result, it was upheld. The election, however, had some surprising consequences.

It seems that, despite Mosley's abject defeat, the enthusiasm generated by the UM electoral campaign energised the movement. According to John Charnley, it 'reached its greatest vigour and

---

[209] See George Gale, 'Election contrast in Portobello Road', *Daily Express*, 5 August 1959.
[210] *Daily Telegraph*, 26 October 1959, press clipping, 'Internees will stay in prison' (Sir Oswald Mosley papers, BU, CRL: OMD/7/1/25).
[211] Grundy, *Memoir of a Fascist Childhood*, pp. 176–77.
[212] Ibid., pp. 189–90.
[213] Ibid., p. 183.
[214] Keith Kyle, 'North Kensington', in D. E. Butler and Richard Rose, *The British General Election of 1959* (Basingstoke: Macmillan, 1999), pp. 174–75.
[215] Ibid., p. 184.

strength in the early sixties;[216] though a rather more objective source saw vigour expressed chiefly in the violent behaviour of 'young racists'.[217] In November 1960, *Action* claimed that the denial of public halls to Mosley had merely led to a great increase in public meetings, and produced a map of England and Wales illustrating the apparent distribution of UM branches: 6 in Wales and 117 in England, concentrated in the greater London area and the midlands,[218] though whether these were thriving centres of UM activity may well be doubted. In September 1962, Mosley claimed that he would soon be holding meetings all over London 'then stretch them out all over the country'.[219] And the impression of a thriving national organisation readying itself for the national crisis that would pave Mosley's path to power was continued in his last major defence of his politics, past and present, *Mosley – Right or Wrong?* (1961). Nor did the fact of African decolonisation undermine Mosley's faith in the African dimension to his Europe-a-Nation policy. That was still feasible so long as Rhodesia and South Africa were white-controlled.[220]

At the same time, UM extended its pro-Irish activities, which included identifying closely with the IRA. In June 1960, Eamonn Bourke condemned Brendan Behan's scurrilous play *The Hostage*, which ridiculed the IRA, denigrating unfairly a movement to which he once owed allegiance as the price of establishment acceptance.[221] This was followed by a critique of movies such as *Odd Man Out*, *Gentle Gunman*, *Beloved Enemy*, *Shake Hands with the Devil* and *A Terrible Beauty*, films which showed the IRA in an unfavourable light or in which an informer is the hero. Despite its lack of substantive political success, Bourke argued, the IRA was a threat because it had a revolutionary focus and was the 'type of organisation anyone in revolt against the contemporary ethos turns to at least with respect, not necessarily agreement', while 'a warm

---

[216] Charnley, *Blackshirts and Roses*, p. 218.
[217] George Thayer, *The British Political Fringe: A Profile* (London: Anthony Blond, 1965), pp. 47–48.
[218] See 'Our national movement grows', *Action* (November 1960).
[219] *Belfast News-Letter*, 19 September 1962, press clipping (Sir Oswald Mosley papers, BU, CRL: OMN/B/9/1/8).
[220] See 'Mosley speaks on Rhodesia', *The National European* (December 1965).
[221] Eamonn Bourke, 'The establishment ticket', *Action* (June 1960).

current of public sympathy keeps it alive': the IRA had been a thorn in the hand of the establishment since Easter 1916 – with the same stubborn refusal to accept the status quo after over 40 years of uncompromising opposition.[222]

Without explicitly saying so, an analogy between the UM and the IRA was drawn on the basis of their anti-establishment identities. Pro-republicanism continued to provide a lens through which to express anti-establishment opinions on other issues. Thus the Katanga tragedy of 1961, in which a number of Irish soldiers died fighting under United Nation Organization direction in its effort to force the Katanga region under the control of the Congo, allowed *Action* to claim that 'these Irish troops were betrayed ... by the same rotten system of tyranny and finance against which other Irishmen gave their lives in 1916'.[223] Nevertheless, despite appearances some things had changed.

By the early 1960s, Cahir Healy was disabused of the idea that partition would be ended at Anglo-Irish governmental level, and pressed for a lesser unity in the form of trade negotiations between north and south. Lord Brookeborough, the northern Prime Minister, however, seeing no reason to entertain this proposal, was happy to leave any such negotiations to the Westminster Government.[224] The only significant complaint the regime expressed at this time was that if the Westminster Government thought it appropriate to ban fascist meetings from Trafalgar Square to prevent disorder, it should also ban the IRA-linked Sinn Fein.[225] And, like Healy, Mosley had also revised somewhat his approach to partition.

His candidature for North Kensington was the first time he had tested his electoral support since 1931, and the first occasion at which he had tested the electoral value of UM's conciliation of the immigrant Irish and Catholic community in an area where that community was well established. The meagre results

[222] Eamonn Bourke, 'The establishment ticket (2)', *Action* (July 1960).
[223] 'U.N.O. unmasked', 'Will these war criminals be tried for Katanga?' *Action*, 1 October 1961.
[224] 'North will not negotiate', *Irish Times*, 18 May 1960.
[225] 'No move to ban Sinn Fein London rally', *Belfast News-Letter*, 18 September 1962.

demonstrated that its support had been greatly overestimated, as had anti-partitionism. Addressing the issue in *Mosley − Right or Wrong?*, Mosley reiterated his belief in the union of Europe as a context in which the Irish border would disappear, together with his anti–Black and Tan activities as a demonstration of his friendship with the Irish people. But he made no mention of Unionist 'oppression' or Northern Ireland as a 'police state' where Catholics were interned at the mere will of the Stormont regime. Indeed, he stated that 'as a loyal Briton I fully recognize the position of the British minority in Northern Ireland'.[226] Mosley did not elaborate on what this would mean in practice, and so long as he entertained parliamentary ambitions − he would stand again unsuccessfully in the 1966 Westminster election − somewhat amended versions of *Ireland's Right to Unite* would continue to be published.[227]

His revised perspective on Northern Ireland, however, was a signal of how he would attempt to contribute to a solution to the Ulster problem from the late 1960s. As to the overall health of the UM at this time, in October 1964 Robert Row produced a depressing report on its strength throughout the country based on municipal election results: the national average was 5.5 per cent, with the highest individual percentage being 13 per cent in East London, followed by 4.8 per cent in Birmingham, 4.4 per cent in Liverpool and 3.3 per cent in Manchester.[228] As for Mosley, his rejection by the electorate in 1966 was complete and he resigned from active politics shortly after. It was a landmark in a number of ways.

For instance, the public platform that had allowed him to demonstrate his formidable oratorical skills was becoming redundant in a developing television age, a medium from which he was effectively barred. But, for our purposes, of particular significance was the complexity of the immigrant Irish community as a constituency to address on the partition issue. Just how complex Enda Delaney's study

---

[226] Mosley, *Mosley − Right or Wrong?*, p. 248.

[227] Oswald Mosley, 'Ireland's right to unite', *The National European* (July 1965); Patrick McGrath, *Union Movement Policy Document No. 2: Ireland's Right to Unite* (Harrow: A. Brown, n.d., [early to mid-1960s]), *passim*.

[228] Robert Row, 'National Support for Union Movement', 1 October 1964 (Sir Oswald Mosley papers, BU, CRL: OMD/7/1/28).

of that community in this period makes clear. He identifies several factors, but for our purposes the most significant are: expectations of a brief stay and corresponding lack of political engagement; social ambition among the aspiring Irish middle-classes for whom nationalist activity was deemed both socially counter-productive and the preserve of a lumpenproletariat from whom it was desirable to keep a social distance; and simple lack of concern about partition together with a developing commitment to the Labour Party.[229]

These were also crucial factors in the progressive disintegration of the distinctive Catholic subculture that had provided a source of social and political support for the UM since the war. As Catholics exploited new opportunities and began to enter the post-war middle-class, 'the assumption that being a Roman Catholic automatically made one distinct from, and opposed to, dominant British principles and structures' lost credibility.[230] It was a process hastened by the reforms of Vatican II (1962), as the Church sought an accommodation with modernity, reflected in enthusiasm for Christian ecumenism and racial unity as opposed to 'a doctrine pregnant with anti-racial hate', something many saw represented by Mosley's meetings: his public speeches in 1962 were occasions for disorder as a range of groups mobilised vigorous opposition.[231] Moreover, as evidenced by the *Catholic Herald*, while European unity was embraced, it was to be achieved on a Christian and moral basis quite different from that proposed by Mosley's Europe-a-Nation plan, especially in its European–African dimension.[232] Subsequent

---

[229] Delaney, *The Irish in Post-War Britain*, pp. 186–87.

[230] See the illuminating essay by Stratford Caldecott, 'The English spring of Catholicism', available online (https://theimaginativeconservative.org/2014/09/english-spring-catholicism.html). Accessed 13 April 2015.

[231] See 'Anti-fascists raid Mosley H.Q.', *Irish Times*, 5 June 1962. 'Mosley knocked down', *Irish Times*, 1 August 1962; 'Behind the street clashes – all deny responsibility', *The Times*, 3 August 1962; '48-hour ban on political marches in London', *Irish Times*, 31 August 1962; 'Police reinforcements in the east end today', *Sunday Times*, 2 September 1962; 'Mosley meeting broken up', *Irish Times*, 3 September 1962; 'Eggs rout Oswald Mosley', *New York Times*, 30 September 1963.

[232] See 'Heythorp [*location of an ecumenical conference*] or Mosley', *Catholic Herald*, 10 August 1962.

issues demonstrated how opposed to Mosley's views developing Catholic values were.[233] But especially important in registering the passing of a political era in the early 1960s was the diminishing significance of partition as a concern of the nationalist minority in Northern Ireland.

The effects of modernity, evident in the socio-economic and educational improvements wrought by the welfare state, had produced a new generation of Catholic middle-class leaders more concerned with the political and socio-economic injustices affecting the Catholic community *within* Northern Ireland than Irish unity, and using the yardstick of modern civic Britishness as the measure of Unionist failure.[234] And for the UM Cahir Healy's retirement from politics in 1965 was no less significant: 'Those of us who shared his [wartime]imprisonment ... will remember him with great admiration, an Irishman we are proud to call a true European'.[235] Earlier that year, in a debate in Queen's University Belfast, Jeffrey Hamm representing the UM, won on the motion, 'This House believes that Britain's first loyalty should be to Europe, not to the Commonwealth'. The debate, however, was apparently devoid of any significant mention of the border issue, a staple of UM propaganda since the late 1940s.[236]

Conclusion

The oft-stated conclusion to a survey of Mosley's post-war career is one of complete failure, though it was not entirely without effect. His influence on later British neo-fascist movements has been traced,[237] and although the UM greatly exaggerated its influence

---

[233] 'New look for democrat', *Catholic Herald*, 4 October 1963; also, 'Catholics and the colour bar', *Catholic Herald*, 12 February 1965.
[234] See, for example, James Loughlin, *The Ulster Question since 1945* (2nd edn, Basingstoke: Palgrave Macmillan, 2004), chap. 1. In April 1963 Mosley sold his Irish estate, saying he 'rarely had time to visit Ireland' (*Irish Times*, 22 April 1963).
[235] 'Mr Cahir Healy', *The National European* (December 1965).
[236] 'Belfast students put Europe first', *The National European* (May 1965); Hamm, *Action Replay*, pp. 199–200.
[237] Poole, 'Oswald Mosley and the Union Movement', pp. 68–79.

on the introduction of the Macmillan's Government's restrictive immigration bill in 1961,[238] it did make some contribution to the climate of opinion that compelled it. On the partition issue, however, neither influence in drawing significant support from the immigrant Irish/British Catholic community nor constitutional effect is evident.

In large part, this was due to the fact that not only was the Irish immigrant community a more complex entity than Mosley and the UM realised, and not amenable to a simple anti-partitionist appeal, but that both anti-partitionists and the UM profoundly underestimated the difficulties in the way of political progress on the issue. In this context, while Mosley could make plausible political points about British history since the Elizabethan era, his understanding of Ireland in the twentieth century – albeit abetted by favourable comments such as those provided by J. D. O'Connell in 1945 – was freeze-framed through the perspective of his anti-Black and Tan activities of the early 1920s. By the same token, the decision to mount an anti-partition campaign in the wake of a war in which the Stormont regime had loyally supported the British war effort while southern Ireland had remained neutral, was misconceived.

In doing so, nationalists were following a traditional approach to the problem: namely, directing their arguments to Westminster over the head of the Unionist community in Northern Ireland, at a time when all Westminster parties supported the Stormont regime on the border question. In retirement, Healy admitted that nationalist anti-partition campaigns made no special effort to attract Protestant support: 'I don't think it would have been worth our while to try to attract Protestants, though we always went to trouble to show we were unsectarian'.[239] It was an approach reinforced by Healy's relationship with Mosley; and yet despite Healy's readiness to assist the UM, his opinion of the Europe-a-Nation context in which Mosley saw Irish unity remains unclear, especially with reference

---

[238] See 'Mr Butler's bill pleases the fascists', *Tribune*, 10 November 1961; for instance, 'Four points justify Union Movement policy', *The National European* (October 1965).
[239] Healy, quoted in Dennis Kennedy, 'NORTHERN LINE-UP-3: Cahir Healy', *Irish Times*, 31 October 1968.

to his own traditional anti-partitionist efforts. Nor for that matter did Mosley press for a unified approach. Cultivating the immigrant Irish and Catholic community in Britain did not appear to require it, only repetition of his past Anglo-Irish record, general statements of commitment, and exposure of Stormont's misdeeds.

The failure of his candidature for North Kensington in 1959, however, demonstrated just how difficult engaging the immigrant Irish community to political effect was. His revised approach to the Ulster problem in the 1960s was, at least, a more realistic one, especially when he sought to contribute to the problem's resolution following the outbreak of civil conflict in 1969.

III

Neo-Fascism and
the Northern Ireland Conflict

5

Northern Ireland

The Mosley and Powell Perspectives

The mid-to-late 1960s registered a number of significant political developments. Oswald Mosley officially retired from politics in favour of developing a role as an influential commentator on national affairs, though his Union Movement (UM) would continue to exist in a diminished form for a number of years, functioning chiefly to propagate Mosley's views through the movement print *Action*; the development of the Ulster troubles naturally attracted his attention. But, just as Mosley was attempting to carve out his new public role, Enoch Powell emerged dramatically in 1968 as a leading figure on the Right with his apocalyptic 'rivers of blood' speech on the national dangers of 'coloured' immigration. As such, he could be seen as usurping Mosley's role in this respect, a figure more relevant to a new era of extreme-Right politics. And, for our purposes, Powell would engage more personally with the Ulster problem than Mosley. This chapter assesses the degree of similarity and difference in their approaches to the subject.

Mosley and Powell: Political Departures

Oswald Mosley's retirement from active politics had the effect of modifying his public perception. It occurred in the context of a largely favourable reception for his autobiography, *My Life*,[1] in both Ireland and Britain, with several leading public figures testifying to his abilities.[2] In this context Mosley sought to reshape his past

[1] Oswald Mosley, *My Life* (London: Nelson, 1968).
[2] Quotations from Malcolm Muggeridge, A. J. P. Taylor, Lord Boothby, R. H. S. Crossman on dust jacket of Mosley, *My Life*; Mosley to Cahir

so as better to exploit this situation. His close associate at this time, Cecil King – whom the security services recorded as having attended one of Mosley's meetings advocating peace with Nazi Germany during the phoney war period of 1940[3] – remarked: 'He is at pains now in interviews to convince everybody that he was never anti-Jewish, never pro-German, and never favoured violence at his meetings. Surely he protests too much.'[4] Mosley had already put in a robust, if not always accurate, defence of his political career during the London Weekend Television broadcast *The Frost Programme*, hosted by David Frost, in November 1967,[5] while at the same time proposed legal action against the BBC for denying him the opportunity to respond to his critics succeeded in its ban on Mosley, in place since 1936, being removed in 1968.[6] Thereafter Mosley had recurrent, if not uncritical, television coverage.[7] These were welcome developments facilitating Mosley's political repositioning, though he never dismissed entirely the prospect of a great national crisis that would result in a call for his services to meet it. He was convinced that British society was in a state of decay, that an economic breakdown was inevitable and that everyone should be ready to deal with that situation.[8] That 1968 was a year of European

Healy, 29 November 1968 (Cahir Healy papers, PRONI: D2991/B/784/3); Michael Foot in Robert Skidelsky, *Oswald Mosley* (London: Macmillan, 1981), pp. 517–18.

[3] Metropolitan Police, Report on Fascist activities, 5 March 1940 (Special Branch files, www.nationalarchives.gov.uk).

[4] Diary entry, 14 November 1968 in Cecil King, *Cecil King Diary, 1965–1970* (London: Jonathan Cape, 1972), p. 217.

[5] *The Frost Programme*, London Weekend Television, broadcast 15 November 1967.

[6] Skidelsky, *Mosley*, pp. 17–18.

[7] See Janet Dack, 'Cultural regeneration: Mosley and the Union Movement', in Nigel Copsey and John E. Richardson (eds), *Cultures of Post-War British Fascism* (London: Routledge, 2015), pp. 22–24.

[8] Diary entries, 14 November 1968; 26 March, 24 April, 9 November 1969, in King, *Cecil King Diary, 1965–1970*, pp. 217, 246–47, 254, 292. In early 1972, Mosley thought that Heath's Government was practically dead and that a Wilson premiership could only be an interim affair. Diary entries, 7 March, 11 November 1972 in Cecil King, *Cecil King Diary, 1970–1974* (London: Jonathan Cape, 1975), pp. 183, 239.

civic upheaval, especially in Paris where the Mosleys lived, could only have stimulated that expectation. Cecil King, no less than Mosley, was convinced of an impending national disaster facing Britain; and also had a similar autocratic disposition, which impelled him in May 1968 to mount a cack-handed attempt to topple the Wilson Government promoted via the pages of the *Daily Mirror*. The consequence was the collapse of his reputation as the most influential newspaper man in the country and losing his positions as controller of the *Daily Mirror* and chairman of the International Publishing Company.[9] Mosley, however, clearly did not regard King's political efforts as directed against his own ambitions. It was Powell who was seen to threaten his political revival.

At a time when the days of oratory as a means of garnering mass support seemed to be over, as Mosley's own experience in the early 1960s appeared to demonstrate, the mass support for Powell's controversial 'rivers of blood' speech in April 1968 in Birmingham – forecasting race war in Britain if 'coloured' immigration was not reversed – could not but be dismaying. If a great national crisis did emerge, there appeared every likelihood that Powell would displace him as national deliverer. Certainly, Powell saw himself in just such a role. The contrast between Powell's isolation from the political mainstream and his popular appeal, argues Robert Shepherd, gave the impression that, like de Gaulle, he was waiting for the call to lead the nation,[10] and he was pleased when an NOP poll found that he was the politician who best understood Britain's problems and those of ordinary people.[11] To the end of his life, Mosley would regard Powell with 'boundless contempt', describing him variously as 'hysterical', 'a Victorian figure' or 'a middle-class Alf Garnett', someone with whom he claimed to have nothing in common: 'Powell is a man of the extreme right and I am a man of the centre'.[12]

[9] See Dominic Sandbrook, *White Heat: A History of Britain in the Swinging Sixties* (London: Abacus, 2006), pp. 650–57.

[10] Robert Shepherd, *Enoch Powell: A Biography* (London: Pimlico, 1997), p. 407.

[11] 'Powell seen as most perceptive', *Irish Times*, 4 December 1972.

[12] Sam White, 'A fascist to the last', *Spectator*, 13 December 1980.

The UM, reasonably enough, denounced Powell as an opportunist, as Mosley had been making similar arguments to his on immigration for the previous ten years,[13] but with only public condemnation as his reward. It was small consolation to Mosley and the UM that the Smithfield porter Dan Harmston, a leading organiser for meetings in support of Enoch Powell, could declare that he was also 'proud to be a friend and colleague of Sir Oswald Mosley'.[14] Yet, despite his antagonism to Powell, Mosley could hardly ignore him. Cecil King recorded that Mosley 'had been seeing something of Enoch Powell',[15] though it is doubtful whether Mosley actually met Powell. Concerned to assert his own greater political credibility, Mosley was moved to critique Powell's solution to the immigration problem with his own, one that was more generous than Powell's and which, privately at least, advanced an additional option – 'the development of the two communities' within Britain. 'Men and women could work together and often play together but are content and proud to live in their own communities for purposes of housing, education and most amenities of social life.' Mosley saw the development of such ideas among 'black intellectuals' in the USA and in Britain, evidenced in the 'advanced communities of the Sikh'. To realise this option Mosley suggested a massive housing scheme 'to rebuild the 1,000,000 homes in Britain now unfit for human habitation', to be tackled by the State 'before there can be any question of it reverting to private enterprise which alone can never solve the half-century old arrears of this problem'.[16] The UM, in making the case for Mosley's more civilised approach to the immigration issue – something the Political Soldier faction of the National Front would also attempt in the 1980s – attacked Powell's 'offensive' references to 'coloured' immigrants,[17] while Mosley would continue to condemn

[13] Paul Foot, *The Rise of Enoch Powell* (Harmondsworth: Penguin, 1969), p. 126.

[14] '"We don't want to integrate" marchers say', *Irish Times*, 25 August 1972.

[15] Diary entry, 14 November 1968 in King, *Diary, 1965–1970*, p. 217.

[16] Mosley to Major Albery, draft (Jeffrey Hamm papers, BU, CRL: MS124/1/1/50).

[17] On UM's criticism of Powell's 'offensive' references to 'coloured' immigrants, see Camilla Schofield, *Enoch Powell and the Making of Postcolonial Britain* (Cambridge: Cambridge University Press, 2015), p. 239.

his arguments throughout the 1970s.[18] And yet, for all Mosley's attempts to create distance between himself and Powell, there were distinct similarities between them, as Mosley's correspondents could recognise.[19]

Both were individuals with a supreme faith in the rightness of their own policies and decisions and with little tolerance for dissenting opinions. Both, if in rather different ways, were impressive orators and had experience of Government. Again, just as Mosley's condemnation of Black and Tan activities in Ireland in the early 1920s derived less from a sympathy with Irish nationalism than from a moral sense of how their activities besmirched Britain's reputation, so too, in a similar way, Powell's condemnation of the killing of eleven indigenous Kenyans on 3 March 1959 at Hola Camp during the Mau-Mau uprising was based less on sympathy for the individuals concerned than a need to redeem the moral reputation of Britain,[20] as indeed, as we have seen, it also was for Mosley. Furthermore, their common opposition to non-white immigration went together with support for white Rhodesia —Powell opposed the Labour Government's economic blockade of Rhodesia following Ian Smith's unilateral declaration of independence in 1965 and also British interference in domestic Rhodesian politics:[21] 'The independence of Rhodesia was something stronger than law'.[22] Powell's ethnocentric disposition was also evidenced in an essay, 'Population figures in the United Kingdom', he contributed to the pro-racist journal, *Mankind Quarterly*, in 1970, a journal whose editor, Professor R. Gyre, subscribed to Nazi race ideology and supported the National Front. Focused on Birmingham, Powell's article, which argued that official figures greatly underestimated the estimated growth of the 'coloured' population, which would be over 20 per cent of the British

---

[18] See Oswald Mosley, *Last Words: Broadsheets, 1970–1980* (London: Black House Publishing, 2012), pp. 27, 32, 39, 67–68, 75, 85, 122–24, 149.
[19] Major Edward Albery to Sir Oswald Mosley, 19 November 1968 (Jeffrey Hamm papers, BU, CRL: MS124/1/1/49).
[20] On the Hola camp atrocity, see Schofield, *Enoch Powell*, pp. 122–27.
[21] Douglas Schoen, *Enoch Powell and the Powellites* (London: Macmillan, 1977), pp. 18–20.
[22] 'Powell says independence for Rhodesia is already fact', *Irish Times*, 7 December 1968.

population by 1979,[23] lent an academic veneer to the populist and emotive warnings of British race vulnerability conveyed in his 'rivers of blood' speech in 1968.[24] If Powell was awaiting the nation's call, his position was only slightly more realistic than Mosley's. And, just as Mosley envisaged the success of his project in terms of a form of national rebirth, so too was this the case for Powell, though the form of which, and the route to it, being different in each case – Europe-a-Nation for Mosley and, as we shall see, triumph over the State's internal and external enemies for Powell.

Similarities between Powell and Mosley can even be found in their approach to British history. Powell found a historical analogy to his own political career in that of Joseph Chamberlain, who forfeited his chance of attaining the Liberal Party leadership when he broke with William Gladstone over Home Rule for Ireland in 1886.[25] Mosley was an admirer of Gladstone, but also of Chamberlain, if in a different way. Chamberlain's ideas on the British Empire and Tariff Reform were an important influence on his own economic thinking.[26] Similarities between both men, moreover, were reflected in how the media dealt with them. A BBC *Panorama* interview with Mosley in 1968, for example, provided the template for the programme's later interview with Powell.[27] And when Powell protested against the residency rights of Irish citizens in Britain, the Labour minister, Tony Benn, saw it as preparing the ground for the exploitation of antisemitism 'as Mosley exploited it before'.[28] Again, there is a similarity between the consequences of their politics for both men.

Just as Mosley suffered social and political ostracism for his political beliefs, so too did Powell – sacked from the shadow cabinet

---

[23] Enoch Powell, 'Population figures in the United Kingdom', *Mankind Quarterly*, vol. 40 (October/December 1970), pp. 87–95.

[24] Michael Billig, *Psychology, Racism and Fascism* (London: Searchlight, 1979), pp. 12–15.

[25] Shepherd, *Enoch Powell*, pp. 436–37.

[26] Bernard Semmel, *Imperialism and Social Reform: English Social-Imperial Thought, 1895–1914* (London: George Allen & Unwin, 1960), pp. 349–57.

[27] See Stuart Hood, 'Up for judgment', *Spectator*, 6 December 1968, pp. 797–98.

[28] Schofield, *Powell*, pp. 284–87.

and ostracised by former colleagues and respectable opinion, but unlike Mosley who was long inured to such ostracism, Powell found it a difficult experience:[29] his life and that of his family was 'totally transformed'; public recognition incurred either adulation or hatred, attacks on his constituency home, and public engagements sometimes attended by rowdy or violent demonstrations.[30]

Throughout it all, like Mosley, Powell refused to accept any responsibility for a situation he had done so much to create: 'Apology was simply unnecessary.'[31] It was a position, as Tom Bower argues, that suggested 'naivete, dishonesty or cowardice', and of these the second was probably most accurate.[32] Apology may have been unnecessary, but Powell was certainly sensitive to the political consequences of his ethnocentrism. Notwithstanding his *Mankind Quarterly* article any association made between his views on race and Nazi or fascist ideas was likely to incur a libel writ, as the *Sunday Times* found in 1969.[33] Certainly, so long as Powell had political ambitions to fulfil racism would be denied: 'The basis of my conviction ... is not racial because I can never discover what "race" means and I have never arranged my fellow men according to their origins.'[34] But in 1995, when political ambition was largely a thing of the past, he felt little compunction in admitting the racist motivation of his 'rivers of blood' speech: 'What's wrong with racism? Racism is the basis of a nationality ... nations are, upon the whole, united by identity with one another, the self-identification of our citizens, and that's normally due to similarities which are regarded as racial differences.'[35] A similar line of thinking can be identified in Powell's attitude to Jews.

[29] Shepherd, *Enoch Powell*, pp. 358–65.
[30] Ibid., pp. 357–58.
[31] Ibid., p. 359.
[32] Tom Bower, 'Immigration', in Lord Howard of Rising (ed.), *Enoch at 100* (London: Biteback, 2012), p. 163.
[33] See 'Powell receives libel apology', *Irish Times*, 22 April 1970.
[34] Powell cited in Shepherd, *Enoch Powell*, pp. 364–65. Powell, however, would contradict this position in 1981 in the context of the first Nationality Bill since 1948, when he protested against the move to assign British nationality to children born in Britain of foreign parents (Schofield, *Powell*, pp. 180–81).
[35] Quoted Shepherd, *Enoch Powell*, p. 365.

Powell was an annual guest and speaker for years at annual dinners hosted by the Jewish community of his Wolverhampton constituency in the 1950s. As such he celebrated the successful dual loyalty of Jews both to Britain and their ancestral middle-east homeland.[36] Paul Foot, however, recounts an occasion in November 1960 when Powell and John Baird, a campaigner for racial equality and tolerance, spoke at a dinner to Jewish ex-servicemen. But while Baird drew parallels between the discrimination both the immigrant Irish and the Jewish community had suffered in the past and the contemporary discrimination suffered by the non-white population, Powell ignored this experience and settled merely for stating that 'Jews are leaders in all fields of human endeavour, and as such I salute them.'[37] Whether his approach to the Jewish community on this occasion implied a concealed hostility, as Foot appears to suggest, might be doubted. In 1994, however, Powell published a study of the St Matthew's Gospel in which he argued, against the verdict of biblical scholarship, that Jesus did not die on the cross but was stoned to death by the Jewish authorities for blasphemy: 'Pilate and the Romans must be exonerated and the blood guilt accepted by the Jewish people.' His response to the accusation that he was reviving the slur that the Jews murdered Christ was to state: 'Well, I can't help it. What I have read, I have read.'[38]

Accordingly, on both race and antisemitism, it can be argued that Powell's thinking was closer to Mosley's than he was willing to admit. But while similarities can be identified, there were also significant differences, in addition to social background and their very different war experiences. They differed on European unity, which Mosley enthused about, and Powell radically opposed; and also on Powell's commitment to free market economics, which was diametrically opposed to Mosley's corporatism. But, most importantly, they differed fundamentally in their diagnoses of the 'crisis' facing Britain in the late 1960s and how it would be best solved.

Mosley's ambition for Britain's role in the creation of Europe-a-Nation with a dependent white African colonial empire in peaceful

---

[36] Schofield, *Powell*, pp. 180–81.
[37] Foot, *Enoch Powell*, p. 58.
[38] Quoted in Shepherd, *Enoch Powell*, p. 500.

coexistence with independent black African states, may have been in part anachronistic in an era of decolonisation, in part hopelessly idealistic in its European aspects. But it was the product of a more flexible mindset than Powell's, and open to adaptation. As we have seen, the development of the EEC was along quite different lines from those proposed by Mosley for Europe-a-Nation in the post-war period, but he nevertheless applauded British entry to it.[39] Moreover, his analysis of the impending disaster facing Britain, even if wrong, was grounded in a sustained analysis of economic factors and conditions.[40] Powell, on the other hand, noted for the 'remorseless logic' of his thinking, quickly developed an increasingly paranoid conspiracy theory of the problems facing the British State and people at odds with their complexity.

Far from economic improvement providing the only stimulus to 'coloured' immigration, Powell argued in 1969–70 that immigration was part of a wider revolutionary agenda by Britain's hard left and anarchists to destabilise society – 'There are some whose intention is to destroy society as we know it, and "race" or "colour" is one of the crowbars they intend to use for the work of demolition'[41] – to the degree that they constituted a 'hidden enemy within' that was putting Britain in 'such peril now as it had been before the two world wars'.[42] For Powell, the nature of the crisis Britain faced was simple: 'the overwhelming majority of people on the one side and a tiny minority', which had a near monopoly of the channels of communication and seemed determined to ignore the national peril.[43] The analytical merits of Powell's assessment of Britain's national 'peril' was in inverse proportion to the popular support he acquired in a period of expanding non-white immigration. A

[39] John S. Cavan, Record of Meeting with Mosley in response to Peter Jenkins's *Guardian* claim that Mosley was politically dead, late July 1971 (Sir Oswald Mosley papers, BU, CRL: OMD/1/2/2/128-9).

[40] See, for instance, 'The coming crisis: markets, exchanges and taxation', in Oswald Mosley, *Policy and Debate* (Washbourne: Euphorion Books, 1954), pp. 22–36.

[41] Quoted in Simon Heffer, *Like the Roman: The Life of Enoch Powell* (London: Weidenfeld & Nicolson, 1998), p. 523.

[42] Ibid., p. 559.

[43] Brian Lee, 'Enoch Powell's language', *New Society*, 23 January 1969.

similar inverse relationship existed between the quality of Powell's analysis of the Ulster problem and the complexity of the issue. In the latter respect, Mosley's analysis demonstrated greater realism but lacked the influence that Powell's political engagement in Ulster politics allowed.

Mosley and the Ulster Crisis: Analysis and Prescription

Mosley's position on Northern Ireland, as we have seen, registered a departure in the early 1960s, from the simple pro-nationalist position on Irish unity that he had held for decades, to one closer to equidistance between the two communities in the region, though it is important to note that 'Europe-a-Nation' still retained the idea of Irish unity.[44] However, the specific nature of a settlement had still to be developed. That deficiency would largely be remedied by Professor Hugh Dominic Purcell, formerly an English lecturer at the Queen's University Belfast, author of a book on the ethnic politics of Cyprus,[45] and who recommended a solution on the lines of ethnic repartition. The Purcell–Mosley connection was effected by Cecil King, all three united in the belief that in Ireland as in Britain time was 'running out'.[46] This is an important background to keep in mind when assessing Mosley's method for effecting Purcell's proposals.

To a limited extent, there was a consensus of sorts between Mosley's *followers*, the Unionists and Powell about the source of the outbreak of conflict in 1969. As would Powell and the Ulster Unionists, the Mosleyite print *Action* had little hesitation in identifying the 'old Red game in a new guise' and of a piece with its intrigues across Europe at the time – though Mosley's published views on Ulster and politics in general in *Last Words* makes no mention of it. Again, like Powell, as we shall see, *Action* saw the Ulster

---

[44] See M. J. McUre to Mosley, [April–May] 1965; Mosley to McUre, 7 May 1965 (Jeffrey Hamm papers, BU, CRL: MS124/1/14/13, 14).

[45] H. D. Purcell, *Cyprus* (New York: Praeger, 1969).

[46] Diary entries, 16, 18 September 1971 in King, *Diary, 1970–1975*, pp. 139–40; [Professor Purcell] to 'Dear Tom [Mosley]', 18 September 1971 (Sir Oswald Mosley papers, BU, CRL: OMN/B/2/4/22).

troubles as likely to be extended to Britain, a society corrupted by 'permissiveness' and in need of 'public order and the eradication of evils which threaten our people'.[47] Unlike Powell and the Unionists, however, it recognised the legitimacy of nationalist grievances, the role of successive British Governments in perpetuating these, and calling for Irish reunification within Europe-a-Nation.[48] Not all republicans were approved of, however: Bernadette Devlin was regarded as a Marxist who would 'land her fellow Catholics into the mire of communism and then see the destruction of Irish religion and pride ... beware of trespassers!'[49] But far from Devlin's selection to stand for Mid-Ulster at a Westminster by-election in June 1969 – occasioned by the death of the sitting MP – being a product of Marxist conspiracy, it was rather the outcome of a confused, ad hoc situation facilitated by her non-party status.[50]

To remedy the situation, now the UM argued for a combination of strong law-and-order policies together with religious leaders being compelled to 'keep their flock in order' and the appointment of a British Minister charged with the task of bringing about Irish unity, thus facilitating 'a united Ireland within a greater union' of Europe-A-Nation.[51] More exactly, as Hamm informed a correspondent, the UM's former policy of simple unity was abandoned in recognition of strong Unionist opposition and in favour of 'a compromise on the lines of a referendum, a further partition of the Six Counties and regional Governments in Dublin and Belfast, within a united Europe'.[52]

These proposals were a generalised description of ideas Mosley had taken from Purcell, who had made him familiar with the

---

[47] 'It's time for a big clean-up', *Action*, 15 January 1970.

[48] 'Communists exploiting the new Ulster troubles', *Action*, 1 September 1969. 'The iniquity of gerrymandering', *Action*, 15 September 1969, *Action*, 1 April 1969; McGrath, *Union Movement Policy Document No.2.*

[49] 'An asp in the Irish bosom', *Action*, 15 November 1970.

[50] For Devlin's account, see Bernadette Devlin, *The Price of My Soul* (London: Panther, 1969), chaps 11–12.

[51] 'The trouble in Ireland', *Action*, 15 July 1970; 'Ireland and Europe', *Action*, 1 April 1971.

[52] Jeffrey Hamm to A. J. Chapman, 1 June 1972 (Jeffrey Hamm papers, BU, CRL: MS124/1/3/31).

original Boundary Commission Report of 1925, published for the first time only in 1969, and which included detailed maps of ethnic settlement in the north of Ireland.[53] It strongly informed Purcell's repartition plan – and Mosley would repeatedly reference it – which involved transferring major Catholic areas of Northern Ireland to the Irish Republic. It also had problematic aspects, especially with respect to the ethnic composition of Belfast, but it attracted Mosley's approval in the main. And the sense of national crisis that informed Mosley's mindset at this time – the prospect of civil war in Ulster spreading to the British mainland – allowed his authoritarian instinct to find expression in a preference for the plan to be 'enforced with a fairly strong hand', given the likely opposition from both north and south; though also, in the manner of authoritarian leaders of the 1930s, with a form of plebiscite thereafter in both jurisdictions on whether the solution was acceptable – 'whether the catholic area was willing to be included in the south and whether the truncated north desired to remain under Stormont or to be incorporated in the U.K.'[54] Mosley elaborated further on his ideas in his first broadsheet on Ulster, 'The Irish problem', of 8 October 1971.

The transfer of the majority Catholic areas to southern jurisdiction would mean that the remaining Catholic areas in the North

> would be an inadequate basis for effective guerrilla action, and reinforcement from the South could be checked ... by lines of wire [along the border] with intersecting block houses in a method long familiar to the British Army and now facilitated by helicopters and highly mobile ground weaponry. This would effectively close the frontier except for the main roads which can easily be controlled by check points.

Mosley conceived such measures as interim, to be pursued while the 'ultimate political settlement of a united Ireland' was achieved. But they were also directed against Enoch Powell. The latter's

---

[53] Geoffrey J. Hand, Introduction to *Report of the Irish Boundary Commission, 1925* (Shannon: Irish University Press, 1969).

[54] Mosley to Cecil King, 13 September 1971 (Sir Oswald Mosley papers, BU, CRL: OMD/1/2/2/112).

suggestion that *every* trouble spot in Northern Ireland should have a permanent army presence would merely have meant sitting targets for snipers – mobility and 'surprise in … fighting is preferable to the role of the sitting duck' – while, less persuasively, Powell's belief that motorised transport was central to IRA operations merely revealed the inadequacy of pedagogy: Powell 'could study with profit and possible sympathy the logistic capacities of the patient donkey'.[55]

Mosley's strategy for solving the Ulster problem – a combination of nationalist/republican conciliation and coercion – suffered from a number of weaknesses, not least a failure fully to take account of how northern and southern Governments would react to it, though, as we have seen, he privately expected opposition. On the other hand, his army background and Irish experiences of the post-1916 period provided timely lessons and warnings on *operational* errors British Governments had to avoid:

> A regular army will always be baffled by well trained guerrillas supported by the national or political sympathy of a courageous population for two main reasons: one, the degree of terror necessary to break the will of the civilians and induce them to betray the guerrillas cannot be applied without raising world opinion to a point that renders continuance impossible; two, the morale of a regular army is broken in the process; you cannot use decent men to torture prisoners to obtain information, bully women and children by burning their houses etc. without destroying the character and discipline of your own men. It was world opinion particularly in America which checked the Black and Tans and obliged peace in 1920.[56]

Written on St Patrick's Day 1971, Mosley's was a timely warning about military and Government excess just five months before the British authorities would proceed to make the very errors he warned against when it enacted internment against the Catholic population: internment, he pointed out shortly after its disastrous effects were

---

[55] See Mosley, 'The Irish problem', in *Last Words*, pp. 38–41.
[56] Mosley to Peregrine Worsthorne, 17 March 1971, copy (Jeffrey Hamm papers, BU, CRL: MS124/1/28/56).

being felt, 'reduces Habeas Corpus to a squalid humbug [and] ... a dozen of his [the interned] relations and friends will feel honour bound to take the place of every Irishman locked up'. On the other hand, the ending of internment and objective army deployment at the border to deter infiltration, together with the creation of a cross-community regiment for internal peace-keeping, properly managed, should create the basis for a final settlement in a European context.[57]

The problem for Mosley, however, was that both his Blackshirt history and fascist identity rendered him a pariah figure whose advice could be easily ignored.[58] And while the UM print *Action* could be relied upon to publicise Mosley's ideas, together with attacks on Powell's politics,[59] its circulation was too small to have a significant public influence. Nevertheless, the ongoing development of the Ulster troubles was closely followed. Thus, the prorogation of Stormont in March 1972, *Action* denounced as too little too late, reinforcing Mosley's argument for a final resolution of the Ulster problem in the European context,[60] a solution, it claimed – not quite accurately – now given an Irish pedigree as it was consistent with Eamon de Valera's proposal of 1957, that of a federal solution to the Irish question with the Protestant parts of the north retaining their own administration until they decided of their own free will to join an all-Ireland parliament, and with southern Ireland re-joining the Commonwealth until then.[61]

Mosley returned to the topic of the Ulster troubles in late 1972, with the same prescription for their resolution as the previous

---

[57] Mosley, 'The Irish Problem', pp. 40–41.

[58] See Mosley to Hugh Massingham, 4 February 1969, requesting space in the *Daily Telegraph* to express his views on the immigration issue; Massingham to Mosley, 12 February 1969 (Jeffrey Hamm papers, BU, CRL: MS124/1/15/39; MS124/1/95/40).

[59] 'The bees in Powell's bonnet', *Action*, 1 July 1972.

[60] 'Tory Irish "initiative" is too little and too late', *Action*, 1 April 1972.

[61] 'The real initiative', *Action*, 1 May 1972. See also 'Ulster tragedy: this way out', *Action*, 1 August 1972; Jeffrey Hamm, 'Their world and ours', *Action*, 1 August 1972. In 1957, however, de Valera's position on proposals involving Ireland re-joining the Commonwealth was simply to state that he was 'open' to their consideration, but without much optimism that they could succeed (Bowman, *De Valera and the Ulster Question, 1917–1973*, pp. 292–93).

year, but with the additional suggestion – apparently informed by his ideas on 'coloured' immigrant repatriation – that Catholics remaining in the now truncated Northern Ireland might be offered generous terms to move to the south if they so wished. He also warned against a trend in British policy of 'differential treatment of the I.R.A. and U.D.A.' and the Government foolishly declaring that it would never meet with the IRA but continue to meet 'ferocity with ferocity'. This was to get 'the worst of all worlds: no peace, scant prospect of enduring military success, some discredit of the British name if words are implemented which are inappropriate to soldier or statesmen'.[62]

The claim that Mosley had the only realistic solution to the Ulster problem that would avoid civil war[63] was apparently validated by the collapse of the power-sharing executive of 1974 under pressure from a loyalist strike organised against it, and the unacceptability of the demands of the Unionist-dominated Constitutional Convention of 1975.[64] And he could only have been confirmed in his analysis of the Ulster problem as a host of politicians and commentators – Sir Gilbert Longden (Tory), Julian Critchley (Tory), John Parker (Labour), Sir David Steel (Liberal), Jo Grimond (Liberal), Nora Beloff (*Observer*), Max Hastings (*Evening Standard*), editorials in the *Daily Telegraph* and *Daily Mail* – came to favour border revision as the only possible solution, something also pressed unsuccessfully in cabinet by Reginald Maudling as Secretary of State for Northern Ireland.[65] Mosley's promotion of the proposal, however, was acknowledged only by *Action*.[66] As the crisis deepened in the 1970s, evidenced by killings such as that of the Tory commentator Ross McWhirter,[67]

[62] Mosley, 'Notes on the situation', in Mosley, *Last Words*, pp. 62–64.
[63] 'Ulster tragedy: this way out', *Action*, 1 August 1972.
[64] 'Ulster: A new settlement now', *Action*, 1 October 1975; 'Ireland – a political solution within Europe', in Mosley, *Last Words*, pp. 108–11.
[65] James Loughlin, *The Ulster Question since 1945* (2nd edn, Basingstoke: Palgrave Macmillan, 2004), p. 77.
[66] 'Rising support for Mosley's idea', *Action*, 15 June 1974. For contemporary interest in the subject, see Liam Kennedy, *Two Ulsters: A Case for Repartition* (Belfast: Queen's University Belfast, 1986), *passim*.
[67] 'Ireland: the only road', *Action*, 15 December 1975. See also 'Letters to the editor: the Irish border', *Action*, 1 February 1976.

Mosley spent considerable time in Britain, Ireland and the USA promoting his autobiography and speaking on the subject of Robert Skidelsky's favourable biography of him to express his opposition to internment without trial, mistreatment of prisoners, supporting the eventual reunion of Ireland within the EEC and the urging of an emergency coalition Government along the line of his post-war UM ideas to meet the socio-economic and political crises Britain appeared to be facing.[68]

Mosley's last broadsheet comment on the Ulster problem came during an Action Society dinner on 19 May 1979, when he again referenced the European context as one in which not only the Ulster issue could be resolved but also such developing issues as Welsh and Scottish devolution, even though he still thought that 'to make the common market before any measure of common government was to put the cart before the horse'.[69] The accession of Margaret Thatcher to power in 1979 did not occasion any revision of his analysis of the problems facing the United Kingdom or how they should be resolved.

Mosley's position on the Northern Ireland troubles of the late twentieth century was born of personal experience and an analysis that long pre-dated them, but which they appeared to validate, and which endured as the context for their resolution changed. But he regarded Ulster fundamentally as a regional issue of a much larger project and he was not *personally* involved in Northern Ireland politics. Powell's case was very different.

[68] See, for instance, Oswald Mosley, 'The Irish problem: interim and Ultimate Solutions', Broadsheet no. 10 (8 October 1971) in Mosley, *Last Words*, pp. 39–41; 'Mosley on Ireland and U.S. Economy', *Irish Times*, 3 February 1972; Oswald Mosley, 'Ireland: A political solution within Europe', Broadsheet no. 26 (19 June 1974) in Mosley, *Last Words*, pp. 108–11; 'Mosley foresees Ireland united within the E.E.C.', *Irish Times*, 14 April 1975; 'Mosley proposes an emergency coalition', *Irish Times*, 5 August 1975; 'Mosley debates with the Irish Prime Minister', in Mosley, *Last Words*, p. 145.
[69] 'Mosley Speaks', *Last Words*, p. 158.

Enoch Powell, the Ulster Problem and Ulster Unionism

Powell's engagement with the subject of Northern Ireland and British nationality has been recently assessed by Paul Corthorn. It is a work that while not ignoring the 'romantic qualities' and the tendency to rely on 'instinct rather than reason' in Powell's thinking on British nationalism has a specific focus – 'to bring to the fore the institutional – parliamentary and legalistic – component of his thought that sat (sometimes uneasily) alongside them'.[70] Powell's approach to the Ulster problem, however, evidences a much sharper right-wing edge than this suggests.

Powell's personal engagement with the Ulster problem was, he would claim, born of a belief in 'self-identification as the touchstone of nationhood', the 'conviction which … obliged me – almost alone among English Members – to enrol in the cause of Ulster Unionism, though I had no personal connection with that province'.[71] But political marginalisation in Britain, the evident synergy between the Ulster Unionist mindset and his own – many Unionists perceived the civil rights campaign in similar terms of an extreme Marxist/IRA conspiracy to destroy 'Ulster',[72] while also sharing his sympathy for white Rhodesia – were significant factors. William Craig,[73] Ian Paisley[74] and James Molyneaux, leader of the Official Unionist Party (OUP), were all supporters of Ian Smith's apartheid regime. Indeed, Molyneux would boast that he had always voted against Rhodesian sanctions.[75] Not surprisingly, Powell's influence was strongest on Molyneaux, who by the early 1980s had also bought into Powell's conspiracy theory of a combined threat to Ulster from secret machinations between London, Dublin and Washington designed to establish Irish unity.

---

[70] Paul Corthorn, 'Enoch Powell, Ulster Unionism and the British nation', *Journal of British Studies*, vol. 51, no. 4 (2012), pp. 970–71.
[71] Quoted in Enoch Powell, *Wrestling with the Angel* (London: Sheldon Press, 1977), pp. 5–6.
[72] See Clifford Smyth, *Ulster Assailed* ([Belfast], n.p., [1970]).
[73] 'Letter from Belfast', *Irish Times*, 5 April 1966.
[74] Redhand, 'Rhodesia', 'UDI', *Protestant Telegraph*, 25 November 1967; 'Wilson and the Rhodesia Hangings', *Protestant Telegraph*, 11 May 1968.
[75] 'Blacks should go back home – Molyneaux', *Irish Times*, 16 February 1978.

Powell visited Northern Ireland shortly after his 'rivers of blood' speech on immigration in April 1968 (a survey by *Gown*, the Queen's University student magazine, found that 60 per cent of students supported his views on 'coloured' immigration: surprising given 'the traditionally more liberal attitude of the University and the fact that there is no significant immigrant problem in Northern Ireland').[76] His arrival caused concern that he might inflame an increasingly fraught situation,[77] concern which Powell's speeches following the outbreak of the troubles in August 1969 hardly assuaged. He was quick to widen the parameters of his anti-immigration theory of the threat to the United Kingdom to include Northern Ireland, and which would develop as the Ulster crisis worsened over the following twenty years.

Although it has been argued that a 'love affair' between Powell and the loyalist population had been going on 'well before civil rights took the stage',[78] it was 1968, in the context of rising nationalist sentiment in Wales and Scotland, that he first addressed the Ulster issue. Powell declared against devolution for both regions, but stated unambiguously that if it was 'the settled view' of the Welsh and Scottish people 'to be themselves a nation then that should not be resisted'. And, referencing the struggle for Irish independence in the post-1916 period, he stated that England would never again repeat such an episode as 'the long and harrowing episode of the coercion of the Irish': 'We have learnt, and learnt once for all, that enforced unity is a curse, to which almost any other consequence or condition is preferable'. Powell's general knowledge of the period, though, was somewhat patchy; he was puzzled by the 1916 Rising, believing mistakenly that the third Home Rule bill already embodied an Irish republic;[79] and while he did not include Ulster in his strictures on British policy in Ireland – 'For Ulster self-government was the outcome not of nationalism ... [Ulster] was not only not demanding autonomy of any kind but was repudiating and resisting

---

[76] 'At the heel of the hunt', *Irish Times*, 15 May 1968; 'The only voice?', *Irish Times*, 13 May 1968.

[77] 'Powell pays a quiet visit to Belfast', *Irish Times*, 11 May 1968.

[78] 'Powell goes west', *Hibernia*, 26 April 1974.

[79] Enoch Powell, 'A myth from start to finish', *Hibernia*, 15 April 1977.

it'[80] – the complexity of the issue was something he either ignored or failed to appreciate. Moreover, the requirements of his political stance on Ulster from the late 1960s necessitated some adjustment of ethnonational designation.

Thus the description of Ulster Protestant opposition to Home Rule in the history of Britain he co-authored with Angus Maude in the mid-1950s as being due to a fear of subordination 'to their Catholic *fellow-Irish*' (my italics),[81] would be a designation he would take care to avoid from 1969. But while an unyielding commitment to the integrity of the United Kingdom and Northern Ireland's place in it would be the cornerstone of Powell's engagement with the Northern Ireland problem, initially his approach might have been rather more open.

According to Cecil King, in September 1969 he enquired if an answer to the problem 'would be to detach Fermanagh, Tyrone and southern Down from Stormont and let them go ahead with an overwhelmingly Protestant three and a half counties', a proposal King rejected citing the likelihood of ethnic cleansing of Catholics from the remaining Protestant-dominated rump State, and retaliation against Protestants in the Irish Republic – as had happened with minority ethnic populations in India and Pakistan. Also, southern refusal to accept any kind of border revision would be inevitable.[82] If King's account of his discussion with Powell is correct, the supposed impracticality of repartition – Mosley's preferred solution –undoubtedly reinforced Powell's commitment to the constitutional integrity argument, something his alignment with Ulster Unionism made imperative and likewise necessitated rejecting the validity of nationalist criticisms of the Stormont regime. Since such criticisms were deemed invalid, Powell was irresistibly drawn to identify them as the product of external plotting by sinister forces, rather than having their source in previous Irish constitutional issues, or decades of sectarian rule in Northern Ireland.

---

[80] 'Powell's view of independence', *Irish Times*, 28 September 1968; Schoen, *Enoch Powell*, pp. 100–01.

[81] Angus Maude and Enoch Powell, *Biography of a Nation: A Short History of Britain* (London: Phoenix House, 1955), p. 173.

[82] Diary entry, 16 September 1969, King, *Diary, 1965–1970*, p. 275.

Thus, Powell, noting that a French and a German student had been jailed for violent behaviour in Derry in August 1969 – 'What is a Frenchman or a German doing throwing petrol-bombs at the police in the United Kingdom?' – saw what he called 'the thing' having 'a great kinship with what had been happening in the universities and cities of the United States, in Paris last year and in Berlin the year before', while 'in London too we have seen a glimpse of its face for a moment now and again'.[83] The remedy for this situation was informed by his solution to Britain's immigration problem – greater control 'over the admission, the movement, and the activities of aliens than is exercised at present', including 'a curb on the Irish in Britain',[84] the latter something he would persist in calling for as the opportunity arose[85] and as the conflict worsened. He argued in February 1970 that the 'nation is struggling as it has never struggled before for a new concept of itself, a new vision of its destiny and a new hope for its future generation. It will not be accomplished unless we of this nation learn to tell the truth about ourselves, and truth about the world in which we live'.[86] Evil influences 'can only be broken by plain truth and common sense, and the will to assert it loud and clear … Without that, there is no escape from the closing trap; no victory over those who hate and wish to destroy Britain'.[87]

By September 1971, with the violent reaction to internment developing, Powell elevated 'the men and women of Ulster' to the front line of the British crisis – 'the forward troops in an exposed position under increasingly heavy attack', made worse both by Westminster neglect and forthcoming entry to the Common Market with its central objective of the unification of the European peoples,

[83] 'Powell urges curb on Irish in Britain', *Irish Times*, 28 August 1969.
[84] Ibid.; 'Powell urges alien status for Irish', *Irish Times*, 9 February 1970.
[85] 'Powell lashes Irish status under [immigration] bill', *Irish Times*, 9 March 1971; '"As you were" for Irish in Britain', *Irish Times*, 19 March 1971. Powell had raised the issue of Irish in Britain in the House of Commons in February 1970 (*Irish Times*, 8 April 1970).
[86] See *Irish Times*, 9 February 1970.
[87] Powell at Birmingham, 13 June 1970, in Rex Collings (ed.), *Reflections of a Statesman: Writings and Speeches of Enoch Powell* (London: Bellew Publishing, 1991), p. 248; 'Civil rights a petty issue – Powell', *Irish Times*, 16 January 1971.

an element of which would be Irish unity. With the imposition of direct rule in April 1972 he urged the abandonment of attempts to find a 'solution' and called for a stern law-and-order policy instead.[88] Reflecting his increasing accommodation to Unionist attitudes, Powell saw the Common Market as little more than a 'Popish Plot',[89] and combined a denial of Catholic grievances with condemnation of all the investigations into regime misdeeds – the Cameron Report (1969), Hunt Report (1969), Scarman Report (1972)[90] – with the suggestion that Catholics fundamentally opposed to his ideas remove themselves to the Irish Republic.[91]

Powell's constitutional anxieties at this time could only have increased as a result of opinion poll findings. For unlike the high level of British popular support for his views on immigration in the late 1960s this did not translate to Northern Ireland's constitutional position, about which the British public was ambivalent. In September 1971, polling showed 32 per cent of respondents wanted Northern Ireland united with the Irish Republic with only a plurality (42 per cent) favouring the status quo of keeping the region in the UK. Respondents also considered Northern Ireland only the fourth most important national problem, 'after the cost of living, unemployment and the Common Market'.[92] After the imposition of direct rule in April 1972, NOP found the percentage of British people favouring Northern Ireland uniting with the Irish Republic rising from 32 per cent to 36 per cent, while those in favour of keeping it in the United Kingdom remained stable at 42 per cent.[93] And Powell could do little to change the Government's political direction on Ulster. He was in a minority of eight British MPs who voted against the Northern Ireland (Temporary Provisions)

[88] 'Powell calls for the re-occupation of no-go areas', *Irish Times*, 24 April 1972; 'End Northern Ireland's "colonial" status – Powell', *Irish Times*, 8 May 1972; 'Powell urges clear and united voice', *Irish Times*, 12 June 1972.
[89] See *Irish Times*, 13 September 1971.
[90] See Paul Bew and Gordon Gillespie, *Northern Ireland: A Chronology of the Troubles, 1968–1999* (1993; 2nd edn, Dublin: Gill & Macmillan, 1999), pp. 17–23.
[91] 'Powell says NI must stay in the U.K.', *Irish Times*, 19 August 1972.
[92] Schoen, *Enoch Powell*, pp. 105–07.
[93] Ibid.

Bill which authorised direct rule. In this context he was inclined to condone loyalist illegality and violence.

Affronted by the existence of 'no-go' areas in Derry and Belfast, in March 1971 Powell condemned large sections of the Catholic and nationalist community as 'enemies' of the United Kingdom. Loyalist extremists, on the other hand, were not enemies of the State, any more than common criminals were, 'even if the former also engaged in violent activities'. The army's function in Northern Ireland was to put down an avowed enemy of the nation which was attacking loyal citizens.[94] Powell would reject Government claims that such utterances bordered on 'incitement to subversion',[95] and would repeat them in September 1972 in the febrile political atmosphere following the prorogation of Stormont. If, as Powell argued, an existential threat to the United Kingdom was at hand, then the most radical measures to thwart it could be justified. And, just as he thought, approvingly, that the white regime of Ian Smith in Rhodesia would prove stronger than British laws enacting sanctions against it, so he sought to excuse the actions of loyalist paramilitaries. As Corthorn notes, insofar as he criticised loyalists, it was merely for their wanting to obey some laws and not others.[96] But their record of sectarian killings mounted steadily in 1971 and 1972, reaching a pitch in the latter year. Of 223 civilians killed, 155 were nationalists/Catholics and 68 Unionists.[97]

Powell would adopt the same attitude in justifying the loyalist strike of 1974 that brought down the power-sharing Sunningdale Agreement of that year.[98] As with white Rhodesia, this was another case of community will being stronger than law; and he was quite willing to meet and cultivate loyalist paramilitary support when he successfully contested the marginal Westminster seat of South

[94] Powell, speech 'To the South Buckinghamshire Conservative Women's annual luncheon, 19 March 1971', in Collings, *Reflections of a Statesman*, pp. 487–89; Schoen, *Enoch Powell*, p. 104.
[95] Powell, speech 'To the County Armagh Unionist Association, Loughgall, 28 July 1972', in Collings, *Reflections of a Statesman*, p. 492.
[96] Corthorn, 'Enoch Powell', p. 990.
[97] Brendan O'Duffy, 'Violence in Northern Ireland 1969–1994: Sectarian or Ethno-national', *Ethnic and Racial Studies*, vol. 18, no. 4 (October 1995), 751.
[98] Shepherd, *Enoch Powell*, p. 472.

Down in October 1974.[99] When sufficient community 'will' was absent, Powell could be disapproving. Thus, in 1977, he attacked Ian Paisley's attempt to repeat the 1974 strike as an act of 'criminal irresponsibility perpetrated against the Province by a small knot of men'.[100] But by then Powell had other reasons for attacking Paisley, just as, at the same time, he was developing increasingly Paisleyite sectarian attitudes.

Having declared himself unperturbed if the Catholic community had to leave Northern Ireland in the event of the 'total' Unionist victory – 'There is no Berlin Wall around Northern Ireland'[101] – as the decade progressed his anti-Catholicism found specific targets for attack in 'dangerous' Catholic clergymen abetting the Provisional IRA and facilitating civil disorder;[102] while in the wider British context he warned against both Prince Charles marrying a Catholic – a Roman Catholic crown would signify the destruction of the Church of England (1978) – and, in 1980, a papal visit to Britain: 'Either the Pope's authority is not universal or the Church of England is not the Catholic and apostolic church in this land.'[103] And just as he denied racist motives when warning against the peril of 'coloured' immigration – he saw intimations of 'civil war' in the Southall riots of April 1979[104] – so Powell denied bigoted, anti-Catholic motives: these issues were not religious, but 'political, national question[s]'.[105] He would add the Archbishop of Canterbury to the list of Catholic clerics encouraging the IRA: 'They treat it as self-evident that the union is foredoomed and that its maintenance, being the cause of the warfare being waged against it, must obviously be abandoned if the warfare is to end.'[106]

[99] Ibid., p. 457; Schoen, *Enoch Powell*, p. 243.

[100] Shepherd, *Enoch Powell*, p. 472.

[101] 'One side or other must prevail', *Irish Times*, 21 October 1974.

[102] 'Powell attacks "dangerous clerics"', *Irish Times*, 5 October 1977.

[103] Martin Cowley, 'Powell opposes papal visit to Britain', *Irish Times*, 6 December 1980.

[104] 'Race riot killing Angers Southall', *Irish Times*, 25 April 1979.

[105] 'Prince Charles must not marry a Catholic – Powell', *Irish Times*, 9 December 1978; also *Irish Times*, 11 December 1978.

[106] 'IRA aided by cardinals, says Enoch Powell', *Irish Times*, 27 September 1979.

Powell would look back on the civil rights phase of the Ulster problem (1968–72) and find – as with Nesta Webster, the conspiracy theory queen of the 1920s – his initial assessment of destructive agitations across the western world, apparently unrelated, but in reality coming together to form a united sinister force, confirmed. To avert its success he argued, echoing his apocalyptic warnings of the early 1970s, there had to be 'a general conviction that there is going to be one society and one particular form of society in Northern Ireland, that is to say one state, one particular form of state and no other'.[107] Nevertheless, despite his warnings, the later 1970s would see the threats to Ulster multiply.

Already, the Birmingham bombs of 1974 had provoked security legislation which effectively quarantined Northern Ireland from the rest of the British State, a development Powell, along with many Unionists, saw as something that would be regarded by the IRA as a victory.[108] In 1976, the EEC prepared to implement rules allowing free entry across the community for migrant workers, leading Powell to envisage his long forecast race war in Britain taking place together with 'havoc' in Ulster from a flood of southern migrants.[109] The culmination would be the destruction of the 'British nation' through 'decomposition' from foreign 'implants'.[110] When Margaret Thatcher came to power in 1979 and failed to deliver on a manifesto promise to restore to Northern Ireland one or more elected regional councils in the absence of devolution, Powell saw reason to extend his conspiracy theory of the Ulster problem from the Northern Ireland Office and the Foreign and Home Offices to include the USA, with whose president, Ronald Reagan, Thatcher had become extremely close. In return for unification, Dublin would renounce its neutrality and join the North Atlantic Treaty Organization

[107] Powell, 'The role of the individual', speech at the Police Federation Seminar, Cambridge, April 1976 in Collings, *Reflections of a Statesman*, pp. 566–67.
[108] See *Irish Times*, 29 November 1974. Powell wanted identity cards for people entering Northern Ireland from the south (*Irish Times*, 9 December 1974); *Irish Times*, 10 January 1975.
[109] 'Powell on dangers to the North of free entry', *Irish Times*, 5 April 1976.
[110] For Powell's warnings on these topics, see *Irish Times*, 7 January, 1, 5, 10 April 1976; 13 September 1977.

(NATO), the result of which would be 'to finally secure the USA's eastern approaches'.[111]

It was indicative of Powell's paranoid mindset at the end of the 1970s that he could claim Humphrey Atkins's devolution initiative, coming a few months after the Mountbatten killings – Powell suggested USA involvement in the murders of both Airey Neave and Lord Mountbatten[112] – was evidence of progress by stealth towards a united Ireland, a product of a secret agreement at the Anglo-Irish summit of 1979.[113] Intellectually arrogant, Powell was immune to counter-argument, dismissing anyone who disagreed with him as disloyal, a traitor to the national interest.[114] Ironically, his certitude about the correctness of his own attitudes would contribute to a division in Unionist ranks at the very time he argued the constitutional threat was greatest and when unity was needed as never before.

Powell and Unionist Divisions

The period from the destruction of the power-sharing executive in May 1974 and the holding of the elections for the Constitutional Convention in May 1975 saw profound differences emerge between Powell and other leaders in the loyalist coalition. While they wanted a strong regional parliament for Northern Ireland regardless of what happened in other parts of the British State, Powell would accept a regional parliament only in the context of such a scheme for the State as a whole.[115] At the same time, his insistence that Ulster Unionists must be unconditionally loyal to 'the Crown in Parliament' was met with severe criticism from Paisley and William Craig's Vanguard.[116]

---

[111] Shepherd, *Enoch Powell*, pp. 479–80.

[112] Ed Moloney, 'Powell Links CIA to Murder of Mountbatten', *Irish Times*, 10 January 1984; Shepherd, *Enoch Powell*, p. 480.

[113] Shepherd, *Enoch Powell*, p. 481.

[114] Ibid., p. 478.

[115] 'Powell's United Kingdom dismays United Unionists', *Irish Times*, 22 April 1975.

[116] 'Loyalist attack on Powell', *Irish Times*, 7 July 1975. Powell was supported by the Unionist MP Jim Kilfedder, who warned that some Unionist were moving towards independence (*Irish Times*, 8 July 1975). But Powell moved

This situation took another turn when William Craig proposed *voluntary* coalition with the SDLP in 1975 and was denounced by other Unionist and loyalist leaders. On this occasion, Powell, at one with Craig's political critics and the paramilitary UVF, was seen as instrumental in swaying many Official Unionist waverers to come down against the proposal in opposition to Craig and the UDA.[117] In Powell's view, power-sharing 'would be the tocsin for a civil war which the U.K. would have instituted on its own soil'.[118]

The 1975 referendum campaign on British membership of the EEC coincided with the start of a turbulent phase in Unionist politics, in which Powell's opposition to devolution for Northern Ireland was a prominent feature, coinciding with the gradual diminishing of Labour's electoral majority at Westminster, and thus allowing him to achieve a significant advance for his integration project when he used his parliamentary influence to obtain an increase in Northern Ireland seats at Westminster from 12 to 17,[119] an exception to Powell's otherwise paranoid conviction of British betrayal of Ulster. His attitude to Margaret Thatcher was significantly revised when she successfully led the campaign to reverse the Argentinian invasion of the Falkland Islands, but his suspicions about US manoeuvring to effect Irish unity remained, to be consolidated by Thatcher's apparent betrayal of Ulster interests in the Anglo-Irish Agreement of 1985.[120]

Clearly influenced by Thatcher's successful defence of the British community in the Falkland Islands, Powell had reassured Jim Molyneaux and the OUP that the discussions between Thatcher and the Irish Taoiseach, Garret FitzGerald, which preceded the Agreement, would come to nothing. The episode dramatically illustrated the limitations of Powell's utility for Ulster Unionism.

---

on to condemn the Constitutional Convention itself as an institution which could 'lead to the destruction of the Union with the United Kingdom': 'Nationalism warning by Powell', *Irish Times*, 28 July 1975.

[117] See *Irish Times*, 11 September 1975.
[118] *Irish Times*, 7 January 1976.
[119] Shepherd, *Enoch Powell*, pp. 465–71.
[120] See Heffer, *Like the Roman*, pp. 860–62, 879, 890–99.

Conclusion

The trajectory of the political departure that Powell's 'rivers of blood' speech at Birmingham in April 1968 occasioned was shaped partly by the stimulus to his deeply held British nativist instincts that non-white immigration provoked, and the avenue, both for their expression and for continued political engagement consistent with his beliefs, that Northern Ireland provided as the Ulster crisis developed from the late 1960s. As the location of an ongoing violent crisis as opposed to the imagined and expected but never quite materialising national disaster in Britain it is not surprising that Powell should position Northern Ireland as a central site of the wider crisis, and that his prescriptions for Ulster should have wider State application.

For our purposes, apart from the insights into Powell's mindset his engagement with the Ulster crisis provides, it also illuminates the extent to which his outlook approximated that of the extreme-Right, covered in the following chapters. It was evident in an obsession with State security; the idea of an 'organic' – white – conception of the British nation; a conspiracy theory that explained the nation's problems; and a preference for severe 'law-and-order' policies to deal with them. But, for the dominant extreme-Right movement of the period, the National Front, Powell's prominence was both encouraging and concerning.

6

The National Front (I)

Negotiating the Ulster Political Terrain, 1967–1985

This chapter explores the ideological and practical interrelationships between the National Front (NF) – the dominant organisation on the British extreme-Right in the 1970s and 1980s – and Ulster loyalism as the Northern Ireland problem developed from the late 1960s to the eve of the Anglo-Irish Agreement of 1985 (AIA). The context is provided by the coincidence, from 1966–68, of the emergence of the NF from a coming together of a number of extreme-Right groups in 1967; the stimulus provided by Enoch Powell's 'rivers of blood' speech in April 1968; Northern Ireland's slide into crisis from October 1968;[1] and, initially, Oswald Mosley's retirement from active politics in 1966.

Thereafter, the extreme-Right groups that would be politically active on the Ulster problem would be mainly of a younger generation who took pains to distinguish themselves from him – regarded as merely a 'Common Fascist'[2] – and align themselves with the Ulster loyalist community, rather than the Catholic and nationalist

---

[1] There is an immense literature on the Northern Ireland conflict. For useful surveys, see the author's *The Ulster Question since 1945* (1998; 2nd edn, Basingstoke: Palgrave Macmillan, 2004); Paul Bew, Peter Gibbon and Henry Patterson, *Northern Ireland, 1921–2001: Political Power and Social Classes* (3rd edn, London: Serif, 2002); Paul Bew and Gordon Gillespie, *Northern Ireland: A Chronology of the Troubles, 1968–1999* (1993; 2nd edn, Dublin: Gill & Macmillan, 1999); Paul Arthur, *Special Relationships: Britain, Ireland and the Northern Ireland Problem* (Belfast: Blackstaff Press, 2000); David McKitterick and David McVea, *Making Sense of the Troubles* (Belfast: Blackstaff Press, 2000).
[2] George Thayer, *The British Political Fringe: A Profile* (London: Anthony Blond, 1965), pp. 14–15; Angelo De Boca and Mario Giovana, *Fascism Today: A World Survey* (London: Heinemann, 1970), p. 267.

minority. This development represented a reconnection with Sir Edward Carson's threatened rebellion against the implementation of Home Rule on Ulster in the pre-Great War period, the stimulus it provided for the emergence of British fascism with the establishment of Rotha Lintorn-Orman's British Fascists in the 1920s, and the continuation of the pro-loyalist strand with Arnold Leese's Imperial Fascist League in the 1930s. But, although Leese would live into the post-war years and his widow continue to promote his ideas, Leese's protégé, Colin Jordan, would take little notice of Northern Ireland.

A graduate of the University of Cambridge, before joining the war effort, Jordan was an English and mathematics teacher at a Coventry Secondary Modern School when he founded the White Defence League, a virulently anti-black organisation, in 1958, thereby initiating a career –initially with John Tyndall – in neo-Nazi, antisemitic politics complete with brown shirts, riding breeches, leather belts and Nazi armlets, punctuated by spells in prison for incitement to race hatred. Jordan's obsession with race, however, was pitched at such a level of generality that conflicts between different sections of the white race, as would occur in Northern Ireland, did not register on his radar, while his overt neo-Nazism and mutual antagonism with other extremists such as John Tyndall – the latter concerned that neo-fascism have a distinctly British persona and mass appeal – made impossible his alignment with the emergent NF.[3]

While the nature of Jordan's race preoccupations explains his ignoring of the Ulster problem, it was not an *immediate* concern of other extreme Rightists either, given Northern Ireland's

---

[3] Dennis Eisenberg, *The Re-emergence of Fascism* (London: MacGibbon & Kee, 1967), pp. 44–45; De Boca and Giovana, *Fascism Today*, pp. 267–68; Thayer, *British Political Fringe*, p. 16; Martin Walker, *The National Front* (London: Fontana, 1977), pp. 27–28; Nigel Fielding, *The National Front* (London: Routledge & Kegan Paul, 1981), p. 22. For Jordan's political interests, see, for example, Colin Jordan, 'Britain: Revival or Ruin?', speech delivered at Birmingham, 20 September 1970 (University of Northampton Archive (UNA), *Searchlight* Archive, Box 2, British Movement: SCH/01/Res/BRI/20/002); Colin Jordan, 'White Power for Britain', speech at Wolverhampton, 15 May 1971 (UNA, *Searchlight* Archive, Box 1, Colin Jordan: SCH/01/Res/BRI/23/02).

constitutional security. In the 1960s, non-Mosleyite extreme-Rightists would come to the Ulster problem only after the most significant factions came together to form the NF, inspired apparently by John Tyndall's attack on the Tory Party following its defeat in the general election of 1966 as a party of national surrender, incapable of holding the support of 'patriotic voters'.[4] Thereafter, three groups – the British National Party (BNP) with 1,500 members; A. K. Chesterton's League of Empire Loyalists (LEL), 2,000 strong, and the Racial Preservation Society, with around 500 members – were joined by a number of smaller groups and Tyndall's Greater Britain Movement. As a result of the amalgamation, the NF could boast around 4,000 members as it began its political life. It also benefited from a range of publications which the various groups had brought with them: Tyndall's *Spearhead*, A. K Chesterton's *Candour*, and later *Nationalism Today*, *National Front News*, *Nationalism*, *Bulldog* and other more ephemeral, temporary prints.[5] As a movement, the NF, initially under Chesterton's leadership, flourished from its inception in 1967 to 1974, benefiting from the controversy over 'coloured' immigration from 1968 and the public response to the influx of Ugandan Asians in the early 1970s, becoming the most successful contemporary extreme-Right movement; and with an expectation of increasing success until its ambitions were undermined by a disastrous performance at the general election of 1979.

Certainly, it faced no serious competitors. Mosley's retirement not only deprived the UM of its most important asset, but Jeffrey Hamm, its effective leader, adopted the impossible position of insisting that the only acceptable basis for cooperation with other extreme-Right organisations was for them to disband and join the UM,[6]

---

[4] Walker, *National Front*, pp. 62–63; Martin Durham, 'The Conservative Party, the British extreme right and the problem of political space, 1967–83', in Mike Cronin (ed.), *The Failure of British Fascism: The Far Right and the Fight For Political Recognition* (Basingstoke: Palgrave Macmillan, 1996), p. 84.

[5] Gerry Gable, 'The far right in contemporary Britain', in Luciano Cheles, Ronnie Ferguson and Michalina Vaughan (eds), *Neo-Fascism in Europe* (London: Longman, 1991), pp. 245–46.

[6] Hamm to ?Carr, 12 May 1971 (Jeffrey Hamm papers, BU, CRL: MS124/1/3/16).

and had no hesitation in terminating the membership of any UM member associated with the pro-loyalist NF. Eventually, the UM also gave up active politics and focused instead on attempting to permeate other organisations with their ideas, believing that a long-foretold national crisis 'is now with us', the only question being 'whether the break-down will come before the break-through'.[7] Thereafter, the only British neo-fascist group supporting Mosleyite anti-partitionism would be the League of St George – a splinter group from the UM in the mid-1970s that would seek to cultivate support from European fascists and the Irish community in Britain.[8]

The early years of the NF would see a changing leadership cadre as prominent members such as the Norfolk landowner Andrew Fountaine left due to policy disputes over issues such as Chesterton's commitment to elections and Chesterton and others' concerns about Tyndall's Nazi past.[9] Nevertheless, Chesterton remained leader until 1970 and it was under his leadership that the NF first adopted a position on the Northern Ireland problem.

Chesterton, the NF and Ulster in the late 1960s

Chesterton's background and upbringing undoubtedly influenced his attitude to Northern Ireland. Although not a Catholic like his cousin, the writer G. K. Chesterton, he had a Catholic mother and was educated at Catholic schools,[10] and could be critical of Ulster Protestants, claiming that when the international Marxist threat was developing in the post-war years, it was British Catholics, not Ulster Protestants – now feeling its sharp end – who attempted to thwart it.[11] Nevertheless, he adopted a largely equidistant position between the Catholic and Protestant communities, hoping for a cross-community

---

[7] On these opinions, see the following correspondence: Jeffrey Hamm to ? (Hull), 1 August 1975; 13 October 1975; Hamm to 'Dear Mr ? [redacted], n.d.; Hamm to Captain ? [redacted], 23 March 1976 (Jeffrey Hamm papers, BU, CRL: MS124/1/2/263, 267, 270, 278).

[8] Gable, 'Far right in contemporary Britain', p. 246; 'Belgian Nazi addresses Irish club', *Searchlight*, July–August 1976.

[9] Durham, 'The Conservative Party, the British extreme right', pp. 81–82.

[10] Chesterton interviewed in *Spearhead*, September 1969.

[11] 'Ulster and the L.E.L.', *Candour*, May 1972.

alliance in support of the Union. At its Annual General Meeting (AGM) on 13 September 1969, both Martin Webster and Denis Pirie, two other leading members, referenced their own Catholic backgrounds, pledging the NF to support loyal citizens of the Queen in the north, regardless of their religion. This point was reaffirmed by D. M. Riddlesdell, the Belfast branch organiser, a former member of Chesterton's LEL and also a Catholic: not 'all Catholics in Northern Ireland support the destruction of that part of the United Kingdom, still less wish to build Bernadette Devlin's … Workers' Republic'.[12] But as the evidence for an Ulster Catholic defence of the Union proved elusive – Riddlesdell's attempt to establish a NF branch in Belfast in the late 1960s failed – Chesterton admitted that if the only committed loyalists in the region 'at this eleventh hour' were militant Protestants, then they must be supported, 'warts and all'.[13] Refusing to believe a report of Protestants shooting at British troops, Chesterton wrongly blamed 'New Left' murderers instead. But, as the conflict developed, he saw the IRA, 'the [Daniel] Cohn-Bendit Brigade' and Bernadette Devlin[14] as mere junior members in the international subversive movement; a movement he believed responsible for the prorogation of Stormont in March 1972, facilitated by a treacherous British political and media establishment, with the prospect 'too horrible to contemplate' of 'British troops and British loyalists fighting each other'.[15]

By late 1972, however, Chesterton's views on the Ulster problem were of less significance than hitherto, being compelled to resign from the NF in late 1970 following a putsch organised by younger members such as Martin Webster, who regarded him as too old and out of touch, blaming him especially for failing adequately to exploit Enoch Powell's raising of the immigration issue in 1968, Powell himself feared as a competitor for the racist vote. Chesterton would identify 2 per cent of NF members as 'really evil men …

[12] 'N.F. Support for Ulster', *Candour*, September 1969.
[13] Chesterton interview, *Spearhead*, September 1969.
[14] Cohn-Bendit was a leading European left-wing radical, Bernadette Devlin a leading socialist republican during the Ulster civil rights agitation.
[15] *Candour*, September, November 1969; April, July 1970; April, May, October 1972.

placed close to the centre of things',[16] an accusation directed at the new leadership: after the brief reign of John O'Brien,[17] John Tyndall assumed the reins of leadership.

Tyndall defined his ideological position against Mosley's 'cosmopolitanism', something not far removed from the 'internationalism which rules our age'.[18] In rejecting Mosley's European project, Tyndall was also rejecting his framework for a resolution of the Ulster problem. Instead, his British nationalism left him, like Powell, committed to an integrationist solution: the region had to be secured 'as a part of Great Britain'.[19] Unlike Chesterton, Tyndall – a descendant of the early Protestant reformer and translator of the Bible into English, William Tyndale (1490–1536) – was from a family with an Irish historical connection going back to the seventeenth century, and which produced Professor John Tyndall (1820–93), physicist and natural philosopher. Though he and both his parents were born in England, Tyndall's paternal grandfather had been a District Inspector of the Royal Irish Constabulary, strongly Unionist and heavily engaged in the struggle against Irish republicanism.[20] With this family background, it is hardly surprising that Tyndall admitted coming to the Ulster problem 'not in a spirit of objectivity, but as a partisan'. More generally, Tyndall argued for the geopolitical, cultural and racial unity of the peoples of the British Isles, on this basis denying the existence of an Irish race or nation. Britain's and Ireland's enemies had worked for 200 years to separate them, with the present Ulster conflict the last phase.[21]

---

[16] Chesterton, quoted in Neill Nugent, 'The political parties of the extreme right', in Neill Nugent and Roger King (eds), *The British Right: Conservative and Right Wing Politics in Britain* (Farnborough: Saxon House, 1977), p. 169; Walker, *National Front*, p. 97.

[17] Walker, *National Front*, pp. 97–107.

[18] 'More about Mosley', *Spearhead*, January/February 1969.

[19] 'Reds behind Ulster agony', *Spearhead*, September 1969; 'Confessions of an IRA Marxist', *Spearhead*, January 1970. For an example of Ulster Unionist argument along the same lines, see Clifford Smyth, *Ulster Assailed* ([Belfast], n.p., [1970]).

[20] John Tyndall, *The Eleventh Hour: A Call for British Rebirth* (1988; 3rd edn, Welling: Albion Press, 1998), pp. 6–8.

[21] Ibid., pp. 369–70.

Tyndall regarded the Ulster loyalist community as a 'people whose qualitative value to the British nation is incomparably greater than that suggested by its size', but a community that Britain's leaders, aided by 'the New World Order' – 'internationalism, liberalism ... controlled by [Jewish] money power', wanted 'isolated out on a limb, so that its influence may not be contagious'.[22] Tyndall believed there were few Protestant or Catholics bigots in Northern Ireland, arguing, accurately enough, that the problem was constitutional in nature.[23] In this regard, at least, Tyndall's understanding, if not in others, was more grounded in reality than that of evangelical Protestants convinced the Roman Catholic Church was organising a campaign to destroy 'Ulster', though there was a clear synergy between Tyndall's view of the morally and nationally corrupting influence of liberal media organisations and the critique of these same forces by Paisley's *Protestant Telegraph*.[24] Tyndall was also at one with Powell and loyalism in rejecting concessions to northern Catholics that would inevitably increase the power of republicanism.[25]

The NF and Ulster: Policy and Implementation

Tyndall's approach to Ulster loyalism has to be seen in the context of the NF's national policy at this time of growing public support[26] – and its dual approach to political success. This entailed both an 'esoteric' appeal to 'intellectual' insiders and a greatly simplified 'exoteric' appeal to the mass membership and the electorate. As Stan Taylor explains, 'the core of the 'esoteric' appeal was the proposition that there has existed for centuries a grand conspiracy by Jews and pro-Zionists to dominate the world, the success of which would entail undermining the dominance of the white 'race', and 'the

---

[22] Ibid. pp. 370–73.
[23] Ibid., pp. 374–75.
[24] On the *Protestant Telegraph*, see David Boulton, *The UVF, 1966–73: An Anatomy of Loyalist Rebellion* (Dublin: Torc Books, 1973), pp. 64–65.
[25] Tyndall, *Eleventh Hour*, p. 375.
[26] Stan Taylor, *The National Front in English Politics* (Basingstoke: Macmillan, 1982), pp. 24–25; Roger Eatwell, 'The esoteric ideology of the National Front in the 1980s', in Cronin, *The Failure of British Fascism*, p. 100.

destruction of nations and nationalism'.[27] Reflecting the pro-Nazi
basis of such beliefs, Joe Pearce, a leading NF member in the late
1970s and early 1980s, pointed out that 'one could not graduate
to the inner-sanctum of the cognoscenti within the Party without
tacitly accepting Nazi ideology and without secretly regretting the
defeat of Hitler and the Third Reich'.[28]

The 'exoteric' vision was designed for the purpose of electoral
appeal, and framed largely in terms of the negative socio-economic
effects of non-white immigration with reference to unemployment,
housing shortages, crime and the welfare state, together with 'the
communist menace' and the Common Market.[29] It was mainly
in the context of its exoteric appeal that the NF's approach to the
Ulster question was framed, with reference to arguments it believed
that 'all decent people' really accepted.[30] Certainly, the antisemitic
dimension of the NF's esoteric ideas would have had little appeal in
Northern Ireland.

The region's politics were not entirely free of a Jewish factor.
Thus traditional anti-papist arguments were updated with the claim
that the Vatican was responsible for the extermination of six million
Jews during the Second World War,[31] while Ian Paisley's wife Eileen,
in contesting a council by-election against Harold Smith, a supporter
of the reformist Prime Minister Terence O'Neill, in October 1966,
used his Jewish religion to argue that as a Jew he 'rejects our Lord
Jesus Christ, the New Testament, Protestant principles, the Glorious
Revolution and the sanctity of the Lord's day'. As such, Smith was
not, and could not be, 'a traditional Unionist. The Protestant Throne
and the Protestant Constitution are nothing to him.' Although it
might seem that Eileen Paisley was appealing 'to an older, more

---

[27] Stan Taylor, 'The National Front: anatomy of a political movement', in
Robert Miles and Annie Phizacklea (eds), *Racism and Political Action in Britain*
(London: Routledge & Kegan Paul, 1979), p. 127.
[28] Joseph Pearce, *Race with the Devil: My Journey from Racial Hatred to Rational
Love* (Charlotte, NC: Saint Benedict Press, 2013), pp. 81–82.
[29] Taylor, *National Front*, pp. 127–29.
[30] Fielding, *National Front*, p. 189.
[31] Ed Moloney, *Paisley: From Demagogue to Democrat?* (Dublin: Poolbeg, 2008),
p. 211.

deep-seated bigotry',[32] in this instance it was more likely that Smith was the target of a variation on the kind of prejudice usually directed at the region's Catholic population.

While the civil disorder of August 1969 in Derry and Belfast persuaded the NF that an international Marxist attack on Northern Ireland and Britain was underway,[33] Ulster as a *major* theme of NF propaganda only becomes evident in March 1971 when it was clear that the troubles would not be of short duration.[34] Leadership commitment, however, was not perfectly mirrored among NF members, who, when asked why they were participating in the first major NF-assisted loyalist demonstration in London, in 1972, referred to 'the Irish thing' or 'Oh, some protest about Ireland or something',[35] though it is worth noting that the NF's far-Left opponents could also 'have very little knowledge or understanding of Irish politics'.[36]

That the NF was the only British party prepared to offer unyielding support should have made it an attractive partner for Ulster loyalism, but while in 1969 the NF claimed 29 'branches or Groups' in England, two in Scotland and one in Belfast,[37] the last was at best notional. It was only in the crisis circumstances attending the prorogation of the old Stormont system in 1972 and the Sunningdale discussions on a power-sharing executive with an all-Ireland council that followed it was something like a functioning NF presence established.[38] But for the NF not only was Government policy in Northern Ireland a focus of attack but so was the leader of the Vanguard movement, William Craig.[39]

For a time, Craig, former Minister of Home Affairs in O'Neill's Government, appeared to be a home-grown neo-fascist leader, 'parading around Fascist-style in heavy leather with an escort of

---

[32] Ibid., p. 137.

[33] 'Exposed: reds behind Ulster agony', *Spearhead*, September 1969.

[34] 'Ulster: time to stand by our friends', *Spearhead*, March 1971.

[35] Fielding, *National Front*, p. 154.

[36] Dave Hann and Steve Tilzey, *No Retreat: The Secret War between Britain's Anti-Fascists and the Far Right* (Lytham: Milo Books, 2003), p. 22.

[37] *Spearhead*, April–May 1969.

[38] 'NF makes entry on Northern Ireland scene', *Spearhead*, July 1973.

[39] 'Failure in Northern Ireland', *Spearhead*, February 1973; 'Craig fails the test', *Spearhead*, March 1973.

motorcycles' and willing on the violent extremes of loyalism with no hint of restraint.[40] In the run-up to the prorogation of Stormont on 24 March 1972 his Vanguard movement developed from attracting a small attendance until on 18 March Craig addressed a crowd of between 20,000 and 60,000 at Ormeau Park, Belfast, on the general theme of a restoration of the pre-1968 political and constitutional status quo. Stimulated by inflammatory rhetoric, including thinly veiled threats on the lives of anyone co-operating with direct rule',[41] he was even apparently contemplating 'an indiscriminate holocaust' against Catholics if it is impossible 'to win our democratic rights without this sort of thing happening'.[42]

For People's Democracy (PD), which had progressed from its university student base in 1969 to become aligned with the Trotskyist Fourth International, and looking at the conflict through a 1930s lens, the prospect of a fully fledged Nazi regime taking over if imperialist aims were not delivered was clear.[43] But Craig's Vanguard movement was only one among a number of organisations and the targeting of loyalist paramilitaries as 'fascist' was a crude simplification.

While Craig appeared to make an NF presence in the North irrelevant, it was his policies rather than neo-fascist appearances that occasioned NF criticism. Craig was at one with the NF in demanding greater UK integration and opposition to the Common Market, but Craig's idea of integration included constitutional reform on the basis of West German federalism – a 'federal United Kingdom',[44] anathema to the NF as being too close to the contemporaneous rise of Scottish nationalism as a threat to the United Kingdom.[45]

[40] 'William Craig', *Fortnight*, 21 September 1972.

[41] Martyn Turner, 'The Vanguard dossier', *Fortnight*, 13 March 1972; Ulster Vanguard (Newtownards Branch), *Government Without Right* … (Newtownards, Co. Antrim, [1972]).

[42] 'Rightists stage big Ulster rally', *New York Times*, 19 March 1972; People's Democracy, *Fascism in the Six Counties* (Belfast: People's Democracy, [1975?]), p. [4].

[43] People's Democracy, *Fascism in the Six Counties*, pp. [2–4].

[44] 'Craig tells Unionists worst yet to come', *Irish Times*, 23 January 1971.

[45] See *Spearhead*, August 1973; 'NF voice vital in Scotland', *Spearhead*, May 1975; 'Scottish nationalism: a design to weaken the UK?', *Spearhead*, March 1976.

And, apart from Craig, more general difficulties persisted. Unlike the NF, which had evolved policies for the UK before the Ulster troubles erupted, loyalist organisations emerged in the throes of a developing crisis – as the kind of solid Westminster support that Ulster Unionism had enjoyed since 1945 was disappearing; as the traditional Unionist monolith was shattering; against a background of impoverished analytical thought about politics within Unionism/loyalism; and with the history of Ulster Unionism having prioritised armed resistance against the papist enemy to defend their interests.

There was thus a disjuncture between the fiercely anti-Catholic ethos of loyalist organisations and the significant Catholic membership of British extreme-Right organisations, especially the leadership of the NF: that the first NF organiser in Belfast, David Riddlesdell, was a Catholic would hardly have been an incentive. Riddlesdell – later killed in a hit-and-run accident – and the NF sympathiser Lindsay Mason were regarded as eccentrics. They had been leading members of a small ultra-loyalist group, the Ulster Constitutional Party (UCP), though Mason has the better claim to political memory, having been elected unopposed to the old Belfast Corporation to represent the nationalist/republican Lower Falls at a by-election in 1972, republicans having boycotted the elections in protest at internment. When the UCP was dissolved in 1974, Mason joined the NF and became effectively its first elected local councillor anywhere in the UK.[46]

In July 1973 an Ulster loyalist overture to the NF occurred when Ulster Volunteer Force (a paramilitary organisation based on Carson's UVF of 1912–14) brigade staff member Billy Mitchell, a committed NF sympathiser, joined the east-Antrim-based Ulster Loyalist Front (ULF) – a grouping highly critical of the Ulster Defence Association (UDA) and the Loyalist Association of Workers (LAW) organisation of Billy Hull, claiming they 'reeked of communist and socialist thinking'. Apparently speaking for the UVF, the ULF contacted the NF, the latter responding with the suggestion of an immediate amalgamation. As a result, in September 1973, talks in London took place, with general agreement found on a joint manifesto that

---

[46] Kerr, 'The history of the National Front in Ulster'; Walter Ellis, 'The Orange front', *Sunday Times*, 4 August 1974.

included NF policies on non-white immigration, 'free enterprise', though not international free trade; restriction of trade union power; the return of hanging; and 'the right of all law-abiding citizens to hold and bear arms'. The ULF deputation, however, was concerned that the NF was largely ignorant of Ulster politics and was shocked to discover that several top NF personnel were Catholics and welcomed Catholic members. They also disagreed with the NF support for internment, as many UVF members were also interned. These would be enduring concerns. Accordingly, the UVF would not consider a merger with the NF, permitting only joint membership.[47]

Nevertheless, 1973 would see a NF presence in Belfast emerge when William Annett formed 'a rudimentary group', and soon after stood as a National Front Loyalist in the South Down constituency at the Northern Ireland Assembly elections of 28 June, though gaining only 591 first preference votes (0.9 per cent).[48] At the February 1974 Westminster election, the OUP candidate Roy Bradford, openly supported by the NF Belfast group, was elected, but its support was hardly central to the result and the group continued to struggle for impact, not least due to the opposition of the largest loyalist organisation, the UDA. This was also the case with the Ulster Workers' Council (UWC) strike of May 1974 that broke the power-sharing executive established under the Sunningdale Agreement.[49] As Ian Wood points out, the UWC strike was successful for reasons unrelated to any support from the NF. Thus, John McMichael, the UDA's second in command, found it easy to give the NF – its members regarded by many loyalists as mere political 'groupies'– short shrift.[50] While the Directorate

[47] See typewritten report, 'The National Front in Northern Ireland', [1975?] (UNA, *Searchlight* Archive, Box 28, National Front: SCH/01/Res/BRI/02/028).

[48] Brian Mercer Walker, *Parliamentary Election Results in Ireland, 1918–92* (Dublin and Belfast: Royal Irish Academy, 1972), p. 86; Kerr, 'The history of the National Front in Ulster'.

[49] See 'National Front opens up in Belfast', *Sunday News*, 12 May 1974.

[50] Kerr, 'The history of the National Front in Ulster'; I. S. Wood, *Crimes of Loyalty: A History of the UDA* (Edinburgh: Edinburgh University Press, 2006), pp. 49, 268, 239.

obtained a mandate to negotiate 'official working alliances' with the region's loyalist movements at the NF annual conference of 1974, UDA investigations into the nature of their new potential allies soon discovered its neo-Nazi character and on 5 September officially proscribed the organisation.[51] But if the NF contributed little to the success of the UWC strike, it was persuaded by its effectiveness to establish an NF Trade Unionists Association in June 1974.[52] And, despite its failure to prosper in Northern Ireland, 1974 saw 'Ulster' emerge as one of four central NF concerns together with 'Europe, trade unions and post-immigration [*opposition to the black community already in the country*]'.[53]

With Ulster a central concern, NF failure in the region to date had simply to be regarded as a learning experience as a new initiative was launched. Tyndall, together with other leading figures such as Webster and John Kingsley Read, made a five-day visit to the region in June 1974, during which they met representatives of the UVF, UDA, UWC, Vanguard and Paisley's Democratic Unionist Party (DUP), together with the NF Belfast Group, which Webster claimed had grown rapidly in recent months and would shortly be certified as an official branch.[54]

Tyndall set out the terms on which Ulster loyalists and the NF would engage with each other: (i) Ulster's place as an authentic member of the UK depended on her contribution to 'reshaping' the State in association with the NF not just political and paramilitary activity in Northern Ireland; (ii) breaking away from Britain – a unilateral declaration of independence (UDI) – to be rejected, as 'Ulster' had more British support than media lies indicated; (iii) joint action in Britain and Northern Ireland to oppose Irish republicanism, power-sharing and a Council of Ireland.[55] Tyndall accurately enough identified the loyalist conception of Britain as that imperial nation 'that once strode the world like a colossus' in the service of which

---

[51] Walker, *National Front*, pp. 159–60.
[52] Ibid., p. 139.
[53] Ibid., p. 153.
[54] Michael Hanna, 'Loyalists: the fascist links', *Hibernia*, 19 July 1974.
[55] Martin Webster, 'Press release', press clipping [late summer 1974] (UNA, *Searchlight* Archive, Box 28, National Front: SCH/01/Res/BRI/02/028).

'Ulstermen played such a proud role'; and set it as the goal they should aim for in the future: 'that British nation will one day rise again ... let us devote ourselves heart and soul to that task'.[56]

The NF–loyalist relationship would never be substantive, but that an approach to the NF came from a significant UVF source, Billy Mitchell, may have conveyed the impression that it could be, an impression sustained by 'Richard Cameron', the editor of the UVF magazine *Combat*, which emerged in early 1974. 'Cameron' could reject the PD accusation of loyalist fascism,[57] while at the same time keenly cultivating the UVF–NF relationship. However, its promotion came at a somewhat confusing time in general for the UVF.

The organisation had declared a ceasefire in November 1973, which initiated a period of politicisation, with the membership urged to consider socio-economic issues such as housing, jobs and social development, together with an opening to the class-oriented Official IRA, which it hoped could undermine the Provisional IRA. Reformism was given an important boost when the Government lifted a ban on the UVF along with Provisional Sinn Fein and as a range of civil servants, academics, religious organisations and the declining Northern Ireland Labour Party (NILP) made contact, thereby influencing the manifesto of the UVF-sponsored Volunteer People's Party (VPP), as it ventured into electoral politics.[58]

Political rethinking, however, faced a significant barrier in that it was mainly the preserve of a relatively moderate leadership and did not translate well among the membership. Violent anti-Catholicism was such an influential factor facilitating UVF membership that moderates were at a distinct disadvantage, incapable of either controlling such members or eliminating them from the organisation. Also, even *within* some individuals, moderating tendencies and politicisation could coexist with a virulent sectarianism: 'By asking the UVF to enter the political world the radicals were challenging much of the

---

[56] See National Front, *Chairman's Ulster Speech* [June 1974] (UNA, *Searchlight* Archive, Box 28, National Front: SCH/01/Res/BRI/02/028).

[57] 'Strikers and fascists', *Combat*, vol. 1, no. 11 [1974].

[58] Sarah Nelson, *Ulster's Uncertain Defenders: Protestant Political, Paramilitary and Community Groups and the Northern Ireland Conflict* (Belfast: Appletree Press, 1984), pp. 172–74.

ideology, ethos and experience of UVF members ... Most members joined as a way of expressing disillusionment with politicians and constitutional methods, and the training they received did not equip them with political skills'.[59] Even VPP political activists were unsure of themselves, feeling incapable of taking on mainstream politicians, while influential loyalists in Belfast, Orangemen and religious fundamentalists waged a campaign against it, with 'allegations of Communism, atheism, pro-republicanism, debauchery and all manner of vices'. Against this background, that the VPP candidate in West Belfast at the October 1974 general election, Ken Gibson, polled only 2,600 votes and lost his deposit proved a fatal verdict on the political experiment.[60]

NF–UVF relations also evidenced loyalist confusion. While the Shankill-based and pro-NF *Loyalist News*,[61] edited by the rabidly anti-Catholic John McKeague, would reproduce an NF leaflet, 'An Open Letter to Ulster Loyalists', reinforcing Tyndall's message,[62] most UVF members, even the most politically minded, had a poor knowledge of the NF political programme, while greater awareness produced either alienation or little of relevance to their situation, not least the organisation's antisemitism and anti-black proposals.[63]

In this context, NF attempts to harmonise its interests and those of loyalists by arguments such as the claim that the EEC would not only facilitate a great increase in alien immigration to Britain, but a similar influx of republican subversives into Northern Ireland from southern Ireland,[64] were wholly inadequate to the task. As such, it was easy for Peter Robinson of the DUP to condemn the NF for 'causing confusion'.[65] Accordingly, when, in the run-up to

[59] Ibid., pp. 177–78.

[60] Ibid., pp. 185–87.

[61] See, for instance, 'Stand by our lads in Ulster', *Loyalist News*, 20 May 1972; 'Red Ulrike [Meinhoff] in Belfast', *Loyalist News*, 3 June 1972; 'Freedom for Ukraine', *Loyalist News*, 2 September 1972.

[62] *Loyalist News*, 11 November 1974.

[63] Nelson, *Ulster's Uncertain Defenders*, pp. 171–73.

[64] 'EEC: huge new immigrant threat', *Spearhead*, August 1975.

[65] See printed sheet, headed, 'Searchlight 6: Ulster National Front, 9/10', n.d. (UNA, *Searchlight* Archive, Box 28, National Front: SCH/01/Res/BRI/02/028).

the Constitutional Convention election of 1975 and in response to calls for loyalist unity, the NF applied for membership of the United Ulster Unionist Council (UUUC), its application was firmly rejected.[66] In fact, the NF itself was in confusion at this time, with stagnant recruitment and beset by internal rows over its direction following the party's poor performance at the October 1974 general election.[67] As for the UVF, it was proscribed for the second time in November 1975 after a savage outburst of sectarian killing and internecine feuding, thereafter losing solidarity and growing increasingly fragmented.[68] NF–UVF, and wider loyalist differences, moreover, intensified in the later 1970s.

NF–Loyalist Antagonism and the Ulster Campaign

Combat reflected the tensions in the now very tenuous UVF–NF relationship, endorsing the exoteric arguments of the NF in Britain in assurances to loyalists that the NF was 'not a Fascist party', only a party 'that wants to see a strong healthy Britain',[69] but also enthusing over Enoch Powell's apparently sectarian condemnation of the idea that Prince Charles might marry a Roman Catholic.[70] For its part, the NF, despite a continued commitment to Northern Ireland's constitutional position, developed, from this point, a distinctly critical attitude to Ulster loyalism. This went together with a reinvigoration of the regional group's activities. Organisers were appointed for areas such as Portadown, Lurgan, Moira, Newcastle and Dromore, under a new Northern Ireland organiser in one Sam McIllwraith,[71] and with its own NF-sponsored print *British Ulsterman*. No great results came of this effort, but *British Ulsterman* does offer useful insights into the mindset of the Ulster NF group.

---

[66] 'National Front in Northern Ireland'; 'Ulster National Front' (UNA, *Searchlight* Archive, Box 28, National Front: SCH/01/Res/BRI/02/028).

[67] Walker, *National Front*, p. 180.

[68] Nelson, *Ulster's Uncertain Defenders*, pp. 170, 190–92.

[69] Samuel Simpson, Joint Press Officer, National Front, Belfast, 'Support for U.V.F. stand against Communism', *Combat*, vol. 1, no. 34 [1974]; 'Is there a UVF–National Front connection?', *Combat*, vol. 2, no. 2 [1975].

[70] 'Well done Enoch', *Combat*, vol. 4, no. 20 [1977].

[71] See printed sheet, headed, 'Searchlight 6: Ulster National Front, 9/10'.

Smarting from the UUUC rebuff, it scornfully questioned the seriousness of the call for unity and accused the organisation of seeking a 'disastrous' alliance with the Conservative Party,[72] while *Spearhead* warned of left-wing infiltration in one of its critics, the UDA.[73] Criticism of individual loyalist leaders and their initiatives continued into the later 1970s, such as the failed loyalist strike of May 1977, led by Revd Ian Paisley and Ernest Baird, the Vanguard leader who communicated the refusal of the NF's UUUC application.[74] The position of *British Ulsterman* and *Spearhead* on Northern Ireland, however, did not always cohere.

Whereas the former, more influenced by local opinion, favoured a restoration of Protestant rule at Stormont while 'anti-loyalist' forces ruled at Westminster,[75] the NF position as defined by *Spearhead* rejected devolution in favour of simple integration with Britain.[76] Again, while an attempt was made at this time to accommodate prosemitic loyalist sentiment in Northern Ireland – and the NF's exoteric political campaign in Britain – by declaring NF respect for 'Jewry' and the achievements of Israel, qualities it averred, now sadly ridiculed in Britain,[77] antisemitism was just too deeply embedded in the NF mindset for it to remain submerged for long. Thus, when Menachem Begin, Prime Minister of Israel, visited London in December 1977, he was picketed by 100 NF members.[78] While differences of policy and ideas go far to explain difficulties in the

---

[72] See John Andrews, 'Is [Harry] West serious about loyalist unity'; 'U.U.U.C. seeks alliance with the Conservative Party'; *British Ulsterman*, no. 3 [1975] (UNA, *Searchlight* Archive, Box 28, National Front: SCH/01/Res/BRI/02/028).

[73] 'Red infiltrators threaten loyalist unity', *Spearhead*, July 1975.

[74] See *Spearhead*, May 1977; also, 'Letter from Belfast', *Spearhead*, March 1978.

[75] *British Ulsterman*, no. 3 [1975] (UNA, *Searchlight* Archive, Box 28, National Front: SCH/01/Res/BRI/02/028).

[76] 'What they are asking about the N.F.', *Spearhead*, June 1977; 'Letter from Belfast', *Spearhead*, March 1978; Robert Gregory, 'Ulster: Action or drift', *Spearhead*, April 1978.

[77] Stuart Balfour, 'Nationhood: the key to our survival', *Spearhead*, October 1976.

[78] 'National Front pickets begin', *Irish Independent*, 5 December 1977.

NF–UVF relationship at this time, arguably a greater problem for the relationship lay in changes in British security policy.

With the Unionist-dominated Constitutional Convention having opted for an unacceptable restoration of Protestant majority rule, the population in general began to settle down, willingly or unwillingly, to acceptance of direct rule; and certainly for Unionists a desire for stronger State action against militant republicanism and other violent extremists. In fact, by 1975, State action had already made significant strides in combating the Provisional IRA,[79] but when the personally forceful Roy Mason replaced Merlyn Rees as Secretary of State for Northern Ireland in September 1976, he appeared to embody the policy. It was against this background that the political alliance of right-wing Unionist parties that made up the UUUC collapsed due to internal differences,[80] and that on 26 November 1977 William Craig declared that Vanguard would cease to function as a political party. A formal declaration to this effect took place on 25 February 1978. As for the NF, progress in Northern Ireland continued to prove difficult – attempts to recruit among Queen's University students were unsuccessful, though some soldiers stationed in Northern Ireland were more amenable.[81] It responded by placing a stronger emphasis on its Ulster-related British activities, even as these were attended by their own problems.

This was evident from 1974, when an NF–Ulster loyalist march in London of around 1,500 on 7 September took place. Intended both as a reply to poll indications that the British people wanted to desert Ulster and to an IRA demonstration in London earlier in the year,[82] the event raised £600,[83] but the marchers had to be protected by 2,000 policemen, harassed all the way by anti-Nazi demonstrators, while 14 people were arrested in scuffles.[84] Advancing the loyalist cause required favourably influencing British political

[79] Loughlin, *The Ulster Question since 1945*, pp. 107–08.

[80] Bew and Gillespie, *Northern Ireland: A Chronology of the Troubles, 1968–1999*, pp. 122–25.

[81] 'Backing the Front', *Hibernia*, 23 February 1978.

[82] 'Ulster: back to square one', *Spearhead*, August 1974.

[83] Fielding, *National Front*, p. 158.

[84] '14 arrested in National Front march', *Irish Press*, 9 September 1974.

and public opinion, but while loyalist–NF action could occasionally derail republican activities,[85] such events were counter-productive, merely reinforcing loyalism's reputation for extremism, and this remained the case until the end of the decade and beyond.[86] For their far-Left opponents fascist-facilitated loyalist marches invariably attracted aggressive opposition, with those in London occasioning a 'national call-out'.[87]

Even IRA bombs in the British midlands failed to create an environment the NF could effectively exploit. From August 1973, until the Birmingham pub bombings of November 1974, 32 bomb incidents took place, but none created a backlash against the local Irish community.[88] That only occurred in the wake of the Birmingham bombings, in which 20 people were killed and over 200 injured. Unsurprisingly, the reaction against the Irish was sharpest in areas and places of work where the NF was well represented. Liverpool, however, which had a considerable Orange population, but lacked an effective NF presence and organisation, saw the NF and the smaller British Movement muster only 50 people on an anti-IRA march; and even in Birmingham the reaction and backlash soon began to cool.[89]

That the NF's Ulster-related activities neither served the loyalist cause nor enhanced its own support was confirmed in a Government report on the organisation provoked by a complaint from Tyndall about supposed State prejudice against NF marches.[90] Increased support for the NF, from 10,000 members in 1974 to 14,000 by 1977 'and still rising' was noted, and with a relationship identified between relative support and proximity to non-white populations

[85] Fielding, *National Front*, p. 182.
[86] 'Derry's Bogside riots re-enacted on London streets', *Sunday Independent*, 14 August 1977. See report of NF march in Bolton, *Irish Independent*, 11 February 1978; also, 'Skirmishes at NF march', *Irish Press*, 13 November 1978; 'National Front in trouble over its race policy', *Irish Press*, 19 April 1979.
[87] Hann and Tilzey, *No Retreat*, p. 256.
[88] *Daily Telegraph*, 11 June 1974; *Guardian*, 18 June 1974, press clippings (Sir Oswald Mosley papers, BU, CRL: OMD/7/1/25).
[89] Ian Walker, 'Backlash in Birmingham', *Hibernia*, 6 December 1974.
[90] John Tyndall to James Callaghan, 18 August 1977 (NAK, Cabinet papers, 'Civil disturbances involving the National Front': PREM16/2084).

in areas where the NF's 2,000 branches were located, especially in London, the Home Counties, West Yorkshire and Leicester. But less than a quarter of the membership was identified 'as active' and, despite a range of activities, 'it owes its support almost entirely to its racial policies, in particular the ending of coloured immigration and the introduction of compulsory repatriation.'[91] Thus both the evidence of the streets and Government assessment illustrated the weakness of the Ulster issue as a factor capable of attracting mass support in Britain.

Quite apart from its own negative reputation with mainstream British public opinion, the loyalist 'product' the NF was trying to sell already had a negative, indeed even 'fascist', reputation in Britain, especially in its Orange dimension,[92] added to which the readership for *Spearhead*'s warnings of disaster in Britain and Northern Ireland[93] was limited to groups of marginal political influence. The limited utility of 'Ulster' for the NF was reflected in its campaign at the general election of 1979.

Martin Webster, distrusted in Northern Ireland because of his Catholicism and a loyalist belief that he had informed on UDA and UVF members organising an arms shipment from Europe[94] (Webster would accommodate the aggressive instincts of many NF supporters by allowing them to transgress the law on minor matters, while taking care to inform the police 'about anybody with a gun or explosives')[95] emphasised the NF's cross-confessional membership, especially that its founder in Northern Ireland was a Roman Catholic. But, more significantly, he lamented the tragedy that people 'of the same [racial] family' should be divided in

---

[91] 'Confidential report on the National Front', 7 February 1978 (NAK, Cabinet papers, 'Civil disturbances involving the National Front': PREM16/2084).
[92] See Johanne Devlin Trew, *Leaving The North: Migration and Memory, Northern Ireland, 1921–2011* (Liverpool: Liverpool University Press, 2013), p. 116; A. F. Parkinson, *Ulster Loyalism and the British Media* (Dublin: Four Courts Press, 1998), pp. 12–16.
[93] See, for instance, 'Too little, too late', *Spearhead*, January 1975; 'End this anarchy', *Spearhead*, November 1975; 'Behind the Ulster strife', *Spearhead*, October 1976; 'Ulster: Britain's shame', *Spearhead*, July 1977.
[94] See 'NF setback in Ulster', *Searchlight*, no. 107 (May 1984).
[95] Gable, 'Far right in contemporary Britain', p. 251.

bitterness, and hoped that '*somehow or other* the people on both sides should be able to find a solution' (my italics).[96] It was a 'reasonable' statement, very much in keeping with the NF's exoteric appeal to the electorate, but was unlikely to be reassuring to a loyalist community anxious for certainty about Northern Ireland's constitutional position.

At the same time, the credibility of the NF claim that it was the only party that could be relied upon to defend Ulster, already doubtful given loyalist suspicions and its failing fortunes, was further diminished when a *World in Action* TV programme in 1978 recorded Tyndall as frankly admitting that he intended to use the NF as a mechanism to build a Nazi party.[97] Together with Margaret Thatcher's stealing of the NF's clothes on immigration, the NF's disastrous showing at the 1979 general election, at which it entered 303 candidates, was only too likely. The party won merely 1.3 per cent of the total vote, compared with 3.1 per cent at the October 1974 general election, and was in a state of demoralisation. Only 400 members attended the NF AGM in October 1979, compared with the 1,000 who had attended the previous two AGMs; and when it sought to exploit the influx of Vietnamese refugees into Britain at the end of the 1970s, in the way it had done to effect on the Ugandan Asian issue earlier in the decade, it failed abysmally. Virtually none of its own members turned out to protest.[98] Again, only 200 NF members turned out to confront a Bloody Sunday march in Birmingham in January 1980 which attracted 2,000 supporters. In resulting conflict with the police, 17 neo-fascists were arrested with two charged with possession of offensive weapons.[99] Far from being able to offer effective support to Ulster loyalists, political survival was now a central concern just as Northern Ireland's constitutional link with Britain seemed to face its most serious threat since 1974.

[96] Isabel Conway, 'Root out non-whites says NF', *Irish Press*, 18 April 1979.
[97] Tyndall, cited in Ray Hill with Andrew Bell, *The Other Face of Terror: Inside Europe's Neo-Nazi Network* (London: Grafton Books, 1988), pp. 84–85.
[98] Taylor, *National Front*, pp. 165–66, 182–83.
[99] Paddy Prendiville, 'National Front faces problems with the Police', *Hibernia*, 31 January 1980.

Ulster and the NF in Crisis

The effects of the electoral collapse of 1979 were profound. The exoteric element of the organisation's politics, deemed crucial to popular support before the election and equally important in restraining the more violent elements of the NF's support base, was now seen to be politically valueless. There was thus no reason for the latter to conceal what they truly believed. Subsequent internal division resulted in the NF splitting into four separate organisations.[100] The NF itself, now under the leadership of Andrew Brons, a Harrogate college lecturer, and Martin Webster, sought to chart a new course – a 'Third Position' based on the ideas of the Strasser brothers, a stance which damned the inequalities and alienation produced by capitalism, but also Hitler for establishing a dictatorship and thus betraying Nazism's early radicalism.[101]

For his part, Tyndall, having left the NF following the refusal of its Directorate to concede him dictatorial authority to run the party, and convinced that Webster's well-known homosexuality and that of his associates had besmirched the NF's reputation, set up the supposedly more morally upright, but more pro-Nazi, New National Front. This proved to be of little account and by 1982 Tyndall had established the British National Party (BNP) which would develop during the 1980s in much the same way as the NF in 1970s but without achieving the same progress: the public's perception of the extreme-Right throughout the 1980s remained dominated by the NF.[102] Yet another, smaller group, the National Front Constitutional Movement, organised by the Norfolk landowner Andrew Fountaine, was another 'respectable' but failed organisation that sought to draw support from the Tory Party's right wing. Finally, the British Democratic Party, based in Leicester and organised by a solicitor, Tony Reed Herbert, collapsed when its members were exposed as part of a gun-running ring in 1981.[103] For our purposes, however, it is enough to note that even though weakened, the NF, with around

---

[100] Hill with Bell, *The Other Face of Terror*, pp. 90–91.
[101] Eatwell, 'The esoteric ideology', p. 107.
[102] Ibid., p. 106.
[103] Hill with Bell, *The Other Face of Terror*, pp. 89–89, 299.

4,000 members, remained the dominant neo-fascist organisation in the early 1980s, though the transformation of Margaret Thatcher's image occasioned by the Falklands Islands victory functioned to ensure that a significant extreme-Right revival was unlikely in this period: At the 1983 general election, the NF's 60 candidates obtained an average vote of only 1.1 per cent of the poll, even worse than in 1979; and despite the internal trauma the Labour Party was experiencing at this time there was no indication that the NF could capitalise on it.[104]

As for its operational structure, while Andrew Brons was the official leader, the NF was being run virtually single-handedly by Martin Webster, editing its publications while paying lip-service to Brons. At the same time a new breed of activists appeared, such as Ian Anderson, educated at Oxford, and Nick Griffin, a Cambridge graduate who soon took over as editor of *Nationalism Today*, the new representative NF print *Spearhead* having departed with Tyndall. Derek Holland was another new graduate activist, while Joe Pearce, a working-class street-fighter from Dagenham, East London, became an important figure in establishing credibility with young working-class skinheads.

Born in February 1961, Pearce had an Irish Catholic grandmother, but his outlook on life was shaped by his father's anti-Irish, antisemitic, anti-Catholic, anti-communist and anti-'coloured' prejudices, prejudices sharpened by a chauvinistic perception of a British empire undermined by decolonisation, and a British nation itself being corrupted by non-white immigration and afflicted by the Northern Ireland troubles in the late 1960s. Pearce joined the NF in May 1976 and enthusiastically embraced its most aggressive activities.[105] He launched *Bulldog* in September 1977, a NF magazine aimed at British youth, and which quickly gained him a racist, neo-Nazi national profile as the magazine's sales rapidly expanded. Pearce modelled it on the lowbrow tabloid press and wrote all the articles, which were kept short and direct to attract 'an angry teenage readership' and 'highly offensive to all but the most racist readers'. The success of his efforts – by January 1978, *Bulldog*'s sales

---

[104] Eatwell, 'The esoteric ideology', pp. 107–08.
[105] Pearce, *Race with the Devil*, pp. 4, chap. 4, 52.

'had expanded ten-fold, from several hundred copies per issue to several thousand' – led him to being taken on at the same time as a full-time paid NF employee: 'I was now living every young radical's dream of being a fully paid, fulltime revolutionary, giving his life for the Cause'; and was soon elected chairman of the newly formed Young National Front (YNF), becoming thereafter a popular NF speaker. His activities, which included a first foray into pro-loyalist Ulster politics when he attended an anti-IRA march in October 1978 at the invitation of a newly established YNF branch in the Waterside (mainly Protestant) area of Derry city, and which led him to join the Orange Order, would result in a term of imprisonment for six months in 1981. From 1978 to 1985, Pearce was a regular visitor to Northern Ireland, becoming closely associated with the UDA leadership, hero-worshipping its leader, Andy Tyrie.[106]

The influence of the new activists was felt at the NF AGM of November 1983, when, in cooperation with Brons, they used the NF rule book to depose Webster.[107] From this point, the new university-educated elite, of which Griffin would become the most prominent, came to be the increasingly dominant faction in the NF organisation, and which *Nationalism Today*, established in 1980 represented. Its content was shaped by its editor, Joe Pearce, in close partnership with Nick Griffin – Pearce had been Best Man at Griffin's wedding – until 1985.[108]

Critical of the theoretically unsophisticated NF of the 1970s, it would begin a process of ideological and organisational development aiming for intellectual, rather than electoral, hegemony among educated groups. Committed to a Strasserite 'Third Position', and influenced by the elitist ideology of the violent Italian Nuclei Armati Rivoluzionari (Armed Revolutionary Nuclei), it was dedicated to the creation of a new society, rejecting the corrupting effects of consumerism through the action of 'Political Soldiers' dedicated to revolutionary struggle.[109] At the same time, it also rejected crude ideas of white racial superiority in favour of an equidistant

---

[106] Ibid., pp. 61–64, 67, 99–103, 108–09.
[107] Gable, 'Far right in contemporary Britain', pp. 252–54.
[108] Pearce, *Race with the Devil*, pp. 74, 76, 175–76.
[109] Eatwell, 'The esoteric ideology', p. 111.

appreciation of racial difference. When finalised, the reformed NF would be explained in *National Front News* in late 1986.[110]

Revolutionary struggle entailed a massive reorganisation and a transformed membership, with most of those over the age of 30 being expelled. Funds from European fascists were acquired to finance the new direction, with the required reading for members transformed to give priority to the 'Third Position'.[111] But although the membership was allowed to run down to just under 1,000 in early 1984, by the end of the year it had recovered to about 3,000, while a new system of recruitment was instituted that gave 'absolute control over the members'. Thus voluntary membership was denied; instead recruits were chosen depending on a perception of their utility at various party levels, whether as an organiser or propagandist, a 'Friend of the Movement', a trainee cadre or a cadre, with further steps up the levels of command possible. Training was provided for the organisation in how to operate in a clandestine manner and how to deal with police interrogations, while young members were instructed to join CND protests against USA bases, following the example of the new Right in Germany, though also arguing that Britain retain its own nuclear deterrent.[112] But, for our purposes, how effective could the new developing policy be in Northern Ireland?

The idea of recruitment through selection rather than voluntary enlistment assumed a significant body of acceptable potential recruits from which a selection could be made. But however feasible this was in Britain, it was clearly not the case in Northern Ireland, where NF numbers were quite abysmal. In excusing the failure of past NF initiatives in the region, Jim Morrison, an NF activist, blamed an RUC 'pogrom' against loyalists – 'putting them in jail for defending their country'.[113] Moreover, while the idea of racial equidistance expounded by the Griffinites could be assumed to be

[110] 'Organising the Movement', *National Front News*, no. 82 [late 1986].
[111] Gable, 'Far right in contemporary Britain', pp. 252–54.
[112] Ibid.; 'Organising the Movement', *National Front News*, no. 82 [late 1986].
[113] Jim Morrison to editor, n.d., *Nationalism Today*, no. 5 [March? 1981]. See also 'Skin' to editor, n.d., *Nationalism Today*, no. 7, July? 1981, to the same effect. There is difficulty in dating exactly the publication of *Nationalism Today* issues, as month and year are rarely provided. Thus issue content has been examined to approximate these, most successfully with year of publication.

unobjectionable in a region which at this time still had no racial problem, the kind of radical national socialism Strasserism entailed was unlikely to be attractive to a Unionist and loyalist community which in the 1970s regarded even relatively mild social reformism as carrying the taint of communism. Nor was the tactic of infiltrating organisations such as CND likely to be feasible in Northern Ireland, as these had no significant presence in the region. Only in one area could the new policy be identified as relatively effective – the cultivation of skinhead activists.[114]

Ulster: Constitutional Initiatives and NF Responses

The years from 1980 to 1985 in Northern Ireland were freighted with political anxiety for Unionism/loyalism, occasioned by developments such as, respectively, the Anglo-Irish summit in 1980 between the Irish Taoiseach Charles Haughey and Margaret Thatcher; the formalisation of relations between Dublin and London through the Anglo-Irish Inter-Governmental Council of November 1981; an Assembly initiated by the Northern Ireland Secretary of State Jim Prior in 1982; the 'supergrass system' – the evidence of one informer to prosecute a number of people – employed against loyalist as well as republican paramilitaries from 1983; the New Ireland Forum of 1983–84, which debated the Ulster problem in the context of new thinking on Irish national identity and new consti-tutional structures; and the consequent talks between Thatcher and the Irish Taoiseach Garret FitzGerald that led to the Anglo-Irish Agreement (AIA) of 1985: in giving the Irish Republic a consul-tative role in the governance of Northern Ireland, it was deeply traumatising for Unionists.[115]

The unfolding of these developments was accompanied by close NF attention with the purpose of expanding the regional branch membership – estimated as 150 in 1981 by Jim Morrison, the local NF organiser[116] – and reflected especially in the *British*

114 Hill with Bell, *The Other Face of Terror*, pp. 173–74.
115 Loughlin, *The Ulster Question since 1945*, pp. 120–21.
116 Joe Pearce, 'Northern Ireland: the third force', *Nationalism Today*, no. 8 [January 1982].

Ulsterman supplement to *Nationalism Today* as Unionists and loyalists demonstrated their opposition. Thus political activism in support of the Unionist community was undertaken, together with enthusiastic promotion of NF literature in the region by leading members such as Pearce and Steve Brady, an Ulster member from a Catholic background.

In February 1980 the NF protested at the USA consulate in Belfast against the American Government's refusal to sell firearms to the RUC.[117] It applauded Ian Paisley's demonstration in early 1981 of 500 men on a hillside waving firearms certificates in protest against Thatcher's dialogue with Charles Haughey as evidence of Ulster's willingness to fight against 'betrayal',[118] while an 'England National Front team' was arranged to play an 'Ulster NF team' when the English football squad refused to travel to Northern Ireland as part of a Home International tournament.[119] The Thatcher Government's defence of the Falkland Islands may have been reassuring to Unionists, but the NF pointed up the contrast with the Ulster problem, which was allowed to persist for 13 years rather than the ten weeks it took to secure the Falklands.[120] The NF, moreover, played to Protestant sectarianism when it criticised Thatcher for not compelling the Pope to excommunicate the IRA before allowing him into Britain,[121] and when it publicised the views of one of its more extreme Ulster supporters, the virulently anti-Catholic George Seawright, a member of both Belfast City Council and the new assembly at Stormont,[122]

An intensified recruitment drive in Northern Ireland took off in 1983 with Jim Morrison claiming the formation of six new 'units', in north and east Belfast, Ballymena, Ballymoney, Enniskillen and Larne, together with more 'overt' activities on Ulster's streets.[123] The

---

[117] Prendiville, 'National Front faces problems with the police', *Hibernia*, 31 January 1980.
[118] 'Ulster will fight', *Nationalism Today*, no. 5 [1981].
[119] See 'N.F. delegation visits Ulster', *British Ulsterman* section of *Nationalism Today*, no. 6 [1981].
[120] 'Falklands versus Ulster', *Nationalism Today*, no. 14 [1983].
[121] See 'Smash the IRA!', *Nationalism Today*, no. 9 [April 1982].
[122] 'An Ulster loyalist speaks out', *Nationalism Today*, no. 18 [1983].
[123] 'Six new units set up: NF', *Belfast Telegraph*, 13 April 1983.

new NF leadership hoped that the removal of Martin Webster at the party's AGM of 1983 would allow the organisation to make greater progress in the region,[124] in the furtherance of which accusations of NF sympathy for Nazism were rejected with reference to the NF's own ex-servicemen's association.[125] At the same time, criticism of the conditions loyalist prisoners in Northern Ireland jails had to endure was emphasised, together with attacks on the 'supergrass system'.[126]

The new Ulster recruitment drive also included meetings and marches in Belfast and Coleraine, the Belfast meeting in early September 1983 (Figure 7) attracting a counter-march by CND, whose principal speaker was Joan Ruddock, its London chairperson.[127] It had been preceded by a meeting in Coleraine Town Hall on 9 July,[128] a meeting repeated when the NF returned to the town on 9 June 1984 and which attracted region-wide opposition by a Labour Movement Campaign against Fascism, concerned that the NF's real purpose was to smash the trade union and labour movement and destroy 'all democratic rights'.[129] But despite appeals for Coleraine Council to cancel the letting of the town hall for the NF event,[130] and for the Secretary of State Jim Prior to intervene,[131] the event went ahead. The significance the NF accorded it was reflected in the roster of speakers which, apart from the chairman, Jim Morrison, the Belfast NF organiser, included Phil Andrews, NF Directorate member; Joe Pearce, Chairman of the YNF; and Ian Anderson, NF Deputy Chairman.[132]

For Unionists the context was especially volatile, given the publication of the New Ireland Report in May. The report departed

[124] Kevin Toolis, 'Opening a new Irish front', *New Statesman*, 15 June 1984.
[125] *Belfast Telegraph*, 20 September 1983, press clipping, 'National Front defended' (UNA, *Searchlight* Archive, Box 28, National Front: SCH/01/Res/BRI/02/028).
[126] 'Smash the supergrass system', *Nationalism Today*, no. 21 [1984].
[127] 'Clash of marches in Belfast tomorrow', *Irish Times*, 2 September 1983.
[128] 'Webster recruiting drive hits Ulster', *Searchlight*, no. 99 (September 1983).
[129] 'Labour challenge to march by NF', *News Letter*, 23 May 1984; also, *Irish News*, 23 May 1984.
[130] 'March of hate', *Irish News*, 8 June 1984.
[131] 'Prior not to ban NF march in Coleraine', *Belfast Telegraph*, 8 June 1984.
[132] 'Coleraine welcomes the Front', *National Front News*, no. 58 [1984].

Figure 7   National Front March, Belfast, September 1983
Courtesy of the *Sunday World*

from traditional nationalist and republican demands for Irish unity by recognising the validity of the Unionist identity and generally opened up the Ulster problem to new interpretations.[133] But all Unionist parties, worried about its implications, rejected it together with the NF. The latter, reflecting the 'revolutionary' political direction the NF was taking under the new leadership, took the opportunity to demonstrate its own new thinking on Ulster by positing the Strasserite Third Position solution: 'The creation of a modern, revolutionary Ulster state within the British family of nations'.[134] In this 'New Ulster' the region's sectarian conflict would be a thing of the past, while the development of a white racially unified British State could even offer membership to southern

[133] Loughlin, *The Ulster Question since 1945*, p. 121.
[134] 'Ulster: no sell-out!', *National Front News*, no. 57 [1984].

Ireland.[135] Moreover, the 'new Ulster' was also offered as a solution to inter-loyalist disunity, something that had usually taken a severe crisis to overcome, as in 1974, but faded once the specific crisis had passed, thus 'paving the way for more Westminster treason'. To resolve this problem, Strasserism proposed a comprehensive programme covering 'social and economic issues' as well as constitutional. Foreign ownership and assets pertaining to Ulster enterprises 'must be taken over and run as workers cooperatives where possible', while private property must be spread to as many people as possible, 'not just a handful of plutocrats', and the banking system reformed. In this way sectional concerns in the loyalist/Unionist community would disappear to be replaced by a community of shared, harmonised interests at the same time as NF policies on immigration, withdrawal from the Common Market, NATO and the UN would end 'control over our affairs' by 'the barons of International Finance and the mass murderers of World Communism'.[136] But, as we have seen, socio-economic and political radicalism of a much lesser order than this found little adherents in the 1970s. Nor was the international dimension of NF activities likely to be better received.

This was intended to establish white racial unity and mobilisation in support of Ulster, the major activist for which being Steve Brady, who had a long record of loyalist and extreme-Right activities, nationally and internationally. From 1980 to 1982, he had attempted to establish a relationship between militant loyalism and European fascists.[137] Such contacts, however, were not attended by success. In April 1983, 15 members of the UVF were jailed for a total of 200 years. During their trial it was revealed that UVF members had been involved in negotiations with Belgian neo-fascists who offered to supply £50,000 worth of guns together with a free supply of

---

[135] Ian Anderson, 'Anti-loyalist campaign smashed', *Nationalism Today*, no. 23 [1984]; 'Ireland must be reborn', *Nationalism Today*, no. 25 [1984].

[136] 'British nationalism: the N.F.'s ideology', British Ulsterman supplement to *Nationalism Today*, no. 20 [1983]. A considerable period of time appears to have lapsed between the publication of this issue and the next, no. 21.

[137] Cathy Johnson, 'The National Front and the Ulster connection', *Fortnight*, 2 July 1986.

explosives in return for a UVF campaign of bomb attacks on Jewish targets in Britain, though the deal eventually fell through.[138] Given the lack of a significant antisemitic tradition in Northern Ireland this is hardly surprising, while for their part, Jews in Northern Ireland remained determinedly neutral in the conflict, rejecting loyalist overtures to facilitate the acquisition of arms from Israel.[139] Attempts to encourage antisemitism in the Ulster context, nevertheless, continued.[140] And despite the failure to effect a loyalist-European fascist alliance – the latter having a strong Catholic dimension – the international context was still seen as one which offered useful lessons loyalists could learn from, not least given how well Irish republicans had mobilised international support for the Provisional IRA, unlike loyalists who had no such connections.

This was a weakness, it was argued, that could be remedied by integrating the Ulster loyalist struggle into the worldwide struggle of the white race for survival against the threats to its existence: once racial nationalists throughout the world saw the loyalists as allies 'against [Jewish] International Finance and World Communism they will begin to actively support the Loyalist Cause'.[141] As such, it would harmonise with the NF's British struggle against the integrated black/republican menace.[142]

White international solidarity, such as it was, however, had little to show for its efforts. While the NF and Ulster loyalism supported white Rhodesia, British-facilitated negotiations saw the Smith regime fall in 1980, to be replaced by a Marxist-oriented Government led by Robert Mugabe. As *Nationalism Today* remarked, 'Within days of coming to power, Thatcher sold out Whites in Rhodesia – Ulster next?'[143] In sum, neither NF domestic nor international activities offered encouraging or effective options

[138] Ibid.

[139] Jim Cusack and Henry McDonald, *The UVF: The Endgame* (revised edn, Dublin: Poolbeg Press, 2008), pp. 116–17.

[140] 'Ex-Terrorists', *Nationalism Today*, no. 20 [1983]; '"Therefore Jew, though justice be thy plea, consider this"', *Nationalism Today*, no. 31 [1985].

[141] 'The role of the N.F. in Ulster politics', *Nationalism Today*, no. 20 [1983].

[142] Steve Brady, 'Ulster points the way to white victory', *Nationalism Today*, no. 8 [1982].

[143] *Nationalism Today*, no. 3, n.d. [early 1981].

for Ulster loyalists. It was reflective of their popular appeal that attendance for the 1984 Coleraine event was estimated at around 150 NF members and supporters, many from England, while around 600 anti-NF demonstrators paraded outside,[144] numbers undoubtedly more realistic than the NF's own estimate of 300, with only 30 from England.[145] The leading Official Unionist MP for North Armagh, Harold McCusker, remarked that anyone coming to Northern Ireland to help with the struggle against the IRA should not be cast lightly aside: 'But, in this case, I think it would do well to remember the saying, "With friends like these, who needs enemies".'[146]

No less telling of the gap between loyalism and the NF was an NF interview in April 1984 with Hugh Smyth, Deputy Lord Mayor of Belfast and leader of the mainly working-class Progressive Unionist Party (PUP). Smyth agreed with NF opposition to the EEC, but otherwise did not believe the IRA could be destroyed, or that 'coloured' immigration was a national problem – thus rejecting one of the major themes in NF attempts to harmonise Ulster loyalist and British neo-fascist interests, namely, that they were part and parcel of the same menace.[147] Nor did Smyth believe that Margaret Thatcher wanted to drive Northern Ireland out of the UK and did not concur with the view that NF supporter George Seawright's extreme British nationalism was necessarily the best way to convey the loyalist message: Smyth rejected 'nationalism', and referenced recent statements by the Queen against it. But probably most disconcerting was Smyth's disapproval of the NF's major pro-loyalist activity in Britain – aggressive opposition to republican demonstrations: the NF should stay within the law and 'concentrate on our democratic and logical ideas of proper representation for the people of Northern Ireland and the extension of full British rights and justice to this region of the United Kingdom'.[148] In fact, despite

[144] Kevin Toolis, 'Opening a new Irish front', *New Statesman*, 15 June 1984.
[145] 'Coleraine welcomes the Front', *National Front News*, no. 58 [1984].
[146] Ibid.
[147] 'Immigrant/IRA links exposed', *National Front News*, no. 58 [1984]; 'Blacks and the I.R.A.', *Nationalism Today*, no. 16 [1983].
[148] 'Hugh Smyth – Deputy Lord Mayor of Belfast', *Nationalism Today*, no. 21 [1984].

the favourable coverage *Nationalism Today* gave to George Seawright, it no less felt obliged to distance itself from his sectarianism: the 'National Front is a secular organisation that welcomes Catholics and Protestants alike into its ranks and, as such, we cannot condone Mr Seawright's views'.[149]

The Smyth interview, part of an NF policy of engaging with leading loyalists with a view to harmonising outlooks and activities, was embarrassing, and given Smyth's refusal to permit editing,[150] damage limitation was attempted by running an article by David Kerr, a leading NF member in the region, alongside the Smyth interview, though Kerr's critcism of the Queen for her commitment to 'the race-mixing, liberal ... World Order' was unlikely to go down well with a loyalist/Unionist community imbued with a pronounced monarchical loyalty.[151] But not only were NF activities in general failing significantly to develop regional support, the one area where they did show some degree of success – aggressive skinhead activity – was hardly conducive to wider Unionist support.

Skinhead activity was cultivated by Joe Pearce, YNF chairman, though Pearce's view that a loyal Northern Ireland Catholic could be British, but not a non-white person,[152] not only jarred with loyalist sensibilities at this time, but also the view of Jim Morrison, the local NF organiser.[153] Pearce had a more welcome reception from Paisleyites, but for aggressive opposition to republican sympathisers in Britain rather than activity in Northern Ireland.[154] However, he was concerned to make a mark in Northern Ireland, and building on his expertise as a street agitator, fertile ground seemed evident in the growth of a skinhead section, especially in Belfast.

A background for its development can be identified in August 1979 when contacts were established between the Belfast NF and

[149] See 'Spotlight on Ulster: the losing of the green', *Nationalism Today*, no. 27 [1985].
[150] 'NF setback in Ulster', *Searchlight*, no. 107, May 1984.
[151] Kerr interview, *Nationalism Today*, no. 21 [1984].
[152] 'Back to front: that's the NF line on Ulster', *News Letter*, 2 June 1981.
[153] Pearce, 'Northern Ireland: the third force'.
[154] Ibid.

'the remains of TARA, one of the North's most sinister loyalist paramilitary groups', most of whom were youthful, chiefly from east Belfast.[155] In this context, strengthening links were noted between the English-based YNF and 'ultra Protestant Ulster Volunteer Force youth groups',[156] or as the leading Scottish print the *Daily Record*, citing police sources, put it, 'Ulster death squads'.[157] Operating under the name 'NF SKINZ', by May 1984 the skinhead group had grown to around 200 members, and already with a well-publicised 'kill' to its credit, some of its members having murdered a Catholic man in the north of the city in 1983.[158] Of course, it required no encouragement from the NF for such a murder to occur, and it is important to record that, as a Catholic convert and having long left the NF behind, Pearce emphasised that he never wanted or encouraged the killing of anyone.[159] The nature of NF literature directed at its Northern Ireland constituency, however, could be distinctly at odds with the 'respectable' cross-confessional arguments directed at all Christian denominations in *Nationalism Today*.

Thus, a form of newsletter, *The Ulster Front Page*, apparently produced by the Ulster YNF for its members and supporters, combined criticism of corrupt Unionist politicians with encouragement of attacks on 'Taigs' [Catholics]. It reflected British NF prejudices when it detailed how NF supporters in the county Down town of Carryduff had prevented 'an invasion of the town by nigger students ... The gang of coons and the white slags who date them', and local loyalist prejudices in accounts of violent attacks on republicans and nationalists in the county Londonderry town of Limavady together with a loyalist invasion of the Catholic village of Ballygawley, county Tyrone, during which the local

---

[155] Chris Doherty, 'National Front links up with Tara', *Hibernia*, 25 October 1979.
[156] 'Recap no. 19: the paramilitary right', *Searchlight*, no. 100 (October 1983).
[157] 'Fear of Front link with death squads', *Daily Record*, 18 June 1984.
[158] 'Belfast killers had links with the National Front', *Irish Times*, 30 April 1984.
[159] Pearce, *Race with the Devil*, p. 112. The *Searchlight* mole in the NF, Tim Hepple, claimed that Pearce had converted to an 'extreme form' of Catholicism: *Searchlight, At War with Society: The Exclusive Story of a Searchlight Mole inside Britain's Far Right* (London: Searchlight, 1993), p. 4.

Catholic church was desecrated. Again, 'a plague of rats' reported at the Catholic Divis Flats in Belfast occasioned the comment that the rats were merely 'joining the human vermin that already lives there ... It is clear that the residents of [Catholic] west Belfast are no better than pigs and behave like pigs'. A forthcoming republican march in Leeds was also referenced and facilities offered for any NF members who wanted to join a counter-march.[160]

To some extent the skinheads might be regarded as an Ulster expression of the 'street-hardened young "political soldiers"'[161] that would become a central feature of the Griffinite NF faction from mid-decade, and *The Ulster Front Page* is revealing of the extent to which the NF would go to cultivate local support. But despite the NF's enhanced activity in Northern Ireland, that its only area of relative growth was among one of the most vicious elements of the loyalist community could hardly be accounted a great success.

It was against this background that an attempt to increase NF–loyalist cooperation was made by resolving an issue that had existed since the NF first organised in the north – whether it was there to compete with indigenous loyalist parties or just to support them. The *British Ulsterman* supplement to *Nationalism Today*, edited by Pearce, declared:

> The NF considers that many organisations in Ulster are doing a first rate job in their fight against Republicanism. For this reason the National Front will seek to assist Loyalist organisations and will not seek to oppose them in any way. We will not stand in elections where other Loyalist parties are standing and our members in Ulster will be encouraged to help in the election campaigning of existing parties.
>
> The most important role that the NF will play in Northern Ireland politics will be in helping to widen Ulster's sphere of influence.[162]

<hr/>

[160] *The Ulster Front Page*, [January 1983?] (UNA, *Searchlight* Archive, Box 6, National Front: SCH/01/Res/EUR/02/006).
[161] Hill with Bell, *The Other Face of Terror*, pp. 295–96.
[162] See 'The role of the N.F. in Ulster politics', *British Ulsterman* supplement to *Nationalism Today*, no. 20 [1983].

Effectively, this was an admission of NF weakness as an independent political force in the region. Nevertheless, despite its political failures, Northern Ireland continued to inspire hope. As the political effects of the New Ireland Forum Report were felt and the groundwork for the AIA laid, the aggression of the loyalist and Unionist reaction was such that it looked as if a constitutional crisis serious enough to carry NF ambitions to fruition had at last arrived.

7

The National Front (II)

Combating the Anglo-Irish Agreement, 1985–1990

The sense of crisis that engulfed Ulster loyalism and Unionism in November 1985 was more intense than that of 1974. Then, the Council of Ireland was the bugbear that effectively brought the Sunningdale Agreement down, through fear of southern influence in Northern Ireland affairs; now, the Anglo-Irish Agreement (AIA) *formalised* southern influence on northern governance, and unlike 1974 there were no established institutions in Northern Ireland at which loyalists could vent their anger and opposition, the meetings of the Agreement being a moveable feast that could be held at any designated location in northern or southern Ireland, or Britain. Signed by Margaret Thatcher and Garret FitzGerald, the Irish Taoiseach, on 15 November 1985, at Hillsborough Castle, county Down, it was an international treaty between the United Kingdom and the Irish Republic, and a multidimensional response to the Ulster problem premised on the understanding that the involvement of both States was an essential basis for any solution, their mutual engagement covering political, legal, economic, social, cultural, constitutional and security cooperation. As such, the Agreement was not intended as a *solution* to the Ulster problem but, with Unionist anxieties in mind, an instrument for addressing nationalist grievances and by doing so compel Unionists to negotiate one, the preferred solution being centred on a form of restored power-sharing Government at Stormont. Until such a Government emerged, however, the Irish Government represented the interests of the Catholic community, its role in the governance of the north facilitated by a secretariat of Irish civil servants at Maryfield, outside Belfast.[1]

---

[1] James Loughlin, *The Ulster Question since 1945* (1998; 2nd edn, Basingstoke: Palgrave Macmillan, 2004), pp. 125–28.

Most worrying for Unionists, not only did the absence of settled institutions in Northern Ireland make the Agreement difficult to oppose, but the element of Irish Republic 'influence' in the governance of Northern Ireland was ambiguous – at what point would it be instrumental or marginal in any given situation? Accordingly, both Unionism and loyalist paramilitarism united in the wake of its announcement. David Kerr, a leading Ulster NF member reflected loyalist paranoia when he claimed that even 'the isolated Whites in Black inner cities have ... more security than border loyalists'. Westminster had betrayed Ulster and the Queen had not lifted a hand to help Ulster loyalists.[2] The AIA would provide the context of Northern Ireland politics until the Belfast/ Good Friday Agreement of 1998. This chapter will attempt to assess how the NF, especially the Griffinite Political Soldier faction, sought to exploit the Northern Ireland problem in the period from the signing of the AIA in November 1985 until the NF collapsed in 1990, for the purpose of creating a revolutionary movement that would establish an independent Ulster and by so doing create the spark for similar revolutionary developments in Europe.

The NF: Internal Division and Its Consequences

The official reorganisation of the NF as a revolutionary movement was completed and publicly explained in 1986 as campaigning against the AIA was developing,[3] and elaborated upon over the next year, especially its new policy on race. Thus there was now approval, not just for white, but for black and 'coloured' leaders such as Louis Farrakhan and Colonel Gaddafi – Farrakhan and Gaddafi were committed antisemites – and the latter's *Green Book* became recommended reading. Libya, Derek Holland averred, was a model of 'direct, or people's democracy, in an actual and practical form'.[4] It has been argued that under the influence of the Political Soldiers

---

[2] David Kerr, 'The crisis in Ulster', *Nationalism Today*, no. 37, March 1986.
[3] 'Organising the movement', *National Front News*, no. 82, November 1986.
[4] Roger Eatwell, 'The esoteric ideology of the National Front in the 1980s', in Mike Cronin (ed.), *The Failure of British Fascism: The Far Right and the Fight For Political Recognition* (Basingstoke: Palgrave Macmillan, 1996), p. 109.

the NF 'reneged on its long-standing commitment to Ulster'.[5] This was not the case, only the objective of its engagement had changed, though not necessarily pursued in a productive way, for the process of reorganisation had produced a split in the organisation.

The Griffinite faction won a bitter court battle that gave it control of the NF organisation, the party's Croydon bookshop, printing works and administrative records, while Griffin, the party's Deputy Chairman, announced the suspension of the Chairman, Martin Wingfield, and three other members of the 18-man National Directorate, accusing them of being State intelligence agents fomenting disaffection among members at a time of 'special potential' – an indirect reference to Northern Ireland which he believed to be in a state of incipient revolution.[6] However, the Griffinites failed to win over the mass of the NF membership.

Wingfield, Ian Anderson (another former chairman), Andrew Brons and Joe Pearce – the last serving a 12-month prison sentence having been convicted on a charge of inciting racial hatred on 12 December 1985[7] – established the Flag faction, named after one of its publications, *The Flag*. The toxicity of the atmosphere between the two factions is reflected in Pearce's criticism of Nick Griffin, his former close friend, whom he accused of 'an ignoble and ignominious act of betrayal ... of mutual friends of ours ... in a scurrilous booklet ... The "facts" published in this booklet were so poisonous that I found it hard to believe that my friend could have been capable of such gutter-scraping mendacity.'[8] It seems clear

---

[5] Nigel Copsey, *Contemporary British Fascism: The British National Party and the Quest for Legitimacy* (2004; 2nd edn, Basingstoke: Palgrave Macmillan, 2008), p. 37.

[6] For the Griffinite account, see 'Attempted murder: the state/reactionary plot against the National Front' [August 1986] (http://www.aryanunity.com/attempted_murder1.html). Accessed 19 February 2017. For further comment on the importance Griffin placed on Ulster as a site of potential revolution, see 'NF gain world-wide support for Ulster's cause', *National Front News*, no. 92, July (1), 1987. For a time in 1987, and probably better to exploit the Ulster crisis, *National Front News* was produced twice monthly.

[7] Joseph Pearce, *Race with the Devil: My Journey from Racial Hatred to Rational Love* (Charlotte, NC: Saint Benedict Press, 2013), pp. 180–81.

[8] Ibid., pp. 76, 188–89.

Pearce was particularly offended by Griffin's targeting of Andrew Brons. During the second half of the 1980s, Pearce was undergoing a gradual and rather difficult personal journey from racist beliefs and politics to conversion to Roman Catholicism, a process completed in 1989;[9] and while on that journey he credits Brons with introducing him to the Catholic ideas of G. K. Chesterton and Hilaire Belloc.[10]

As opposed to the Political Soldiers, the Flag membership was generally 'made up of the more working-class and lower middle-class side of the party. In the late 1980s this group had perhaps 2000 members, compared to the Political Soldiers, who numbered at most a few hundred'.[11] Its political position was outlined in the first issue of *Vanguard*.

Rejecting the 'leadership cult' and intellectual theorising on the basis of foreign models of the Griffinites, it emphasised the importance of speaking plain English, 'the language of the people', with native English thinkers such as Hilaire Belloc and G. K. Chesterton as models, together with the development of a mass base and a focus on electoral success. As against the Griffinite emphasis on a leadership cadre that would direct a revolution in conditions of State crisis, the Flag faction pointedly remarked, 'unless our support base is expanded we will be too small to take advantage of a crisis'. At the same time, and despite the Flag leadership's warning to 'avoid thuggish behaviour' that damaged the party image and brought State repression,[12] the mass base of a neo-fascist organisation was only too likely to be physically aggressive; and indeed it was not something Brons was concerned about in the early 1980s.[13] As one former Flag activist has put it: 'The last thing we wanted to do was sit down in some strange farmhouse and be questioned by some Political Soldier about our revolutionary and religious convictions. Everyone was

---

[9] Ibid., pp. 194, 203.

[10] Ibid., pp. 157–58.

[11] Eatwell, 'The esoteric Ideology', p. 113.

[12] 'Loyalty is forever', *Vanguard*, no. 1, August 1986.

[13] Matthew Collins, 'The National Front at 50; Part II' (https://www.hopenothate.org.uk/2017/12/15/national-front-50-part-ii-hope-not-hate-magazine/). Accessed 23 March 2018.

welcome in our idea of the party, particularly those with a relaxed attitude to violence ... The minute someone started toying with the mechanics of this well-oiled machine, it fell to fucking pieces.'[14]

In its resistance to the ideological theorising based on foreign models on which the Political Soldier position was based, the Flag rank and file mentality, at one level, might be seen as closer to that of loyalist paramilitaries; nevertheless, Brons claimed that the NF (Flag faction) had evolved: from a party 'that knew exactly what it opposed, but not what it stood for, to a Radical Racial Nationalist Party with a comprehensive ideology and a comprehensive policy'.[15] This took the form predominantly of Distributism, a socio-economic policy which married nationalism and individual initiative for societal good through eliminating harmful internal division within the nation; harmonising maximum individual self-advancement and societal well-being; and by increasing the sense of initiative and responsibility of the nation. Accordingly, Distributism, with its emphasis on national harmonisation and cooperative ownership was deemed much superior to the corporatism traditionally associated with radical nationalism. Corporatism, it was claimed, *constitutionalised* the antagonistic categories of capitalist and worker rather than eliminated them.[16] Yet, despite the existence of different factions in the NF, it is important, as Roger Eatwell argues, not to impose neat ideological divisions 'when the reality was often confused'.[17] Distributism also had its adherents among the Political Soldiers,[18] not least the Political Soldier faction in Northern Ireland which would claim it as their socio-economic policy, married to the 'revolutionary' solution of Ulster independence.[19]

This solution to the conflict, however, sat in stark opposition to that of the Flag faction, which resolutely rejected breaking the Union and effecting the 'complete fragmentation of the indigenous

---

[14] Matthew Collins, *Hate: My Life in the British Far Right* (London: Biteback Publishing, 2011), p. 58.
[15] Quoted, ibid. See also 'Loyalty is forever', *Vanguard*, no. 1, August 1986.
[16] Eatwell, 'The esoteric ideology ', pp. 113–14.
[17] Ibid., p. 115.
[18] Collins, 'The National Front at 50; Part II'.
[19] See John Coulter, 'Front poses sinister new threat', *News Letter*, 29 September 1986.

"races" inhabiting the British Isles'.[20] Ulster had to be defended 'as we would defend Wales, Kent and Yorkshire', and in cooperation with the Democratic Unionist Party (DUP) and Official Unionists, rather than, as was the Griffinite approach, attacking them.[21] The Flag position was undoubtedly reinforced by the close relationship, if not actual membership by some Flag members of loyalist organisations and the Orange Order in Britain.[22] The two factions were united in wanting the most severe security measures to defeat the Provisional IRA, but radically opposed in constitutional remedies for the Ulster conflict, and in this context the Political Soldier faction was at a distinct disadvantage, for a position in line with loyalist thinking was more likely to be sellable than Ulster independence, though it is important not to overstate Flag influence. An NF consumed by internal conflicts in which bitter personal animosities, sabotage, incompetence and ideological conflict were all intertwined, ensured that both factions were weakened. By 1990, the Political Soldier faction had practically broken up, and although the Flag faction staggered on, a continuing 'haemorrhage of NF members meant that by the early 1990s it was the BNP that was the main organisation on the far right'.[23]

The NF and the Unionist Agitation against the AIA

The Griffinite analysis of the Ulster problem, as defined by Steve Brady – aligned with the Political Soldier faction in late 1985 – rightly argued that it was not about theological differences but political ideas. He also claimed the population was overwhelmingly loyal, consisting not only of the 59 per cent Protestant and Unionist community but also at least one-third of 'the 41 per cent Catholic

[20] Andrew Tyler, 'Rupture in the Front', *Time Out*, May 1986 (UNA, *Searchlight* Archive, Box 6, Ulster: SCH/01/Res/EUR/02/006).
[21] 'NF Ulster Policy Statement', National Front [Flag], *The Newsletter*, [c.1986–87] (UNA, *Searchlight* Archive, Box 6, Ulster: SCH/01/Res/EUR/02/006).
[22] 'UDI row fuels Front split', *Searchlight* (June 1986). For more on factional differences, see also 'Loyalty is forever', *Vanguard*, no. 1, August 1986 (UNA, *Searchlight* Archive, Box 6, Ulster: SCH/01/Res/EUR/02/006).
[23] Eatwell, 'The esoteric ideology', pp. 114–15.

electorate', leaving only 20 per cent to 25 per cent of the electorate seriously committed to republicanism. This cross-community loyal majority, betrayed by the British Government and persecuted by Provisional IRA terrorism, was now demanding the right to self-determination: 'the Loyalist people are now beginning to stir'. An accompanying argument by Derek Holland, who had visited Northern Ireland, was rather more realistic about the problems of inter-community differences, but still promoted Ulster independence as the best hope for a solution.[24]

Brady's analysis of the Ulster conflict was a combination of the sound and erroneous. He was right in thinking that republicanism was supported by only a minority of the population, but clearly erroneous in his assertion that a third of the Catholic community was 'loyalist'. Again, while he was right in asserting that the conflict was not about theological differences, he ignored the fact that loyalist paramilitaries selected their victims in the great majority of cases on a simple sectarian basis – their Catholic religion. And despite the NF's proclaimed anti-sectarian stance, pride of place was given in the December 1985 issue of *Nationalism Today* to the viciously anti-Catholic, George Seawright, a member of the Northern Ireland Assembly and NF supporter.[25] But more seriously erroneous was the faction's claim of an Ulster loyalist demand for independence: this proposal was never influential in the Unionist community.

Given the wider ideological framework of the Political Soldier faction, and the NF more generally, it was natural for the AIA 'sell-out' phase of the Ulster conflict to be seen in the context of the collapse of white Rhodesia, and for the Political Soldier faction tempting to accuse the Flag faction of regarding Ulster, like Rhodesia, as a lost cause.[26] But, the Griffinite faction argued, white Rhodesia fell because it had become 'too effete, bourgeois and materialist'. Ulster was different. Its people never had a soft life;

[24] Steve Brady, 'Ulster – the slippery road towards civil war'; Derek Holland, 'A Catholic visits Ulster', *Nationalism Today*, no. 31, October 1985.
[25] 'Ulster', *Nationalism Today*, no. 32, August 1985; see also 'Spotlight on policy: Ulster', *Nationalism Today*, no. 38, April 1986.
[26] 'Ulster must fight', *Nationalism Today*, no. 37, March 1986.

rather, their resistance had been deepened and hardened by 20 years of republican terrorism. Moreover, when Rhodesia fell, the NF was an impotent spectator. In the coming Ulster revolution there was a real prospect of the NF playing a decisive political role, with the repercussions felt not only throughout Britain but throughout Europe.[27] As Griffin later explained: 'If one of the British nations can be wrested from the grip of the American/Zionist/Capitalist axis, then the liberation of the rest will not be far behind. And when Britain awakes, Europe's long drugged sleep will be at an end. Ulster is where it will begin.'[28]

In pursuit of that objective Brady and Jim Morrison, the Belfast NF organiser, mobilised the recent history of IRA atrocities and Westminster betrayal to inflame loyalist opinion: the AIA was a reward for terrorism and the channel for future betrayals. Even the guarantee for Northern Ireland's constitutional position so long as a majority existed to maintain it was nothing new: it was part of the Sunningdale Agreement of 1973, but did not negate the 'imperialistic' claims in the Irish constitution over the whole territory of Ireland.[29] And Unionist concerns were heightened further by the limited success of their attempts to mobilise opposition to the AIA, not least in Britain.

Unionist MPs in Northern Ireland sought to demonstrate the degree of regional opposition to the AIA by resigning their seats and forcing by-elections with the target of obtaining 500,000 votes. But only 418,230 anti-AIA votes were registered, with one seat actually being lost to the nationalist Social Democratic and Labour Party (SDLP). A similar attempt to impress the Thatcher Government by contesting British elections was a greater failure, while a projected campaign of mass demonstrations in Britain fizzled out when only 100 people turned out for the first such meeting in Liverpool. Moreover, a Friends of the Union group established within the

[27] Ibid.
[28] 'NF gain world-wide support for Ulster's cause', *National Front News*, no. 92, July (1), 1987.
[29] Steve Brady, 'Murdering bastards!'; Jim Morrison, 'Ulster: no sell-out', *National Front News*, no. 73 [December 1985]. Incomplete dating means that this is sometimes determined from issue content.

Conservative Party in May 1986 to coordinate the campaign had little effect on Tory elite and popular opinion.[30] In fact, when Unionists travelled to Britain to assess the prospects of influencing public opinion, they were shocked at the total lack of sympathy for, or understanding of, Unionism.[31] Accordingly, Unionist opposition to the AIA would have a primary focus on activity within Northern Ireland, and since the 'loyalist' third of the Catholic community that Brady identified failed to make its presence felt, a close alignment with loyalist paramilitarism was inevitable.

Thus, the Ulster Clubs that the DUP formed in conjunction with loyalist paramilitaries in early November 1985 to oppose the forthcoming AIA – it would grow to around 88 units in Northern Ireland and about 20,000 members[32] – was approved by the Griffinite Ulster faction, as a widespread campaign of political and civil disobedience, which included boycotts of the Northern Ireland Office and Westminster, protests in the Northern Ireland Assembly, mass public protests, a one-day general strike attended by intimidation, non-payment of rent and rates and the refusal to set local government rates, got under way.[33] In early 1986, loyalist paramilitarism added to these activities with a campaign of violence against policemen deemed to be collaborating in implementing the AIA and – though not something the NF could endorse – an enhanced sectarian murder campaign against the Catholic community.[34] But while the failure of these activities to have their intended effect was highly disappointing to Unionists and loyalists, this was not the case for the Griffinite faction, for whom aggressive community action served a quite different purpose: revolution was unlikely to come from Westminster amelioration of Unionist concerns and had to appeal to both communities. For this to occur such action needed to be extended and to have a wider scope. More exactly, it was necessary that the existing loyalist paramilitary and

---

[30] Loughlin, *The Ulster Question since 1945*, pp. 98–99.
[31] Feargal Cochrane, *Unionist Politics and the Politics of Unionism since the Anglo-Irish Agreement* (Cork: Cork University Press, 1997), pp. 222–23.
[32] Peter Taylor, *Loyalists* (London: Bloomsbury, 2000), p. 180.
[33] Loughlin, *The Ulster Question since 1945*, pp. 129–30.
[34] Ibid., p. 130.

Unionist leadership be condemned and removed: 'the old failed Establishment politicians [and] ... the so-called Loyalist politicians who have grown fat on promoting bigotry'. Only their removal could lay the foundation to resolve the problems an independent Ulster would face – sectarian hatred, violence, unemployment, bad-housing, and, 'to cap it all, a Chinese immigration problem'.[35] Moreover, for the purpose of taking 'power in Ulster' the Griffinites proposed adding a VAT tax strike and a television licence strike to the existing Unionist activities, together with a rejection of the RUC in favour of loyalist self-policing and a programme to rebuild 'our communities'.

Non-cooperation with State authorities was not unique, such a policy having been pursued by the nationalist community in protest against internment in the early 1970s. The distinctiveness of the Griffinite ideas, however, was expressed in Distributivist proposals that included the creation of an Ulster business co-op – removing Ulster businesses from international and Government control and transferring control to local workers and managers.[36] Past experience of loyalism had clearly indicated such radical ideas would be unacceptable, but the Griffinites believed that their support for militant loyalism was appreciated and influential – when some Griffinite members in the north were remanded in custody *National Front News* associated their imprisonment with that of loyalist internees, bringing the issue to British popular attention in association with the 'independence of Ulster' demand.[37]

Evidence of the Political Soldiers' increasing influence in Northern Ireland was read into its paper sales in the region in 1986, which 'rose rapidly from 300 to over 1,000 (equivalent to a circulation of 50,000 on the mainland)' and continued to soar,[38] while individual NF units could be relied upon to spread the Griffinite message, such as that in

[35] 'Victory to Ulster!', *British Ulsterman* supplement to *National Front News*, no. 75 [March 1986].
[36] 'Preparing for power in Ulster', *National Front News*, no. 79 [August 1986]; 'Victory to Ulster', *British Ulsterman*, no. 75 [March 1986].
[37] 'Internment on remand', *National Front News*, no. 80 [October 1986]; 'Magilligan P.O.W.'s eight demands', 'Barking', *National Front News*, no. 84, February (1), 1987.
[38] 'Attempted murder: the state/reactionary plot against the National Front'.

Portadown, which produced its own leaflet, *Ulster Patriot*.[39] Again, the commitment of the Belfast NF formation to the 'revolutionary' position had been demonstrated in April 1986 when its Belfast organiser Andrew McLorie, a schoolteacher, was prosecuted and later imprisoned for two years for participating in petrol bombing an RUC sergeant's home, the incident getting widespread coverage in the Irish and British press,[40] though an association was made between NF meetings and attacks on Catholic residences in the region.[41] And, as in the past, NF activities failed to produce significant political influence, while its internal divisions were easily exacerbated.

Thus, a week-long investigation by the *Yorkshire Post* of the Political Soldiers' 'revolutionary' activities in Northern Ireland was regarded by the Griffinites as 'designed to frighten the N.F. away from involvement in Ulster (which it failed to do) and to scare the [Flag] reactionaries into trying to ditch the new militancy. In this at least, it achieved its objective.'[42] For its part, the Flag faction regarded the *Yorkshire Post* report as media lies promoted by the National Union of Journalists,[43] and was 'horrified' that a major newspaper regarded the Political Soldier faction as representative of the NF in general. As expressed by Martin Wingfield, the Flag position sought to mitigate the impression of a profoundly divided organisation, taking a position synonymous with the Griffinites on respect for 'different races', 'coloured' immigrant repatriation, and on punishing NF members engaged in racial attacks, but rejecting foreign influence

[39] 'Ulster', *National Front News*, no. 95, September 1987.
[40] See 'The National Front "is behind attacks on the police"', *Daily Telegraph*, 11 April 1986; 'Belfast bomb: NF link denied', *Morning Star*, 12 April 1986; 'Bombings denied by Front', *Irish Press*, 12 April 1986; 'Teacher in NF denies bombing', *News Letter*, 12 April 1986; 'Bomb charge teacher says "I'm in NF"', *Irish News*, 12 April 1986.; 'National Front role denied', *Irish Times*, 12 April 1986; also in similar vein, *Morning Star*, 12 April 1986; *Irish Press*, 12 April 1986; *Daily Telegraph*, 11 April 1986, press clippings (UNA, *Searchlight* Archive, Box 28, National Front: SCH/01/Res/Bri/028).
[41] See, for instance, *Edinburgh Evening News*, 23 April 1986; *Shropshire Star*, 23 April 1986, press clippings (UNA, *Searchlight* Archive, Box 28, National Front: SCH/01/Res/Bri/028).
[42] 'Attempted murder: the state/reactionary plot against the National Front'.
[43] 'Nailing the media lies', *National Front News*, no. 75 [March 1986] (UNA, *Searchlight* Archive, Box 28, National Front: SCH/01/Res/Bri/028).

on NF policies together with 'revolutionary' or 'terrorist', as opposed
to electoral, activity. In this context, Wingfield denied that the NF
was a recruiting agent for the UDA in Britain, but admitted that it
sold publications by all Unionist and loyalist groupings,[44] while at
a Directorate meeting, he rejected the Political Soldier support for
loyalist attacks on the RUC, urging instead a strictly law-abiding
policy. He was overruled, as was his later proposal – so the Griffinites
argued – for the NF to abandon the Ulster issue completely.[45]

The Flag faction's differences with the Griffinites also found
expression in NF Ulster-focused activities in Britain, with
Wingfield opposing UDI for Ulster at a rally against a 'Bloody
Sunday' march in London at the start of February 1986.[46] It
also rejected Griffinite advice to refuse cooperation with the
Metropolitan Police on arrangements for the NF counter-meeting
in protest against police harassment of NF activists; and also advice
to oppose American bases in Britain, from which Gaddafi's Libya
was attacked. Wingfield, the Griffinites argued, 'may have excellent
credentials as a racialist, but so has the extreme right-wing of
the Tory party, which is where Wingfield belongs'.[47] As for the
Bloody Sunday demonstration, the NF counter-demonstration still
managed to create disorder which received negative State-wide
publicity.[48] But what was for the Political Soldiers a brave act by the
only group determined enough to confront republican terrorists,[49]
did absolutely nothing for the anti-AIA campaign, nor for their
objective of an independent Ulster.

[44] Ibid.
[45] 'Attempted murder: the state/reactionary plot against the National Front'.
[46] Ibid.
[47] Ibid.
[48] 'NF men attack march', *Northern Echo*, 3 February 1986; 'Marchers
ambushed by NF mob', *Oxford Mail*, 3 February 1986; 'National Front in
demo clash', *Western Mail*, 3 February 1986; 'NF group clash with marchers',
Eastern Daily Press, 3 February 1986; 'Missiles hurled', *East Anglican Daily
Times*, 3 February 1986; also 'NF attacks Bloody Sunday marchers', *News
Letter*, 3 February 1986; 'NF violence at march', *Irish Press*, 3 February 1986,
press clippings (UNA, *Searchlight* Archive, Box 28, National Front: SCH/01/
Res/Bri/028).
[49] 'Front Stand Alone', *National Front News*, no. 75 [March 1986].

266 Fascism and Constitutional Conflict

A *Searchlight* report of April 1986 brought together a variety of British press items on NF–loyalist connections to demonstrate a widespread cross-fertilisation of activities from gun running to individual acts of violence, together with aggressive participation in marches.[50] It was clearly with reference to such activities that Sir John Herman, Chief Constable of the RUC, warned of some Ulster politicians having close paramilitary links and connections with other extremists involved in orchestrating the current anti-RUC campaign.[51] Or, as the *Daily Telegraph* put it: 'The National Front is behind attacks on the police.'[52]

The exposure of the NF's Ulster links inevitably placed strain on the already failing Unionist/loyalist campaign against the AIA. That was an alliance born of necessity, and for the more respectable elements – especially the Official Unionist Party (OUP) led by Jim Molyneaux – political extremism was something the Thatcher Government would use against them. Molyneaux had warned loyalist leaders at the beginning of 1986 of the dangers of the NF connection,[53] which appeared to have some effect. A directive from the UDA, 'United Kingdom Command', apparently from this period, ordered 'all members … to withhold active support of the National Front until otherwise instructed'.[54] Molyneaux's anxieties about the NF, however, were not so quickly taken on board by Ian Paisley's more radical DUP.

In July 1986, it was embarrassed when the *Today* newspaper ran a front page spread on the NF–loyalist connection, with a picture of Nick Griffin and John Field – the latter a Welshman resident in Northern Ireland and later to be the Ulster organiser – recruiting at the 12 July Orange demonstrations, while also claiming that David Kerr and Field flanked Ian Paisley when he led a loyalist takeover

---

[50] 'Comrades in arms', *Searchlight*, no. 130, April 1986.
[51] John Blevins, 'Fascist support for Unionists', *Morning Star*, 12 April 1986, press clipping (UNA, *Searchlight* Archive, Box 28, National Front: SCH/01/Res/Bri/028).
[52] *Daily Telegraph*, 11 April 1986, press clipping (UNA, *Searchlight* Archive, Box 28, National Front: SCH/01/Res/Bri/028).
[53] 'National Front and loyalists fall out', *Searchlight*, no. 128, February 1986.
[54] Ulster Defence Association: United Kingdom Command, circular, n.d. (UNA, *Searchlight* Archive, Box 28, National Front: SCH/01/Res/Bri/028).

of the town of Hillsborough (location of the monarch's residence in Northern Ireland) on 10 July 1986.[55] Paisley and Peter Robinson, DUP deputy leader, denied that the party had any connection with UDI-supporting neo-fascist organisations,[56] but the DUP's association with political extremism came to the fore again on 7 August 1986, when Robinson led a disruptive loyalist 'invasion' of the county Monaghan village of Clontibret in the Irish Republic, for which episode he was arrested and in January 1987 brought to court where the judge branded him a 'senior extremist politician' and imposed a fine of £15,000.[57] On 10 November 1986, Paisley presided over the formation of Ulster Resistance in the Ulster Hall, Belfast,[58] an organisation which apparently existed to control popular loyalism by bringing a number of organisations of varying degrees of extremism under its direction,[59] but which fed the extremist image: David Kerr, publisher of *Ulster Sentinel*, a journal dedicated to 'the cause of World White Solidarity and National Revival', claimed he was invited to the ticket-only occasion,[60] while the organisation, together with the UDA and UVF, would be involved in gun-running in this period,[61] indications of which caused Ian Paisley and Peter Robinson to dissociate themselves from the organisation.[62] Extremism associated with the Unionist anti-AIA campaign culminated on 15 November 1986, the anniversary of the signing of the AIA, with a major Unionist–NF protest at Bridgwater, Somerset, in the constituency of Tom

[55] 'Paisley's fascist sidesmen', *Today*, 15 July 1986, press clipping (UNA, *Searchlight* Archive, Box 6, Ulster: SCH/01/Res/EUR/02/006).

[56] 'Nazis push for Ulster UDI', *Tribune*, 21 July 1986, press clipping (UNA, *Searchlight* Archive, Box 6, Ulster: SCH/01/Res/EUR/02/006).

[57] Paul Bew and Gordon Gillespie, *Northern Ireland: A Chronology of the Troubles, 1968–1999* (1993; 2nd edn, Dublin: Gill & Macmillan, 1999), p. 202.

[58] Ibid., p. 204.

[59] Brendan O'Brien, 'Inside the loyalist terror machine', *Irish Independent*, 19 November 1986.

[60] Kerr, 'The history of the National Front in Ulster'.

[61] Jim Cusack and Henry McDonald, *The UVF: The Endgame* (revised edn, Dublin: Poolbeg Press, 2008), pp. 219–22.

[62] Ed Moloney, *Paisley: From Demagogue to Democrat?* (Dublin: Poolbeg, 2008), pp. 318–19.

King, Secretary of State for Northern Ireland, accompanied by a simultaneous loyalist rally in Northern Ireland. But, as an event intended to advance the Unionist case in Britain, it was entirely counterproductive, raising anxieties among the local population, attracting anti-fascist counter-demonstrators, and with ensuing trouble between the latter and the Ulster loyalist/ NF/ Friends of British Ulster/ British National Party members.[63]

Addressed by Martin Wingfield of the Flag faction and the OUP MP Fraser Agnew, together with a message of support from the Revd Ian Paisley, the disorder provoked by the protest was universally blamed on the Unionist/far-Right contingent and linked by the press both to NF violence in Manchester and loyalist attacks on Catholic areas of Northern Ireland during which an elderly woman died.[64] In November 1986, the Students' Union at Queen's University Belfast declared it would oppose any attempt by the NF to organise among students,[65] while John McMichael, UDA vice-Chairman, in accepting NF support in opposing the AIA, warned that this did not 'commit the UDA to support for its larger aims'.[66]

Loyalist awareness of these 'larger aims' had been facilitated greatly by a major article on the NF in the region's leading Unionist print, *News Letter*, by the journalist John Coulter. This followed the Griffinite faction's outline of its Ulster objectives in August,[67] and which Coulter viewed as a 'sinister new threat'. He interviewed John Field, the new regional organiser following the imprisonment of

---

[63] See 'Town's Ulster demo fear', *Western Daily Press*, 15 November 1986; 'Woman dies as loyalists rampage', *Birmingham Post*, 17 November 1986; 'Ulster march trouble sparks ban call', *Western Daily Press*, 18 November 1986; 'Violence flares at Bridgwater', *Western Gazette*, 21 November 1986; 'Demo arrests', *Peterborough Evening Telegraph*, 24 November 1986 (UNA, *Searchlight* Archive, Box 26, National Front: SCH/01/Res/EUR/02/026).
[64] 'Demo arrests', *Peterborough Evening Telegraph*, 24 November 1986 (UNA, *Searchlight* Archive, Box 26, National Front: SCH/01/Res/EUR/02/026).
[65] 'Union vows to fight Front', *News Letter*, 4 November 1986.
[66] 'Opening a second front for fascism', *Scotsman*, 31 January 1987, press clipping (UNA, *Searchlight* Archive, Box 6, Ulster: SCH/01/Res/EUR/02/006).
[67] 'Preparing for power in Ulster', *National Front News*, no. 79 [August 1986].

McLorie, on the NF's Ulster polices, especially on the independent Ulster the Griffinite faction envisaged:

> By independence we mean negotiated independence from the British state. The only thing we wish to sever is a corrupt political link. The cultural, spiritual, racial and historical link between Ulster and the mainland will remain forever. People will always remember the sacrifice Ulster made in two world wars and the Falklands. What makes an Ulsterman feel British is the same as what makes an Englishman feel British – it is a gut feeling.[68]

Under negotiated independence Britain would assist Ulster financially in return for facilitating 'Northern Ireland's vital strategic importance to NATO'.[69] Field refused to disclose what specific relations the NF had with paramilitary groups – 'in general, we support all loyalist paramilitaries'[70] – but claimed that as a member of the NF Directorate he would be the link man with loyalist organisations and envisaged a vital role for the Ulster Clubs in an independent Ulster, which he urged the NF's own supporters to join: they would form the basis of an alternative welfare state and civil service in an economic system based on Distributism.[71] In furtherance of NF–loyalist cooperation, the Ulster formation called for a Bill of Rights to protect the loyalist right of public assembly in protests against the AIA.[72]

For a loyalist community which had seen its anti-AIA activities fail over the previous year, activities directed to securing Northern Ireland's constitutional position *within* the United Kingdom, the radicalism of a party whose presence was marginal in Northern Ireland had little practical to offer. Thus it was easy for *Combat*, the UDA magazine, to reject the NF as an evil, race-hate peddling organisation for which there was no place in

[68] John Coulter, 'Front poses sinister new threat', *News Letter*, 29 September 1986.

[69] Ibid.

[70] Ibid.

[71] Ibid.; 'National Front aims for growth in north', *Irish Times*, 5 November 1986.

[72] 'NF bid to combat "Repressive laws"', *News Letter*, 18 December 1986.

Northern Ireland.[73] The Griffinites would reject this criticism, emphasising their anti-racism,[74] but to little effect.

In sum, by the end of 1986 it was clear that whatever hopes had been invested in the loyalist–NF link at the beginning of the year had been shown to be entirely misplaced. Aggressive rhetoric aside, the Ulster Unionist case was ultimately directed to the Westminster Government – the most important player in the Ulster conflict – and British public opinion. In this context any association with the NF was entirely counter-productive. It was a reality the Griffinites refused to acknowledge, professing satisfaction with their progress. By November 1986, the faction had established a Belfast base, with a permanent office and bookshop in Templemore Avenue in east Belfast,[75] and looked forward to political success in 1987.

Political Soldiers: Expectations and Experience

It says much about the Griffinite mentality in 1987 that it would confidently call for a complete boycott of the Westminster general election of May that year on the grounds that Westminster would never do justice to the Ulster people.[76] It was a wholly unrealistic expectation, but part of a wider attempt by the Griffinites to shape a narrative of acute crisis that would culminate in 1987 against a background of Unionist leadership failure to undermine the AIA, Thatcher's determination to hand Northern Ireland over to the Irish Republic and with even the moderate SDLP accused of facilitating gun-running for the IRA. And NF efforts were pressed with some urgency as Unionist politicians resumed the socio-political roles they had formerly abandoned: 'time is running out fast. Ulster's loyalists must decide soon whether their loyalty is to the decaying

---

[73] See *Combat*, vol. 6, no. 3, 22 December 1986.
[74] 'Unionists get it wrong', *National Front News*, no. 84, February (1), 1987. The paper was published fortnightly for a time.
[75] 'Ulster NF shop open', *National Front News*, no. 82 [November 1986].
[76] 'The system says the same', *National Front News*, no. 89, May (1) 1987; 'Ulster: for the nation against the state, no. 90, *National Front News*, no. 90, June (1) 1987.

old "Union" with corrupt Westminster above all else – or to Ulster first and foremost.'[77]

In July it declared the complete failure of all attempts to prevent the Ulster sell-out project, with the ultimate decision about the region's future now imminent. A 'special bulletin' for all 'cadres' in the region was started, cross-community activism was claimed in its 'thriving' Larne unit, the Rathcoole unit of north Belfast was considering contesting a vacant local council seat, and violent attacks on the RUC and 'innocent Catholics' were discouraged as the movement made progress towards the independence that would provide a solvent for all the region's problems.[78]

In this context it was clearly intended that the mass mobilisation of Orangemen at the twelfth of July celebrations would provide the tipping point for the advance of the independence project. But July came without the expected tipping point. Indeed, it registered a Griffinite setback. Despite extensive selling of its literature across the north there was a significant drop in sales as compared with July 1986, partly attributed to more subdued parades, a perceived result of Unionist failure. But other reasons were sought and found, partly in increased harassment of NF members by police and bigoted senior Orange officials. But particular attention was paid to a 'smear' story by John Coulter in the *News Letter* days before the Orange celebrations.

Just as Coulter had 'smeared' the NF in 1986, he did so again, identifying the Griffinites as extremists opposed by a 'moderate' faction, in fact the 'reactionary' Flag faction:[79] 'The article gave the impression that the reactionaries are a credible force rather than a failed splinter group. Their leaders were given big photo puffs and their promise to bring over three mini-bus loads of papers sellers were taken seriously'. To this was added lies about Griffinite arms dumps and training, together with alliances with European

---

[77] 'Ulster: it's time to decide', *National Front News*, no. 85, March (1) 1987; 'Yank arms deal helps Ulster sell-out', *National Front News*, no. 86, March (2) 1987; 'Assault', *National Front News*, no. 89, May (1) 1987; 'Ulster awake', *National Front News*, no. 91, June (2) 1987.

[78] 'No surrender to Thatcher', 'Ulster', 'Independence will bring social justice for all in Ulster', *National Front News*, no. 92, July (1) 1987.

[79] John Coulter, 'Movement dedicated to an independent Ulster', *News Letter*, 8 July 1987.

terrorists. Coulter's family connection with the old Unionist and Orange establishment was exposed and seen as evidence of the latter's determination to destroy the independence project and of the threat the Political Soldiers presented to their power.[80] What this assessment evidenced, however, was Griffinite blindness to the actual reasons for their lack of regional influence and the consequences of their increasingly difficult relationship with the Unionist and loyalist communities.

Initial Unionist confidence that their efforts would succeed had led them to assert that they would not negotiate with the Government until the AIA was removed. But as their anti-Agreement efforts failed, they had painted themselves into a corner which ensured that the crisis over the AIA would be prolonged. As it did so, strains within the alliance of Unionist and loyalist paramilitary forces increased, exacerbated by the association between criminality, Unionism, loyalist paramilitarism and their NF supporters that continued to grab British press headlines into 1987.[81] Additionally, a much publicised and avoidable error occurred when the OUP Member of the European Parliament, John Taylor, transferred his parliamentary allegiance from the European Democrats with which the Conservatives were aligned to the European Right Group, a faction which included the neo-fascist and antisemitic Front National of France, led by Jean-Marie Le Pen, a party Taylor seems to have had an imperfect knowledge of, but which had condemned the AIA.[82]

---

[80] 'John Coulter', *National Front News*, no. 93, August (1) 1987.

[81] 'Paisley's National Front henchmen', *Today*, 9 February, 1987; 'Paisley's NF connection', *Asian Times*, 20 February 1987; 'Front threat', *Time Out*, 25 February 1987, press clippings (UNA, *Searchlight* Archive, Box 6, Ulster: SCH/01/Res/EUR/02/006); 'Candidates win court injunctions', *The Independent*, 20 February 1987; 'Accused tells of link with National Front' *Scotsman*, 24 February 1987; 'Loyalist trial told of NF infiltration claim', *Scotsman*, 26 February 1987; 'Speak out', *Dunfermline Press*, 27 February 1987; 'Man guilty of UDA terror conspiracy', *Glasgow Herald*, 5 March 1987; 'Kingsley's capers', *Searchlight*, no. 143 (May 1987), press clippings (UNA, *Searchlight* Archive, Box 26, National Front: SCH/01/Res/BRI/02/026); 'NF in UDA gun running', *Searchlight*, no. 142 (April 1987).

[82] 'I'm no fascist', *Today*, 11 February 1987, press clipping (UNA, *Searchlight* Archive, Box 6, Ulster: SCH/01/Res/EUR/02/006).

The furore caused by Taylor's action provoked a hurried disowning by his party of any extreme-Right link,[83] but political embarrassment nevertheless ensued. For the socialist leader in the European Parliament, 'The timing is hardly coincidental. Just as the National Front is recruiting in Northern Ireland the extreme right in the EEC has recruited leading Ulster Unionist John Taylor'.[84]

For the Griffinite Ulster faction, however, the durability of the crisis encouraged the belief that their Ulster independence proposal was the only credible alternative, and keenly interpreted ongoing political developments in ways that appeared to substantiate that belief. Thus, when Alan Wright, leader of the Ulster Clubs, suggested they could take the place of the AIA-enforcing RUC,[85] and that their 'Strategy for Victory' document – calling for all Unionist MPs and other loyalist organisations to constitute themselves as a Northern Ireland Grand Committee to coordinate opposition to the AIA – be acted upon, the Griffinite faction gratefully saw 'our ideas beginning to be taken up by others. There is a long way to go but we regard the formation of the Northern Ireland Grand Committee as the long overdue first step towards the formation of an Ulster Provisional Government.'[86] Less satisfying, however, were the consequences of attacking loyalist leaders.[87] When Gusty Spence, one of the most authoritative figures in Ulster loyalism, denounced the NF as dangerous Nazis who 'must be stopped', John Field replied by criticising Spence as 'a faintheart' misled by media lies,[88] a retort that reportedly resulted in his being driven out of Belfast by loyalist paramilitary pressure.[89]

It was indicative of the political distance between the Political Soldier faction in Northern Ireland and loyalist paramilitarism that on 29 January 1987 the UDA's think tank, the New Ulster Political Research Group, produced *Common Sense*, its own document for an

---

[83] 'Unionists disown link with right', *Guardian*, 17 February 1987.
[84] 'Taylor hits back at "Smear Tactics"', *News Letter*, 21 January 1987.
[85] Moloney, *Paisley: From Demagogue to Democrat?*, p. 312.
[86] 'Forward to victory', *National Front News*, no. 88, April (2) 1987.
[87] 'Ulster's time to decide', *National Front News*, no. 85, March (1) 1987.
[88] 'Former loyalist killer slams Front', *Searchlight*, no. 141, March 1987.
[89] 'NF in UDA gun-running', *Searchlight*, no. 142, April 1987.

Ulster settlement, based on a form of proportional power-sharing.[90] But it owed little to the ideas of the NF, rather the power-sharing experiment of the mid-1970s, which would find expression again in the Belfast/Good Friday Agreement of 1998.[91] The UDA, moreover, saw its implementation as something to be pursued, not by itself, but by Unionist party leaders. They, however, simply sidelined it on the basis of the Unionist commitment not to negotiate for a settlement until the AIA was removed. But even selling it to the UDA rank and file was difficult. As Steve Bruce puts it:

> loyalists could only be won over to 'proportionality' if the IRA stopped killing Protestants, and the only way to ensure that was to kill a lot of IRA men. Provided that such killing was followed quickly by political innovation then Catholics would accept it and there would be no surge of IRA recruitment ... there was no conflict between the political and military sides of the UDA.[92]

Promoted on this basis there was no prospect of the plan finding cross-community acceptance, not least because UDA killers usually made no distinction between the Provisional IRA and ordinary Catholics. But, arguably, the real significance of the UDA proposal was less its feasibility than its indication of the Unionist direction of travel. That became clearer in July 1987 when the Unionist Task Force, consisting of Harold McCusker, Peter Robinson and Frank Miller, produced *An End to Drift*.

The document suggested devolutionary alternatives to the AIA starting with 'talks about talks', and warning that if this initiative failed independence would be considered as an option.[93] But,

---

[90] Bew and Gillespie, *Northern Ireland: A Chronology of the Troubles, 1968–1999*, p. 205; Loughlin, *The Ulster Question since 1945*, p. 132.

[91] See also the discussion in Peter Taylor, *Loyalists* (London: Bloomsbury, 2000), pp. 197–99.

[92] Steve Bruce, *The Red Hand: Protestant Paramilitaries in Northern Ireland* (Oxford: Oxford University Press, 1992), pp. 238–39. See also Mark Langhammer and David Young, 'The UDA plan: opening for dialogue or sectarian fix?', *Fortnight*, no. 249 (March 1987), pp. 14–15; Loughlin, *The Ulster Question since 1945*, pp. 100–01.

[93] Cochrane, *Unionist Politics*, pp. 227–28.

unlike the detail the NF Political Soldiers provided on the kind of Ulster independence they would pursue, this was never given specific form,[94] being really no more than a threat to compel British compliance with Unionist demands. Unionist leaders effectively shelved the document; nevertheless, 'It was no longer a question of whether the unionists would negotiate, it was simply a matter of when and on what basis.'[95] Thus, not only had the period from January to July 1987 failed to deliver the independence tipping point the Griffinites hoped for but indications of a Unionist climbdown on the AIA were increasingly clear.

At the same time, the Griffinite faction also came under renewed attack from members of the Flag faction in Northern Ireland,[96] committed to working with mainstream Unionism and pursuing its own political strategies. Thus, whereas the Political Soldiers urged non-cooperation with the RUC, the Flag faction focused on division *within* the police about the role they were forced to play in combating loyalist activities. Accordingly, it threw its support behind the Police Federation, the representative body of ordinary RUC members, as against Sir John Hermon, the RUC Chief Constable, attacked for his role in using the police to implement the AIA: 'Slowly, the majority of Northern Ireland's policemen are beginning to realise that, first and foremost, above all else, they are Loyal Ulstermen.'[97] And, as with mainstream Unionism, it took the position that independence was to be opted for only if it became obvious that Britain had actually abandoned Ulster, not something to be actively campaigned for.[98]

It was concerned that Unionist criticism of the NF over the previous year had often failed to distinguish between the two factions and their different political positions on Northern Ireland, a concern that underlay an article by Steve Brady in July 1987. Now aligned with the Flag faction, Brady bluntly pointed out that loyalists and Unionists were regarded as extremist bigots in Britain and that,

---

[94] Anne Purdy, *Molyneaux: The Long View* (Antrim: Greystone Books, 1989), pp. 158–59.
[95] Ibid., p. 251.
[96] 'Warning police at Work', *National Front News*, no. 92, July (1) 1987.
[97] 'Anglo-Irish Agreement splits Ulster's police', *Vanguard*, no. 7, April 1987.
[98] 'UDA tries recruiting from National Front', *Guardian*, 18 August 1986.

like it or not, the NF Flag faction 'is Ulster's only potential base of mass support outside its own people. And we've got potential.'[99] So far, however, that potential had failed to be delivered on.

A Flag assessment of UK strength in February 1987 identified only two groups in Northern Ireland, though their factional designation is not specified, while, as for sales of its print *Vanguard*, the Coleraine unit was recorded sixteenth in the top 20 branches in May 1987, but by July 1987 had completely fallen out of the list.[100] Moreover, a series of British opinion polls over the period from 1986 to 1993 indicated not increasing popular British support for Northern Ireland's constitutional position but alienation.[101] As for Brady, despite his commitment to Ulster loyalism, he also held membership of the anti-partitionist League of St George and the Michael Collins Association. Neither was active on the Ulster problem, their purpose apparently being to draw Irish youth into the worldwide neo-fascist and white racist movement, Ulster being but one site of conflict in a much more extensive struggle.[102] For the Griffinites, however – the faction with the most ambitious constitutional plans for Northern Ireland – the reality was that by mid-1987 the 'revolutionary' moment they had perceived in the wake of the AIA was passing, though they failed to realise it.

The Independence Project: A Renewed Campaign

On any objective assessment, the prospects for the Griffinite Political Soldiers by the late summer of 1987 were bleak. It was a reality obscured from their view by ideological obstinacy and the fact that the constitutional crisis persisted. Thus, despite the poor return for their efforts so far in 1987, in August the Griffinites claimed their

---

[99] Steve Brady, 'Why loyal Ulster should support the NF', *Vanguard*, no. 10, July 1987.

[100] *Vanguard*, no. 5, January 1987; no. 10, July 1987.

[101] James Loughlin, *Ulster Unionism and British National Identity since 1885* (London: Pinter, 1995), pp. 212–13.

[102] 'Ulster: fascism', *The Northern Star*, 20 July 1991; Steve Brady, 'Ulster: how can the National Front help?'; 'Why the NF supports loyal Ulster', *Vanguard*, no. 3, December 1986.

'big summer drive' to build support was making 'a major impact'.[103] With this mentality, autumn would see a renewed effort to promote the independence cause, energised by perceived positive indicators of progress, such as the fact, or so it was claimed, that the faction had Catholic members in their 'thriving' Larne unit and that their Rathcoole unit was energetically promoting Griffinite literature: it would make a venture into electoral politics on 17 September when David Kerr stood as a local election candidate for Newtownabbey council.

He would represent local interests by opening up all council business to public scrutiny and also to demonstrate that the NF was 'to be taken seriously as a locally-based political force and not some sort of youth cult'.[104] Furthermore, the emergence of a group of disgruntled rank-and-file Unionists promoting their own Ulster Movement for Self-Determination, which had a close similarity with the Griffinites' own views, was welcomed as evidence that their ideas were gaining increased popular currency, though the new movement was faulted for organisational inexperience, lack of *concrete* proposals and the promotion of a Protestant ethos that would undermine their project from the start.[105] Yet another positive indicator would be identified in the Catholic Church's forthright condemnation of the Provisional IRA following the Enniskillen Remembrance Day bombing of 8 November 1987, which killed 12 people and injured 68, and with a call for loyalists to make a reciprocal gesture.[106]

This unrealistically optimistic mood persisted in face of clear evidence to the contrary, such as the fact that David Kerr received only 27 votes at the Newtownabbey by-election, a result excused on the basis that the region's population had never had the chance to be

---

[103] 'Those worried men of privilege', *National Front News*, no. 94, August (2) 1987.

[104] 'National Front to contest election', *News Letter*, 10 September 1987; 'Front-line action', *National Front News*, no. 92, July (1) 1987; 'Front-line action: Ulster', *National Front News*, no. 94, August (2) 1987.

[105] 'A welcome development in Ulster', *National Front News*, no. 95, September 1987. Only one issue appeared in September.

[106] 'At last', *National Front News*, no. 99, December (1), 1987.

fully conversant with the Griffinites' independence plan.[107] Instead, optimism about its progress went together with urging the loyalist population to emulate the UVF in 1912–14 and embark on armed struggle to effect independence.[108] In fact, the closest such armed struggle came to realisation in this period was when John McMichael suggested a *coup d'état* in the region, for the purpose of which the UDA set about acquiring arms from abroad, especially the apartheid regime of South Africa. This proved highly controversial when the transaction in Paris, involving a South African diplomat handing weapons to UDA representatives, was exposed and those involved arrested, and as the Irish Anti-Apartheid Movement charted the history of previous loyalist contacts with the apartheid regime.[109] Moreover, the envisaged coup proved abortive when the Unionist leaders, Peter Robinson and Harold McCusker, were unresponsive and when the UVF refused to commit, preferring to oppose the AIA by increased violence.[110] And, even then, McMichael's proposal owed nothing to Griffinite ideas. Meanwhile, the signs of failure continued to increase.

An essential element of developing an Ulster nation was the creation of a supportive 'national' myth; and for this purpose a promising text appeared to have been found in Ian Adamson's *The Cruthin*,[111] which sought to locate the Protestant people as an authentic community in Ulster since ancient times rather than a historically recent community of planters in the seventeenth century, and with its own set of historical heroes and sites, in Cuchulain and Navan Fort, outside Armagh city. Indeed, the Flag, no less than the Political Soldier faction, was supportive of nation-making based on ancient Ulster myth such as Adamson attempted,[112] but with little success. The loyalist rank and file proved as resistant

---

[107] 'Hope for the future', *National Front News*, no. 98, November (2), 1987.

[108] '1912 – "Ulster will fight": 1987 Ulster must fight', *National Front News*, no. 95, September 1987.

[109] See 'Arrested in Paris': Louise Asmal, Irish Anti-Apartheid Movement to the editor, *Irish Times*, 27 April 1989.

[110] Cusack and McDonald, *UVF: The Endgame*, pp. 219–20.

[111] Ian Adamson, *The Cruthin* (1974; Bangor: Pretani Press, 1986).

[112] 'Ulster: A nation', *National Front News*, no. 96, October (1) 1987; 'Cuchulainn – hampion of Ulster', *Vanguard*, no. 8, May 1987.

to education on this subject as it had to political education in the past: ancient Ulster was simply too remote to identify with,[113] added to which was loyalist suspicion of the Celtic Cross, the emblem of the worldwide Aryan movement, but to loyalist minds having a perceived association with Irish republicanism.[114] But a greater threat to Griffinite hopes lay in its support for Colonel Gaddafi's Libya as a model of direct democracy.

The Political Soldiers' erroneous insistence that Libya had no connection with militant Irish republicanism was exposed when, in an interview with the Irish Republic's State broadcaster in October 1986 Gaddafi called on Irish youth, north and south, to participate in the 'struggle for the liberation of Ulster',[115] support confirmed at the beginning of November 1987 when the *Eksund* was stopped off the French coast with a large cache of arms and ammunition destined for the Provisional IRA.[116] Emphasising the significance of his other national policies,[117] Griffinites attempted to dismiss Gaddafi's pro-IRA sympathies as 'misplaced', but it was hardly persuasive. Nor when, as a result of loyalist contacts, Gaddafi rejected Irish republicanism in 1988, did the Griffinites gain anything from loudly publicising the fact.[118]

The Gaddafi issue was a gift to the Flag faction as it continued its efforts to discredit the Political Soldier project: 'Make no mistake, the bullets going into the backs of soldiers and civilians in Ulster come from Gaddafi.'[119] Nor was Griffinite support for Palestinian rights[120] likely to garner loyalist support in a region where prosemitism was strong among loyalists. And, to add to the faction's difficulties, a leaflet it had produced making the tercentenary connection between the Stuart 'tyranny' of 1688 and the AIA was changed to Stuart

[113] See Bruce, *Red Hand*, pp. 232–36.
[114] G. Burgess to the editor, *Vanguard*, no. 9, June 1987.
[115] Bew and Gillespie, *Northern Ireland: A Chronology of the Troubles, 1968–1999*, p. 204.
[116] Kerr, 'The history of the National Front in Ulster'.
[117] 'Qadhafi, Ulster and the IRA', *National Front News*, no. 105, June (1) 1988.
[118] 'Libya condemns the IRA', *National Front News*, no. 110, September 1988.
[119] Martin Wingfield, in 'Ulster's agony', *The Flag*, no. 21, July 1988.
[120] 'Hitting back at Zionism', *National Front News*, no. 109, August 1988; 'Support the Intifada', *National Front News*, no. 121, August 1989.

'dynasty' by an English NF official, thereby diminishing its Ulster Protestant resonance. They were no less irritated when an article on 'Alternative Ulster' intended for the July 1988 issue of *National Front News* was replaced 'without our knowledge by a bizarre historical article on the Fenian Cycle from Irish mythology topped by a huge green Celtic knotwork shamrock!' In protest, and in order to ensure no repetition, permission from the National Directorate was obtained 'to produce a local A4 paper, the original Ulster Nation'.[121] If there was any small consolation in this situation, it lay in the fact that politically the Flag faction fared no better.

Its plans for a celebration to mark the tercentenary of the 'Glorious Revolution' in Exeter, caused consternation when news of 'the NF and Orange Order' celebration became public.[122] The same consternation resulted in Exeter University cancelling acceptance of an Orange Order – 'known to have links with far-Right organisations' – application for accommodation during the celebrations.[123] For the same reason, the Devon and Cornwall Chief Constable Donald Elliott temporarily deferred a decision on an 'Orange–NF' march in September 1988.[124]

For the Griffinites, what sustained their optimism in the face of meagre results – to which was added an opinion poll finding of April 1988 which showed only 6 per cent of people in the region favoured an independent Northern Ireland[125] – were developments in the wider international context in which its Ulster activities were placed. Thus, as the Soviet Union came under constitutional stress from nationalist agitations across the State in the late 1980s, together with other international developments, *National Front News* exulted at what it saw as the emerging triumph of its own 'Third Way': '*Co-operative economics; political de-centralisation; popular participation in government and defence; respect for the environment – these*

---

[121] Kerr, 'The history of the National Front in Ulster'.

[122] 'Green light for Devon Orangemen', *Searchlight*, no. 155, May 1988 (UNA, *Searchlight* Archive, Box 35, Regional Flag Groups and National Front: SCH/01/Res/BRI/02/035).

[123] 'Orange campus visit axed', *Western Morning News*, 7 September 1988 (UNA, *Searchlight* Archive, Box 26, National Front: SCH/01/Res/BRI/02/026).

[124] 'Way clear for Orange-NF link up', *Searchlight*, no. 157, July 1988.

[125] Robin Wilson, 'Poll shock for the accord', *Fortnight*, April 1988.

NF ideas form the basis of our "Green Revolution".[126] Despite lack of success in Northern Ireland, progress towards the realisation of the Griffinite project more widely was seen as ongoing. The continuing efforts of mainstream Unionism to move away from negative and fruitless opposition to the AIA to more positive engagement with the Government,[127] however, clearly indicated that Ulster's 'revolutionary' moment had passed. Finally recognising this, the Political Soldiers registered alarm,[128] and did some rethinking about their approach to Northern Ireland.

Little new was offered in terms of the core Political Soldier positions on race, international issues, power-sharing and socio-economic issues,[129] but past strategy was examined and found wanting. In late March, an 'Ulster National Front' seminar decided that its attempt to ingratiate itself with 'the various Unionist and loyalist groups', instead of building up an active, strong local presence, had been an error: 'The NF will not repeat this mistake ever again!'[130] Also, it was decided that *Ulster Nation* would be an organ for worldwide distribution to counter the republican 'lie machine', something loyalist organisations had failed effectively to do.[131] As to elections, 'units' in Belfast, county Armagh, county Antrim and county Londonderry would contest local elections due in May 1989, though in the event only two seats were actually fought under the NF banner. And, while other, albeit tiny, independence organisations were emerging in Northern Ireland, such as the Ulster Independence Committee and the aforementioned Movement for Self Determination, campaigning together on a broad front was rejected on the grounds that 'pro- and anti- capitalist factions' would be falsely "united"' and would inevitably split.[132]

---

[126] 'The new alliance', *National Front News*, no. 103, March (1) 1988.

[127] Cochrane, *Unionist Politics*, pp. 226–27.

[128] '"Talks about talks" mean SELL OUT', *National Front News*, no. 103, March (1) 1988.

[129] *Ulster Nation*, no. 1 [1988] (UNA, *Searchlight* Archive, Box 6, Ulster: SCH/01/Res/EUR/02/006).

[130] 'Seminars from Ulster', *National Front News*, no. 105, June (1) 1988.

[131] 'Front "Not on paper chase"': Stuart McCullough to editor, *Sunday News*, 27 November 1988.

[132] 'Ulster arise!', *Ulster Nation*, no. 2 [November/December 1988] (UNA, *Searchlight* Archive, Box 6, Ulster: SCH/01/Res/EUR/02/006).

In the run-up to the local elections the new politically independent stance drew fierce loyalist criticism, partly due to the Griffinites' support for Gaddafi[133] and partly by a Griffinite election leaflet attacking not just republicanism but loyalists for failing to secure the interests of their communities in a context where Westminster had effectively expelled Ulster from the UK.[134] *Ulster* declared that the Griffinite 'perverts', criticism from whom the UDA would not tolerate, were not to be confused with the loyalist-supporting Flag faction.[135]

Warned by the UDA to 'put up or shut up!', Stuart McCullough, Belfast organiser, responded robustly to what he saw as an attempt to drive the Ulster NF out of Belfast,[136] though a popular belief that McCullough declared, 'If the UDA want a war, they can have a war', is something David Kerr dismisses: 'I doubt if he would have been stupid enough to shout "bring it on" to a well-organised army of scary men with guns.' His later departure from Northern Ireland, Kerr claimed, followed an RUC warning that his name was on a Provisional IRA death list.[137] As for the local elections, at which Kerr stood in the Belfast Doagh Road ward and McCullough in the Pottinger ward, Kerr gained 41 first-preference votes and McCullough 27. And yet poor as these results were Kerr found a rationalisation, respectively, in press misrepresentation; inability to produce enough election material; and a self-denying cross-community approach which sacrificed 'possible votes for longer term considerations': addresses were sent to Catholic parts of wards – areas where no 'unionist' bigot would ever bother to send an election address, 'just as the "non-sectarian" Marxist bigots of Sinn Fein never send their leaflets to Protestant areas'. Their own analysis of first- and second-preference votes 'indicated that at least 20 per cent of the NF votes came from Catholics', while a large number

[133] 'Editorial board clarifies policy on "Ulster"', *Ulster*, April 1989.
[134] See 'We're not moving NF tell loyalists', *Sunday News*, 14 May 1989; National Front, *Ulster Patriot* (Belfast: Beacon Books, 1989).
[135] 'Editorial board clarifies policy on "Ulster"', *Ulster*, April 1989.
[136] See 'We're not moving NF tell loyalists', *Sunday News*, 14 May 1989; National Front, *Ulster Patriot*.
[137] Kerr, 'The history of the National Front in Ulster'.

of second-preference votes came from loyalists, demonstrating that support for a 'new Ulster' had cross-community support.[138] But this would be the last occasion on which the Political Soldier project would be electorally tested.

In the way that hope springs eternal, the 'progress' evident at the election was sought to be built on through the distribution of the NF's forthcoming publication, *Alternative Ulster*, and a sticker campaign in Catholic and Protestant areas of Belfast denouncing Unionism, republicanism and the sectarian chains in which they had constrained their communities. This was done in support of a stronger, non-sectarian effort by a more regionally grounded NF formation, though maintaining a close relationship with the parent NF body in Britain.[139]

In fact, problems facing the Political Soldiers in Britain would fatally affect the Ulster formation. The former had come to be seen as a cult in the second half of the 1980s: its 'separate but equal' racial view, together with the slogan 'Fight Racism', were internally alienating factors, and when the March 1988 edition of *Nationalism Today* featured pictures of Gaddafi, Iran's Ayatollah Khomeini and the US black separatist Louis Farrakhan on the front cover a wave of resignations followed.[140] In 1989, both Flag and Griffinite factions faced each other at a parliamentary by-election in Vauxhall, London. Neither performed well, with 127 votes cast for the Political Soldier candidate Patrick Harrington and 83 for Edward Budden, the Flag representative, representing 0.4 and 0.3 percentage of the total vote, respectively. Further fragmentation followed in 1990, with the Political Soldiers splintering into Griffin's International Third Position (ITP) and Harrington's Third Way, respectively, with the Flag faction under Anderson and Wingfield continuing alone. Only at this late stage was it acknowledged that the negative imagery and reputation associated with the title 'National Front' was such that

---

[138] 'Ulster NF break through old divide in May elections', *National Front News*, no. 119, June 1989.

[139] 'NF starts new push with "no sectarian" pledge', *Irish News*, 21 August 1989.

[140] Daniel Trilling, *Bloody Nasty People: The Rise of Britain's Far Right* (London: Verso, 2012), p. 48.

284 Fascism and Constitutional Conflict

it had to be abandoned.[141] Griffin, moreover, had further problems, partly involving political estrangement from Derek Holland and Roberto Fiore, fellow ITP members, but both Catholics who had introduced 'an increasing amount of religious rhetoric into the organisation's doctrine'; and personally when he lost the sight of one eye as the result of a bonfire accident,[142] though not in Northern Ireland.

Against this background, the Ulster formation would continue its activities, including the production of *Alternative Ulster* and associated literature.[143] But, not only was it delusional to expect an uplift in the group's fortunes from yet another restatement of its policies, the contemporaneous disintegration of the British Political Soldier formation ensured that an important source of support had disappeared. Certainly, there was no evidence that the traditional narratives of identity that lay at the heart of the Ulster problem were losing their community hold. And, like the British formation, the Ulster body would also formally cease activities in 1990. When it did, it did not even have an office to close, the Templemore Avenue premises having already been lost due to financial difficulties.[144] Many years later, David Kerr would admit of this time that the revolutionary moment in Northern Ireland had indeed passed: 'but we just didn't notice it'.[145] If any doubt existed about it, the entry of Unionist leaders to talks with Peter Brooke, a new Secretary of State for Northern Ireland, in 1990, put the issue beyond question.

Conclusion

In his study of the NF in the mid-1970s, Martin Walker makes the important point that it was very much out of its depth in Ulster, knowing little of the communal roots of loyalism and the complex

---

[141] 'For a third way', *National Front News*, no. 126, January 1990.
[142] Trilling, *Bloody Nasty People*, pp. 48–49.
[143] Ulster National Front, *National Front Launches Pro-Independence Document* (Belfast: Ulster National Front, 1989); *Alternative Ulster* (Belfast: Ulster National Front, 1989), p. [2] (UNA, *Searchlight* Archive, Box 6, Ulster: SCH/01/Res/EUR/02/006).
[144] Kerr, 'The history of the National Front in Ulster'.
[145] Ibid.

social traditions which held loyalists together, thinking simplistically that their kind of nationalism was the same as the NF's own.[146] Walker's argument, however, is much stronger for the mid-1970s than for the mid-1980s, when the British extreme-Right had ample time to become familiar with the dynamics of loyalism, not least from its own foot soldiers in the region, limited in number though they were. Yet we find the same unrealistic expectations being reproduced in the mid-1980s as had existed a decade earlier.

In part, this was due to the fact that the Political Soldier faction which took 'official' control of the NF operation, though better educated than previous cadres, came to the Ulster problem overly influenced by revolutionary theory drawn largely from the European extreme-Right, which retained its credibility despite sitting just as awkwardly with loyalist thinking as NF policies in the 1970s. It was sustained by the fact that the crisis of the mid-1980s was of a more serious and enduring nature than that of the mid-1970s – resolved in the loyalist interest by paramilitary action in 1974. Despite the manifest failure of efforts to expand the Political Soldier support base in the region, so long as the crisis endured the hopes of a revolutionary opening to change that situation also endured. But the faction's ideological rigidity also left it ill-equipped to recognise changes in the north's political environment pointing clearly to the passing of the 'revolutionary' moment and to the debilitating effects of the internal divisions in the NF. As we have seen, insofar as loyalists found the NF brand attractive, it was in its Flag manifestation, committed to a UK integrationist solution to the Northern Ireland problem. And yet, the Flag faction proved no more successful in its Northern Ireland efforts than the Griffinite Political Soldiers. The intensity of the Ulster conflict left little space for external groups, especially those whose British political promise in the early 1970s had so completely evaporated.

[146] Martin Walker, *The National Front* (London: Fontana, 1977), pp. 159–60.

8

The British National Party and Ulster

Neo-Fascism in a Context of Political Agreement

The British National Party (BNP)'s prominence in the 1990s was not an overnight phenomenon. From its beginnings in the early 1980s as John Tyndall's response to his failed attempt at an authoritarian reconstruction of the National Front (NF) its organisational structure accorded with his ideas, but its ideology and political objectives, as Nigel Copsey points out, merely followed generally in the NF Flag vein, needing no change.[1] For the rest of the decade, the party focused on long-term organisational development – attempts to forge an alliance with the NF Flag faction in 1987 failed on Tyndall's authoritarian insistence on being leader of the merged organisation[2] – rather than electoral conflict. Its poor performance in the 1983 general election when its 53 candidates averaged only 1.3 per cent of the vote demonstrated that fighting elections only highlighted party weakness.[3] As it entered the 1990s, therefore, the BNP had failed to make a decisive political breakthrough; nevertheless, with the collapse of the NF it was now the major vehicle of extreme-Right opinion,[4] while the problem of moving from the British political margins would gradually be solved mainly through the efforts of Nick Griffin.

---

[1] Nigel Copsey, 'Contemporary fascism in the local arena: the British National Party and "Rights for Whites"', in Mike Cronin (ed.), *The Failure of British Fascism: The Far Right and the Fight For Political Recognition* (Basingstoke: Palgrave Macmillan, 1996), pp. 120–21; also, Matthew Goodwin, *New British Fascism: Rise of the British National Party* (London: Routledge, 2011), pp. 37–40.

[2] Copsey, 'Contemporary fascism in the local arena', p. 122.

[3] Ibid., pp. 121–22.

[4] Ibid., p. 124.

Griffin found his way back into the extreme-Right centre initially through engaging in controversial debate on the Holocaust; and having begun the 1990s arguing against engaging in electoral contests, by mid-decade had changed tack and was now enthusiastically promoting it.[5] Griffin's political rise was aided by Tyndall's mistakes. As the BNP became more prominent it attracted the aggressive attention of anti-Nazi activists. In response, Combat 18 (C18), led by one Charlie Sargent, emerged from BNP ranks in 1992 as a party protection force. Openly neo-Nazi, and promoting a race war, it rapidly became a problem as it turned on party activists who favoured contesting elections. Encouraged by a BNP council by-election victory (by seven votes) in the Tower Hamlets ward of Millwall, London, in September 1993, Tyndall declared C18 a proscribed organisation. But little was done to enforce proscription and C18 continued to have a debilitating effect on the party, even creating its own political wing, the National Socialist Alliance. At this time, BNP membership, as estimated by party activist (and *Searchlight* mole) Tim Hepple, who accessed its membership cards, was over 3,000. And while this made it the largest of the far-Right parties it hardly suggested a movement gaining mass support, though C18 was estimated to have only 80 members and there was no indication that it was likely to become a major movement.[6]

At the same time, Tyndall's position was coming under threat, facing a possible leadership challenge from a pro-election wing of the party led by Eddie Butler, arguing for a softening of the party's policy on immigration and the abandonment of compulsory repatriation if it was to be electorally successfully. In this context Tyndall responded favourably to Griffin's offer to work with the BNP on the basis of a physically aggressive 'hard-line and principled stance', Griffin rapidly proving his hard-line credentials

---

[5] Daniel Trilling, *Bloody Nasty People: The Rise of Britain's Far Right* (London: Verso, 2012), pp. 66–67.
[6] See *Searchlight, At War with Society*, p. 23; David Matas, 'The extreme right in the United Kingdom and France', in Aurel Braun and Stephen Scheinberg (eds), *The Extreme Right: Freedom and Security at Risk* (Boulder, Colo.: Westview Press, 1997), pp. 87–88, 90. Matas put BNP membership at around 2,500.

by activities for which he was prosecuted under the Public Order Act. He joined the BNP in 1995, proving his commitment by assisting Tyndall in moving decisively against C18.[7] In 1996 he became editor of *Spearhead*.[8] From this position he enhanced his extremist positions, while at the same time planning to overthrow Tyndall.

All BNP factions had fascist backgrounds,[9] but not all adhered rigidly to one strategy on expanding party support: Tyndall favoured hard-line street activity to facilitate the BNP bullying its way into power; Griffin, influenced by the success of Jean-Marie Le Pen's Front National in France, sought to combine street action with electoral success from local to national level, while at the same time preparing to 'seize power when the opportune moment arose', a strategy his position as *Spearhead* editor and then publicity director left him well placed to promote. He was aware of a perceived need to 'adopt modern presentational techniques'. In February 1998, he proposed a new language in which the BNP could present its nativist ideas informed by the four fundamental concepts: freedom, social security, popular democracy and identity – national survival depended on the reversal of the cultural trends of recent decades if the British native peoples were to have a future.[10] Griffin argued: 'Internally we need to provide a sense of belonging, something very special, but ordinary electors should see us as just another choice on the political scene.'[11] To this end the BNP website was modernised and a Media Monitoring Unit established to facilitate members' complaints about derogatory references to the party, resulting in a modification of description by some outlets – 'far-right' or 'ultra-nationalist' rather than 'fascist' or 'Nazi'. In his own case of inciting racial hatred Griffin produced a black American separatist, Osiris Akkebala, to testify in his favour, claiming pride in one's race was

---

[7] Nigel Copsey, *Contemporary British Fascism: The British National Party and the Quest for Legitimacy* (2004; 2nd edn, Basingstoke: Palgrave Macmillan, 2008), pp. 66–69.
[8] Trilling, *Bloody Nasty People*, pp. 68–69.
[9] Goodwin, *New British Fascism*, pp. 37–40.
[10] Trilling, *Bloody Nasty People*, pp. 72–73.
[11] Griffin, quoted ibid., p. 74.

natural and that he was not offended by Griffin's race arguments: Griffin got off with a suspended sentence. Furthermore, the party got seriously involved in community politics focused on local issues, such as food delivery rounds for housewives; running taxi services for OAPs and women; and arranging football teams and outings for neglected youngsters – all of which were combined with political work designed to 'sink roots in target wards'.[12]

On this basis, in November 1998, Griffin criticised Tyndall's leadership, attacking 'extremism' within the party, and in February 1999 launched an official challenge, arguing that the European election campaign of that year would be part of the leadership campaign. The campaign was a total failure, but Tyndall, who had sought to have the 'vicious and divisive' leadership contest stopped,[13] got the blame. At the end of September 1999, the results of the leadership election showed that Griffin had won 1,082 votes to Tyndall's 411. With a turnout of 80 per cent of members, this was a resounding victory: Tyndall had to resign.[14] But what were the implications of these developments for BNP policy on Northern Ireland in the 1990s?

Framing an Ulster Policy

Although the BNP would not establish an Ulster presence until the early 1990s, it had already indicated its determination to have a Northern Ireland base with a propaganda campaign at the 12 July Orange celebrations of 1988 and with BNP activists having propagated their pro-loyalist cause in Scotland.[15] Its Liverpool branch subsequently mounted an attack on the Ulster Griffinite faction in 1989 largely on Flag lines.[16] This was hardly coincidental. As noted, the Flag faction of the NF had been seeking collaboration

---

[12] Ibid., pp. 75–76.
[13] 'BNP in peril: help us save it!', *Spearhead*, no. 366, August 1999.
[14] Trilling, *Bloody Nasty People*, pp. 76–79.
[15] 'BNP joins loyalist celebrations', *The Flag*, no. 22, August 1988 (UNA, *Searchlight* Archive, Box 35, Regional Flag Groups and National Front: SCH/01/Res/BRI/02/035).
[16] 'View points', *Ulster Nation*, no. 3 [1989] (UNA, *Searchlight* Archive, Box 6, Ulster: SCH/01/Res/EUR/02/006).

with John Tyndall's BNP for some time.[17] Moreover, at the same time as the BNP was in the process of becoming Britain's leading extreme-Right organisation, a transformation in the leadership of loyalist organisations in Northern Ireland was also occurring.

By 1990, the UDA old guard had been discredited and replaced. Their Intelligence Officer, Brian Nelson, was exposed as a Government agent provocateur, while the racketeering activities of another leader, James Pratt Craig, were exposed on British television. Also, John McMichael, the UDA second in Command, had been assassinated by an IRA bomb planted under his car in late December 1987: a killing, police suggested, facilitated by other UDA figures as part of an internal feud,[18] while other leading members were imprisoned. 'The old regime was replaced, leaving no one from the pre-1974 leadership in senior positions.'[19] For a new, younger leadership the extreme Right's association with Hitlerism was much less offensive than it had been for its predecessor, making for a more congenial relationship. Thus, Mark Cotterill, a former member of the NF National Directorate, along with Steve Brady and other extreme Rightists, organised a trip for loyalists to the USA in 1991, with Cotterill later writing it up in the UDA magazine *Ulster*.[20] Cotterill also laid a UDA wreath during the 12 July Orange celebrations in Northern Ireland.[21] Critics could claim that the developing extreme-Right connection with the UDA was due to the latter's political immaturity rather than deliberate intent,[22] but this is unlikely. Brady, for instance, had a long-established neo-fascist reputation in the region and a loyalist–extreme-Right relationship of varying significance had existed since the early 1970s. But did a closer extreme-Right–loyalist relationship imply greater progress for neo-fascism as a force?

[17] Copsey, *Contemporary British Fascism*, p. 37.
[18] Paul Bew and Gordon Gillespie, *Northern Ireland: A Chronology of the Troubles, 1968–1999* (1993; 2nd edn, Dublin: Gill & Macmillan, 1999), p. 211.
[19] Nick Lowles, *White Riot: The Violent Story of Combat 18* (2001; revised edn, Croydon: Milo Books, 2014), pp. 64–65.
[20] Mark Cotterill, 'Loyalists visit America', *Ulster*, July/August 1991 (UNA, *Searchlight* Archive, Box 6, Ulster: SCH/01/Res/EUR/02/006).
[21] Lowles, *White Riot*, p. 62.
[22] 'Ulster: fascism', *The Northern Star*, 20 July 1991 (UNA, *Searchlight* Archive, Box 6, Ulster: SCH/01/Res/EUR/02/006).

Certainly, 1990 was not 1985. The uproar in the Unionist and loyalist community then, which seemed freighted with Rightist revolutionary potential, had now disappeared. Also, the late 1980s had seen the Provisional IRA campaign stall – singular strikes against the security forces could not disguise the fact that the organisation was incapable of winning the 'war', while at the same time their activities offered a rationalization for an intensified loyalist murder campaign. This background provided the context for the political path to a solution favoured by Gerry Adams, the republican leader, at the same time as the new Secretary of State for Northern Ireland, Peter Brooke, un-associated with the implementation of the AIA, took office, hinting clearly that if republican violence ended political engagement was possible. Brooke signalled his seriousness of intent in January 1990 when he initiated talks between the north's constitutional parties,[23] followed by ongoing discussions and, in December 1993, the Downing Street Declaration: John Major and Albert Reynolds, the Irish Taoiseach, pledged their two Governments to work for a constitutional settlement of the Ulster problem. And, despite the Unionist community being given guarantees on Northern Ireland's constitutional position, the Declaration's direction was very much that of conciliating republicanism. It was widely welcomed in Britain and Ireland, with even mainstream Unionists, after an uncertain start, putting up no significant protest against it.[24]

The BNP might howl 'Sell-Out!',[25] but it didn't provide a rallying cry for British popular outrage. As with the region's issues in general, British public opinion proved difficult to activate on Northern Ireland, leaving British Governments with a generally free hand to proceed as they wished. And with the path to an Ulster settlement advancing along difficult but distinctly traditional lines extreme-Right parties, as in the past, were faced with ploughing a difficult political field.

---

[23] James Loughlin, *The Ulster Question since 1945* (1998; 2nd edn, Basingstoke: Palgrave Macmillan, 2004), chap. 4.

[24] Bew and Gillespie, *Northern Ireland: A Chronology of the Troubles, 1968–1999*, pp. 282–83; Loughlin, *The Ulster Question since 1945*, p. 154.

[25] 'Sell-Out!', *British Nationalist*, January 1994.

The general lines of the BNP's Ulster policy were established in the early 1990s. The Warrington bombs of 1993 demonstrated that Tory Government involvement in the Ulster talks process was not only encouraging IRA violence[26] but was also a negative index of relative national virility in the international context: 'If the IRA ever succeed, all our nation's enemies, at home and abroad, would conclude that we British had become a pushover. In these conditions we could expect a lot more trouble.'[27] The Warrington bombs also prompted a detailed exposition of the BNP's position on Northern Ireland by its regional organiser and former member of the Griffinite Ulster National Front, Greg Cumming.

'A new way forward needed for Ulster' posited Northern Ireland's complete integration with Britain, together with an opening to the rest of Ireland. Religious intolerance and the 'clown' who was its leading exponent, Ian Paisley, were denounced together with his pro-Zionist DUP; they caused Ulster loyalists to be branded as bigots and made the Provisional IRA seem like far-sighted progressives – 'rational, tolerant people of understanding and moderation'. But all of Northern Ireland's political parties were condemned as mere pawns of Westminster's 'homosexual and Masonic mandarins, who exercise joint authority with the Government of the Irish Republic'. Cumming was much more forgiving of loyalist paramilitaries who had now, he argued erroneously, 'given up senseless sectarian killings in favour of specifically targeted hits on legitimate republican enemies'.[28] Of the independence option he was committed to in the 1980s, it remained now only as a last desperate measure to avoid Irish unity, and hardly more attractive than the European superstate 'of the banker and the businessman', flooded with economic immigrants undermining European jobs, people and blood. As for domestic Ulster issues, the BNP would provide a solution to the region's socio-economic problems, such as a chronic housing shortage and an unemployment

[26] 'Smash the IRA', *British Nationalist*, March, May, July 1993.
[27] 'Peace at any price?', *British Nationalist*, May 1993; 'Exterminate the IRA!', *British Nationalist*, October 1994; also 'Britain betrayed to IRA by traitors', *British Nationalist*, March 1995.
[28] Greg Cumming, 'A new way forward needed for Ulster', *Spearhead*, no. 290, April 1993.

problem exacerbated by terrorism, though, among much that was familiar in the extreme-Right perspective on Northern Ireland, Cumming signalled a major issue of the future when he referenced the presence of 22,000 'Oriental', mainly Chinese, immigrants in Northern Ireland.[29]

However, despite the fact that their own activities were energised by atrocities such as the Warrington bombs, which created outrage in both Britain and Ireland[30] (the second of which, on 20 March 1993, killed two children, Jonathon Ball aged 3 and Tim Parry aged 12, and injured 56), the BNP gained little political advantage from them. Moreover, while loyalist paramilitaries agreed with the BNP that political talks on Ulster meant a 'sell-out', when they looked for British allies to support the enhanced campaign of violence, they pursued to undermine them, it was to the more violently inclined C18 that they looked. Furthermore, and as with neo-fascists in the past, establishing an *effective* BNP presence in loyalist areas was extremely difficult.

The BNP by-election success in Tower Hamlets in 1993 was significant only in the context of its otherwise political marginalisation, but, as we have seen, even that limited success was beyond the reach of the extreme Right in Northern Ireland, a region where even indigenous political parties linked to loyalist paramilitarism have struggled to make progress. Accordingly, while the BNP carried on the NF policy of aggressive opposition to the IRA, its chief centre of activity, as with the NF, remained Britain – mainly opposing republican and 'Bloody Sunday' marches.[31] And yet, given the UK framework of its politics, a Northern Ireland presence was necessary.

It was established in Belfast in 1992, and, against a background of perceived State treachery and a continuing republican threat, began expanding its presence in mid-1994, claiming an enthusiastic reception 'on the doorstep', especially, in addition to Belfast, east Ulster towns that were the traditional focus of extreme-Right

---

[29] Ibid.
[30] 'Hang child murderers!', *British Nationalist*, April 1993.
[31] 'BNP attacks IRA march', *British Nationalist*, July 1991; 'BNP stops Bloody Sunday mob', *British Nationalist*, February, March 1992.

activities – Coleraine, Newtownards, Ballymena, Ballmoney and Portadown – taking encouragement from the apparently 'panic' reaction to its presence in the regional press.[32] It was already seeking pro-loyalist credibility through activity on issues such as a campaign to have Neil Latimer, a Ulster Defence Regiment soldier, convicted of the sectarian murder of a Catholic, released.[33]

Loyalism, Combat 18 and the Struggle against Constitutional Treachery

As British 'treachery' towards Ulster dominated loyalist thinking, a 'doomsday' situation presented itself to the UDA and C18, one in which Labour Party personalities (a frisson of fear was created when opinion polls mistakenly suggested that Labour, perceived as anti-partitionist, would win the general election of 1992) such as Ken Livingstone and Diane Abbot would be targeted, in association with a strategy of bomb attacks in the Irish Republic.[34] And the new UDA leadership, with others in the UVF such as Johnny Adair and Billy Wright, were more viciously sectarian. Adair already had neo-fascist connections and many of his most ardent supporters in the second battalion Ulster Freedom Fighters (UFF) shared his background, becoming more violent when secret British communications with the republican leadership were revealed: the most infamous loyalist terrorist to have open links with C18 was Steve Irwin, a UFF killer who would be sentenced to life imprisonment for his part in the attack on the Rising Sun pub in Greysteel, county Londonderry, which left seven people dead.[35]

To facilitate their upgraded campaign of violence, the UDA requested assistance from Sargent's C18 in the acquisition of sophisticated weaponry, especially bomb-making materials,[36] activity

[32] See *Belfast Telegraph* article, 'BNP set to fight seats in Ulster', *British Nationalist*, August 1994.
[33] 'Ulster BNP joins fight to free jailed UDR soldier', *British Nationalist*, October 1992.
[34] 'The Terror Squad', *World in Action*, Granada Production for ITV, broadcast 19 April 1993.
[35] Lowles, *White Riot*, pp. 74–76.
[36] Ibid., pp. 69–70.

facilitated by the fact that while the UDA was declared illegal in Northern Ireland in 1992 it remained legal in Britain.[37] In fact, C18 was already making a contribution to their joint enterprise through the targeting of anyone in Britain who expressed support for republicanism, multi-culturalism and/or the Troops Out movement, with the UDA in each area providing the list of targets.[38] It says much for the marginalisation of the BNP in Northern Ireland – the UDA was increasingly disenchanted with both it and the near moribund NF[39] – that its proscription of C18 was no restraint whatsoever on the UDA's embrace of the group; and to effect improved cooperation with C18 the UDA reorganised in Britain.

The London UDA commander was replaced by the younger, more 'bullish' members such as Frank Portinari and Eddie Whicker. Under orders from UDA headquarters in Belfast, Portinari was determined to place the UDA on a more active footing in the capital. As for Whicker, he moved into the UDA orbit, ferrying senior UDA officials on their brief visits to London, while both he and Portinari were frequent visitors to the loyalist drinking dens of Belfast.[40] In the *World in Action* programme on C18, Whicker was shown with the UDA emblem tattooed on his arm, and when asked if he approved of the murder of Catholics refused to answer.[41] The UDA's links with British neo-Nazis did not go uncriticised by Unionist politicians, but to little effect. Expressing his confidence in the security of the C18–UDA relationship in the UDA magazine *Warrior*, Whicker declared: 'regardless of what you think of their [C18] political beliefs ... they can easily be classed better Loyalists than some of our so-called political representatives here in Ulster!'[42] He evidenced this by arranging a major UDA/C18 attack on the annual Troops Out-organised Bloody Sunday march of 30 January 1993 with the intention of first doing 'the march and then ... [torching] Kilburn', a major area of Irish residence in north

---

[37] 'Neo-nazi intelligence-gathering network', *Searchlight*, September 1992.
[38] 'The Terror Squad', *World in Action*; Lowles, *White Riot*, pp. 67–69, 78.
[39] 'NF thug's Ulster fate', *Searchlight*, February 1992.
[40] Lowles, *White Riot*, pp. 67–69.
[41] 'The Terror Squad', *World in Action*.
[42] Whicker, quoted in Lowles, *White Riot*, pp. 75–76.

London. According to a former C18 member, 'Some of us would have went [on the anti-Bloody Sunday demonstration] anyway, but a lot more went because of the UDA's active involvement'. On the day, over 600 neo-Nazi supporters, football hooligans and loyalists massed, their purpose thwarted only by effective police action, entailing 376 arrests.[43] Just under two months later the Provisional IRA's Warrington bombs occasioned mob attacks on Kilburn.[44]

Whicker's reign as terror organiser, however, was to be short-lived, undone by the publicity the *World in Action* programme brought to his UDA/C18 activities: he was arrested at the beginning of June 1993, caught in the act of gun-running.[45] Together with the police mass round-up at the Bloody Sunday march, which brought the UDA and its supporters unwelcome publicity, Whicker's arrest and imprisonment was a damaging development, as were further arrests, such as that of Frank Portinari, jailed for five years for attempted gun-running to loyalists, and that of other violent C18 members, especially Johnny Adair. Such arrests reduced the sectarian edge of C18 activities at the same time as a younger generation came to the fore with a somewhat new political outlook. C18 would regularly turn out at loyalist and Apprentice Boys marches in Britain, but mainly hoping to confront 'Reds'. As C18 developed a 'Race and Nation' policy as against the more narrow nationalism of the BNP, it saw the Irish conflict as increasingly futile and counter-productive. This was reflected in its attendances at loyalist events in Britain: only 50 C18 supporters came out to provide protection for the annual Derry Apprentice Boys march in March 1995, a mainstay of the loyalist calendar in central London, while the march was ignored by the Left and by republican groups. Only 30 C18 activists turned out for the same march in 1996, and by 1997, C18 numbers had dwindled to 15. It 'signified a downgrading of Loyalism within C18 circles and vice versa'.[46] Interestingly, when C18 established

---

[43]   Ibid., pp. 72–73.

[44]   Ibid., pp. 73–74.

[45]   'Senior Nazi arrested', *Statewatch*, July 1993; 'South Africa and the UDA', *Statewatch*, May 1993 (UNA, Searchlight Archive, Box 4, Ulster and Ireland: SCH/01/Res/EUR/02/004).

[46]   Lowles, *White Riot*, pp. 78–79.

the NSA as a political front, Sargent drew comparisons with the IRA/Sinn Fein relationship rather than Ulster loyalism,[47] though C18 graffiti can still be found in loyalist areas. Other developments, however, should be noted that bear on C18's gradual disengagement from the Ulster problem, such as the fight-back launched by Tyndall and Griffin against C18 in 1995. But much more important were developments in the Northern Ireland peace process in the mid-1990s.

A combination of American pressure, constitutional guarantees for Unionism, British facilitation and the creation of a 'pan-nationalist alliance' that convinced the republican leadership that a *political* road to Irish unity now existed, culminated in the declaration of a 'complete cessation of violence' by the Provisional IRA on 31 August 1994, with the loyalist UDA and UVF following suit on 10 October. These were major developments in an ongoing and difficult peace process that would, if by fits and starts, lead eventually to the Belfast/Good Friday Agreement of Easter 1998.[48] With the violent paramilitary phase of the Ulster problem moving towards an end – though there would be temporary breakdowns to come – the loyalist/C18 connection lost much of its *raison d'être*. It is somewhat ironic, however, that just as that relationship was diminishing, C18 would have its greatest publicity in association with Northern Ireland.

This was occasioned by an Irish Republic–England football match at Lansdowne Road, Dublin in mid-February 1995, which, due to the violence provoked by the English fans, had to be abandoned. Given its notoriety, the trouble was widely assumed to be the work of C18, especially as Charlie Sargent was only too willing to cultivate that impression and the assumption that it was related to the Ulster problem. But while C18 material was found in the ground, few C18 members it seems actually attended the match – the extremist/hooligan presence was more varied and extensive, the reality more complex. A number of factors were at play: minimal legal consequences for football violence in Dublin; Irish police acceptance of British intelligence on English football hooligans but decline of practical British police assistance and

---

[47] Ibid., p. 78.
[48] See Loughlin, *The Ulster Question since 1945*, chap. 4.

presence in the football ground (too politically sensitive); chaotic sale of tickets allowing English and Irish fans to intermingle; inefficient stewarding of fans; insufficient and inefficient policing. In sum, 'shambolic and amateurish preparations and policing of the match gave the hooligans the opportunity to cause chaos'. Nevertheless, Sargent's boasting and a media willingness to find a simple cause pinned the blame on C18, and it worked to the group's detriment.

A new police squad was established to deal with C18, together with another *World in Action* investigation which reinforced its violent nature. The Dublin episode would be a significant factor in C18's demise,[49] which took off with an internal feud at the end of December 1996 and climaxed in 1997,[50] due to a controversy over Sargent apparently being an informant for British Intelligence, and his later conviction for murder as a result of the internal conflict.[51]

The BNP and the Belfast/Good Friday Agreement

Despite Tyndall's proscribing of C18 the association between the two organisations remained in the public mind, reinforced by reporting of the Dublin controversy which tended to describe C18 as the 'armed wing of the BNP', irritating at a time when the latter was striving for respectability. Its members were English patriots, as opposed to racists hating the 'blacks, Asians, the Irish and Jews', and none were involved in the Dublin disorder;[52] its approach to Ulster was more respectable. Moreover, dissatisfied with the politically inadequate publications of loyalist organisations, the Ulster group, along with 'like-minded loyalists', would produce an Ulster-focused publication in 1996, *True Brit*, focused on framing the ongoing Ulster problem within the wider perspective of BNP concerns, especially the supposed destruction of the British nation: 'The same

---

[49] For an effective assessment of the Dublin trouble, see Lowles, *White Riot*, chap. 10.

[50] Copsey, *Contemporary British Fascism*, p. 69.

[51] Matthew Collins, *Hate: My Life in the British Far Right* (London: Biteback Publishing, 2011), p. 302.

[52] Rachel Borrill, 'Right-wing riot links with UDA alleged', *Irish Times*, 17 February 1995.

sick, corrupt and decadent system that allows IRA terrorists to murder at will is the same system that is systematically attempting to destroy the whole fabric of our Nation through mass coloured immigration against the will of our people.'[53]

Cumming's outline of the BNP's Ulster policy owed much to previous extreme-Right thinking, but not only did it face familiar problems of popular persuasion, the Ulster integration proposal was now significantly out of kilter with the direction the peace process was taking, especially given that the main loyalist organisations were not only on ceasefire, but were also participants in that developing process: they would vehemently reject Ian Paisley's call to oppose the Belfast/Good Friday Agreement in 1998. The Ulster issue, thus, was moving gradually into a post-conflict stage, posing questions for the BNP as to its viability in the region and when it had denounced the only major Unionist party also committed to the belief that the peace process entailed constitutional betrayal, Paisley's DUP.[54] Moreover, for a party that indexed its political respectability by opposition to race attacks, that such attacks would proceed to a point where the region became branded the race-hate capital of Europe hardly suggested a significant regional impact, not least because the overwhelming number of race incidents occurred, and still occur, in loyalist areas, the main areas of BNP activity, and which a persuasive argument recently sourced largely to the nature of loyalist prejudice.[55]

If the political environment offered any hope for the BNP in the mid-1990s, it lay in the fact that while David Trimble's Official Unionist Party (OUP) was the main Unionist participant in the peace process, its impact at Westminster – effectively keeping John Major's Tory Party, elected with a marginal majority, in office – gave it significant influence on Major's approach to the talks, especially in insisting that the Provisional IRA disarm before being allowed to participate in political negotiations. The longer the talks process

---

[53] *True Brit*, vol. 1, no. 1, autumn 1996 (UNA, *Searchlight* Archive, Box 18, BNP: SCH/01/Res/BRI/03/018).

[54] See, for instance, *The New Protestant Telegraph*, May 1993.

[55] See Robbie McVeigh, 'Racism in the six counties', in J. V. Ulin, Heather Edwards and Sean O'Brien (eds), *Race and Immigration in the New Ireland* (Notre Dame, Ind.: University of Notre Dame Press, 2013), *passim*.

dragged on so the possibility existed of constitutional 'treachery' being averted.[56] Accordingly, when political stalling provoked the Provisional IRA to break their ceasefire with the Baltic Exchange bombing of 1996, its meaning, for the BNP, was obvious: republicans thought talks might achieve their objectives; when this was shown not to be true 'they resorted once again to murder'. And Tony Blair, elected on a landslide majority in May 1997, was among the 'fools' calling for a restoration of the peace process. Only the BNP remained consistent in its approach to the Northern Ireland problem, demanding the extermination of the IRA: 'A BNP government would stop the terror within three weeks. What will Tony Blair do?'[57] In fact, thanks to encouraging signals from Blair, the Provisional IRA reinstated its ceasefire on 20 July 1997, leaving the evidentiary basis for the viability of the BNP's Ulster policy resting on attacks perpetrated by smaller republican groups such as the Irish National Liberation Army (INLA) – responsible for killing the notorious leader of the Loyalist Volunteer Force (LVF), Billy Wright, *inside* the Maze prison on 27 December 1997.[58]

If the peace process denied the opportunity for a significant political advance, its wider setting nevertheless presented controversies the BNP might exploit, such as the banning or restriction of Orange marches through Catholic districts, especially the July parade to Drumcree Anglican Church outside Portadown, and which, until 1995 had proceeded without legal restriction. Signalling the prominence 'Drumcree' would have following the signing of the Belfast/Good Friday Agreement in 1998, the success of the Orange Order in forcing the RUC to rescind a ban on it marching through a Catholic area on its return journey from Drumcree in 1996 was recommended as an effective example of extra-parliamentary street activity to thwart the forthcoming constitutional 'treachery'.[59] Additionally, Unionist opinion was cultivated with the promise of

---

[56] 'The IRA – when will Major act?', *British Nationalist*, July 1996.
[57] 'Intern the terrorists', *British Nationalist*, July 1997.
[58] See Chris Anderson, *The Billy Boy: The Life and Death of the LVF Leader Billy Wright* (Edinburgh and London: Mainstream, 2002); 'Back to war', *British Nationalist*, January 1998.
[59] See 'Parade lessons', *True Brit*, vol. 1, no. 1, autumn 1996.

its Ulster's message being conveyed to the people of Britain via a BNP television broadcast the following year. It would look forward to the collapse of 'the present anti-British party system'.[60]

Evidencing Nick Griffin's growing influence in the BNP, *True Brit* exulted over electoral successes achieved by Jean-Marie Le Pen's Front National at the French elections of February 1997 as something that heralded not only a solution to the Ulster problem but would actually restore the constitutional unity that existed under the Act of Union between Britain and Ireland from 1800 to 1922: when Le Pen obtained power in France, he would take it out of the EEC, which would then collapse and thus deprive the Irish Republic of the large subsidies that kept its economy afloat, resulting in it being driven to seek re-entry to the United Kingdom.[61]

The peace process, however, proceeded on its halting way to deliver a political agreement on Good Friday 1998. Consisting of three strands – internal Northern Ireland governance based on power-sharing; cooperation between Northern Ireland and the Irish Republic; and cooperation between the Irish Republic and Britain. Also, impartiality of treatment for all sections in Northern Ireland was provided for, together with a provision for everyone in the region to decide whether to identify themselves as British or Irish, or both. But it also came with serious concerns, such as the early release from jail of paramilitary prisoners, allowing republicans into Government in Northern Ireland without prior decommissioning of their weapons, and reform of the RUC, seen by Unionists as a serious reflection on the reputation of a blameless body of men who had bravely combated republican terrorism for 25 years.[62] And others emerged, such as the Government providing the republican leaders Gerry Adams and Martin McGuinness with handguns for their own protection.[63] Unionist concern was compounded when

[60] Ibid.
[61] 'The establishment quakes as France awakes!', *True Brit*, vol. 1, no. 2, spring 1997.
[62] For further discussion of the Agreement, see Loughlin, *The Ulster Question since 1945*, chap. 5.
[63] See *British Nationalist*, July 1998. For a thoughtful rejection of the

Northern Ireland suffered the worst atrocity of the troubles era, when 28 people were killed in a dissident IRA bomb in Omagh, county Tyrone in August 1998.

In this context, while a June 1998 referendum in Northern Ireland on the Agreement produced a 71 per cent approval for it, within the Protestant community only just over half approved. Indeed, for a time, the Tory Party leadership was tempted to join the Agreement's opponents before being compelled by support for it in Britain and Ireland to desist.[64] And while anti-Agreement Unionism was united behind the powerful negativism of Ian Paisley's DUP, supported by six of the ten United Ulster Unionist MPs at Westminster and the Orange Order, what kept the Agreement in place was the failure of its opponents to produce a viable alternative that would eliminate the effects of the hated AIA of 1985.

Against this background, the controversy over contentious Orange marches made that issue the centre ground of anti-Agreement activity, and for a while it seemed a highly effective one. Paisley, the most impressive mass orator in the region, had warned loyalists at Drumcree in July 1995: 'If we don't win this battle all is lost, it is a matter of life or death. It is a matter of Ulster or the Irish Republic. It is a matter of freedom or slavery.'[65] A hyperbolic outburst in 1995 seemed to many anti-Agreement loyalists in 1998 a simple statement of fact. By then, Drumcree had indeed become a synecdoche for the Ulster problem in general, the part that consumed the whole. It received widespread British media attention, attracting a BNP visit. Subsequently, *British Nationalist* readers were treated to a pro-Orange account of the episode, and an indication of what political advantage the BNP expected from it:

> On the positive side ... the fact that all the mainland political parties now openly support the Irish imperialism of the

Agreement by the now much reduced National Front, see 'The long Good Friday', *Vanguard*, no. 53 [1998].
[64] Matthew Parris, 'Up the creek with Paisley', *The Times*, 3 July 1998; Eric Waugh, 'Hague sees opportunity to exploit Ulster divisions', *Belfast Telegraph*, 23 January 1999.
[65] Paisley, quoted in Bew and Gillespie, *Northern Ireland: A Chronology of the Troubles, 1968–1999*, p. 108.

Pan-Republican Front can only help to boost sympathy for the British National Party in Ulster. This can only encourage the growth of our organisation there, and ensure that future BNP visitors have an even warmer welcome than we did.[66]

It was in this state of optimism about Ulster that Nick Griffin was elected leader of the BNP in 1999.

Nick Griffin, Ulster and Political Modernisation

While the argument that 'the people of Northern Ireland have been duped into accepting a phoney "peace" deal',[67] remained fundamental to the BNP approach to the Ulster problem when Nick Griffin became leader, that the Agreement was in place and the institutions of Government it embodied were being prepared were facts that could not be ignored. The first period of devolved Government in Northern Ireland may have lasted only from 2 December 1999 to 11 February 2000, due mainly to a failure of the Provisional IRA to decommission its weapons, but the Agreement endured, something the BNP could do little about. Indeed, despite the claim in 1996 that the BNP's Ulster case would be aired to the British population in the party's TV election broadcast of 1997, when aired, the broadcast made no mention of Ulster; nor was Ulster mentioned in the BNP broadcasts for the European elections of 1999 and 2004.[68] In fact, not until February 2011 would the BNP be actually registered as a political party in Northern Ireland.

Accordingly, the BNP's modernisation project – which would survive a BBC *Panorama* exposure in August 2000 of the party's antisemitic mentality and the criminal background of many leading members[69] – entailed a shift in Ulster's significance for the party.

[66] See 'Butlins meets Bosnia: Colin Smyth reports on a visit to Drumcree', *British Nationalist*, August 1998; 'Freedom tattered at Drumcree', *Spearhead*, no. 354, August 1998.

[67] 'The peace process', *British Nationalist*, June/July 1999.

[68] BNP election broadcasts, 1997, 1999, 2004; conference speeches, 1998 (YouTube). Accessed 20 March 2017.

[69] See *Panorama*, 'Under the Skin', BBC1 television, broadcast 25 November 2000.

Condemnation of the Agreement would still be made,[70] but, for Griffin, extreme-Right failure in Northern Ireland since the early 1970s could hardly be ignored: the region would not be a springboard into the British political mainstream; moreover, care was needed to ensure that BNP coverage of Ulster issues conformed to the needs of the modernisation project.

This was promoted mainly via a glossy publication, *Identity*, which rejected nostalgia for the disastrous Hitler: the future lay with 'Democracy not dictatorship, cultural identity not racial superiority'.[71] Similarly, the Golden Dawn movement in Greece was defined as 'Neo-Fascism', something the BNP had long rejected, evident in its call to 'reject Judeo-Obsessiveness': no vast Jewish conspiracy was responsible for the nation's predicament, only 'treacherous capitalism',[72] though the 'war criminals' running the Israeli Government would be attacked, along with Blair's plans for the invasion of Iraq, plans that would merely serve the interests of US oil companies as well as Israel.[73] At the same time, the emergence of the United Kingdom Independence Party (UKIP) was dismissed as an example of mere 'civic nationalism', whereas the movement of the future was the BNP's 'modern nationalism'.[74]

Political modernisation in the Ulster context was evident as early as 2000 in an equidistant approach to paramilitary prisoners: early releases under the Agreement had included 'some of the most despicable characters to have emerged in the so-called "loyalist" paramilitaries'.[75] In October 2002, Griffin boasted that the Ulster BNP group had a cross-community membership – 'looking for

[70] See, for instance, John Tyndall, '"Peace" in Ulster: the pathetic delusion', *Spearhead*, January 2000; '"Real IRA" prepare for bloodbath', *Truth* (issued in support of the NF), 12 August 2000 (UNA, *Searchlight* Archive, Box 26, National Front: SCH/01/Res/BRI/02/026).
[71] See 'Moving forward for good', *Identity: Magazine of the British National Party*, June 2002.
[72] 'Hitler in reverse', *Identity*, March 2006; 'Modern nationalism – the new force in politics', *Identity*, April 2006.
[73] See 'Against the war for our troops', *Identity*, April 2003.
[74] 'Hitler in reverse', *Identity*, March 2006; 'Modern nationalism – the new force in politics', *Identity*, April 2006.
[75] 'Ulster sell-out continues', *Voice of Freedom*, August 2000.

an alternative to sectarianism'. It was a distinct departure from the BNP's pro-Orange stance on the Drumcree issue of 1998. In the same vein, the Belfast/Good Friday Agreement, based on governance by national/republican and Unionist blocs, was itself sectarian in nature, a criticism made not just by the BNP, and a critique that ran in tandem with other, more traditional extreme-Right issues that other parties avoided, such as the negative effects of the EU and immigration.[76] Moreover, attacks on Sinn Fein now tended to fall within mainstream Unionist lines, such as the fact that *abstentionist* Sinn Fein MPs were drawing their Westminster parliamentary allowances while at the same time police were arresting loyalists. In a similar vein, when power-sharing resumed in Northern Ireland in 2007 after an absence of five years, and involving Sinn Fein and the DUP, now the two largest parties on each side of the political divide, the BNP argued merely that Tony Blair had conceded too much in his negotiations with republicans and thereby done much to undermine moderate politics.[77] And while it was suggested that Nick Griffin *might* be a target of the INLA,[78] such concerns were not exceptional for Unionist or loyalist politicians in Northern Ireland.

BNP modernism was also evident in a more conciliatory approach to the Irish Republic, with Griffin citing his own Irish origins in the village of Ballygriffin in west Cork, a place he liked to take his children on holiday,[79] and with a stated intention of political recruitment based on the supposed racial unity of all ethnic groups in the British Isles: 'The Marxist IRA does not represent Ireland.'[80] Accordingly, in early 2004, a short-lived 'Keep Ireland Irish' campaign was launched. It was not entirely altruistic. Ireland was a 'backdoor' route for immigrants coming to Britain: 'It's therefore in our direct self-interest to help the Irish to organise so as to shut their

[76] Mary Fitzgerald, 'BNP to contest seats in Ulster', *Belfast Telegraph*, 31 October 2002.

[77] John Bean, 'Sinn Fein given too much', *Identity*, April 2007.

[78] *Identity*, August 2004; *Identity*, April 2006.

[79] Gemma O'Doherty, 'Next stop Ireland for the British neo-Nazis', *Irish Independent*, 27 April 2002.

[80] See, for example, Nick Griffin, 'The Celts', *Identity*, May 2003; 'Nationalist groups of the British Isles must stand together, or we will hang separately', *Identity*, May 2004.

own gates.'[81] The initiative came to nothing, the WikiLeaks exposé of BNP membership in 2007 would identify only two members in the Irish Republic, one of whom was an English retiree.[82] Ireland, however, was to provide a source of inspiration for the BNP more generally when Irish electors rejected the EU's Lisbon Treaty in 2008 in the first (but not the second) of two referendums on the issue. John Bean, *Identity* editor, opined that it 'raises a nostalgic yearning that the British community of nations could once again include a United Ireland'.[83] Moreover, despite its criticism of the republican movement, having acquired a copy of a Sinn Fein electoral campaign report in 2005, the BNP leadership was so impressed that it recommended the party to adopt it wholesale: ignore 'all the republican propaganda … and for "Sinn Fein" read BNP'.[84]

The transformation in BNP comment on Northern Ireland has to be seen in the context of its successful modernisation project in Britain in this period. In 2002, it had three BNP councillors elected in Burnley, in 2003, eight, indicating that it was 'far more adept at targeting resources and courting the media than it has been in the past',[85] and would go on to a tally of 60 British councillors at its peak.[86] But the BNP's Ulster formation failed to achieve anything like the same success. Despite an intention to stand a candidate in the European Parliament election of 2005, it came and went without a BNP presence. However, any account of the Ulster formation's political failure in this period has to take note of how it was affected by the fall-out from the BNP's modernisation project, especially the emergence in the region of the rabidly racist White Nationalist Party (WNP).

[81] Sandra Hurley, 'British neo-Nazis in Irish campaign', *Sunday Independent*, 7 March 2004.
[82] 'Two members of BNP living here', *Irish Independent*, 20 November 2008.
[83] John Bean, 'Irish shock waves expose the EU', *Identity*, August 2008.
[84] 'The case for a campaigning party', *Identity*, November 2005.
[85] Gary Younge, 'A land fit for racists', *Guardian*, 4 May 2002.
[86] Sonia Gable, 'New leader takes BNP back to basics', *Searchlight*, 9 September 2014 (http://www.searchlightmagazine.com/archive/new-leader-takes-bnp-back-to-basics). Accessed 5 March 2015.

The WNP, BNP and Ulster

Certainly, Northern Ireland with its developing racism problem appeared to provide fertile ground for recruitment. The Protestant community had experienced both greatly diminished political power and loss of cultural dominance since the outbreak of the troubles in 1969, with the result that the Belfast/Good Friday Agreement was viewed as a necessary compromise, and not, as for the Catholic community, something to be enthusiastically embraced. Unionist leaders signed the Belfast/Good Friday Agreement reluctantly, failing enthusiastically to endorse it, with the result that in the referendum on the Agreement of May 1998 only 55 per cent of Protestants approved. By October 2002, only 32 per cent of Protestants approved of the Agreement, while 67 per cent disapproved, mainly because of a belief that the Agreement had benefited Catholics and nationalist/ republicans to a greater extent than Unionists and loyalists.[87] A toxic and paranoid atmosphere was developing evidenced in loyalist and interface areas by 'a significant increase in sectarian activity', a situation exacerbated by Government conciliation, as opposed to taking a firm security approach, to loyalist criminality.[88]

In this context, Ulster's Catholic and nationalist/republican community was seen as a 'pan-nationalist front', and for the most extreme anti-Agreement loyalists a legitimate target for physical attack.[89] Overlapping extremist groupuscules, such as the Orange Volunteers and the Red Hand Defenders, emerged precisely to do that, their main areas of operation being those in which extreme-Right activity had long been established.[90] And to these groups

[87] See Paul Dixon and Eamonn O'Kane, *Northern Ireland since 1969* (Harlow: Longman, 2011), p. 96.

[88] For an insightful discussion of these issues and possible remedies, see Mark Langhammer, 'Cutting with the grain: how to make change in the Protestant community', *Fortnight*, May 2004.

[89] For an illuminating discussion focused on the murder of the Catholic journalist Martin O'Hagan, see Susan McKay, 'Faith, hate and murder', *Guardian Weekend*, 17 November 2001.

[90] See Liam Clarke and Vincent Kearney, 'Religious fanatic leads loyalist rebels', *Sunday Times*, 14 February 1999; Martin Fletcher, 'Extremist few strive to keep the hatred alive', *The Times*, 19 February 1999.

can be added, despite the organisation's collapse in 1997, an Ulster element of C18 combining soccer hooliganism with sectarian violence: it had assisted the notorious mid-Ulster loyalist killers, the LVF, to murder Rosemary Nelson, a solicitor specialising in defending nationalists and republicans, in 1999.[91] At the same time, the increase of the immigrant community in Northern Ireland has energised its activities.[92]

Only 25 racial incidents were reported in the region in 1997, but 13,655 were registered by 2012, with only 12 cases successfully prosecuted.[93] In December 2013, the Institute of Race Relations in Northern Ireland concluded that 'a staggering amount (about 80 per cent) of racially aggravated crime continues to go unreported'.[94] At the same time, antisemitism was reported as developing in the north and increasing in the south.[95] That the great majority of racist incidents occurred, and occur, in loyalist areas (in Belfast only loyalist areas have a supply of vacant housing, the Catholic west of the city being heavily overcrowded) made it all the easier for C18 to make its own contribution. And while the BNP could take satisfaction in having dissociated itself from C18,[96] commentators didn't always acknowledge the separation.[97] This was also the case with the WNP.

The group emerged in May 2002, established by Eddy Morrison

---

[91] Henry McDonald, 'LVF link to neo-Nazis unearthed', *Guardian*, 2 April 2000.

[92] The 2011 census found that 32,400 people – 1.8 per cent of the usually resident population – belonged to ethnically minority groups, more than double the proportion ten years earlier, when the figure stood at 0.8 per cent.

[93] Jonathan McCambridge, '900% increase in race hate crimes', *Belfast Telegraph*, 30 October 2003; Richard Montague, 'Racism a legacy of troubles', *Belfast Telegraph*, 23 May 2014.

[94] Gerard Stewart, 'An assessment of racial violence in Northern Ireland', 12 December 2013 (https://www.irr.org.uk/news/an-assessment-of-racial-violence-in-northern-ireland/). Accessed 14 October 2016.

[95] James Fitzgerald, 'Anti-Semitic acts prompt calls for tougher laws', *Irish Times*, 18 June 2005; Henry McDonald, 'Belfast Jewish community submitted to antisemitic online abuse', *Guardian*, 17 February 2017.

[96] See *Spearhead*, May 1998.

[97] Colin O'Carroll, 'Fears rise as soccer matches embroiled in sectarian scandals', *Irish News*, 12 January 1998; 'Combat 18', *Irish Independent*, 8 May 1999; "Neo-Nazi fanatics for Derry parade", *Derry Journal*, 6 July 2001.

and six others, ex-BNP and NF, as the British political wing of Aryan Unity. From an Anglo-Catholic background and with family connections going back to Mosley's BUF in the 1930s, Morrison had been a member of several extreme-Right organisations and in 1989 had re-joined the BNP at Tyndall's invitation, where he stayed until the late 1990s, provoked to leave by the national and racial betrayals he saw in Griffin's modernisation project: 'to sacrifice our very Racialist beliefs for the sake of a handful of crumbs from ZOG's [Zionist Occupation Government] table in the shape of a few council seats and votes was out of the question'. He then re-joined the NF in July 1999, but by October 2000, after failed attempts to reorganise what was by now a largely moribund organisation, he left. The experience, however, had alerted him to the importance of the internet as a medium of communication.[98]

Expecting a slow development and conceived mainly as a web-based organisation, recruitment, according to Morrison, proved so good that the WNP soon had dedicated units throughout Britain, 'with an especially strong movement building up in Ulster'. A regular monthly bulletin, *White Sentinel*, and a monthly magazine, *White Nationalist World*, were produced together with 'the Celtic Cross as the vanguard symbol of a new renaissance Nationalist Movement'.[99] The WNP held its first meeting on 9 November 2002, declared as a great success heralding a bright future.[100] Its propaganda covered a variety of problems affecting the British State – social, economic, immigration, etc. – together with opposition to the impending invasion of Iraq, the latter chiefly for its own ideological reasons: the defeat of Saddam Hussein would secure the Israeli State.[101]

---

[98] Eddy Morrison, 'Memoirs of a street soldier: a life in white nationalism', part 15 (http://www.aryanunity.com/memoirs15.html). Accessed 20 December 2013.

[99] Eddy Morrison, 'Memoirs of a street soldier: a life in white nationalism', part 17.

[100] 'Historic first meeting of the White Nationalist Party!', *White Sentinel*, November 2002 (UNA, *Searchlight* Archive, Box 1, White Nationalist Party: SCH/01/Res/BRI/11/01).

[101] See WNP press item, 'White nationalist news round', [March 2003] (UNA, *Searchlight* Archive, Box 1, White Nationalist Party: SCH/01/Res/BRI/11/01).

The WNP campaign in Northern Ireland was determined and energetic, justifying the claim that Ulster members had made their formation 'one of the best organised and most active regional groups'. This was affirmed at a 'flagship' Ulster meeting of 18–20 July 2003, part of a range of events also covering Hull, Leeds and Burnley;[102] and, unlike C18, which, though no less extreme and violent, had tended to be spontaneous in activity, lacking coherent organisation. Moreover, believing that all publicity was good publicity, the WNP website reproduced hostile articles from the Northern Ireland press; despite their hostility they tended to lend credibility to WNP claims of strong expansion.[103]

The WNP's area of operation, however, remained the same as that of other extreme-Right organisations since the 1970s – Belfast, Lisburn, Lurgan, Portadown, Coleraine, Ballymoney and Larne, all urban areas of east Ulster; and, as such, a highly problematic factor for the BNP Ulster faction as it attempted to promote its more 'moderate' version of neo-fascism[104] in opposition to 'openly racist, white supremacists who may be connected to loyalist paramilitaries'. Local BNP members were warned that any association with the WNP would entail expulsion.[105] Nevertheless, that both the WNP and the BNP exploited the same range of issues and that the former did so aggressively, meant that in the resultant controversies the identities of the two organisations were easily confused.

Coleraine, for instance, was a prominent WNP recruitment target,[106] and when it held a day of action in the town on 16 August 2003, the *Coleraine Times*, in raising alarm, framed its account in the context of the BNP's electoral successes in Burnley.[107] The

[102] *White Sentinel*, June 2003 (UNA, *Searchlight* Archive, Box 1, White Nationalist Party: SCH/01/Res/BRI/11/01).
[103] *Ballymoney* Times, 14 May, 4 June 2003; *Belfast Telegraph*, 1 May 2003; 'More media hysteria over the rise of the WNP in Ulster!', *Sunday World*, 25 May 2003.
[104] *White Sentinel*, July 2003.
[105] 'BNP members warned over White Nationalist Party', *UTV Newsroom*, 21 August 2003.
[106] Kyle White, 'WNP "to step up campaign"', *Coleraine Times*, 18 March 2003.
[107] David Rankin, 'White Nationalist Party targets Coleraine', *Coleraine Times*, 20 August 2003; 'WNP flag controversy whipped up in Ballymena',

BNP was not the only political party to be discomfited by WNP activities. This was also true of leaders of loyalist organisations, such as David Irvine of the PUP, engaged in promoting respectable identities in the hope of electoral progress,[108] but whose members had made the WNP welcome and 'supported most of what we stand for'.[109]

In large measure, these embarrassing associations were a product of the WNP method of operation, which, in the traditional extreme-Right manner, sought to integrate its own agenda with community concerns on a range of local issues, as in Ballymoney where it combined extensive leafleting with support for an anti-lignite protest campaign.[110] In east Belfast the WNP supported parents' rights to access the sex offenders register, together with distribution of 'Hang IRA Scum' leaflets. In Ballymena, it made its own contribution to an ongoing sectarian flag controversy by erecting the Celtic Cross flag, whose colours were the same as the Swastika banner – red, white and black – across the street from the town's social security and housing agency, the offices to which newly arrived immigrants went to enquire about benefits and accommodation.[111] In the same vein, the WNP enthusiastically supported local residents in the Portadown area – a location of recent notoriety due to the Drumcree dispute – in their campaign against the building of a mosque for the area's 200-strong Muslim community.[112] Racist motivation was denied, citing sewerage problems and land unsuitability, but one leading Unionist activist illustrated the essentially nativist nature of the anti-mosque campaign when he claimed that

---

Ballymena Guardian, 23 July 2003; 'Racist flag "put up to cause offence"', *Belfast Telegraph*, 23 July 2003.

[108] Kitty Holland, 'The grim reaper of racism', *Irish Times*, 17 January 2004; 'WNP has nothing to do with UDA fumes Wright', *Coleraine Times*, 25 August 2003.

[109] *White Sentinel*, July 2003.

[110] See 'UDA signs up with hate mob', *Sunday World*, 25 May 2003; *Ballymoney Times*, 4 June 2003.

[111] 'WNP flag controversy whipped up in Ballymena', *Ballymena Guardian*, 23 July 2003; 'Racist flag "put up to cause offence"', *Belfast Telegraph*, 23 July 2003.

[112] 'Trimble steps into mosque dispute', *Sunday Times*, 19 January 2003.

312 Fascism and Constitutional Conflict

Muslims were 'out to wipe out Christianity'; 'Christianity is the enemy of the Muslim'.[113]

The 'WNP anti-Mosque campaign' and related concerns in east Ulster and England garnered much publicity from the beginning of 2003, the year of the WNP's most sustained activity.[114] And though the Portadown campaign failed, it still served the WNP's purpose of demonstrating its credibility as a defender of local ethnic interests, and played into the central WNP theme in Northern Ireland of integrating race and opposition to the nationalist/ republican threat to Unionism: Sinn Fein/IRA wanted not just Irish unity but the creation of a multi-racial Ulster 'just so they can lead a "United Ireland" into a one world government'.[115] A republican victory would 'spell the end of the white race worldwide'.[116] The WNP made little distinction between Sinn Fein and the moderate nationalist SDLP, the latter often the chief target of WNP/loyalist attack due to its calls for the Human Rights and Equality Commissions to investigate the WNP and others groups espousing racism for breaches of Northern Ireland legislation;[117] though attempts to engage Unionist support for such efforts could stall on the latter's insistence that nationalist opposition to Orange marches in Catholic areas was also racist.[118]

By late 2003, the rise in racist attacks in Northern Ireland was such that ethnic minorities were more likely to suffer racial violence there than in England or Wales.[119] WNP and extreme-Right activity generally in Northern Ireland continued in the same

[113] 'Race Attacks "rise" in Northern Ireland', *BBC News Online*, 13 October 2003.
[114] 'Fantastic publicity in Ulster as WNP anti-mosque campaign hots up!' WNP press item, January 2003 (UNA, *Searchlight* Archive, Box 1, White Nationalist Party: SCH/01/Res/BRI/11/01).
[115] See 'SINN/IRA WORK FOR A MULTI RACIAL ULSTER', Reproduction of republican declaration of anti-racist intent, to be subscribed to by local councillors, in WNP press item [2003] (UNA, *Searchlight* Archive, Box 1, White Nationalist Party: SCH/01/Res/BRI/11/01).
[116] 'New target for race hate group, *Sunday World*, 20 July 2003.
[117] 'WNP should be investigated', *Ballymoney Times*, 13 August 2003.
[118] 'Council clash over racism', *Ballymena Times*, 14 August 2003.
[119] '"North is facing a racism crisis"', *Irish News*, 22 October 2005.

aggressive manner into 2004,[120] though now significant levels of opposition began to develop. In areas where loyalism was relatively weak, such as Derry city, extreme-Right activities were much less evident and opposition effective,[121] to which can be added a 'Fascists Out' group confronting the WNP and C18 in north Antrim,[122] while public condemnation was expressed about a WNP sticker carrying an image of the Battle of the Somme with the accompanying legend: 'They did not die for a multi-racial Ulster.'[123] The most serious blow the WNP suffered in 2004, however, was occasioned when, following a dispute with Morrison, Mark Cotterill, among others, broke away as a group under the title, England First Party. By mid-2005, Morrison had also left the WNP and on 6 June the WNP National Council decided to pass out of existence. Thus, just as suddenly as it emerged in Northern Ireland, it disappeared.

With the WNP gone, the BNP formation in the region sought to make a fresh start. Kieran Dinsmore, having replaced the former NF Political Soldier Andy McLorie as regional organiser, hoped the then stalemate over power-sharing and the increase of the region's immigrant population offered hopeful electoral prospects. Inspired by the local electoral success the BNP's new modernised image was delivering in Britain,[124] the organisation expanded its efforts outside east Ulster to Derry city, claiming to be responding to local enquiries; moreover, the region's proportional electoral system was something the BNP believed would work to its advantage.[125] These

---

[120] Dan Kernan, 'Belfast man was told not to rent to immigrants', *Irish Times*, 10 January 2004; David Rankin, 'WNP stage day of action', *Coleraine Times*, 28 January 2004.

[121] 'Londonderry to help stamp out racism and sectarianism', *Londonderry Sentinel*, 24 March 2004.

[122] See 'White Nationalist Party: WNP/C18 fascists driven out of Portrush', *indymedia Ireland* (https://www.indymedia.ie/article/64287?userlanguage=ga&save_prefs=true). Accessed 7 November 2012; 'Opposition to fascist rock gig growing', *Belfast Telegraph*, 18 May 2004.

[123] See 'Condemnation over racist sticker found in town', *Larne Times*, 27 May 2004.

[124] Ciaran Barnes, 'Race-hate British National Party planning to reorganise in north', *Daily Ireland*, 19 April 2006.

[125] 'BNP to seek Derry members', *Derry Journal*, 4 July 2007.

expectations, however, would be undone when Sinn Fein and Ian Paisley's DUP agreed to go into Government together in 2007, giving the Belfast/Good Friday Agreement a basis of security that would endure until 2017. And a different kind of blow was delivered when the entire BNP membership list was exposed on the internet by WikiLeaks. The leak revealed that in December 2007, Northern Ireland had 30 members out of a UK total of 12,656; in April 2009, a further leak disclosed 47 members in a UK total of 11,820. About a quarter that could be personally identified had apparently been inactive for around 12 years.[126]

That BNP failure in Northern Ireland was so complete illustrates just how problematic the region was for external parties seeking to advance their interests. In the 1970s, the explanation was that racism and antisemitism were negligible factors, but failure endured even when they did develop.[127] One academic study sources the race issue to the 'parity of esteem' dimension of the Belfast/Good Friday Agreement, a central element of the peace process – it had initiated a sense of loyalist cultural threat that was easily translated into a much higher level of anti-immigrant sentiment and targeting among Protestants.[128] With reference to the Catholic population, in 2014 a 110 per cent increase was registered in Catholic west Belfast over previous years.[129] However, the Catholic community had never been attracted to the British extreme Right and despite the claims of the latter, that community was not the chief target of its activities. As for antisemitism, the Arab–Israeli conflict which has done much

[126] 'BNP membership list', *Guardian* Datablog, 19 October 2009 (https://www.theguardian.com/politics/interactive/2009/oct/19/bnp-membership-uk-map). Accessed 30 April 2017; 'Ulster's doomed!: That BNP list again' (https://ulstersdoomed.blogspot.com/2009/10/that-bnp-list-again.html). Accessed 25 March 2014.

[127] 'Anti-Semitic incidents in Britain have risen 50 per cent in the last year', *The Independent*, 30 July 2015; 'Rise in anti-Semitic hate incidents as 557 cases reported from January to June', *Belfast Telegraph*, 4 August 2016.

[128] See Samuel Pehrson, M. A. Gheorghiu and Tomas Ireland, 'Cultural threat and anti-immigrant prejudice: the case of Protestants in Northern Ireland', *Journal of Community and Applied Social Psychology*, vol. 22, no. 2 (March/April 2012), 111–24.

[129] 'Race, crime and punishment', *Spotlight*, BBC Northern Ireland, 2014.

to stimulate it had, and has, been subsumed within the region's sectarian framework,[130] with Unionists and nationalists identifying with Israelis and Palestinians, respectively,[131] though antisemitism and legitimate criticism of Israeli State policies in the occupied Palestine territories can be easily confused.

In Britain, 2009 would see the triumph of Griffinite modernism and the pinnacle of Griffin's career, when he and Andrew Brons, exploiting the immigration issue to much better effect than the BNP's Ulster faction, gained election to the European Parliament.[132] By 2010, 'Ulster' had virtually disappeared as a subject from *Identity*, though the Northern Ireland formation, finding inspiration in Griffin's and Brons's success, looked forward to contesting the Northern Ireland Assembly election of May 2011, which, like the European election, was also based on a proportional system.[133] Its three candidates, however, standing in Belfast East, East Antrim and South Antrim, respectively garnered a grand total of only 1,250 votes and no seats.[134]

The failure of 2011 was repeated at the Northern Ireland local elections of 2014, undoubtedly made all the more galling by UKIP successes. Whereas the BNP's two candidates failed abysmally, three UKIP representatives were elected, while a Unionist member of the Northern Ireland Assembly, David McNarry, had switched to UKIP in 2013. In this context it is worth noting that whereas the NF and the BNP actively engaged with loyalist sentiment and their local issues, this was not the case with UKIP's national leadership. When Nigel Farage visited Northern Ireland during the 2014 European

---

[130] See 'Outrage as Belfast synagogue targeted twice in hate attacks', *Belfast Telegraph*, 22 July 2014.
[131] Henry McDonald, 'Anti-Semitism bred by ignorance … just look at our attitudes to Israel–Palestine', *Belfast Telegraph*, 29 August 2016; 'Rabbi says anti-Semitism is "on the rise" in Northern Ireland', BBC News, 2 October 2016 (https://www.bbc.co.uk/news/uk-northern-ireland-37533746). Accessed 7 April 2017.
[132] Martin Wainwright, 'EU elections: BNP's Nick Griffin wins seat in European Parliament', *Guardian* (8 June 2009).
[133] '"At last – a real choice!" First British National Party candidates ever in the province', *Voice of Freedom*, no. 122, April 2011.
[134] BBC News. 'Northern Ireland elections', 8 May 2011.

parliamentary election campaign, he resolutely refused to comment on local sectarian issues, despite local party members claiming he would.[135] This was a telling local illustration of a more general national fact: namely, that by 2014 UKIP was providing a more respectable home for radical Right opinion than the BNP, generally free of any overt neo-Nazi or racist reputation, street violence and thuggery. That at the same time the BNP was imploding only assisted the UKIP advance.[136]

An element of that implosion was the departure from the party of Jim Dowson. A Scottish businessman based in Northern Ireland and with a history of membership of the Orange Order and anti-abortion activism, he came to prominence in the BNP in 2007 when, having persuaded Griffin he could professionalise the party organisation, he took charge of its finances and would claim to have raised £4,000,000. Griffin acknowledged that without his contribution the BNP would never have won seats in the European Parliament, but also that Dowson had a tendency to 'piss people off'. This apparently derived from Dowson's requirement that BNP members demonstrate a much higher degree of commitment to its activities than a party of volunteers was used to.[137] However (and apparently for other reasons), his relations with Griffin also became highly fractious and he left the BNP in 2010, thereafter becoming involved in founding Britain First, an organisation he used to attack Griffin. He was also active in loyalist flag protests in Belfast in 2012, provoked by the city council's decision to restrict the flying of the Union flag. Yet Dowson's membership of Britain First was short-lived. He resigned in 2014, having disagreed with its policy of aggressive action towards Muslims, including 'invasions' of Mosques.[138]

---

[135] Liam Clarke, 'Treading carefully in political minefield', *Belfast Telegraph*, 15 May 2014.

[136] For a comprehensive discussion on this topic, see Robert Ford and Matthew Goodwin, *Revolt on the Right: Explaining Support for the Radical Right in Britain* (London and New York: Routledge, 2014), pp. 84, 89, 147, 200, 243.

[137] Trilling, *Bloody Nasty People*, pp. 174–75.

[138] See 'Scots ex-BNP chief seen fuelling Union flag riots in Belfast', *Daily Record*, 9 January 2013; Hope not Hate, 'Hate files: the British National Party'

For Nick Griffin, 2014 was the nadir of his fortunes. Declared bankrupt, he lost his European Parliament seat, and his party leadership role (he became party 'President'). The party's European election vote was derisory while its council seats were reduced from 60 to two. He was blamed for this state of affairs, for concentrating on European and international issues when he should have been emphasising Britain's: 'We are the British National party, not the European National Party.'[139] In this situation of party decline and personal difficulty Griffin abandoned any pretence of non-sectarian impartiality as his traditional alignment with Ulster loyalism was resumed. In October 2012, he attended a centenary parade commemorating the 100th anniversary of the Ulster Covenant of 1912. But his presence provoked embarrassing questions to the Orange Order, while he was also under police investigation for derogatory remarks he had made about Catholics on social media.[140] No less problematic for the BNP were its attempts to exploit the controversy over the flying of the Union flag at Belfast City Hall: the protest leaders rejected BNP support as an attempt 'by sinister elements to undermine support for perfectly legitimate protests'.[141] The party's last elected local councillor, Brian Parker, in Pendle, east Lancashire, retired from politics in the run-up to the local elections of May 2018.[142]

(https://web.archive.org/web/20150206073711/http://www.hopenothate.org.uk/hate-groups/bf/); 'Britain First founder quits over mosque invasions which "attract racists and extremists"', *Daily Mirror*, 27 July 2014.

[139] Gable, 'New leader takes BNP back to basics'.

[140] 'Why was BNP leader at Ulster Covenant event? – Anderson', *Derry Journal*, 1 October 2012.

[141] Hope not Hate report, in Peter Walker, 'Support for British far-right groups hits 20-year low', *Guardian*, 14 January 2015; Deborah McAleese, 'Former BNP man and Nick Griffin ex-crony Paul Goldring flies to Belfast for loyalist flag protest', *Belfast Telegraph*, 15 December 2015; 'Stay away, protesters tell BNP', *News Letter*, 31 December 2012.

[142] Helen Pidd, 'As the BNP vanishes, do the forces that built it remain?', *Guardian*, 2 May 2018.

Conclusion

The historical trajectory of the British extreme-Right over the period covered by this study has been from the centre of British politics with the Ulster crisis of 1912–14 to its extremes. Ulster 1912–14 was serious, not only in itself, but because it was the focal point of a fundamental crisis of the British State, as popular democracy and a rising labour movement aligned with Irish nationalism in support of self-Government for Ireland. For the elite Right – a historical formation that had ruled the State for centuries – the crisis appeared to threaten the destruction of the United Kingdom and its empire. Only the outbreak of the Great War defused a crisis that had the potential of developing into civil war.

Tory encouragement of loyalist rebellion against the Liberal Government in 1912–14 may have seemed indicative of a brief extremist phase of the party's history that was unrepeatable, which is how British historians have generally treated it. But, as we have seen, this is not how George Lansbury and other Labour leaders of the time regarded it. 'Ulster' remained in Labour calculations in the inter-war period as an indicator of what the Tories were capable of with reference to fascist possibilities in a period of mass unemployment and economic distress with capitalism appearing to be in crisis. Against an academic perception of fascism as a political option *destined* to fail in Britain, the Left was much less sure. Then, as in the later historiography, there was no consensus on a definition of fascism. A variety of possibilities were under consideration; Mosley's movement did not by any means exhaust fascist potentiality in the British context.

Certainly for later pro-loyalist extreme-Right organisations the threatened Ulster rebellion of 1912–14 seemed freighted with a fascist potential that contemporary problems – especially those provoked by the grievances of the region's disaffected Catholic minority and the constitutional and paramilitary campaigns to free Northern Ireland from British control they led to from 1969 – provided a likely basis for delivering on. At the same time, the British fascist presence in Northern Ireland over the last century was also to a large extent a function of political developments in Britain.

For Rotha Lintorn-Orman, the inspiration Edward Carson's threatened rebellion provided for her own movement was an aspect of a perceived general State crisis, while the extension of BF activities into Northern Ireland was occasioned by the split associated with the General Strike of 1926 and the need to repair membership losses. For Mosley's Blackshirt movement in its regional manifestation, the Ulster Fascists, it was driven by the palingenetic expectations produced by the great upsurge in Blackshirt support that followed his compact with Lord Rothermere. Even the miniscule presence of Arnold Leese's Imperial Fascist League was largely a function of Anglo-Irish difficulties in the mid-1930s and how de Valera's dismantling of the Irish Free State's imperial links appeared to offer a wider threat to the British Empire. Again, the presence in Northern Ireland of Admiral Sir Barry Domvile's pro-Nazi organisation The Link was driven chiefly by the desire to evidence a thriving state-wide organisation.

The post-war period registered a new context for the relationship of British fascist organisations with Northern Ireland. The constitutional security resulting from Northern Ireland's contribution to the British war effort meant that for the next 20 years there was no – and apparently no need for a – pro-loyalist fascist presence in the region. As we have seen, the Duke of Bedford's British People's Party gave the subject only momentary consideration. For anti-partitionist fascism, however, as represented by Mosley and his Union Movement, the absence of a presence in Northern Ireland – the Ulster Fascist experience in the 1930s cautioned against another fascist agitation in the region and there would be no anti-partitionist fascist or neo-fascist presence in Northern Ireland thereafter – went together with a deep engagement with the question.

This was driven by its respectability as an issue in Anglo-Irish relations in a period when Mosley's fascist background rendered him a pariah figure. It provided a pathway to more respectable political activity and immigrant Irish support through contacts with, especially, the Westminster MP from Northern Ireland Cahir Healy (less successfully though with the wider anti-partition campaign); and by a focus on exploiting Northern Ireland's political system as an egregious example of the failures and corruption of representative democracy in general – an argument in direct continuity from the BUF's anti-partition case in the 1930s. What was distinctive now, however, was the context envisaged for the issue's resolution: Mosley's new political project, Europe-a-Nation (a replacement for the New Empire Union of Fascist States that he envisaged in the inter-war period). The full title of Mosley's anti-partition publication being *Ireland's Right to Unite When Entering European Union* (1948) – Irish unity was *conditional* on Ireland's membership of Europe-a-Nation. Only as his political ambitions were seen to fail in the late 1950s and early 1960s – especially the failure of his efforts to cultivate support from the immigrant Irish community – did his position on Northern Ireland begin to change. The result was a more credible acknowledgement of the nature of the problem, especially an acceptance of the British identity of the Unionist community and what that might imply about constitutional change. Moreover, having moved from a propagandist to a more empirical approach to the problem, Mosley, as the Troubles took off from the late 1960s, was able to make some soundly based warnings against ill-advised and morally corrupting Government security policies drawing on his own Irish experience of Ireland in the post-1916 period.

While the contrast between Mosley's approach to the Northern Ireland problem and that of the National Front from the late 1960s is stark, Enoch Powell represents something of a transitional figure. Having similarities with Mosley in terms of personality, Government experience, support for white Africa and concern about 'coloured' immigration, with its supposedly negative consequences for the British nation, the difference emerges in their perceptions of the 'crisis' Britain faced in this period.

On Ulster, Powell combined the attitude of the Edwardian Tory leader and later (post-war) Prime Minister, Andrew Bonar Law

– an ardent supporter of Carson and the UVF – with the mentality of Nesta Webster and the National Front, a mentality shaped by conspiracy theories of enemies within and without attempting to destroy the British State and nation, and with Northern Ireland as merely the latest site of conflict. In this respect, Powell evidenced a degree of political paranoia absent in Mosley. Also, unlike Mosley, Powell advocated a coercive and repressive 'solution' to the Troubles at one with the extreme-Right, targeting variously – together with treacherous British politicians and Irish republicanism/nationalism in Northern Ireland – the USA, the Irish community in Britain and the Irish Republic as threats to the United Kingdom. And yet, while Powell did much to encourage the National Front, he was also regarded as a threat to their own ambitions.

The NF's engagement with Northern Ireland was occasioned by the worst Irish constitutional crisis since the post-Great War period, suggesting a situation it could exploit. But the passage of time since a British fascist organisation was last present in the region, perhaps made it possible for it to overlook the central lesson of the inter-war period: namely, that all British fascist organisations attempting to organise in Northern Ireland faced the same problems – issues of limited relevance in the region and intensely held political identities expressed in organisations that left little room, ideologically or spatially, for external parties to occupy, though something that was true for British Tories operating in Northern Ireland as recent decades have shown and not just the extreme Right. For the Front's leader for most of the 1970s, John Tyndall, his engagement with the conflict and hope for success in the region was informed by a very personal dimension – a grandfather whose membership of the Royal Irish Constabulary involved conflict with militant republicanism – something which facilitated the positing of the Ulster Unionist community as exhibiting the best aspects of British character and an example for the people of Britain to follow. Even so, Tyndall was incapable of extending the operational space for the NF in Northern Ireland. Our understanding of NF difficulties in Northern Ireland is enlarged by an examination of the situations of, and relationships between, loyalist paramilitaries and the wider Unionist community and the British extreme Right and wider British society.

Insofar as loyalists were prepared to condone and perpetrate violence outside the *official* sanction of the law to secure the integrity of the British State, they can, arguably, be said to exhibit in this respect a similar 'nationalist' mentality to that of the extreme Right. And just as the latter justified its existence and activities because British Governments were failing to address the problem posed to the British nation by threats such as 'coloured' immigration, loyalist paramilitaries justified theirs because a similar threat posed by nationalists and republicans in Northern Ireland was not being addressed by treacherous British administrations. No less a similarity of motive can be identified in concern about a 'takeover' of material advantage – for the former in the supposed privileges in employment and housing 'coloured' immigrants received over whites,[1] for the latter in the supposed advantages Catholics received in terms of State benefits over loyalists.[2] As for recruitment, just as the extreme-Right recruited 'best among the very young, the least educated, and the working class',[3] so too was this the case with loyalist paramilitary organisations,[4] while a similarity exists also in the political orientations of people attracted to loyalist organisations and the extreme-Right. A founding member of the reconstituted UVF in the late 1960s could describe its membership as 'a broad alliance ... communists, fascists, liberals, Tories, democratic socialists. All kinds of people',[5] which was also very much the case for British fascist organisations since the 1920s. Nor does loyalist membership of the British army and involvement in the war against Nazi Germany register a radical difference from neo-fascist experience: they could also point to a history of involvement in the war against Nazi Germany. Certainly,

---

[1] Stan Taylor, 'The National Front: anatomy of a political movement', in Robert Miles and Annie Phizacklea (eds), *Racism and Political Action in Britain* (London: Routledge & Kegan Paul, 1979), p. 133.

[2] Susan McKay, *Northern Protestants: An Unsettled People* (Belfast: Blackstaff Press, 2000), p. 42.

[3] Taylor, 'The National Front: anatomy of a political movement', p. 137.

[4] Sarah Nelson, *Ulster's Uncertain Defenders: Protestant Political, Paramilitary and Community Groups and the Northern Ireland Conflict* (Belfast: Appletree Press, 1984), ch. 11.

[5] Jim Cusack and Henry McDonald, *The UVF: The Endgame* (revised edn, Dublin: Poolbeg Press, 2008), pp. 213–14.

pro-fascist sympathies and a concern for strong national defences often went together, as the examples of Admiral Sir Barry Domvile and Major-General J. F. C. Fuller indicate – the latter a leading member of Mosley's organisation but also an expert on tank strategy, this accounting for his freedom at a time when Mosley and other leading members of his organisation were suffering internment.[6] Moreover, both fascists and loyalist paramilitaries often defined their enemies collectively rather than individually: ethnicity, colour and religion being the markers that defined legitimate victims for attack. And just as the degree to which the NF attracted mainstream support was due to the perceived salience of the 'coloured' threat – at its height in the early to mid-1970s, tapering off towards the end of the decade as Margaret Thatcher took up the immigration issue – so too, for loyalist paramilitaries, wider Unionist community engagement with their activities peaked during the loyalist strike against the Sunningdale Agreement in 1974 with its power-sharing executive and threatening Council of Ireland, tailing off thereafter, and as was the case also in the wake of the AIA as the political cost of their alliance with paramilitaries became apparent. Yet again, we might note how attempts to create a more politically congenial image for the UVF through the organisation's paper, *Combat* and the Volunteer Peoples Party, were undone in the mid-1970s by more extreme elements following dismal results in the October 1974 general election, were 'mirrored' in how the NF's attempt to develop a more voter-friendly public image in the 1970s was undone by similar elements within the organisation as its public support dissipated in the last year of the decade.

In sum, the similarity of characteristics and experience between Ulster loyalism and the British extreme-Right suggest that, even if the latter was better attuned ideologically and politically to Northern Ireland, the space and conditions for political success in the region simply did not exist. Nor did the Front's connection with Ulster do anything for its popular support in Britain: the sectarian nature of the Unionist regime; the links between loyalism and the

[6] See Maj.-General J. F. C. Fuller, 'These weapons will decide!', *Sunday Pictorial*, 6 September 1942; 'Fuller says – "The Rhine has proved a ditch"', *Sunday Pictorial*, 11 March 1945.

extreme-Right in the acquiring of arms; and the aggressive nature of loyalist and pro-loyalist neo-fascist demonstrations in Britain meant that the British press found it easy to establish a negative synergy – 'Orange-NF' – between the two. While their similarities naturally and obviously attract the label 'right wing' some commentators have contested the application of that label to loyalist paramilitaries, arguing that such an erroneous label can be accounted for in terms of how left-wing propaganda has reported the Ulster conflict.

Thus Steve Bruce claims that an unintended consequence of 'the IRA's success in portraying itself as an anti-imperialist liberation movement – that is left-wing – is the perception of the UDA and UVF as "right wing", and the curious suitors such a depiction has attracted'.[7] Jim Cusack and Henry McDonald argue, 'If the IRA was anti-imperialist then loyalists must be right-wing and reactionary.'[8] The view that loyalists were simply the victims in a zero-sum game of left-right nomenclature, however, is unconvincing. If this were the case, one would not expect to find a clear left-right division in the wider causes republicans and loyalists identified with. But, as we have seen, there is a significant and definable affiliation of Ulster loyalism/Unionism with cognate groups in former imperial territories such as apartheid South Africa and especially white Rhodesia. Paisley's expanding movement in the late 1960s enthusi-astically supported Ian Smith's declaration of UDI, while admiration for Ian Smith and his white regime came from both the Vanguard leader, William Craig, and James Molyneaux, leader of the Official Unionist Party. To this we can contrast republican alignment with liberation movements in Palestine, south America and South Africa, though whether the Provisional IRA had the same justification for armed revolt can certainly be questioned. Where the major loyalist formations differed radically from the extreme Right was in recognising the significance of the Provisional IRA ceasefire of August 1994 and in responding accordingly, thereby making a significant contribution to the peace process and the making of the Belfast/Good Friday Agreement; and by doing so helping to reduce

[7] Steve Bruce, *The Red Hand: Protestant Paramilitaries in Northern Ireland* (Oxford: Oxford University Press, 1992), pp. 150–51.
[8] Cusack and McDonald, *The UVF: The Endgame*, pp. 214–16.

the already much diminished British extreme-Right prospects in Northern Ireland.

Never bright and sustained largely by ideological blinkers, the effective closure of the conflict that the Agreement registered was something that could not be ignored, though the improvement of the BNP's electoral prospects in Britain which began at the same time as the Agreement was taking effect made the 'loss' easier to take. Gradually, 'Ulster' as an issue disappeared from the BNP's literature, while a more extreme organisation such as the White Nationalist Party lasted less than two years, even as the race issue on which it traded worsened massively in the region. And yet it might be unwise to conclude that 'Ulster' is a dead issue for the British extreme Right, so long as the Irish border is capable of creating complications in Anglo-Irish relations, as in regard to Brexit at present;[9] as loyalist groups such as 'Kick the Pope' bands associated with the miniscule British Ulster Alliance provide a congenial environment – evidenced by neo-Nazi emblems appearing alongside loyalist insignia;[10] and so long as the Belfast/Good Friday Agreement, which allows for polls on the abolition or maintenance of the border, leaves the finalisation of Northern Ireland's constitutional status in question.

[9] 'Dublin stance on post-Brexit border could provoke loyalist paramilitaries, says [David] Trimble', *Guardian*, 7 April 2018.
[10] See "Right-wing neo Nazi grouping joins loyalists for march in Northern Ireland", 5 September 2006 http://oreaddaily.blogspot.co.uk/2006/09/right-wing-neo-nazi-grouping-joins.html). Accessed 1 March 2017; 'Nazi and Confederate flags have appeared on lamposts in County Antrim', *Belfast Telegraph*, 7 August 2015.

Bibliography

Manuscript Sources

Irish National Archives, Dublin
Department of Defence papers
Department of External Affairs papers
Department of Justice papers

King's College London (Liddell Hart Military Archives)
Arthur Bryant papers

National Archives, Kew
Cabinet papers: Civil Disturbances involving the National Front
Home Office papers
Metropolitan Police papers
Race Relations Board: Minutes and papers
Security Service Files: 'The Link'
Security Service Files: Union Movement
Security Service: Fascist Activity in the United Kingdom
Security Service: Revolutionary Organisations and Sentiment

National Maritime Museum, Greenwich
Admiral Sir Barry Domvile Diaries

Public Records Office of Northern Ireland
British Fascists documents
Cabinet papers
Cahir Healy papers
Church of Ireland Young Men's Literary and Debating Society Record Book
Department of Commerce papers
Edward Carson papers
Home Affairs papers
Lady Craigavon Diary
Londonderry papers
Royal Ulster Constabulary records

University of Birmingham, Cadbury Research Library
Jeffrey Hamm papers
Lady Mosley papers
Nicholas Mosley deposit
Oswald Mosley papers

University of Northampton Archive
Searchlight Archive

Online/Audio-Visual Sources

'Attempted murder: the state/reactionary plot against the National Front'
    [August 1986] (http://www.aryanunity.com/attempted_murder1.html).
    Accessed 19 February 2017.
BBC News, 'Northern Ireland elections', 8 May 2011.
—— 'Rabbi says anti-Semitism is "on the rise" in Northern Ireland', BBC
    News, 2 October 2016 (https://www.bbc.co.uk/news/uk-northern-
    ireland-37533746). Accessed 7 April 2017.
BNP election broadcasts, 1997, 1999, 2004; conference speeches, 1998
    (YouTube). Accessed 20 March 2017.
'BNP Members warned over white nationalist party', *UTV Newsroom*,
    21 August 2003.
'BNP membership list', *Guardian* Datablog, 19 October 2009 (https://www.
    theguardian.com/politics/interactive/2009/oct/19/bnp-membership-uk-
    map). Accessed 30 April 2017.
Caldecott, Stratford, 'The English spring of Catholicism' (https://theimagi-
    nativeconservative.org/2014/09/english-spring-catholicism.html).
    Accessed 13 April 2015.
Collins, Matthew, 'The National Front at 50; Part II' (https://www.
    hopenothate.org.uk/2017/12/15/national-front-50-part-ii-hope-not-
    hate-magazine/). Accessed 23 March 2018.
Friends of Oswald Mosley (https://www.oswaldmosley.com/).
Gable, Sonia, 'New leader takes BNP back to basics', *Searchlight*,
    9 September 2014 (http://www.searchlightmagazine.com/archive/
    new-leader-takes-bnp-back-to-basics). Accessed 5 March 2015.
Hope not Hate, 'Hate files: the British National Party' (https://web.
    archive.org/web/20150206073711/http://www.hopenothate.org.uk/
    hate-groups/bf/). Accessed 1 November 2018.
Kelly, James, Veteran newspaper reporter. Information on Job Stott supplied
    to the author on 20 March 2003.
Kerr, David, 'The history of the National Front in Ulster', *Civil Liberty*
    (https://www.civilliberty.org.uk/resources/nf_ulster.html). Accessed
    11 December 2016.

—— '*Mein Kampf* – publish or burn?' BBC Radio 4, broadcast 14 January 2015.

Metropolitan Police, Special Branch files (www.nationalarchives.gov.uk).

Military Service Records: Job Stott, Army Roll of Honour 1939–45 database (Naval and Military Press Ltd, 2010) (https://search.findmypast.co.uk/search-world-records-in-military-armed-forces-and-conflict).

Morrison, Eddy, 'Memoirs of a street soldier: a life in white nationalism' (http://www.aryanunity.com/memoirs15.html). Accessed 20 December 2013.

Mosley, Oswald, Interview, *The Frost Programme*, London Weekend Television, broadcast 15 November 1967.

Murphy, John, 'Why did my grandfather translate *Mein Kampf*?', *BBC News Magazine*, 14 January 2015 (https://www.bbc.co.uk/news/magazine-30697262). Accessed 15 January 2015.

'No more Blooms: Ireland's attitude to the Jewish refugee problem, 1933–46' (Dublin: Radio Telefís Éireann, 1997).

Panorama, 'Under the skin', BBC1 television, broadcast 25 November 2000.

'Race attacks "rise" in Northern Ireland', BBC News Online, 13 October 2003.

'Right-wing neo Nazi grouping joins loyalists for march in Northern Ireland', 5 September 2006 (https://oreaddaily.blogspot.com/2006/09/right-wing-neo-nazi-grouping-joins.html). Accessed 1 March 2017.

Spotlight, 'Race, crime and punishment', BBC Northern Ireland, 2014.

Stewart, Gerard, 'An assessment of racial violence in Northern Ireland', 12 December 2013 (https://www.irr.org.uk/news/an-assessment-of-racial-violence-in-northern-ireland/). Accessed 14 October 2016.

'The terror squad', *World in Action*, Granada Production for ITV, broadcast 19 April 1993.

Trilling, Daniel, 'Britain's last anti-Jewish riots', *New Statesman*, 23 May 2012 (https://www.newstatesman.com/2012/05/britains-last-anti-jewish-riots). Accessed 28 April 2014.

'Ulster's doomed!: That BNP List Again' (https://ulstersdoomed.blogspot.com/2009/10/that-bnp-list-again.html). Accessed 25 March 2014.

'Under the skin', *Panorama*, BBC1 television, broadcast 25 November 2000.

Waring, D. G., Wartime broadcasts (http://genome.ch.bbc.co.uk/search/0/20?adv=0&q=D.G.+Waring&Media=all&yf192). Accessed 15 November 2015.

'White Nationalist Party: WNP/C18 fascists driven out of Portrush', *indymedia Ireland* (https://www.indymedia.ie/article/64287?userlanguage=ga&save_prefs=true). Accessed 7 November 2012.

Works of Reference

Burke's Peerage, Baronetage & Knightage (London: Burke's Peerage, 1959).

Butler, D. E. and Richard Rose, *The British General Election of 1959* (Basingstoke: Macmillan, 1999).

Connolly, S. J. (ed.), *The Oxford Companion to Irish History* (2nd edn, Oxford: Oxford University Press, 2002).

Gardiner, J. and N. Wenburn (eds), *The History Today Companion to British History* (London: Collins & Brown, 1995).

Hand, Geoffrey J., *Report of the Irish Boundary Commission, 1925* (Shannon: Irish University Press, 1969).

Hansard Parliamentary Debates (House of Commons)

Hansard Parliamentary Debates (House of Lords)

Hawkins, J. M. (ed.), *The Oxford Reference Dictionary* (Oxford: Oxford University Press, 1988).

Keesing's Contemporary Archives

National Council for Civil Liberties, *Report of a Commission of Inquiry on Special Powers Acts, Northern Ireland* (London: NCCL, 1936).

Northern Ireland Parliamentary Debates

Theimer, Walter, *The Penguin Political Dictionary* (Harmondsworth: Penguin, 1939).

Walker, Brian Mercer, *Parliamentary Election Results in Ireland, 1918–92* (Dublin and Belfast: Royal Irish Academy, 1972).

Magazines and Newspapers

Action (1930s)
Action (post Second World War)
Anglo-German Review
Ballymena Guardian
Ballymoney Times
Belfast News-Letter (later *News Letter*)
Belfast Telegraph
Blackshirt
British Fascism
British Lion
British Nationalist
British Ulsterman
Candour
Catholic Herald
Catholic Times
Coleraine Times

Combat
Cookstown News
Cork Examiner
Daily Express
Daily Ireland
Daily Mail
Daily Mail Atlantic Edition
Daily Mirror
Daily Record
Daily Telegraph
Derry Journal
Derry Standard
Down Recorder
The European
The Fascist
Fascist Bulletin
Fascist Week
Fermanagh Herald
Fermanagh Times
The Flag
Fortnight
The Guardian
Guardian Weekend
Hibernia
Identity
Illustrated London News
Impartial Reporter
The Independent
Irish Democrat
Irish Examiner
Irish Independent
Irish News
Irish Press
Irish Times
Kerryman
Larne Times
Londonderry Sentinel
Loyalist News
Morning Post
Mourne Observer
The National European
National Front News

Nationalism Today
New Dawn
New Protestant Telegraph
New Society
New Statesman
New York Times
Newry Telegraph
Newsletter (Belfast)
Northern People
Northern Star
Northern Whig
Picture Post
Protestant Telegraph
Searchlight
Southern Star
Spearhead
Sunday Independent
Sunday News
Sunday Pictorial
Sunday Times
Sunday World
Time Out
The Times
True Brit
Ulster
Ulster Blackshirt Bulletin (Cabinet papers, PRONI, CAB 9B/216)
Ulster Patriot
Ulster Sentinel
Union
United Irishman
Vanguard
Voice of Freedom
Weekly Irish Times
Weekly Telegraph
White Sentinel

Theses

Moore, Gerald, 'Anti-Semitism in Ireland' (PhD thesis, Ulster Polytechnic, 1984).
Morgan, Craig, 'The British Union of Fascists in the Midlands, 1932–40' (PhD thesis, University of Wolverhampton, 2008).

Works Published in the Period to 1939

Allen, W. E. D., 'The fascist idea in Britain', *Quarterly Review*, vol. 261, no. 518 (October 1933).

Armour, W. S., *Mankind at the Watershed* (London: Duckworth, 1936).

Blakeney, R. B. D., 'British fascism', *Nineteenth Century*, vol. 97 (January 1925).

Brady, R. A., *The Spirit and Structure of German Fascism* (London: Gollancz, 1937).

British Fascists, *The 'Red Menace' to British Children* (2nd edn, London: British Fascists, [1926]).

Bryant, Arthur, *Humanity in Politics* (London: Hutchinson, [1938]).

Catlin, George, 'Fascist stirrings in Britain', *Current History*, vol. 39 (February 1934).

Chesterton, A. K., 'The problem of decadence', *Fascist Quarterly*, vol. 2, no. 1 (January 1936).

—— *Oswald Mosley: Portrait of a Leader* (London: Action Press, 1937).

Crawford, Virginia, 'The rise of fascism and what it stands for', *Studies*, vol. 12 (1923).

Crofts OP, A. M., *Catholic Social Action: Principles, Purpose and Action* (London: Catholic Book Club, 1936).

D'Arcy, C. F., *The Adventures of a Bishop* (London: Hodder & Stoughton, 1934).

de Broke, Lord Willoughby, 'The constitution and the individual', in *Rights of Citizenship: A Survey of Safeguards for the People* (London: Warne, 1912).

de Poncins, Vicomte Leon, 'Oliveira Salazar', *British Union Quarterly*, vol. 1, no. 1 (January/April 1937).

Domvile, Admiral Sir Barry, *By and Large* (London: Hutchinson, 1936).

—— *Look to Your Moat* (London: National Book Association, 1937).

Drennan, James (W. E. D. Allen), *B.U.F.: Oswald Mosley and British Fascism* (London: John Murray, 1934).

—— 'The Nazi movement in perspective', *Fascist Quarterly*, vol. 1, no. 1 (January 1935).

Edwards, H. W. J., 'The dissidents', *British Union Quarterly*, vol 2, no. 3 (July/September 1938).

Gibbons, John, 'Salazar of Portugal: portrait of a dictator', *Action*, 19 June 1937.

Gloag, John, *Word Warfare: Some Aspects German Propaganda and English Liberty* (London: Nicholson and Watson, 1939).

Hamilton, Lord Ernest, *Forty Years On* (London: Hodder & Stoughton, 1922).

Hammond, J. L., *Gladstone and the Irish Nation* (London: Longman, 1938).

Haslip, Joan, *Parnell* (London: Cobden-Sanderson, 1936).

Haxey, Simon, *Tory M.P.* (London: Gollancz, 1939).

Hitler, Adolf, *My Struggle* (abridged edn, London: Hurst & Blackett, 1936).

Ireland, Denis, *From the Irish Shore: Notes on My Life and Times* (London: Rich and Cowan, 1936).

Joyce, William, 'Collective security', *Fascist Quarterly*, vol. 1, no. 4 (1935).

—— 'Notes on the difference between observing and preserving the British constitution', *Fascist Quarterly*, vol. 2, no. 1 (January 1936).

—— 'Quis separabit' [obituary of Lord Carson], *Fascist Quarterly*, vol. 2, no. 1 (January 1936).

—— 'Analysis of Marxism', *Fascist Quarterly*, vol. 2, no. 4 (October 1936).

Kipling, Rudyard, 'The Army of a Dream', in *Traffics and Discoveries* (London: Macmillan, 1904).

Lane, Col. A. H., *The Alien Menace: A Statement of the Case* (2nd edn, London: Boswell, 1928).

Laski, Harold, Foreword to Robert A. Brady, *The Spirit and Structure of German Fascism* (London: Gollancz, 1937).

Laurie, A. P., *The Case for Germany: A Study of Modern Germany* (Berlin: Internationaler Verlag, 1939).

'Linum', 'Flax culture in the British Isles', *Fascist Quarterly*, vol. 2, no. 4 (October 1936).

Lorimer, E. O., *What Hitler Wants* (Harmondsworth: Penguin, 1939).

McEvoy, Francis, 'Anglo–Irish reconciliation through cultural renaissance' in *British Union Quarterly*, vol. 1, no. 2 (April/June 1937).

McNeill, Ronald, *Ulster's Stand for Union* (London: John Murray, 1922).

Maule Ramsay, Captain Archibald H., *The Nameless War* (1952; 2nd edn, London: Britons Publishing Society, 1954).

Morton, J. B., *The New Ireland* (London: Paladin Press, 1938).

Muggeridge, Malcolm, *The Thirties in Great Britain* (1940; London: Fontana, 1971).

Murphy, James, '*Mein Kampf*: An appreciation of the new unabridged edition', *Anglo-German Review* (March 1939).

—— Translator's introduction to Adolf Hitler, *Mein Kampf* (London: Hurst & Blackett, 1939).

National Council for Civil Liberties, *Report of a Commission of Inquiry on Special Powers Acts, Northern Ireland* (London: NCCL, 1936).

Ridley, F. A., *The Papacy and Fascism: The Crisis of the Twentieth Century* (London: Martin Secker and Warburg, 1937).

Rudlin, W. A., *The Growth of Fascism in Great Britain* (London: Allen & Unwin, 1935).

Somervell, D. C., *The Reign of King George V: An English Chronicle* (London: Faber & Faber, 1935).

Stott, Job, *The Case against Prohibition and the Local Veto* (Belfast: Ulster Anti-Prohibition Council, 1927).

Strachey, John, *The Menace of Fascism* (London: Gollancz, 1933).

Ulster Fascists, *Fascism in Ulster* (Belfast: Ulster Fascists, [1933]).

Waring, D. G., *Nothing Irredeemable* (London: John Long, 1936).

—— *The Oldest Road* (London: John Long, 1938).

—— *The Day's Madness* (London: John Long, 1939).

Webster, Nesta, *World Revolution: The Plot against Civilisation* (London: Constable, 1921).

—— *Secret Societies and Subversive Movements* (London: Boswell, 1924).

—— *Spacious Days: An Autobiography* (London: Hutchinson, 1949).

Wilkinson, Ellen Cicely and Edward Conze, *Why Fascism?* (London: Selwyn & Blount, 1934).

Willoughby de Broke, Lord, 'The constitution and the individual', in *Rights of Citizenship: A Survey of Safeguards for the People* (London: Frederick Warne, 1912).

Works Published in the Period after 1939

Adamson, Ian, *The Cruthin* (1974; 2nd edn, Belfast: Pretani Press, 1986).

Allen, W. E. D., *David Allen's: The History of a Family Firm, 1857–1957* (London: John Murray, 1957).

Anderson, Chris, *The Billy Boy: The Life and Death of the LVF Leader Billy Wright* (Edinburgh and London: Mainstream, 2002).

Anderson, John, 'A face in the crowd', *Comrade: Newsletter of the Friends of Oswald Mosley*, no. 60 (April 2006).

Arthur, Paul, *Government and Politics of Northern Ireland* (London: Longman, 1984).

—— *Special Relationships: Britain, Ireland and the Northern Ireland Problem* (Belfast: Blackstaff Press, 2000).

Bardon, Jonathan, *Belfast: An Illustrated History* (Belfast: Blackstaff Press, 1982).

Bean, John, *Many Shades of Black* (London: New Millennium, 1999).

Beckman, Morris, *The 43 Group: Battling with Mosley's Blackshirts* (2nd edn, Stroud: History Press, 2013).

Bell, J. B., *The Secret Army: A History of the IRA* (London: Sphere, 1972).

Benewick, Robert, *The Fascist Movement in Britain* (London: Allen Lane, 1972).

Bew, Paul, *Land and the National Question in Ireland, 1858–1882* (Dublin: Gill & Macmillan, 1979).

Bew, Paul and Gordon Gillespie, *Northern Ireland: A Chronology of the Troubles, 1968–1999* (1993; 2nd edn, Dublin: Gill & Macmillan, 1999).

Bew, Paul, Peter Gibbon and Henry Patterson, *Northern Ireland, 1921–1996: Political Forces and Social Classes* (London: Serif, 1995).

—— *Northern Ireland, 1921–2001: Political Power and Social Classes* (3rd edn, London: Serif, 2002).

Billig, Michael, *Psychology, Racism and Fascism* (London: Searchlight, 1979).

Blake, Robert, *The Unknown Prime Minister: The Life and Times of Andrew Bonar Law, 1858–1923* (London: Eyre & Spottiswoode, 1955).

Boulton, David, *The UVF 1966–73: An Anatomy of Loyalist Rebellion* (Dublin: Torc Books, 1973).

Bowd, Gavin, *Fascist Scotland: Caledonia and the Far Right* (Edinburgh: Birlinn, 2013).

Bowen, B., 'South-East Fingal', *Dublin Historical Record*, vol. 18, no. 3 (June 1963).

Bower, Tom, 'Immigration', in Lord Howard of Rising (ed.), *Enoch at 100* (London: Biteback, 2012).

Bowman, John, *De Valera and the Ulster Question, 1917–73* (Oxford: Oxford University Press, 1983).

Bowyer Bell, J., *The Secret Army: The IRA* (3rd edn, Dublin: Poolbeg Press, 1998).

Brewer, John, *Mosley's Men: The British Union of Fascists in the West Midlands* (Aldershot: Gower, 1984).

Bruce, Steve, *No Pope of Rome: Anti-Catholicism in Modern Scotland* (Edinburgh: Mainstream, 1985).

—— *The Red Hand: Protestant Paramilitaries in Northern Ireland* (Oxford: Oxford University Press, 1992).

Buckland, Patrick, *Irish Unionism 1: The Anglo-Irish and the New Ireland, 1885–1922* (Dublin: Gill & Macmillan, 1972).

—— *The Factory of Grievances: Devolved Government in Northern Ireland, 1921–39* (Dublin: Gill & Macmillan, 1979).

—— *A History of Northern Ireland* (Dublin: Gill & Macmillan, 1989).

Camrose, Viscount, *British Newspapers and Their Controllers* (London: Cassell, 1947).

Canning, Paul, *British Policy towards Ireland, 1921–1941* (Oxford: Oxford University Press, 1985).

Carr, E. H., *Conditions of Peace* (London: Macmillan, 1943).

Cesarani, David, 'The anti-Jewish career of Sir William Joynson-Hicks, Cabinet Minister', *Journal of Contemporary History*, vol. 24, no. 3 (July 1989).

—— 'Joynson-Hicks and the radical right in Britain after the First World War', in Tony Kushner and Kenneth Lunn (eds), *Traditions of Intolerance: Historical Perspectives on Fascism and Race Discourse in Britain* (Manchester: Manchester University Press, 1989).

—— *Disraeli: The Novel Politician* (New Haven, Conn. and London: Yale University Press, 2016).

Charnley, John, *Blackshirts and Roses: An Autobiography* (1990; 2nd edn, London: Black House Publishing, 2012).

Clayton, Pamela, *Enemies and Passing Friends: Settler Ideologies in Twentieth-Century Ulster* (London: Pluto Press, 1996).

Clough, Bryan, *State Secrets: The Kent–Wolkoff Affair* (Hove: Hideaway, 2005).

Clump SJ, Cyril, *A Catholic's Guild to Social and Political Action* (revised edn, Oxford: Catholic Social Guild, 1955; 2nd impression, 1957).

Cochrane, Feargal, *Unionist Politics and the Politics of Unionism since the Anglo-Irish Agreement* (Cork: Cork University Press, 1997).

Cockett, Robert, *Chamberlain, Appeasement and the Manipulation of the Press* (New York: St Martin's Press, 1989).

Cole, J. A., *Lord Haw Haw: The Full Story of William Joyce* (London: Faber & Faber, 1964).

Collings, Rex (ed.), *Reflections of a Statesman: Writings and Speeches of Enoch Powell* (London: Bellew Publishing, 1991).

Collins, Matthew, *Hate: My Life in the British Far Right* (London: Biteback Publishing, 2011).

Coogan, T. P., *The I.R.A.* (London: Pall Mall Press, 1970).

—— *The I.R.A.* (revised edn, London: HarperCollins, 2000).

Conway, Martin, *Catholic Politics in Europe, 1918–1945* (London: Routledge, 1997).

Copsey, Nigel, 'Contemporary fascism in the local arena: the British National Party and "Rights for Whites"', in Mike Cronin (ed.), *The Failure of British Fascism: The Far Right and the Fight for Political Recognition* (Basingstoke: Macmillan, 1996).

—— *Contemporary British Fascism: The British National Party and the Quest for Legitimacy* (2004; 2nd edn, Basingstoke: Palgrave Macmillan, 2008).

Copsey, Nigel and John E. Richardson (eds), *Cultures of Post-War British Fascism* (London: Routledge, 2015).

Cothorn, Paul, 'Enoch Powell, Ulster Unionism and the British nation', *Journal of British Studies*, vol. 51, no. 4 (2002).

—— 'W. E. D. Allen, Unionist politics and the New Party', *Contemporary British History*, vol. 23, no. 4 (2009).

—— 'Enoch Powell, Ulster Unionism and the British nation', *Journal of British Studies*, vol. 51, no. 4 (2012).

Crockett, Richard, *Twilight of the Truth: Chamberlain, Appeasement and the Manipulation of the Press* (London: Weidenfeld & Nicolson, 1989).

Cronin, Mike (ed.), *The Failure of British Fascism: The Far Right and the Fight for Political Recognition* (Basingstoke: Macmillan, 1996).

—— *The Blueshirts and Irish Politics* (Dublin: Four Courts Press, 1997).

Cross, Colin, *The Fascists in Britain* (London: Barrie and Rockliff, 1961).

Crowson, N. J. (ed.), *Fleet Street, Press Barons and Politics: The Journals of Collin Brooks* (Cambridge: Cambridge University Press for the Royal Historical Society, 1998).

Cullen, Stephen, 'Another nationalism: the British Union of Fascists in Glamorgan, 1932–40', *Welsh History Review*, vol. 17, no. 1 (June 1994).

——— 'The fasces and the saltire: the failure of the British Union of Fascists in Scotland, 1932–1940', *Scottish Historical Review*, vol. 87, no. 2 (October 2008).

Curran, Frank, *Ireland's Fascist City* (Londonderry: Derry Journal, 1946).

Cusack, Jim and Henry McDonald, *The UVF: The Endgame* (revised edn, Dublin: Poolbeg Press, 2008).

Dack, Janet, 'Cultural regeneration: Mosley and the Union Movement', in Nigel Copsey and John E. Richardson (eds), *Cultures of Post-War British Fascism* (London: Routledge, 2015).

De Boca, Angelo and Mario Giovana, *Fascism Today: A World Survey* (London: Heinemann, 1970).

Delaney, Enda, *The Irish in Post-War Britain* (Oxford: Oxford University Press, 2007).

Devlin, Bernadette, *The Price of My Soul* (London: Panther, 1969).

Devlin, Paddy, *Yes, We Have No Bananas: Outdoor Relief in Belfast* (Belfast: Blackstaff Press, 1979).

Dixon, Paul and Eamonn O'Kane, *Northern Ireland since 1969* (Harlow: Longman, 2011).

Domvile, Admiral Sir Barry, *From Admiral to Cabin Boy* (1947; Uckfield: Historical Review Press, 2008).

Dorril, Stephen, *Blackshirt: Sir Oswald Mosley and British Fascism* (London: Penguin, 2007).

Douglas, R. M., 'The swastika and the shamrock: British fascism and the Irish question, 1918–1940', *Albion*, vol. 29, no. 1 (1997).

——— *Architects of the Resurrection: Ailtirí na hAiséirghe and the Fascist 'New Order' in Ireland* (Manchester: Manchester University Press, 2009).

Duggan, Christopher, *Fascist Voices: An Intimate History of Mussolini's Italy* (London: Bodley Head, 2014).

Duggan, John P., *Neutral Ireland and the Third Reich* (Dublin: Lilliput Press, 1989).

Durham, Martin, 'The Conservative Party, the British extreme right and the problem of political space, 1967–83', in Mike Cronin (ed.), *The Failure of British Fascism: The Far Right and the Fight for Political Recognition* (Basingstoke: Macmillan, 1996).

Eatwell, Roger, *Fascism: A History* (London: Chatto & Windus, 1995).

——— 'The esoteric ideology of the National Front in the 1980s', in Mike Cronin (ed.), *The Failure of British Fascism: The Far Right and the Fight for Political Recognition* (Basingstoke: Macmillan, 1996).

Eisenberg, Dennis, *The Re-emergence of Fascism* (London: MacGibbon & Kee, 1967).

English, Richard, *Armed Struggle: The History of the IRA* (London: Pan, 2012).

Fanning, Ronan, *Eamon de Valera: A Will to Power* (London: Faber & Faber, 2016).

Farr, B. S., *The Development and Impact of Right-Wing Politics in Britain, 1903–1932* (New York: Garland, 1987).

Farrell, Michael, *Northern Ireland: The Orange State* (London: Pluto Press, 1976).

—— *Arming the Protestants: The Formation of the Ulster Special Constabulary and the Royal Ulster Constabulary, 1920–1927* (Dingle: Brandon Books, 1983).

Fielding, Nigel, *The National Front* (London: Routledge & Kegan Paul, 1981).

Fisk, Robert, *In Time of War: Ireland, Ulster and the Price of Neutrality, 1939–45* (London: Paladin, 1987).

Foot, Paul, *The Rise of Enoch Powell* (Harmondsworth: Penguin, 1969).

Ford, Robert and Matthew Goodwin, *Revolt on the Right: Explaining Support for the Radical Right in Britain* (London and New York: Routledge, 2014).

Friers, Rowel, *Drawn from Life: An Autobiography* (Belfast: Blackstaff Press, 1994).

Gable, Gerry, 'The far right in contemporary Britain', in Luciano Cheles, Ronnie Ferguson and Michalina Vaughan (eds), *Neo-Fascism in Europe* (London: Longman, 1991).

Gainer, Bernard, *The Alien Invasion: The Origins of the Aliens Act of 1905* (London: Heinemann, 1973).

Gillespie, Gordon, 'The secret life of D. G. Waring', *Causeway* (spring 1998).

Goodwin, Matthew, *New British Fascism: Rise of the British National Party* (London: Routledge, 2011).

Gottlieb, J. V., *Feminine Fascism: Women in Britain's Fascist Movement* (London: I.B. Tauris, 2003).

Graves, Robert and Alan Hodge, *The Long Weekend: A Social History of Great Britain 1918–1939* (London: Readers' Union, 1941).

Griffin, Roger, *The Nature of Fascism* (London: Pinter, 1991).

—— *Modernism and Fascism: The Sense of a New Beginning under Mussolini and Hitler* (Basingstoke: Palgrave Macmillan, 2007).

Griffiths, Richard, *Fellow Travellers of the Right: British Enthusiasts for Nazi Germany* (Oxford: Oxford University Press, 1983).

—— *Patriotism Perverted: Captain Ramsay, The Right Club and British Anti-Semitism, 1939–40* (London: Constable, 1998).

—— 'The reception of Bryant's *Unfinished Victory*: insights into British public opinion in early 1940', *Patterns of Prejudice*, vol. 38, no. 1 (2004).

Grigg, John, *The Young Lloyd George* (London: Methuen, 1973).

Grundy, Trevor, *Memoir of a Fascist Childhood: A Boy in Mosley's Britain* (London: Heinemann, 1998).

Hamilton, Alastair, *The Appeal of Fascism* (London: Anthony Blond, 1971).

Hamm, Jeffrey, *Action Replay* (London: Howard Baker, 1983).

Hanley, Brian, *The IRA, 1926–1936* (Dublin: Four Courts Press, 2002).

Hann, Dave and Steve Tilzey, *No Retreat: The Secret War between Britain's Anti-Fascists and the Far Right* (Lytham: Milo Books, 2003).

Harbinson, J. F., *The Ulster Unionist Party, 1882–1973: Its Development and Organisation* (Belfast: Blackstaff Press, 1973).

Heffer, Simon, *Like the Roman: The Life of Enoch Powell* (London: Weidenfeld & Nicolson, 1998).

Hibbert, Christopher, *Mussolini: A Biography* (London: Reprint Society, 1962).

Hill, Ray with Andrew Bell, *The Other Face of Terror: Inside Europe's Neo-Nazi Network* (London: Grafton Books, 1988).

Hillman, Nicholas, "'Tell me chum, in case I got it wrong. What was it we were fighting for during the war?'": the re-emergence of British fascism, 1945–58', *Contemporary British History*, vol. 15, no. 4 (2001).

Holmes, Colin, *Anti-Semitism in British Society, 1876–1939* (London: Edward Arnold, 1979).

—— *Searching for Lord Haw-Haw: The Political Lives of William Joyce* (London and New York: Routledge, 2016).

Hope, John, 'Fascism and the state in Britain: the case of the British Fascist, 1923–31', *Australian Journal of Politics and History*, vol. 39, no. 3 (1993).

Hyde, H. M., *Carson* (London: Heinemann, 1953).

Jackson, Alvin, *Sir Edward Carson* (Dundalk: Dundalgen Press, 1993).

Jackson, D. M., *Popular Opposition to Irish Home Rule in Edwardian Britain* (Liverpool: Liverpool University Press, 2009).

Jayson, Gerald, 'The farm', *AJR Journal: Association of Jewish Refugees*, vol. 10, no. 2 (February 2010).

Jeffery, Keith, 'Curragh incident', in S. J. Connolly (ed.), *The Oxford Companion to Irish History* (2nd edn, Oxford: Oxford University Press, 2002).

Kelly, James, *Bonfires on the Hillside: An Eyewitness Account of Political Upheaval in Northern Ireland* (Belfast: Fountain Press, 1995).

Kennedy, David, 'Catholics in Northern Ireland 1926–39', in Francis MacManus (ed.), *The Years of the Great Test, 1926–39* (Cork: Mercier Press, 1967).

Kennedy, Dennis, *The Widening Gulf: Northern Attitudes to the Independent Irish State 1919–49* (Belfast: Blackstaff Press, 1988).

Kennedy, Liam, *Two Ulsters: A Case for Repartition* (Belfast: Queen's University, 1986).

Keogh, Dermot, *Jews in Twentieth-Century Ireland: Refugees, Anti-Semitism and the Holocaust* (Cork: Cork University Press, 1998).

Kershaw, Ian, *Making Friends with Hitler: Lord Londonderry, the Nazis and the Road to War* (London: Penguin, 2005).

King, Cecil, *Cecil King Diary, 1965–1970* (London: Jonathan Cape, 1972).

—— *Cecil King Diary, 1970–1974* (London: Jonathan Cape, 1975).

Kitchen, Martin, *Fascism* (Basingstoke: Macmillan, 1982).

Kyle, Keith, 'North Kensington', in D. E. Butler and Richard Rose, *The British General Election of 1959* (Basingstoke: Macmillan, 1992).

Laffan, Michael, *The Partition of Ireland, 1911–1925* (Dundalk: Dundalgen Press, 1983).

Laqueur, Walter (ed.), *Fascism: A Reader's Guide* (Harmondsworth: Penguin, 1979).

Laski, Harold, *Where Do We Go from Here? An Essay in Interpretation* (Harmondsworth: Penguin, 1940).

Lebzelter, Gizela C., *Political Anti-Semitism in England, 1919–1939* (London: Macmillan, 1978).

—— 'Anti-Semitism: a focal point for the British radical right', in Paul Kennedy and Anthony Nicholls (eds), *Nationalist and Racialist Movements in Britain and Germany before 1914* (Basingstoke: Macmillan, 1987).

Lee, Brian, 'Enoch Powell's language', *New Society*, 23 January 1969.

Leese, Arnold, *Out of Step: Events in the Two Lives of an Anti-Jewish Camel Doctor* (Guildford: Arnold Leese, [1951]).

Lenaghan, Joe, 'The long road to good race relations', *Fortnight*, April 2004.

Lewis, D. S., *Illusions of Grandeur: Mosley, Fascism and British Society, 1931–81* (Manchester: Manchester University Press).

Linehan, Thomas, *British Fascism, 1918–39: Parties, Ideologies and Culture* (Manchester: Manchester University Press, 2000).

Linz, Juan, 'Some notes towards a comparative study of fascism in sociological perspective', in Walter Laqueur (ed.), *Fascism: A Reader's Guide* (Harmondsworth: Penguin, 1979).

Longford, Frank Pakenham, Earl and Thomas P. O'Neill, *Eamon de Valera* (London: Arrow Books, 1974).

Loughlin, James, *Gladstone, Home Rule and the Ulster Question, 1882–93* (Dublin: Gill & Macmillan, 1986).

—— 'Northern Ireland and British fascism in the inter-war years', *Irish Historical Studies*, vol. 29, no. 116 (November 1995).

—— *Ulster Unionism and British National Identity since 1885* (London: Pinter, 1995).

—— 'Consolidating "Ulster": regime propaganda and architecture in the inter-war period', *National Identities*, vol. 1, no. 2 (1999).

—— 'Mobilising the sacred dead: Ulster Unionism, the Great War and the politics of remembrance', in Adrian Gregory and Senia Paseta (eds), *Ireland and the Great War: 'A War to Unite Us All?'* (Manchester: Manchester University Press, 2002).

—— *The Ulster Question Since 1945* (1998; 2nd edn, Basingstoke: Palgrave Macmillan, 2004).

—— 'Rotha Lintorn-Orman, Ulster and the British Fascists movement', *Immigrants & Minorities: Historical Studies in Ethnicity, Migration and Diaspora*, vol. 32, no. 1 (March 2014).

—— 'Hailing Hitler with the Red Hand: The Link in Northern Ireland, 1937–40', *Patterns of Prejudice*, vol. 50, no. 3 (July 2016), 276–301.

Lowles, Nick, *White Riot: The Violent Story of Combat 18* (2001; revised edn, Croydon: Milo Books, 2014).

Lunn, Kenneth, 'The impact and ideology of the British fascists in the 1920s', in Tony Kushner and Kenneth Lunn (eds), *Traditions of Intolerance: Historical Perspectives on Fascism and Race Discourse in Britain* (Manchester: Manchester University Press, 1989).

Lynn, Brendan, *Holding the Ground: The Nationalist Party in Northern Ireland, 1945–72* (Aldershot: Ashgate, 1997).

McGarry, Fearghal, *General Eoin O'Duffy: A Self-Made Hero* (Oxford: Oxford University Press, 2005).

McGrath, Patrick, *Union Movement Policy Document No. 2: Ireland's Right to Unite* (Harrow: A. Brown, n.d. [early to mid-1960s]).

McKay, Susan, *Northern Protestants: An Unsettled People* (Belfast: Blackstaff Press, 2000).

Macklin, Graham, *Very Deeply Dyed in Black: Sir Oswald Mosley and the Resurrection of British Fascism after 1945* (London: I.B. Tauris, 2007).

McMahon, Deidre, *Republicans and Imperialists: Anglo-Irish Relations in the 1930s* (New Haven, Conn. and London: Yale University Press, 1984).

—— 'Economic war', in S. J. Connolly (ed.), *The Oxford Companion to Irish History* (2nd edn, Oxford: Oxford University Press, 2002).

MacManus, Francis (ed.), *The Years of the Great Test, 1926–39* (Cork: Mercier Press, 1967).

McVeigh, Robbie, 'Racism in the six counties', in J. V. Ulin, Heather Edwards and Sean O'Brien (eds), *Race and Immigration in the New Ireland* (Notre Dame, Ind.: University of Notre Dame Press, 2013).

Mandell, Richard, *The Nazi Olympics* (London: Souvenir, 1971).

Manning, Maurice, *The Blueshirts* (Dublin: Gill & Macmillan, 1970).

Mansergh, Nicholas, 'Irish foreign policy, 1945–51', in K. B. Nowlan and T. D. Williams (eds), *Ireland in the War Years and after 1939–51* (Dublin: Gill & Macmillan, 1969).

—— *The Unresolved Question: The Anglo-Irish Settlement and its Undoing, 1912–1972* (New Haven, Conn. and London: Yale University Press, 1991).

Matas, David, 'The extreme right in the United Kingdom and France', in Aurel Braun and Steven Scheinberg (eds), *The Extreme Right: Freedom and Security at Risk* (Boulder, Colo.: Westview Press, 1997).

Maude, Angus and Enoch Powell, *Biography of a Nation: A Short History of Britain* (London: Phoenix House, 1955).

Maume, Patrick, 'Herbert Moore Pim, 1883–1950', in James Quinn and Patrick Maume (eds), *Ulster Political Lives, 1886–1921* (Dublin: Royal Irish Academy, 2016).

Miles, Robert and Annie Phizacklea (eds), *Racism and Political Action in Britain* (London: Routledge & Kegan Paul, 1979).

Moloney, Ed., *Paisley: From Demagogue to Democrat?* (Dublin: Poolbeg Press, 2008).

Morris, Benny, *The Roots of Appeasement: The British Weekly Press and Nazi Germany during the 1930s* (London: Routledge, 1991).

Mosley, Diana, *A Life of Contrasts* (London: Hamish Hamilton, 1977).

Mosley, Nicholas, *Beyond the Pale: Sir Oswald Mosley, 1933–1980* (London: Secker & Warburg, 1983).

Mosley, Oswald, *My Answer* (2nd edn, Ramsbury: Mosley Publications, 1946).

—— *The Alternative* (Ramsbury: Mosley Publications, 1947).

—— *Policy and Debate* (Washbourne: Euphorion Books, 1954).

—— *Ireland's Right to Unite When Entering European Union* (1948; 2nd edn, London: Sanctuary Press, 1957).

—— *Mosley: The Facts* (London: Euphorion Distribution (England), 1957).

—— *Mosley – Right or Wrong?* (London: Lion Books, 1961).

—— *My Life* (London: Nelson, 1968).

—— *Last Words: Broadsheets, 1970–1980* (London: Black House Publishing, 2012).

Mowat, C. L., *Britain between the Wars, 1918–1940* (London: Methuen, 1966).

Muggeridge, Malcolm, *The Thirties* (1940; London: Fontana, 1971).

Mulcahy, Risteard, *Richard Mulcahy (1886–1971): A Family Memoir* (Dublin: Aurelian Press, 1999).

Mullally, Frederic, *Fascism inside England* (London: Claud Morris, 1946).

Munck, Ronnie and Bill Rolston, *Belfast in the 1930s: An Oral History* (Belfast: Blackstaff Press, 1987).

Nelson, Sarah, *Ulster's Uncertain Defenders: Protestant Political, Paramilitary and Community Groups and the Northern Ireland Conflict* (Belfast: Appletree Press, 1984).

Norton, Christopher, 'The internment of Cahir Healy M.P., Brixton Prison, July 1941–December 1942', *20th Century British History*, vol. 18, no. 2 (2007).

—— *The Politics of Constitutional Nationalism in Northern Ireland, 1932–70* (Manchester: Manchester University Press, 2014).

Nugent, Neill, 'The ideas of the British Union of Fascists', in Neill Nugent and Roger King (eds), *The British Right: Conservative and Right Wing Politics in Britain* (Farnborough: Saxon House, 1977).

O'Driscoll, Mervyn, *Ireland, Germany and the Nazi: Politics and Diplomacy, 1919–39* (Dublin, Four Courts Press, 2004).

O'Duffy, Brendan, 'Violence in Northern Ireland 1969–1994: sectarian or ethno-national', *Ethnic and Racial Studies*, vol. 18, no. 4 (October 1995).

O'Leary, Cornelius, 'Northern Ireland, 1945–72', in J. J. Lee (ed.), *Ireland, 1945–72* (Dublin: Gill & Macmillan, 1979).

O'Sullivan, Donal, *The Irish Free State and its Senate* (London: Faber & Faber, 1940).

Parkinson, A. F., *Ulster Loyalism and the British Media* (Dublin: Four Courts Press, 1998).

Payne, Stanley, *Fascism: Comparison and Definition* (Madison: University of Wisconsin Press, 1980).

Pearce, Joseph, *Race with the Devil: My Journey from Race Hatred to Rational Love* (Charlotte, NC: Saint Benedict Press, 2013).

Pehrson, Samuel, M. A. Gheorghiu and Tomas Ireland, 'Cultural threat and anti-immigrant prejudice: the case of Protestants in Northern Ireland', *Journal of Community and Applied Social Psychology*, vol. 22, no. 2 (March/April 2012).

Peoples Democracy, *Fascism in the Six Counties* (Belfast: Peoples Democracy, [1975?]).

Phoenix, Eamon, *Northern Nationalism, Partition and the Catholic Minority in Northern Ireland, 1890–1940* (Belfast: Ulster Historical Foundation, 1994).

—— 'The history of a newspaper: the *Irish News*, 1855–1995', in Eamon Phoenix (ed.), *A Century of Irish Life: The Irish News and 100 Years of Ulster History, 1890s–1990s* (Belfast: Ulster Historical Foundation, 1995).

—— 'Cahir Healy (1877–1970) Northern Nationalist leader', in A. F. Parkinson and Eamon Phoenix (eds), *Conflicts in the North of Ireland, 1900–2000* (Dublin: Four Courts Press, 2010).

Pitchford, Mark, *The Conservative Party and the Extreme Right, 1945–75* (Manchester: Manchester University Press, 2011).

Poole, Anne, 'Oswald Mosley and the Union Movement: success or failure', in Mike Cronin (ed.), *The Failure of British Fascism: The Far Right and the Fight for Political Recognition* (Basingstoke: Macmillan, 1996).

Powell, Enoch, 'Population figures in the United Kingdom', *Mankind Quarterly* (October 1970).

—— *Wrestling with the Angel* (London: Sheldon Press, 1977).

—— *Collected Poems* (London: Bellew Publishing, 1990).

Pugh, Martin, *'Hurrah for the Blackshirts!': Fascists and Fascism in Britain between the Wars* (London: Jonathan Cape, 2005).

Purcell, H. D., *Cyprus* (New York: Praeger, 1969).

Purdy, Anne, *Molyneaux: The Long View* (Antrim: Greystone Books, 1989).

Rawnsley, Stuart, 'The membership of the British Union of Fascists', in Kenneth Lunn and Richard Thurlow (eds), *British Fascism* (London: Croom Helm, 1980).

Roberts, Andrew, 'A Nazi sympathiser and supreme toady', *Spectator*, 23 July 1994.

Sandbrook, Dominic, *White Heat: A History of Britain in the Swinging Sixties* (London: Abacus, 2006).

Saikia, Robin (ed.), *The Red Book: The Membership List of The Right Club, 1939* (London: Foxley Books, 2010).

Sanfey, Michael, 'On Salazar and Salazarism', *Studies*, vol. 95, no. 368 (2003).

Saunders, F. S., *The Woman Who Shot Mussolini* (London: Faber & Faber, 2010).

Scharf, Andrew, *The British Press and Jews under Nazi Rule* (Oxford: Oxford University Press, 1964).

Schoen, Douglas, *Enoch Powell and the Powellites* (London: Macmillan, 1977).

Schofield, Camilla, *Enoch Powell and the Making of Postcolonial Britain* (Cambridge: Cambridge University Press, 2013).

Searchlight, At War with Society: The Exclusive Story of a Searchlight Mole in Britain's Far Right (London: Searchlight, 1993).

Semmel, Bernard, *Imperialism and Social Reform: English Social-Imperial Thought, 1985–1914* (London: George Allen & Unwin, 1960).

Shaffer, Ryan, 'British, European and White: cultural constructions of identity in post-war British fascist music', in Nigel Copsey and John E. Richardson (eds), *Cultures of Post-War British Fascism* (London: Routledge, 2015).

Sharf, Andrew, *The British Press and Jews under Nazi Rule* (Oxford: Oxford University Press, 1964).

Shearman, Hugh, *Not An Inch: A Study of Northern Ireland and Lord Craigavon* (London: Faber & Faber, 1942).

Sheehy, Michael, *Divided We Stand: A Study of Partition* (London: Faber & Faber, 1955).

Shepherd, Robert, *Enoch Powell: A Biography* (London: Pimlico, 1997).

Sherman, A. J., *Island Refuge: Britain and Jewish Refugees From the Third Reich, 1933–1939* (London: Elek, 1973).

Skidelsky, Robert, 'Great Britain', in S. J. Woolf (ed.), *European Fascism* (New York: Random House, 1968).

—— *Oswald Mosley* (London: Macmillan, 1981).

Smith, D. M., *Mussolini* (London: Paladin, 1993).

Smyth, Clifford, *Ulster Assailed* ([Belfast], n.p., [1970]).

Staunton, Enda, *The Nationalists of Northern Ireland, 1918–1973* (Blackrock: Columba Press, 2001).

Stephan, Enno, *Spies in Ireland* (London: Four Square Press, 1965).

Sternhell, Zeev, 'Fascist ideology', in Walter Laqueur (ed.), *Fascism: A Reader's Guide* (Harmondsworth: Penguin, 1979).

Stevenson, John, 'Conservatism and the failure of fascism in inter-war Britain', in Martin Blinkhorn (ed.), *Fascists and Conservatives: The Radical Right and the Establishment in Twentieth Century Europe* (London: Routledge, 1990).

Stone, Dan, 'The "Mein Kamp Ramp": Emily Overend Lorimer and Hitler translations in Britain', *German History*, vol. 26, no. 4 (2008).

Svirsky, Leon (ed.), *Your Newspaper: Blueprint for a Better Press* (New York: Macmillan, 1947).

Taylor, Peter, *Loyalists* (London: Bloomsbury, 2000).

Taylor, Stan, 'The National Front: anatomy of a political movement', in Robert Miles and Annie Phizacklea (eds), *Racism and Political Action in Britain* (London: Routledge & Kegan Paul, 1979).

—— *The National Front in English Politics* (Basingstoke: Macmillan, 1982).

Thayer, George, *The British Political Fringe: A Profile* (London: Anthony Blond, 1965).

Thorpe, Andrew (ed.), *The Failure of British Fascism in Inter-War Britain* (Exeter: University of Exeter Press, 1989).

Thurlow, Richard, *Fascism in Britain: A History, 1918–1985* (Oxford: Blackwell, 1987).

—— 'The failure of the fascists', in Andrew Thorpe (ed.) *The Failure of British Fascism in Inter-War Britain* (Exeter: University of Exeter Press, 1989).

—— 'The guardian of the "sacred flame": the failed political resurrection of Oswald Mosley', *Journal of Contemporary History*, vol. 33, no. 2 (1998).

Tillies, Daniel, *British Fascist Anti-Semitism and Jewish Responses, 1932–40* (London: Bloomsbury, 2014).

Trew, Johanne Devlin, *Leaving the North: Migration and Memory, Northern Ireland, 1921–2011* (Liverpool: Liverpool University Press, 2013).

Trilling, Daniel, *Bloody Nasty People: The Rise of Britain's Far Right* (London: Verso, 2012).

Tyndall, John, *The Eleventh Hour: A Call for British Rebirth* (1988; 3rd edn, Welling: Albion Press, 1998).

Ulster Vanguard, Government without Right ... (Newtownards: Ulster Vanguard, [1972]).

Villis, Tom, *British Catholics and Fascism: Religious Identity and Political Extremism between the Wars* (Basingstoke: Palgrave Macmillan, 2013).

Vincent, John (ed.), *The Crawford Papers: The Journals of David Lyndsey, Twenty-Seventh Earl of Crawford and Tenth Earl of Balcarres, 1871–1940 during the Years 1892 to 1940* (Manchester: Manchester University Press, 1984).

Waddington, G. T., '"An idyllic and unruffled atmosphere of Anglo-German understanding": aspects of the operation of the *Dienststelle Ribbentrop* in Great Britain 1934–38', *History*, vol. 82, no. 265 (January 1997).

Walker, Graham, *The Politics of Frustration: Harry Midgley and the Failure of Labour in Northern Ireland* (Manchester: Manchester University Press, 1985).

—— '"Protestantism without Party": the Ulster Protestant League in the 1930s', *Historical Journal*, vol. 28, no. 4 (1985).

—— *A History of the Ulster Unionist Party: Protest, Pragmatism and Pessimism* (Manchester: Manchester University Press, 2004).

Walker, Martin, *The National Front* (London: Fontana, 1977).

Warm, David, 'The Jews of Northern Ireland', in Paul Hainsworth (ed.), *Divided Society: Ethnic Minorities and Racism in Northern Ireland* (London: Pluto Press, 1998).

Webber, G. C., 'Patterns of membership and support for the British Union of Fascists', *Journal of Contemporary History*, vol. 19, no. 4 (1984).

—— 'Tolerance and discretion: conservatism and British fascism, 1918–1926', in Tony Kushner and Tony Lunn (eds), *Traditions of Intolerance: Historical Perspectives on Fascism and Race Discourse in Britain* (Manchester: Manchester University Press, 1989).

Webster, Nesta, *Spacious Days: An Autobiography* (London: Hutchinson, 1949).

West, Nigel, *MI5: British Security Service Operations, 1909–45* (London: Triad Granada, 1983).

Williams, T. D., 'DeValera in Power', in Francis MacManus (ed.), *The Years of the Great Test, 1926–39* (Cork: Mercier Press, 1967).

Winter, Sir Ormonde, *Winter's Tale: An Autobiography* (London: Richards Press, 1955).

Wiskemann, Elizabeth, *Fascism in Italy: Its Development and Influence* (London: Macmillan, 1969).

Wood, I. S., *Crimes of Loyalty: A History of the UDA* (Edinburgh: Edinburgh University Press, 2006).

Wood, Nancy, *Vectors of Memory: Legacies of Trauma in Postwar Europe* (Oxford: Berg, 1998).

Woodbridge, Steven, 'Fraudulent fascism: the attitude of the early British Fascists towards Mosley and the New Party', *Contemporary British History*, vol. 23, no. 4 (2009).

Woodcock, George, *Who Killed the British Empire?* (London: Reader's Union, 1974).

Index